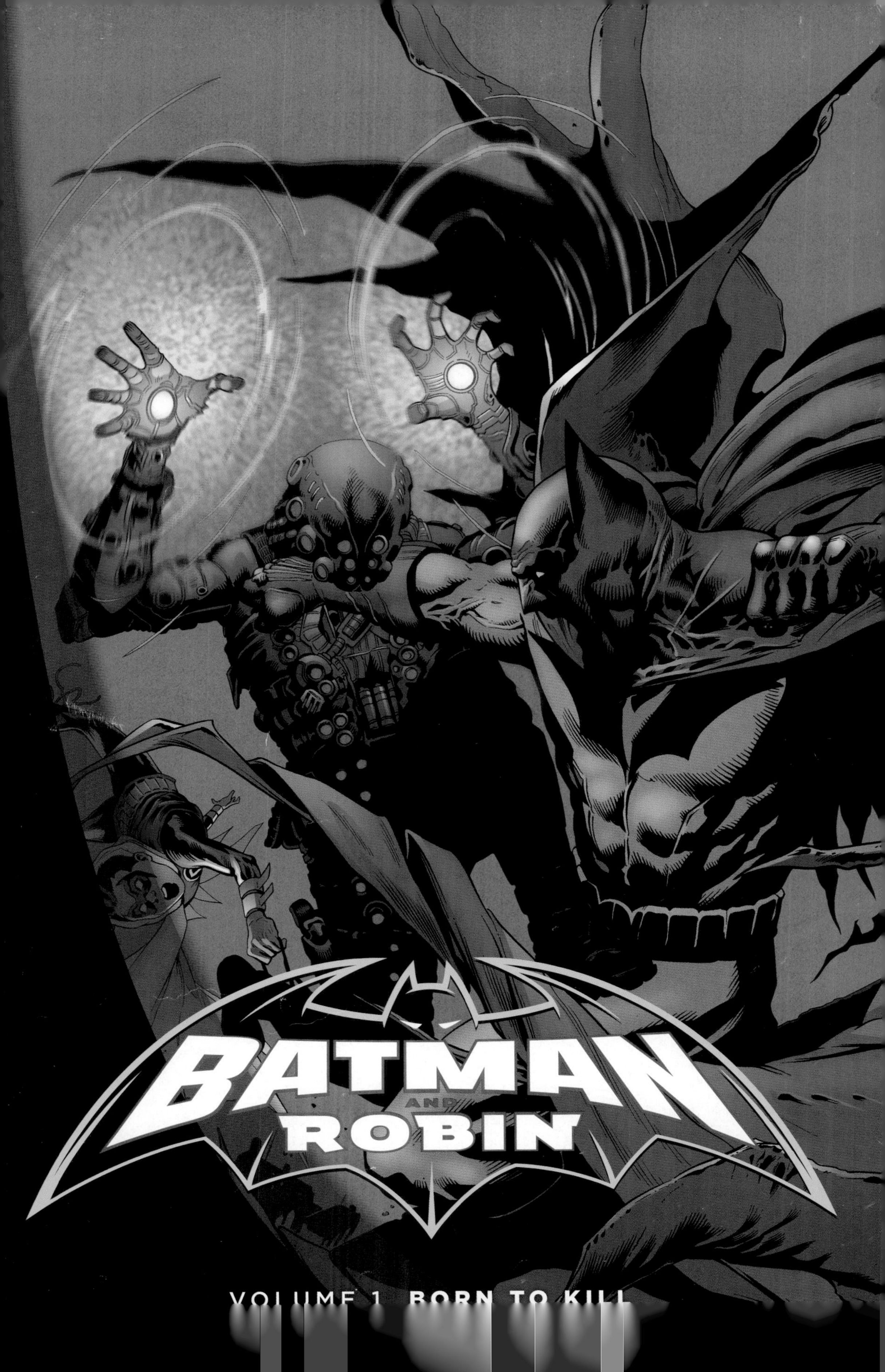
BATMAN AND ROBIN
VOLUME 1 BORN TO KILL

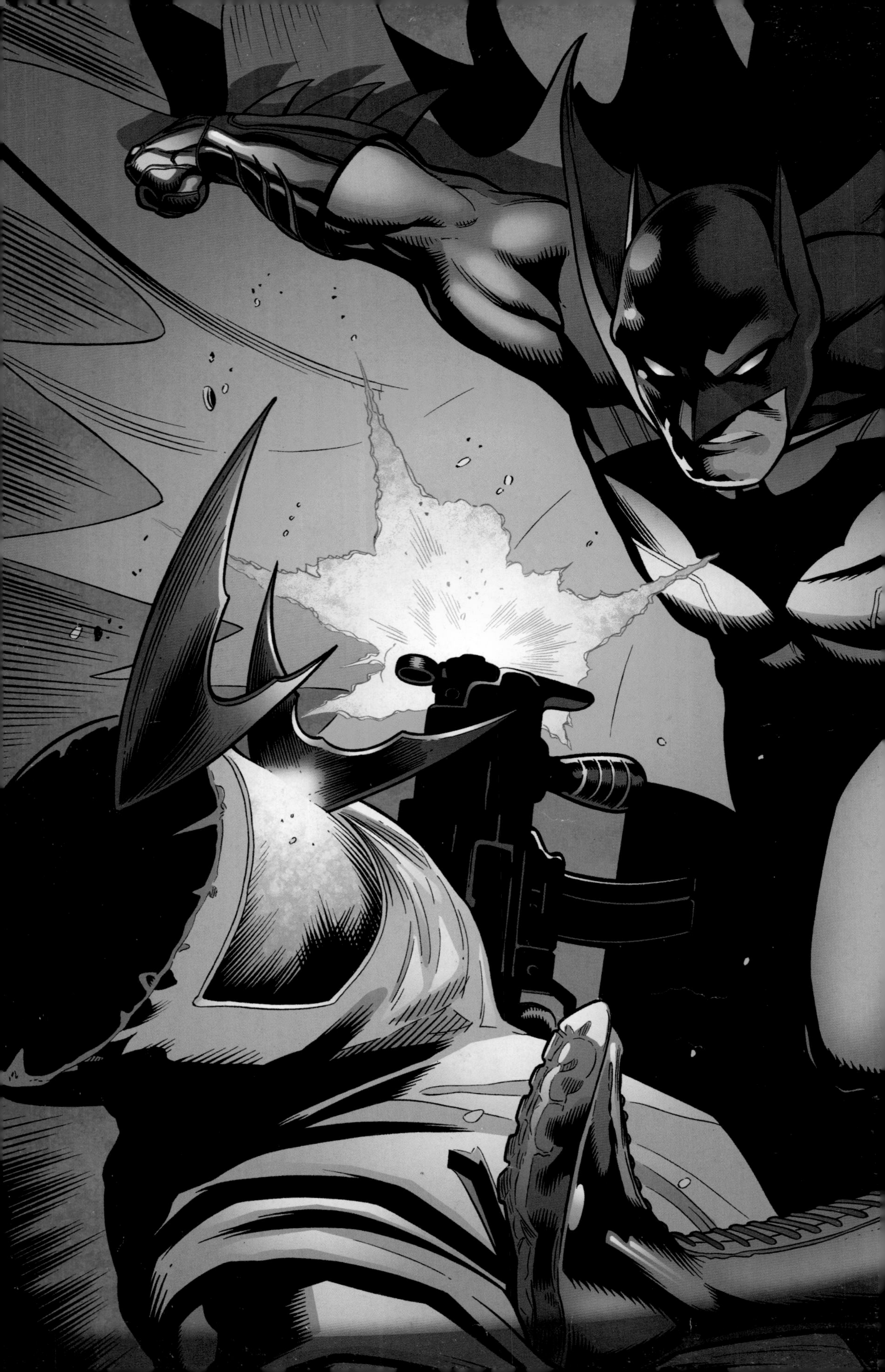

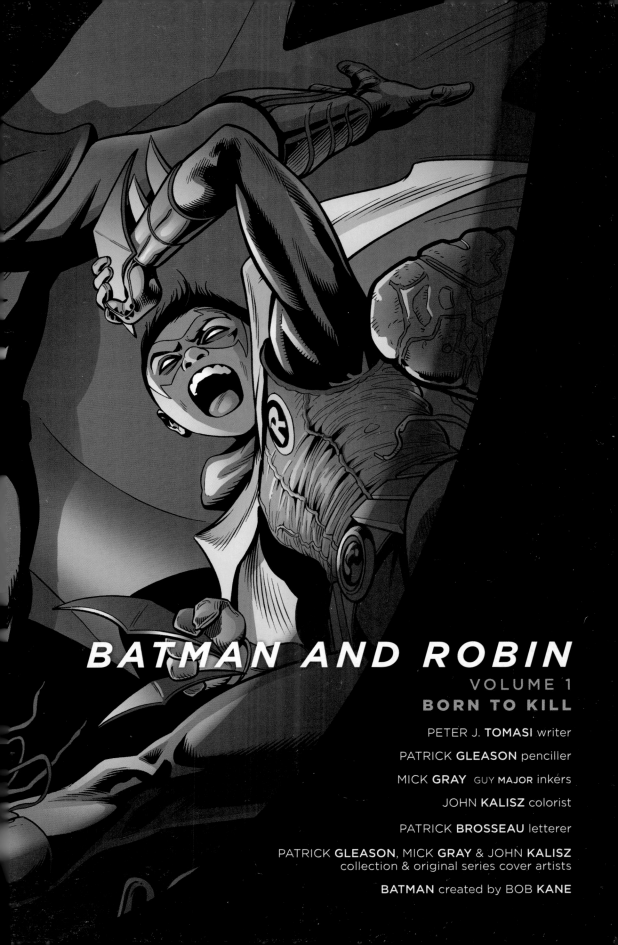

BATMAN AND ROBIN

VOLUME 1
BORN TO KILL

PETER J. **TOMASI** writer

PATRICK **GLEASON** penciller

MICK **GRAY**   GUY **MAJOR** inkers

JOHN **KALISZ** colorist

PATRICK **BROSSEAU** letterer

PATRICK **GLEASON**, MICK **GRAY** & JOHN **KALISZ**
collection & original series cover artists

BATMAN created by BOB **KANE**

MIKE MARTS Editor – Original Series HARVEY RICHARDS Associate Editor – Original Series
KATIE KUBERT Assistant Editor – Original Series PETER HAMBOUSSI Editor
ROBBIN BROSTERMAN Design Director – Books ROBBIE BIEDERMAN Publication Design

BOB HARRAS VP – Editor-in-Chief

DIANE NELSON President DAN DIDIO and JIM LEE Co-Publishers
GEOFF JOHNS Chief Creative Officer
JOHN ROOD Executive VP – Sales, Marketing and Business Development
AMY GENKINS Senior VP – Business and Legal Affairs NAIRI GARDINER Senior VP – Finance
JEFF BOISON VP – Publishing Operations MARK CHIARELLO VP – Art Direction and Design
JOHN CUNNINGHAM VP – Marketing TERRI CUNNINGHAM VP – Talent Relations and Services
ALISON GILL Senior VP – Manufacturing and Operations DAVID HYDE VP – Publicity
HANK KANALZ Senior VP – Digital JAY KOGAN VP – Business and Legal Affairs, Publishing
JACK MAHAN VP – Business Affairs, Talent NICK NAPOLITANO VP – Manufacturing Administration
SUE POHJA VP – Book Sales COURTNEY SIMMONS Senior VP – Publicity
BOB WAYNE Senior VP – Sales

BATMAN AND ROBIN VOLUME 1: BORN TO KILL

DC Comics, 1700 Broadway, New York, NY 10019
A Warner Bros. Entertainment Company
Printed by RR Donnelley, Salem, VA, USA. 6/1/12. First Printing.

HC ISBN: 978-1-4012-3487-4
SC ISBN: 978-1-4012-3838-4

SUSTAINABLE
FORESTRY
INITIATIVE

Certified Chain of Custody
At Least 25% Certified Forest Content
www.sfiprogram.org
SFI-01042
APPLIES TO TEXT STOCK ONLY

Library of Congress Cataloging-in-Publication Data

Tomasi, Peter.
Batman and Robin. Volume 1, Born to kill / Peter J. Tomasi, Patrick Gleason.
p. cm.
"Originally published in single magazine form in BATMAN AND ROBIN 1-8"—T.p. verso.
ISBN 978-1-4012-3487-4
1. Graphic novels. I. Gleason, Patrick. II. Title. III. Title: Born to kill.
PN6728.B36T64 2012
741.5'973—dc23
                                                              2012010314

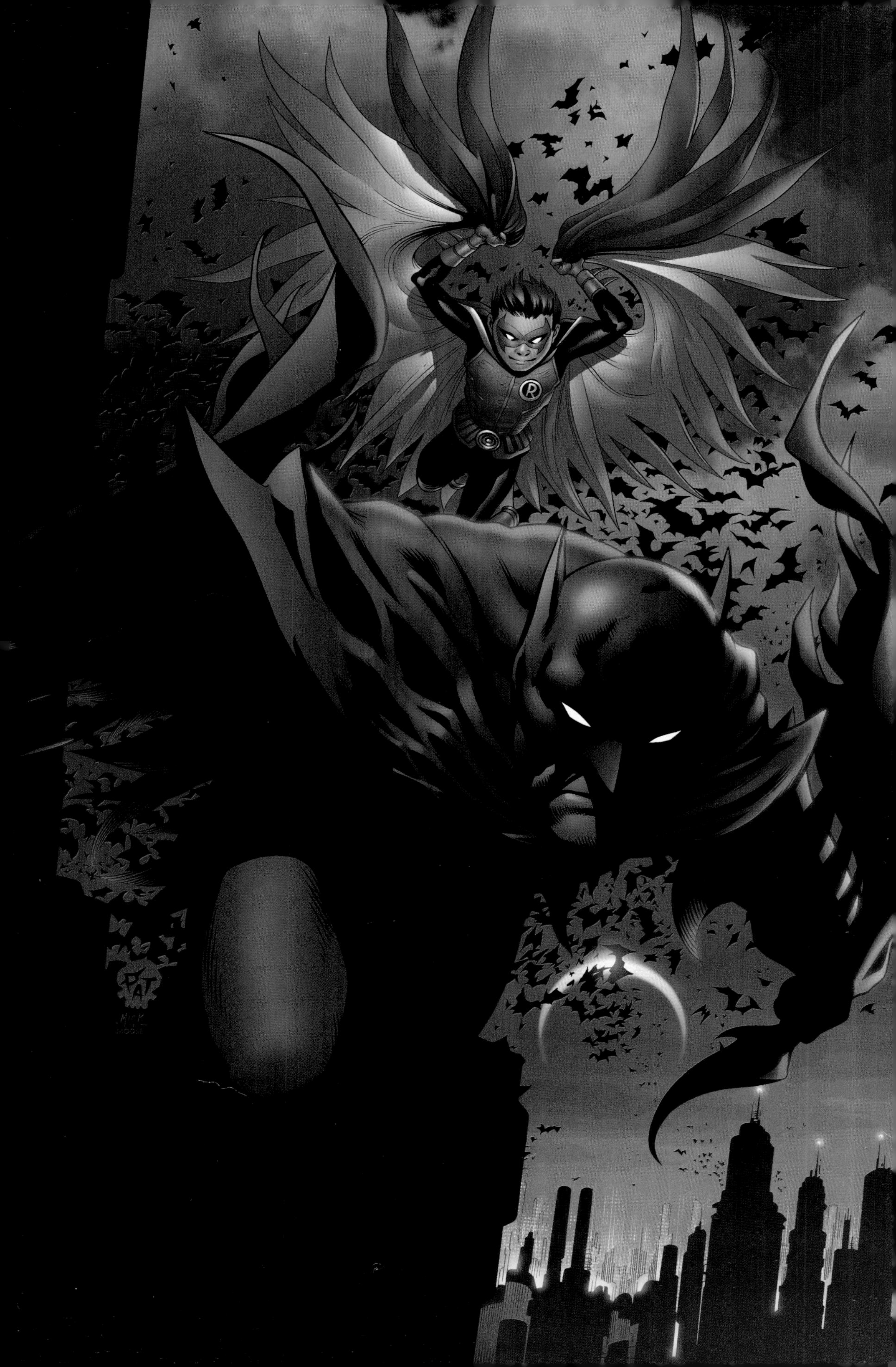

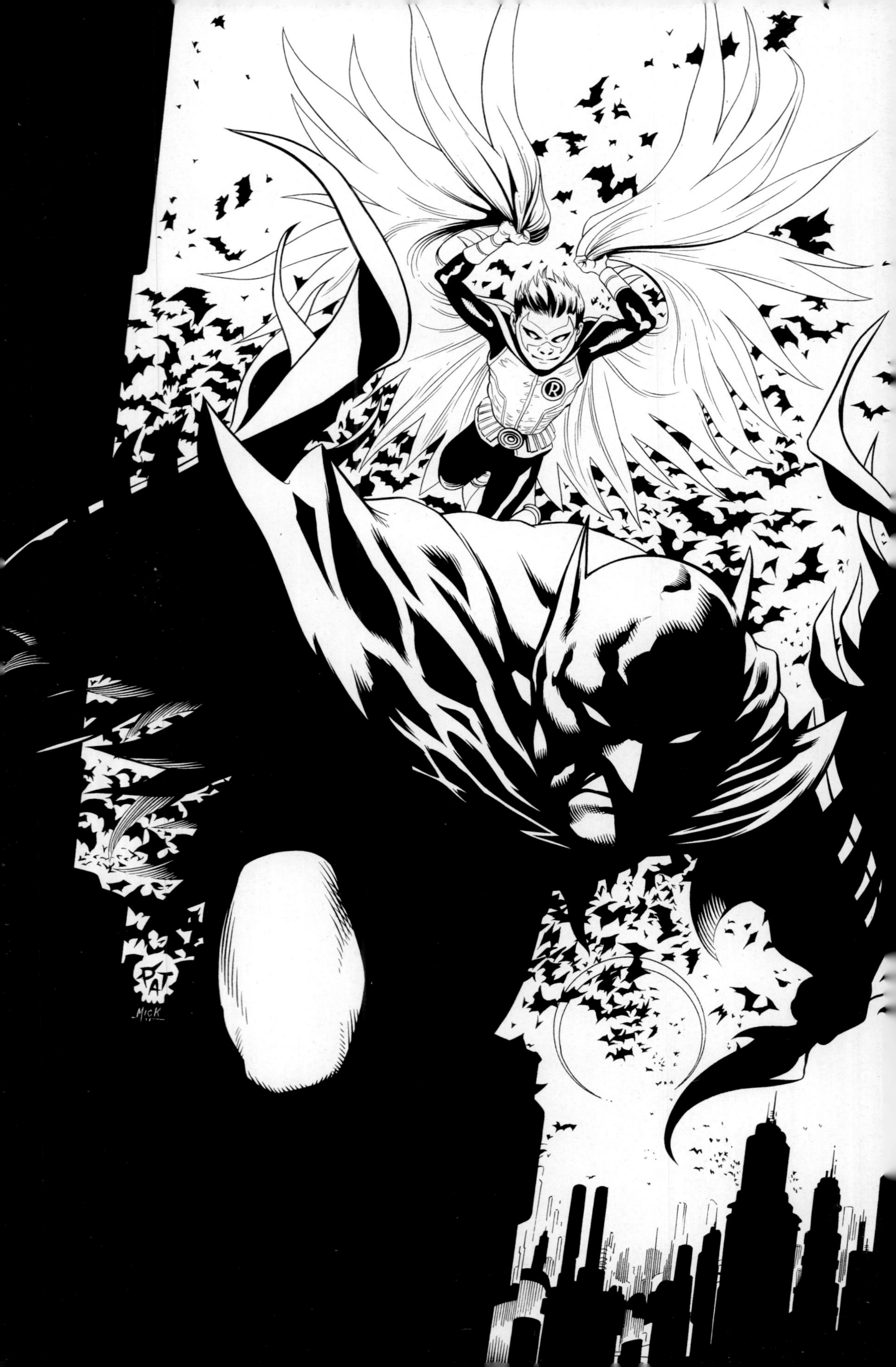
PAT
MICK

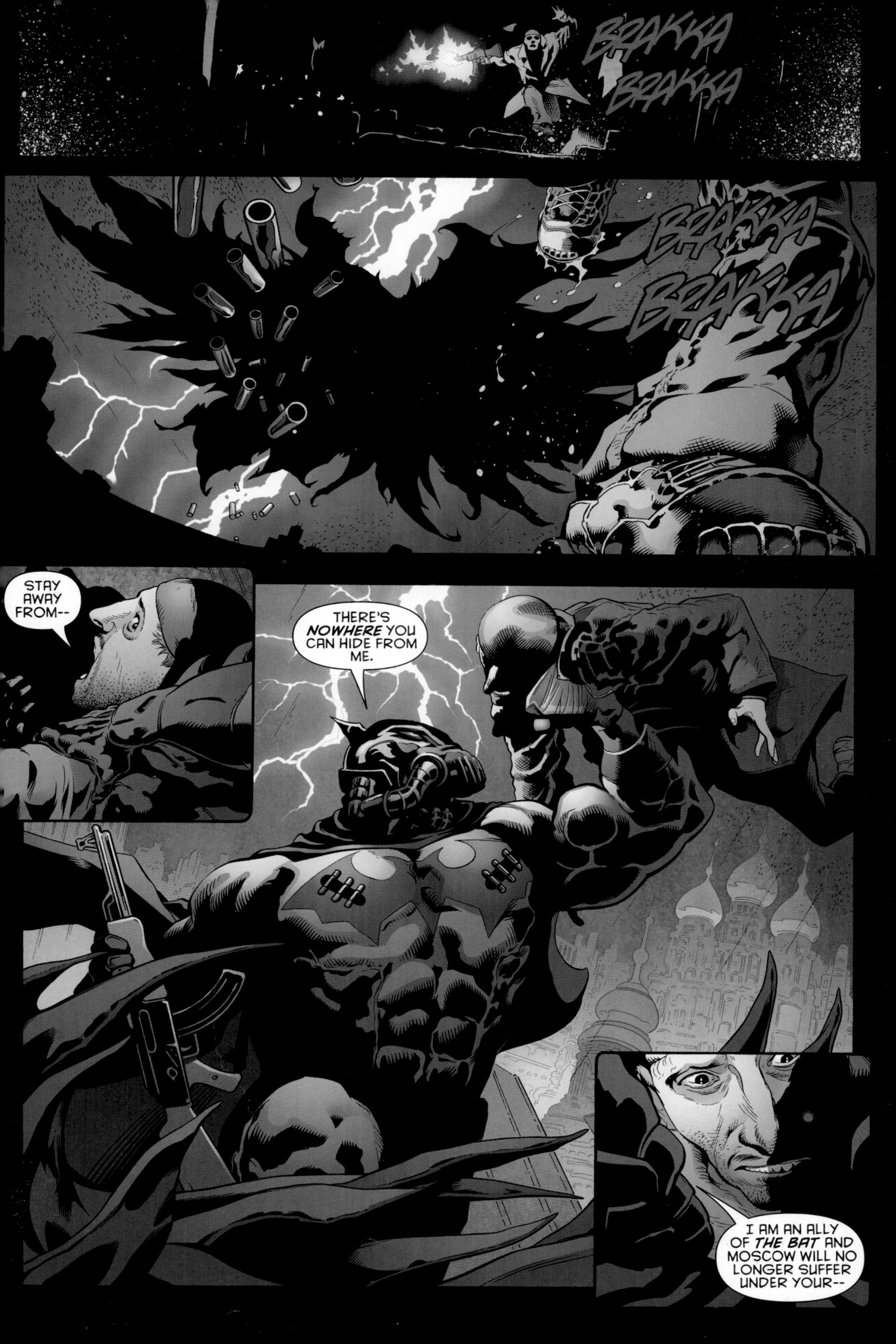
BRAKKA
BRAKKA
BRAKKA
BRAKKA
STAY AWAY FROM--
THERE'S NOWHERE YOU CAN HIDE FROM ME.
I AM AN ALLY OF THE BAT AND MOSCOW WILL NO LONGER SUFFER UNDER YOUR--

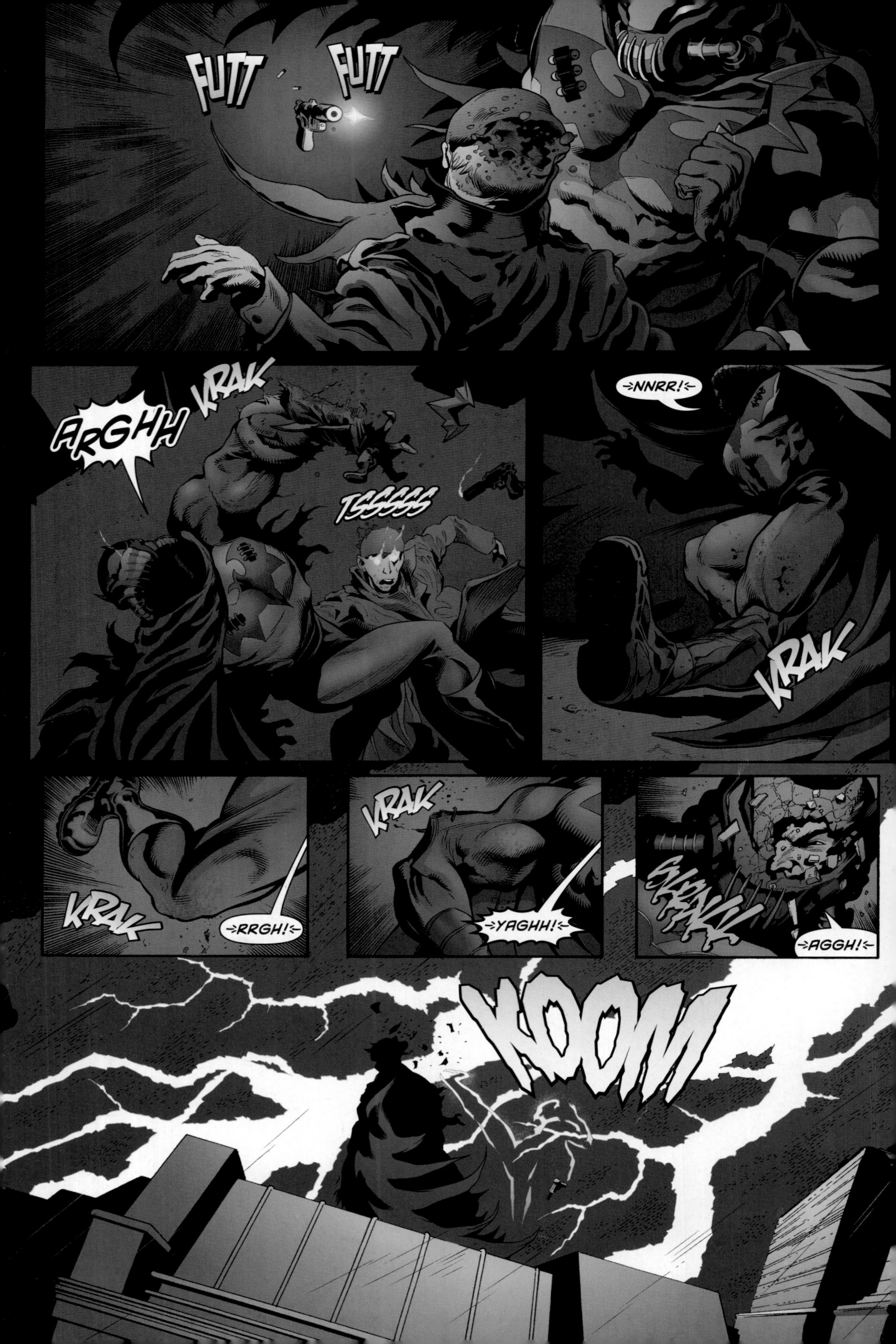
FUTT
FUTT
ARGHH
KRAK
TSSSSS
NNRR!
KRAK
KRAK
RRGH!
KRAK
YAGHH!
AGGH!
KOOM

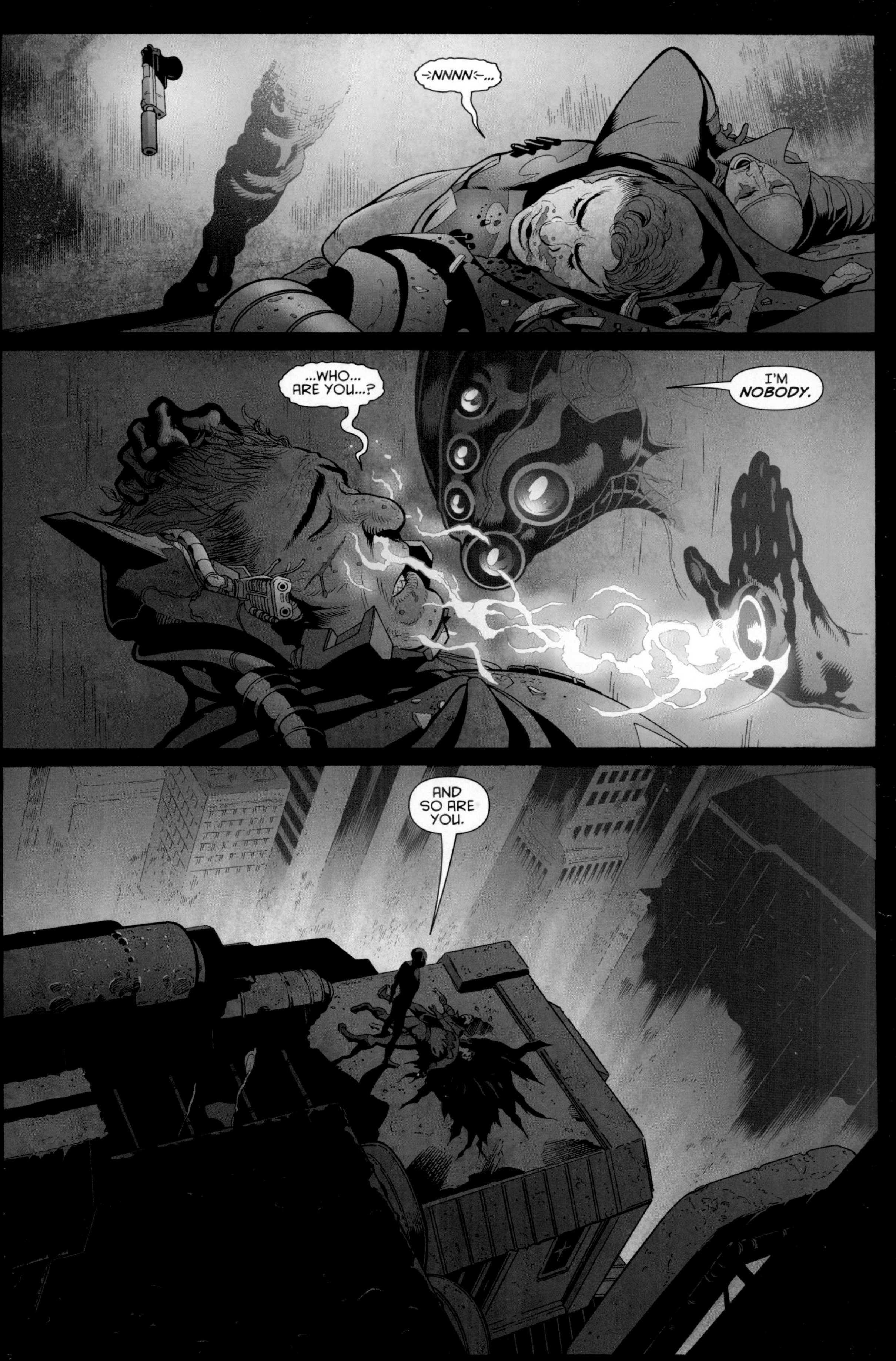
-NNNN-...
...WHO... ARE YOU...?
I'M *NOBODY.*
AND SO ARE YOU.

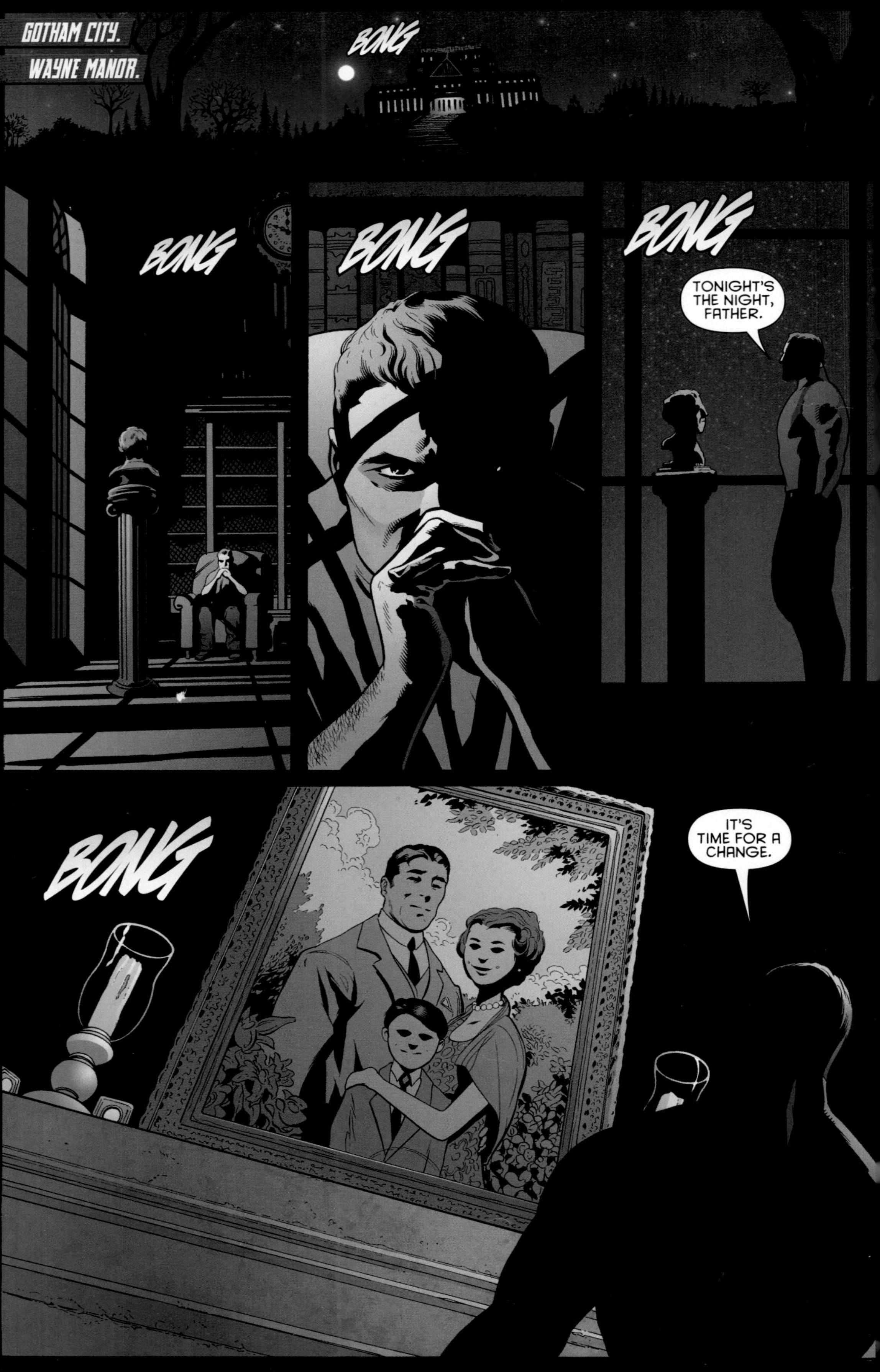
GOTHAM CITY.
WAYNE MANOR.
BONG
BONG
BONG
BONG
TONIGHT'S THE NIGHT, FATHER.
BONG
IT'S TIME FOR A CHANGE.

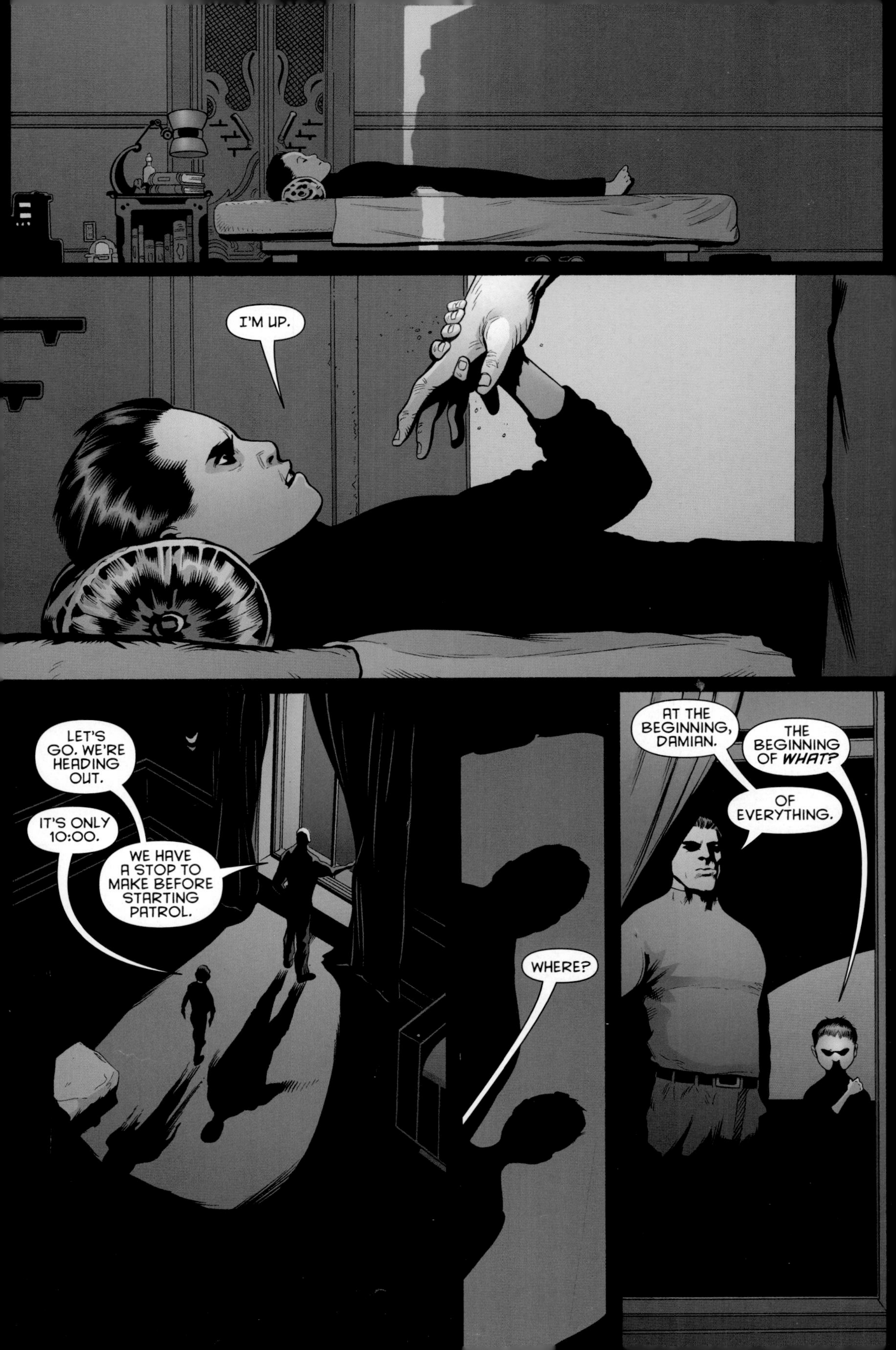
I'M UP.
LET'S GO. WE'RE HEADING OUT.
IT'S ONLY 10:00.
WE HAVE A STOP TO MAKE BEFORE STARTING PATROL.
WHERE?
AT THE BEGINNING, DAMIAN.
THE BEGINNING OF *WHAT?*
OF EVERYTHING.

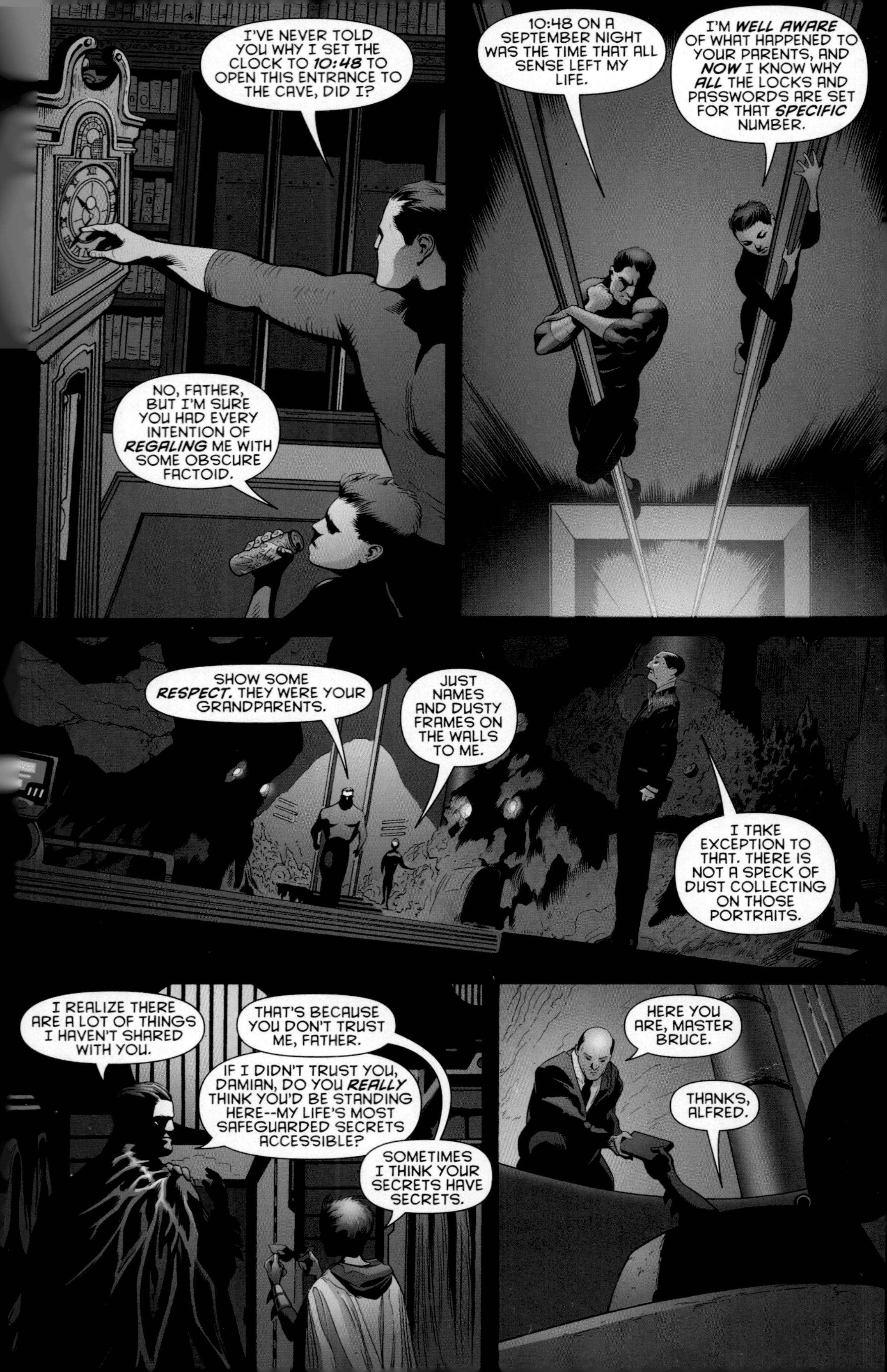
I'VE NEVER TOLD YOU WHY I SET THE CLOCK TO 10:48 TO OPEN THIS ENTRANCE TO THE CAVE, DID I?
NO, FATHER, BUT I'M SURE YOU HAD EVERY INTENTION OF REGALING ME WITH SOME OBSCURE FACTOID.
10:48 ON A SEPTEMBER NIGHT WAS THE TIME THAT ALL SENSE LEFT MY LIFE.
I'M WELL AWARE OF WHAT HAPPENED TO YOUR PARENTS, AND NOW I KNOW WHY ALL THE LOCKS AND PASSWORDS ARE SET FOR THAT SPECIFIC NUMBER.
SHOW SOME RESPECT. THEY WERE YOUR GRANDPARENTS.
JUST NAMES AND DUSTY FRAMES ON THE WALLS TO ME.
I TAKE EXCEPTION TO THAT. THERE IS NOT A SPECK OF DUST COLLECTING ON THOSE PORTRAITS.
I REALIZE THERE ARE A LOT OF THINGS I HAVEN'T SHARED WITH YOU.
THAT'S BECAUSE YOU DON'T TRUST ME, FATHER.
IF I DIDN'T TRUST YOU, DAMIAN, DO YOU REALLY THINK YOU'D BE STANDING HERE--MY LIFE'S MOST SAFEGUARDED SECRETS ACCESSIBLE?
SOMETIMES I THINK YOUR SECRETS HAVE SECRETS.
HERE YOU ARE, MASTER BRUCE.
THANKS, ALFRED.

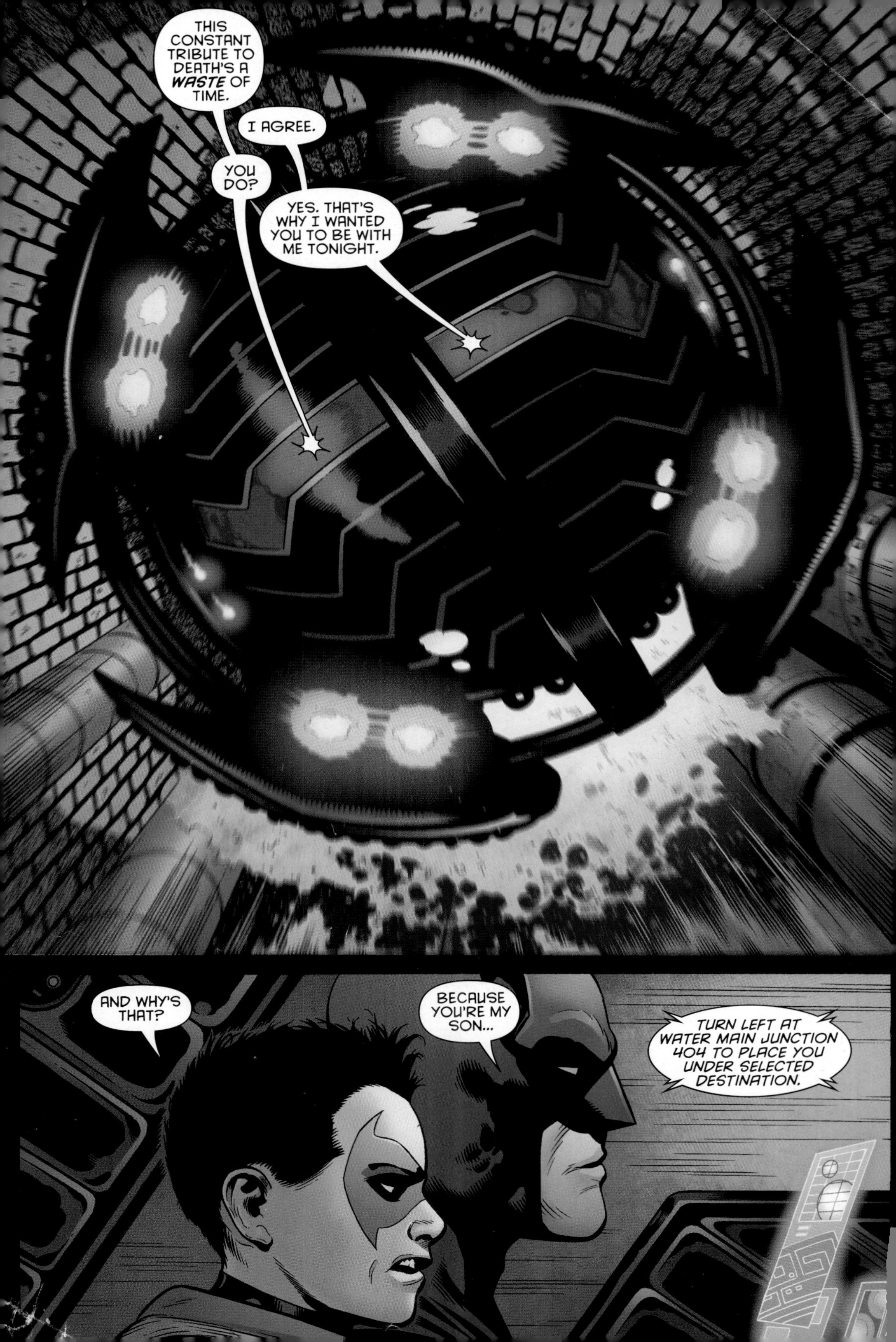
THIS CONSTANT TRIBUTE TO DEATH'S A *WASTE* OF TIME.
I AGREE.
YOU DO?
YES. THAT'S WHY I WANTED YOU TO BE WITH ME TONIGHT.
AND WHY'S THAT?
BECAUSE YOU'RE MY SON...
TURN LEFT AT WATER MAIN JUNCTION 404 TO PLACE YOU UNDER SELECTED DESTINATION.

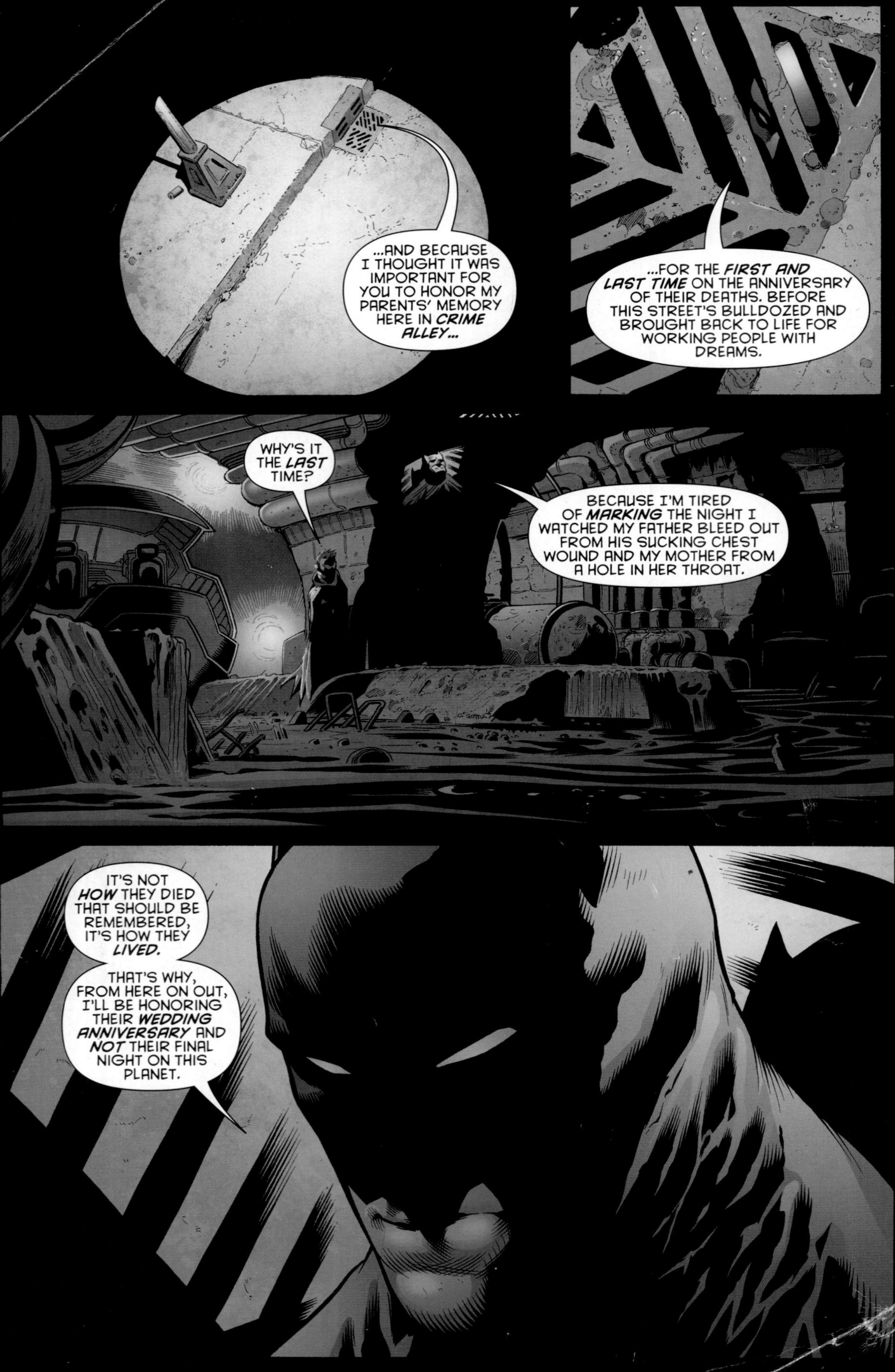

...AND BECAUSE I THOUGHT IT WAS IMPORTANT FOR YOU TO HONOR MY PARENTS' MEMORY HERE IN ***CRIME ALLEY***...
...FOR THE ***FIRST AND LAST TIME*** ON THE ANNIVERSARY OF THEIR DEATHS. BEFORE THIS STREET'S BULLDOZED AND BROUGHT BACK TO LIFE FOR WORKING PEOPLE WITH DREAMS.
WHY'S IT THE ***LAST*** TIME?
BECAUSE I'M TIRED OF ***MARKING*** THE NIGHT I WATCHED MY FATHER BLEED OUT FROM HIS SUCKING CHEST WOUND AND MY MOTHER FROM A HOLE IN HER THROAT.
IT'S NOT ***HOW*** THEY DIED THAT SHOULD BE REMEMBERED, IT'S HOW THEY ***LIVED.***
THAT'S WHY, FROM HERE ON OUT, I'LL BE HONORING THEIR ***WEDDING ANNIVERSARY*** AND ***NOT*** THEIR FINAL NIGHT ON THIS PLANET.

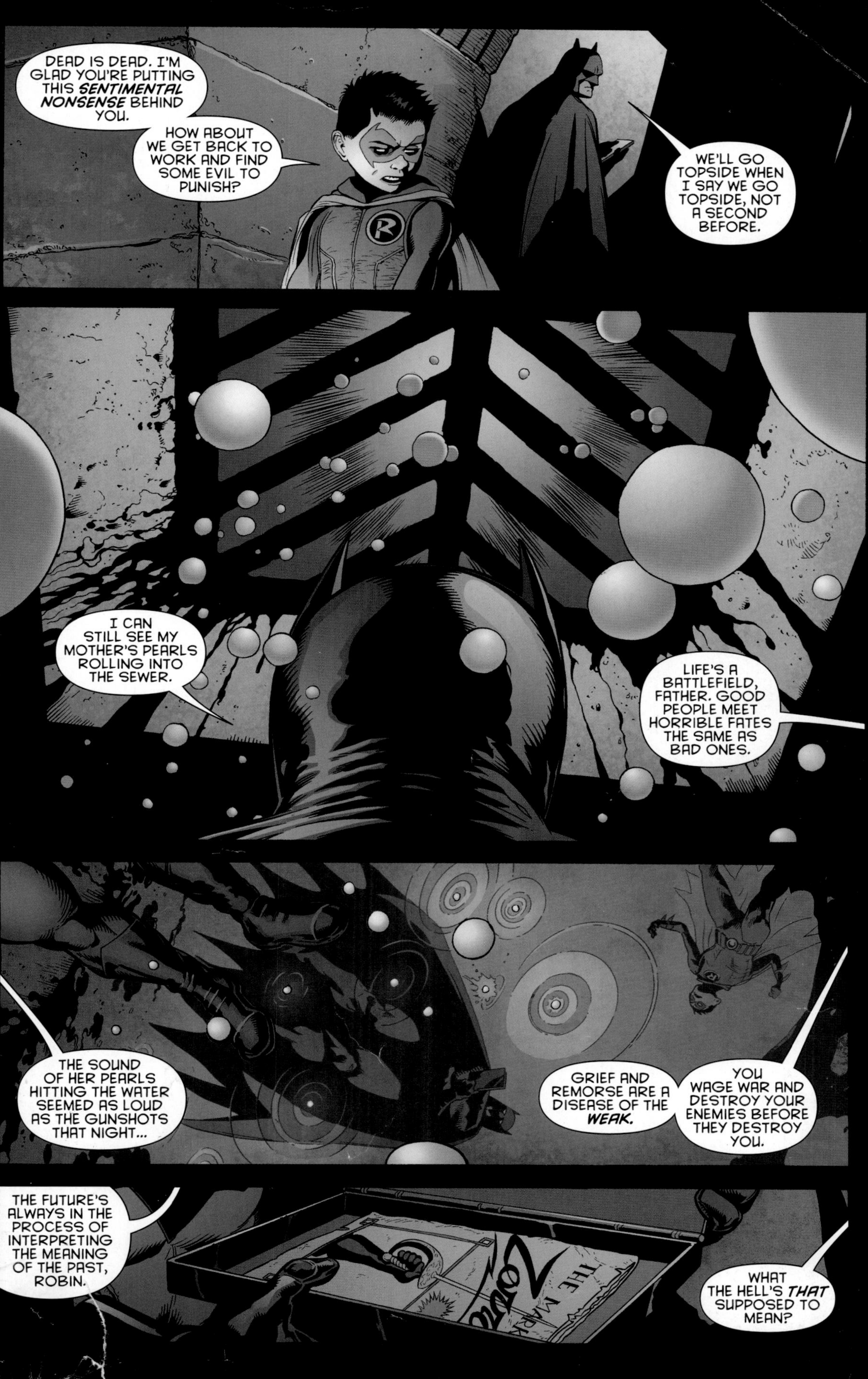
DEAD IS DEAD. I'M GLAD YOU'RE PUTTING THIS ***SENTIMENTAL NONSENSE*** BEHIND YOU.
HOW ABOUT WE GET BACK TO WORK AND FIND SOME EVIL TO PUNISH?
WE'LL GO TOPSIDE WHEN I SAY WE GO TOPSIDE, NOT A SECOND BEFORE.
I CAN STILL SEE MY MOTHER'S PEARLS ROLLING INTO THE SEWER.
LIFE'S A BATTLEFIELD, FATHER. GOOD PEOPLE MEET HORRIBLE FATES THE SAME AS BAD ONES.
THE SOUND OF HER PEARLS HITTING THE WATER SEEMED AS LOUD AS THE GUNSHOTS THAT NIGHT...
GRIEF AND REMORSE ARE A DISEASE OF THE ***WEAK.***
YOU WAGE WAR AND DESTROY YOUR ENEMIES BEFORE THEY DESTROY YOU.
THE FUTURE'S ALWAYS IN THE PROCESS OF INTERPRETING THE MEANING OF THE PAST, ROBIN.
WHAT THE HELL'S ***THAT*** SUPPOSED TO MEAN?

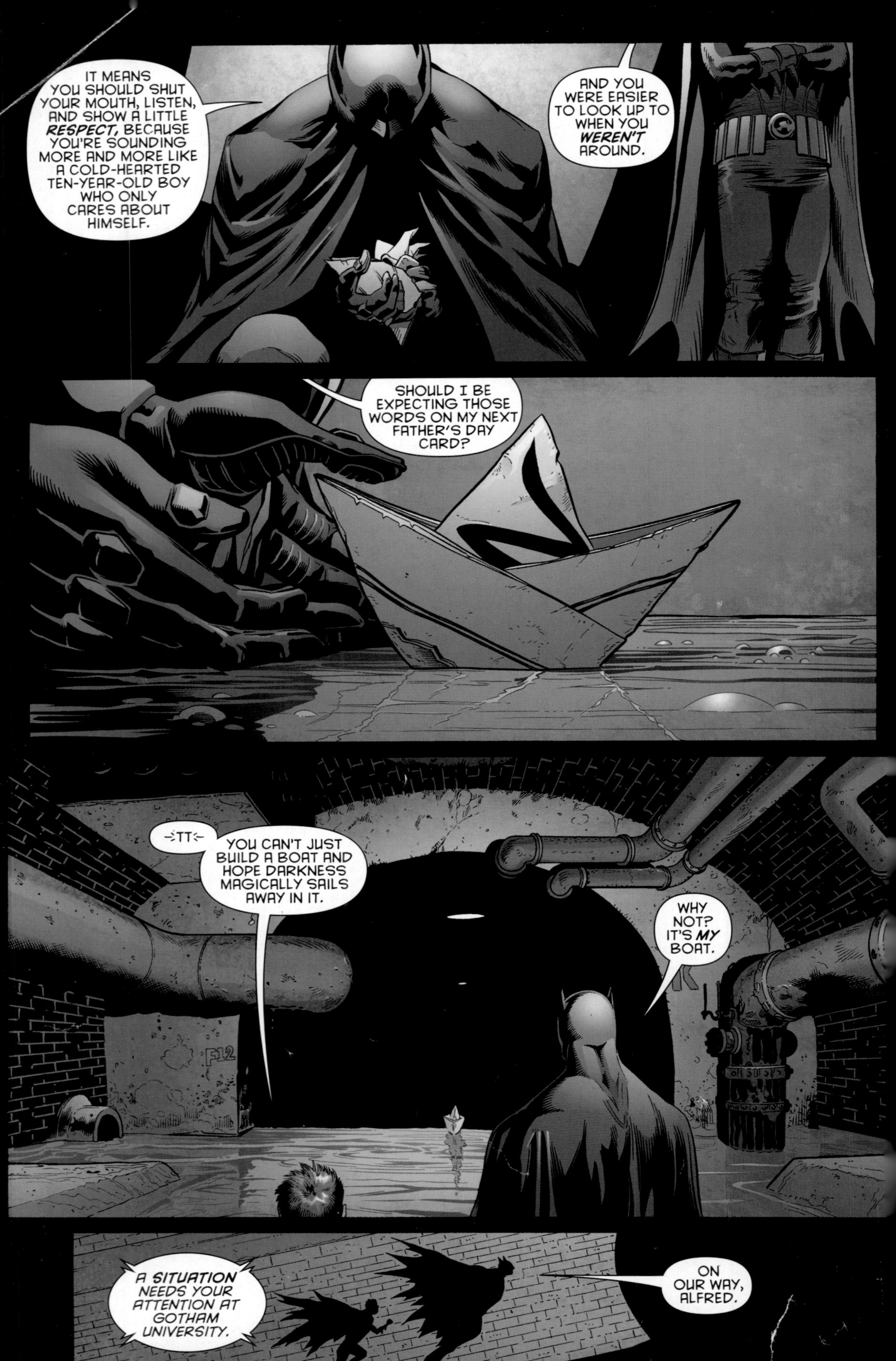
IT MEANS YOU SHOULD SHUT YOUR MOUTH, LISTEN, AND SHOW A LITTLE *RESPECT,* BECAUSE YOU'RE SOUNDING MORE AND MORE LIKE A COLD-HEARTED TEN-YEAR-OLD BOY WHO ONLY CARES ABOUT HIMSELF.
AND YOU WERE EASIER TO LOOK UP TO WHEN YOU *WEREN'T* AROUND.
SHOULD I BE EXPECTING THOSE WORDS ON MY NEXT FATHER'S DAY CARD?
-TT-
YOU CAN'T JUST BUILD A BOAT AND HOPE DARKNESS MAGICALLY SAILS AWAY IN IT.
WHY NOT? IT'S *MY* BOAT.
F12
A *SITUATION* NEEDS YOUR ATTENTION AT GOTHAM UNIVERSITY.
ON OUR WAY, ALFRED.

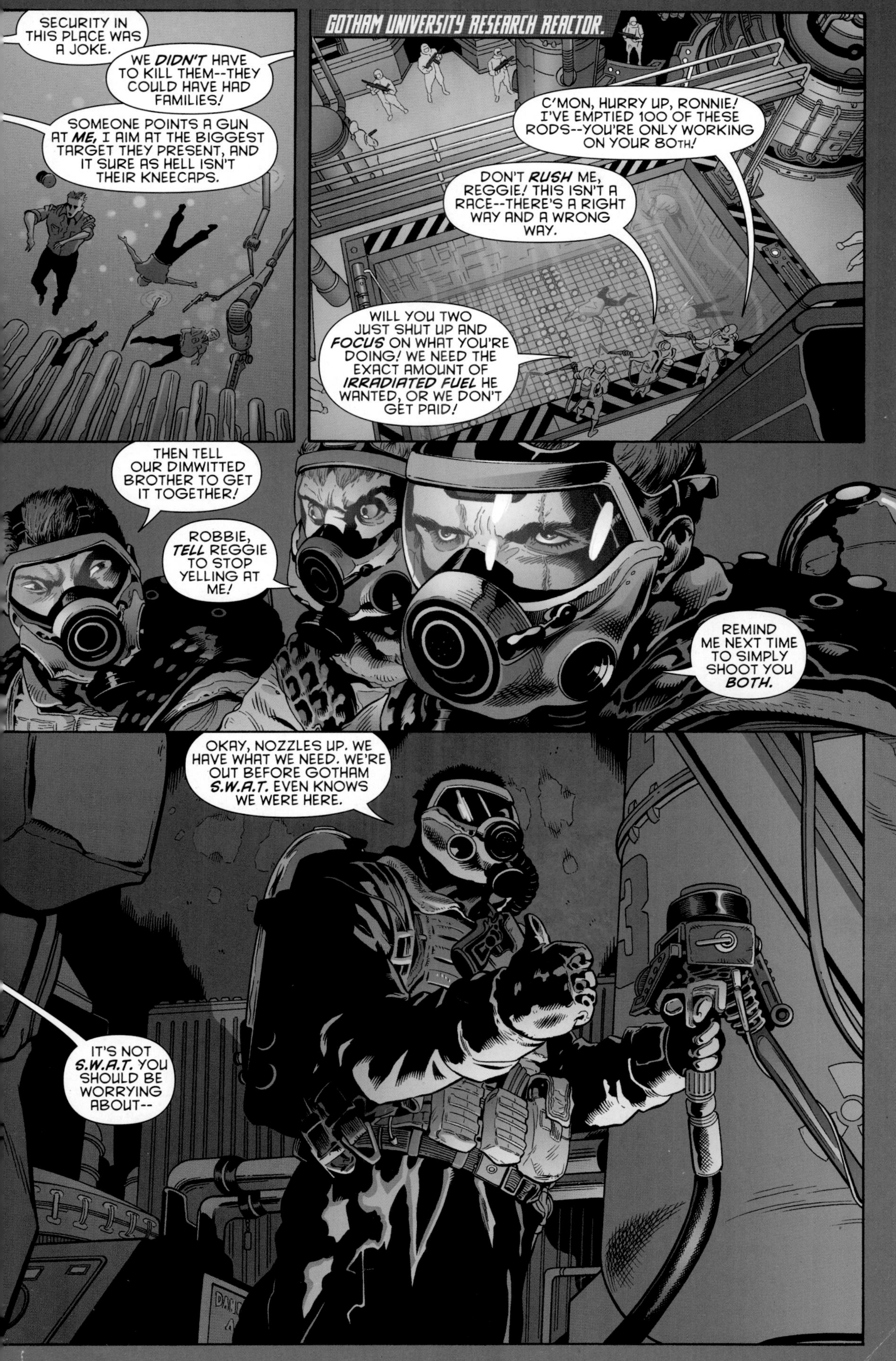
SECURITY IN THIS PLACE WAS A JOKE.
WE DIDN'T HAVE TO KILL THEM--THEY COULD HAVE HAD FAMILIES!
SOMEONE POINTS A GUN AT ME, I AIM AT THE BIGGEST TARGET THEY PRESENT, AND IT SURE AS HELL ISN'T THEIR KNEECAPS.
GOTHAM UNIVERSITY RESEARCH REACTOR.
C'MON, HURRY UP, RONNIE! I'VE EMPTIED 100 OF THESE RODS--YOU'RE ONLY WORKING ON YOUR 80TH!
DON'T RUSH ME, REGGIE! THIS ISN'T A RACE--THERE'S A RIGHT WAY AND A WRONG WAY.
WILL YOU TWO JUST SHUT UP AND FOCUS ON WHAT YOU'RE DOING! WE NEED THE EXACT AMOUNT OF IRRADIATED FUEL HE WANTED, OR WE DON'T GET PAID!
THEN TELL OUR DIMWITTED BROTHER TO GET IT TOGETHER!
ROBBIE, TELL REGGIE TO STOP YELLING AT ME!
REMIND ME NEXT TIME TO SIMPLY SHOOT YOU BOTH.
OKAY, NOZZLES UP. WE HAVE WHAT WE NEED. WE'RE OUT BEFORE GOTHAM S.W.A.T. EVEN KNOWS WE WERE HERE.
IT'S NOT S.W.A.T. YOU SHOULD BE WORRYING ABOUT--

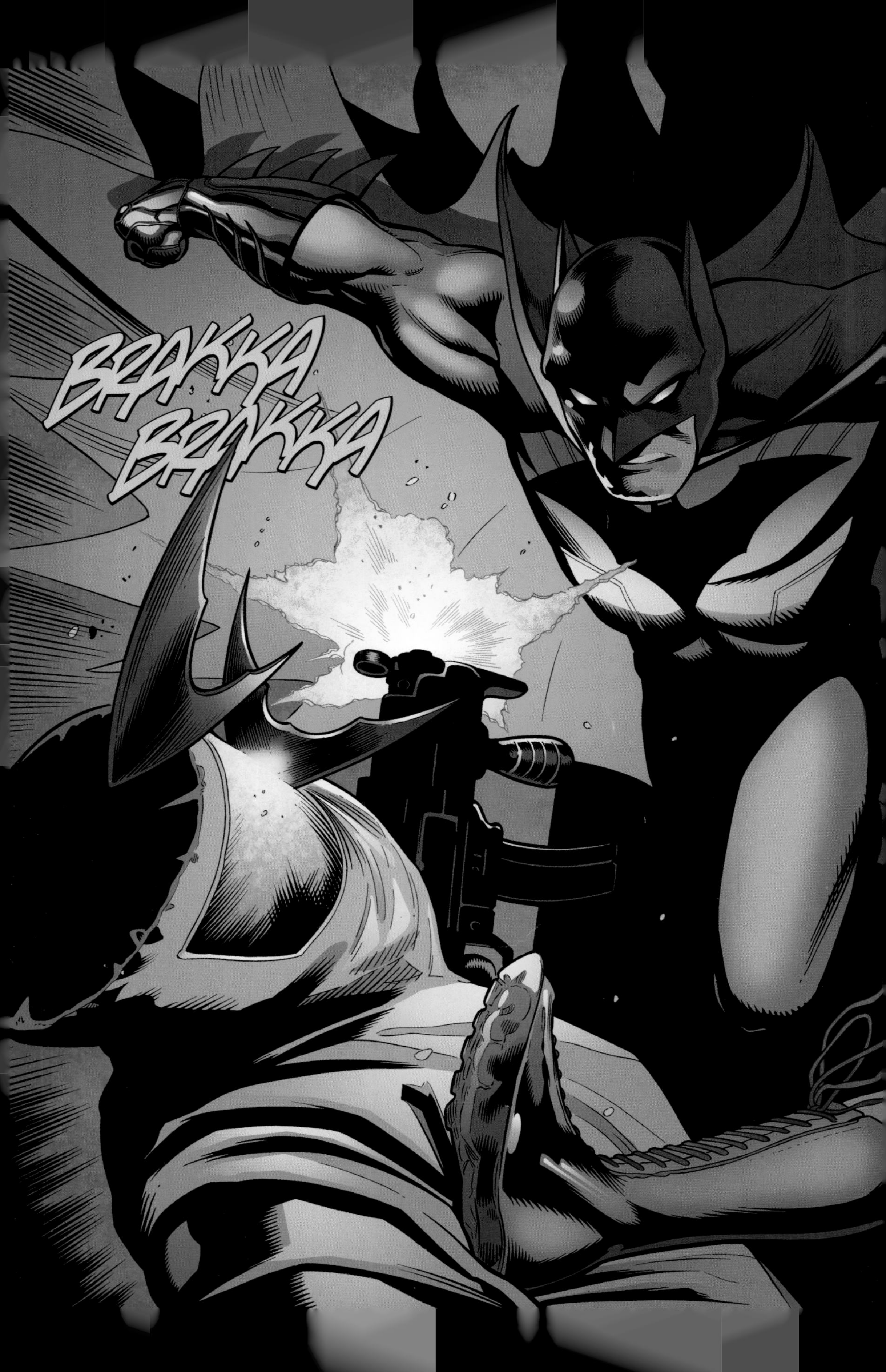
BRAKKA
BRAKKA

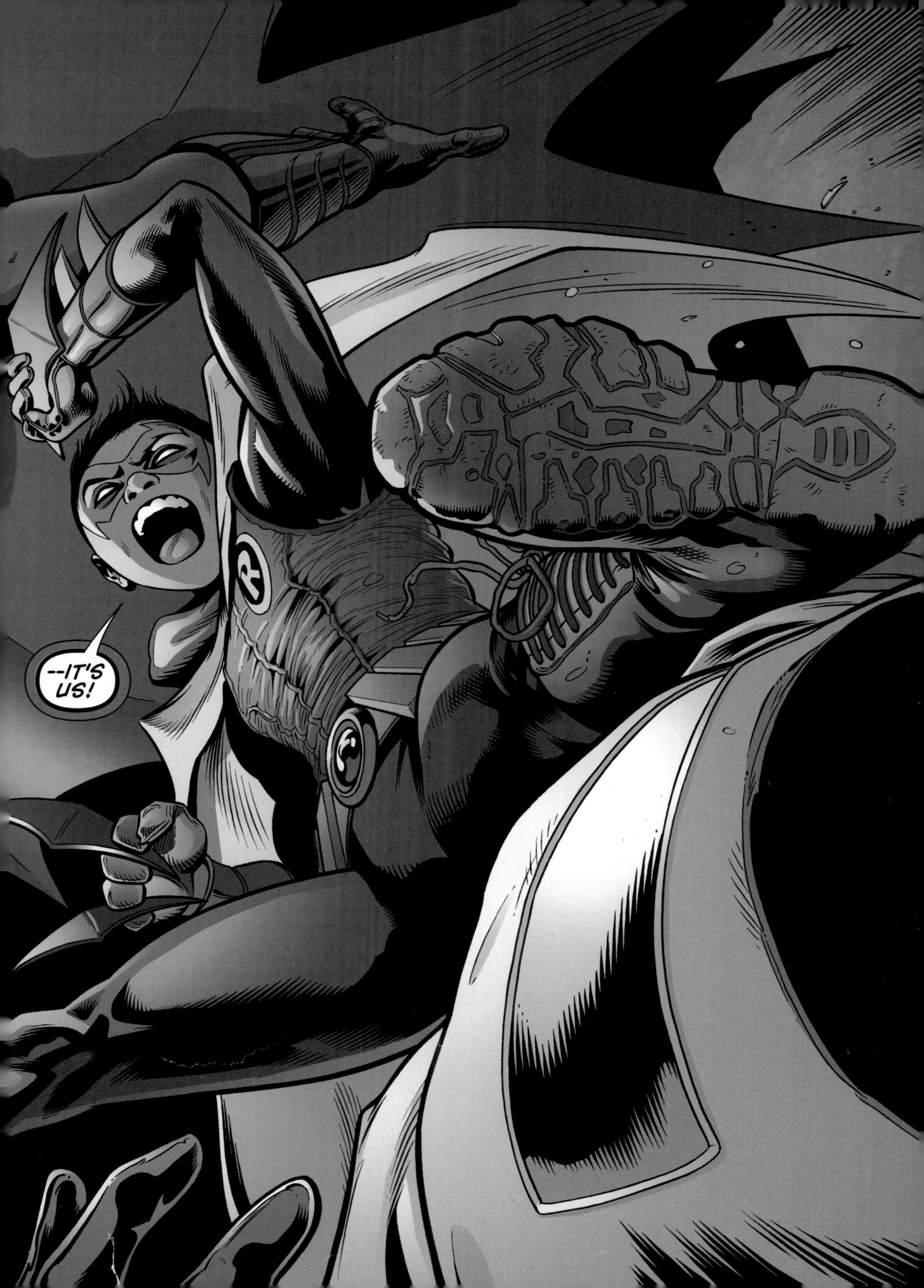
--IT'S US!

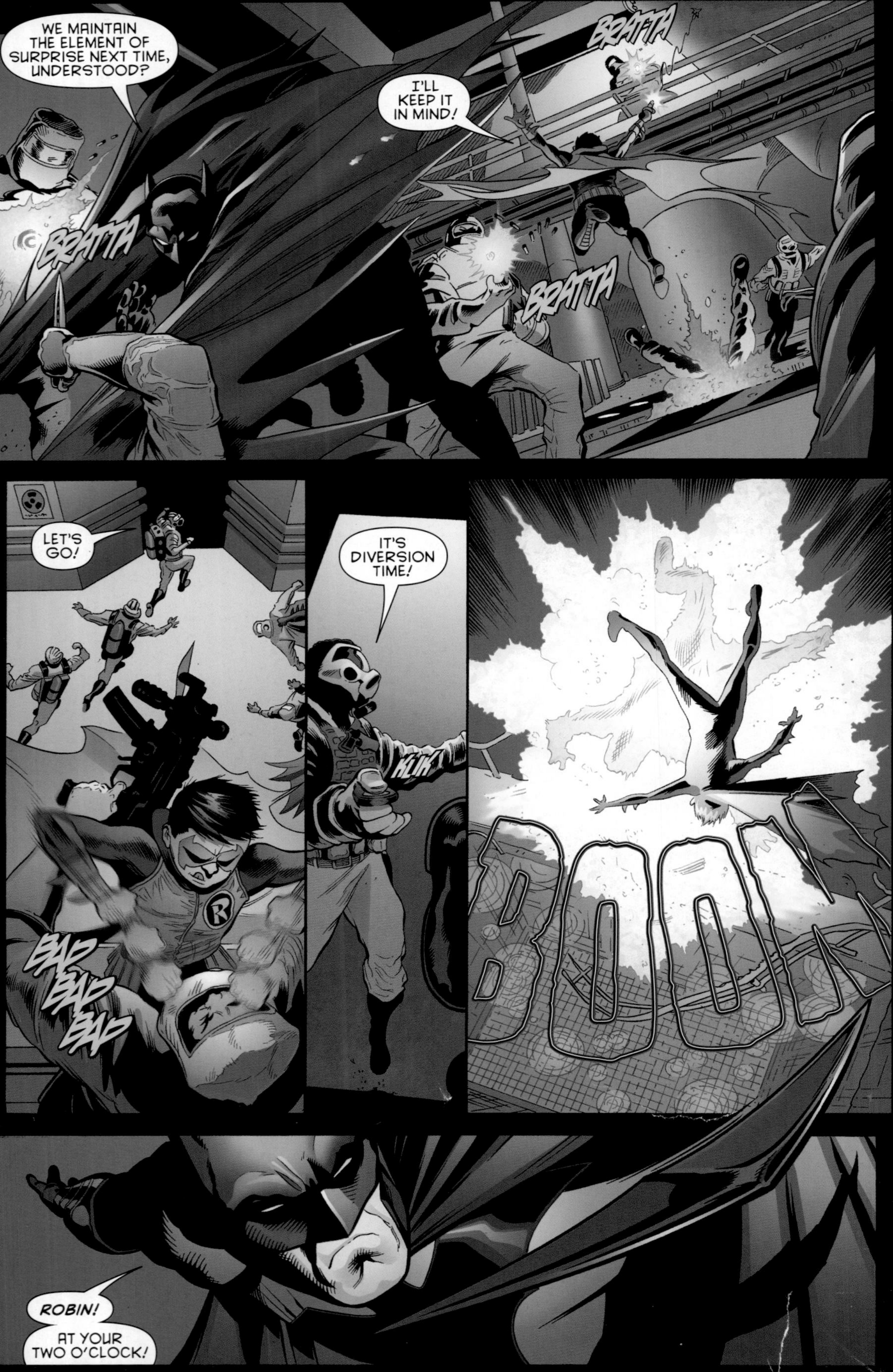
WE MAINTAIN THE ELEMENT OF SURPRISE NEXT TIME, UNDERSTOOD?
BRATTA
BRATTA
I'LL KEEP IT IN MIND!
BRATTA
LET'S GO!
BAP BAP BAP
IT'S DIVERSION TIME!
KLIK
BOOM
ROBIN!
AT YOUR TWO O'CLOCK!

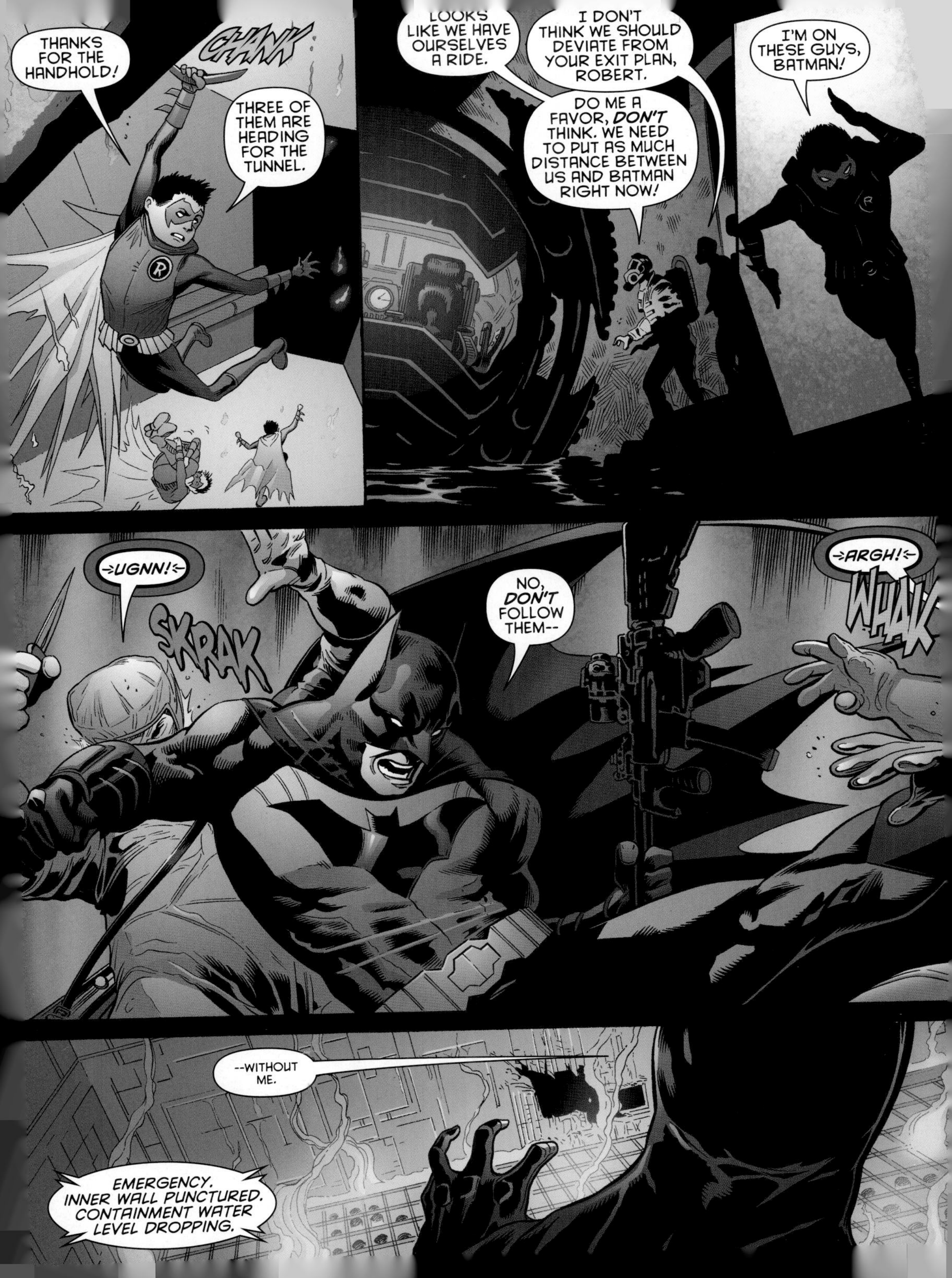

THANKS FOR THE HANDHOLD!
CHANK
THREE OF THEM ARE HEADING FOR THE TUNNEL.
LOOKS LIKE WE HAVE OURSELVES A RIDE.
I DON'T THINK WE SHOULD DEVIATE FROM YOUR EXIT PLAN, ROBERT.
DO ME A FAVOR, DON'T THINK. WE NEED TO PUT AS MUCH DISTANCE BETWEEN US AND BATMAN RIGHT NOW!
I'M ON THESE GUYS, BATMAN!
UGNN!
SKRAK
NO, DON'T FOLLOW THEM--
ARGH!
WHAK
--WITHOUT ME.
EMERGENCY. INNER WALL PUNCTURED. CONTAINMENT WATER LEVEL DROPPING.

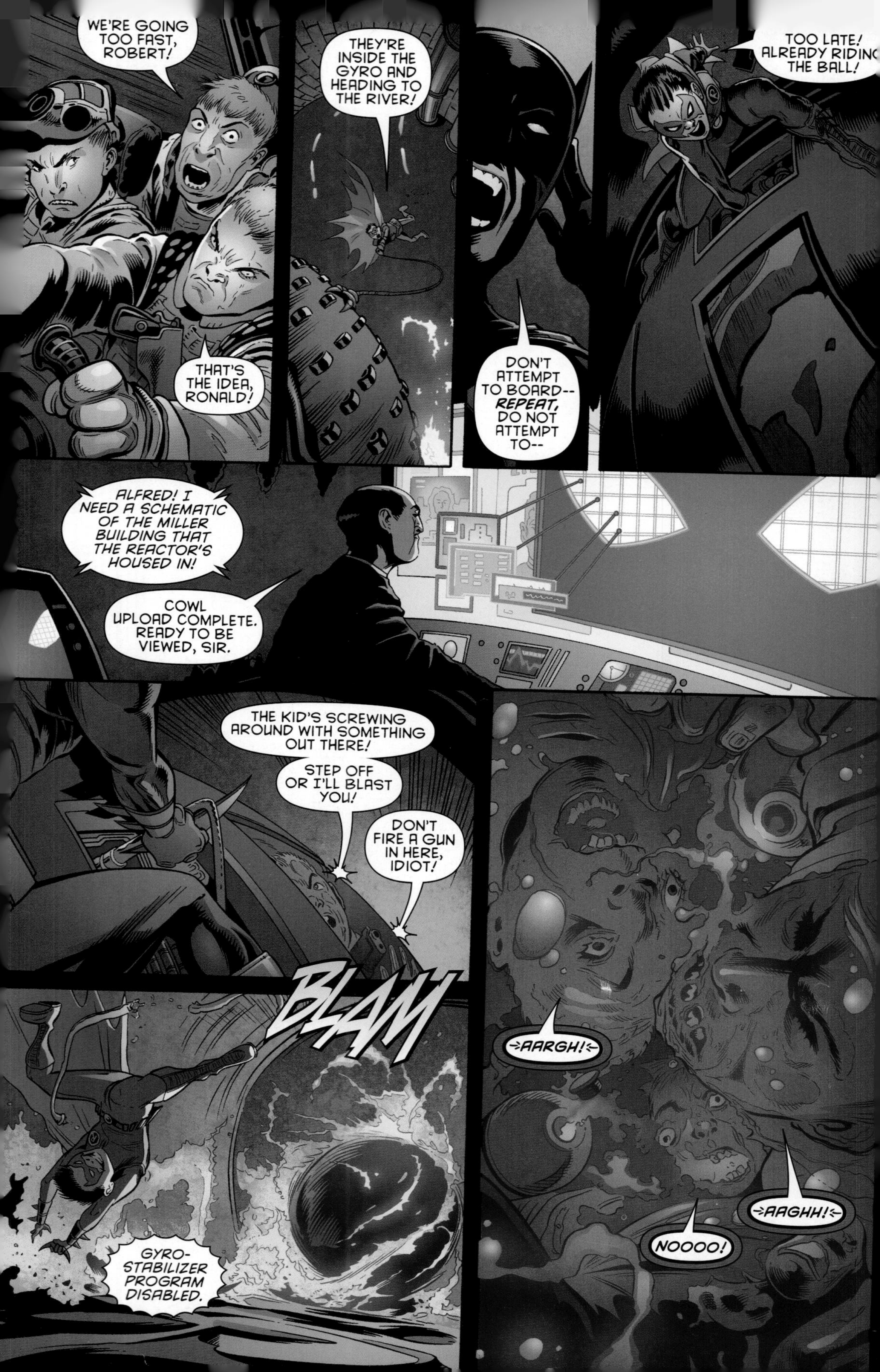
WE'RE GOING TOO FAST, ROBERT!
THAT'S THE IDEA, RONALD!
THEY'RE INSIDE THE GYRO AND HEADING TO THE RIVER!
DON'T ATTEMPT TO BOARD-- REPEAT, DO NOT ATTEMPT TO--
TOO LATE! ALREADY RIDING THE BALL!
ALFRED! I NEED A SCHEMATIC OF THE MILLER BUILDING THAT THE REACTOR'S HOUSED IN!
COWL UPLOAD COMPLETE. READY TO BE VIEWED, SIR.
THE KID'S SCREWING AROUND WITH SOMETHING OUT THERE!
STEP OFF OR I'LL BLAST YOU!
DON'T FIRE A GUN IN HERE, IDIOT!
BLAM
GYRO-STABILIZER PROGRAM DISABLED.
AARGH!
NOOOO!
AAGHH!

POOM

FSSSS

I'M SEALING THE CONTAINMENT RUPTURE, ALFRED.

POOM

CONTACT COMMISSIONER GORDON AND GET A *N.A.I.R.* TEAM HERE NOW--

TWEET

PUSH OFF THAT WALL! FASTER, ADAMS!

BOOM
BOOM
BOOM
BOOM

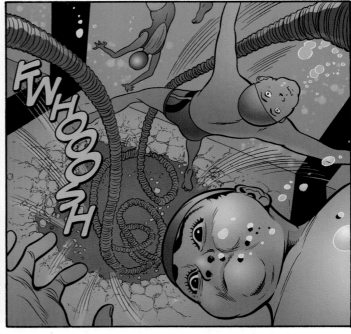

KWHOOOH

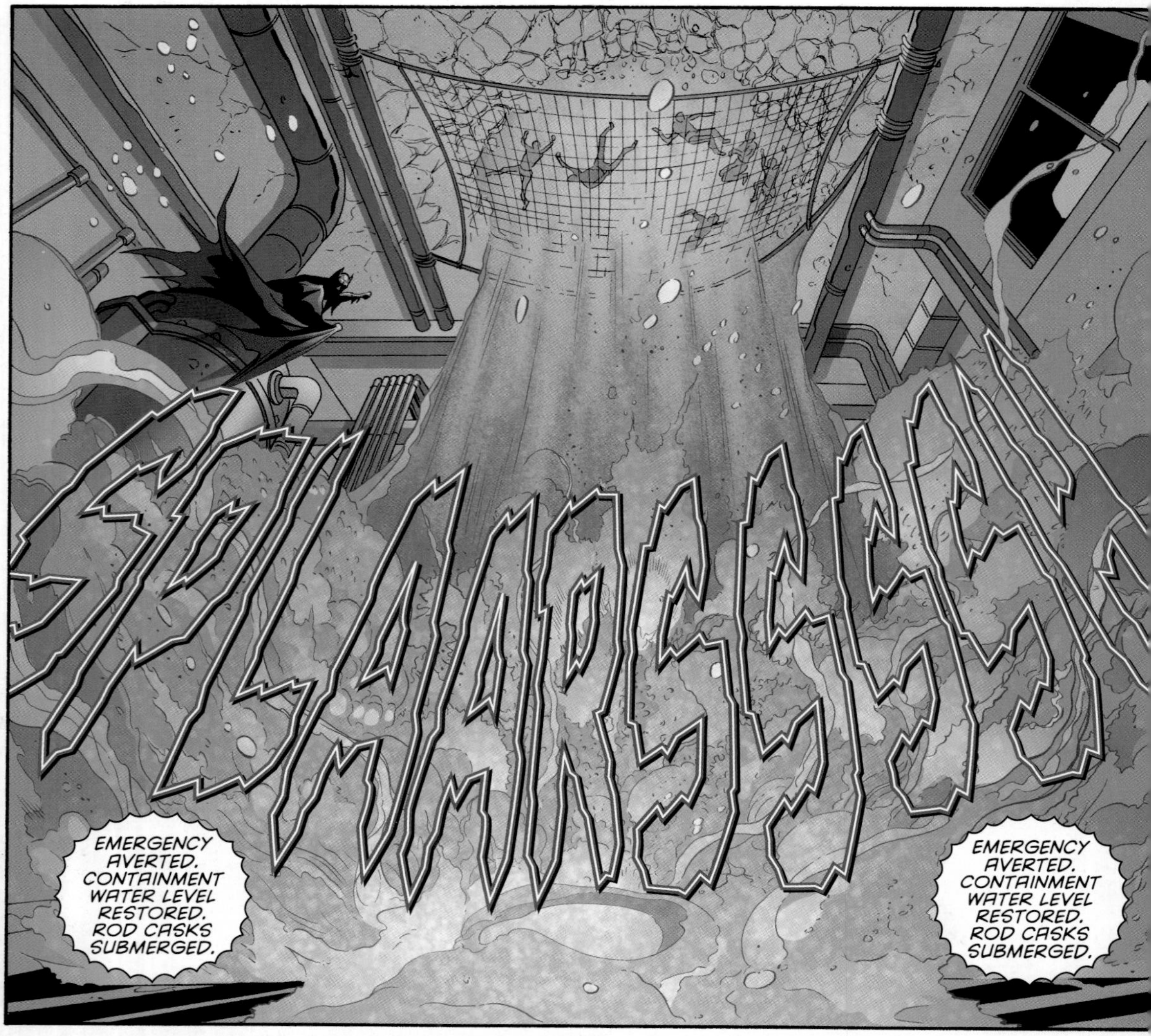
SPLAARSSSSSH
EMERGENCY AVERTED. CONTAINMENT WATER LEVEL RESTORED. ROD CASKS SUBMERGED.
EMERGENCY AVERTED. CONTAINMENT WATER LEVEL RESTORED. ROD CASKS SUBMERGED.

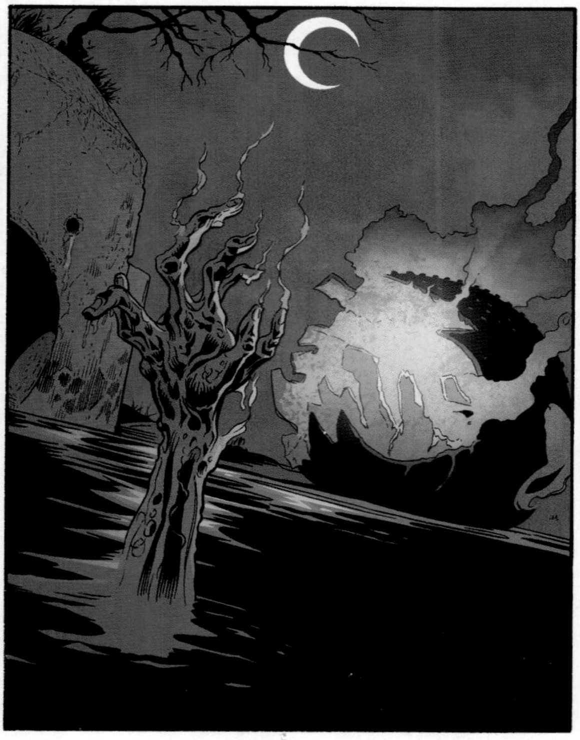

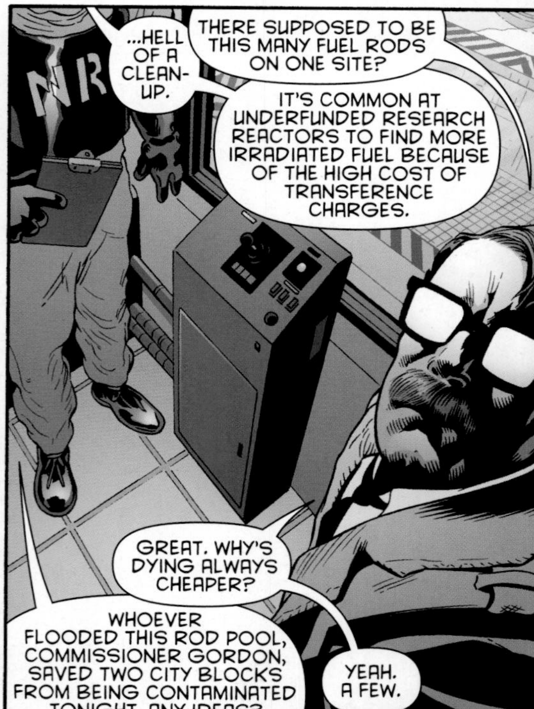
...HELL OF A CLEAN-UP.
THERE SUPPOSED TO BE THIS MANY FUEL RODS ON ONE SITE?
IT'S COMMON AT UNDERFUNDED RESEARCH REACTORS TO FIND MORE IRRADIATED FUEL BECAUSE OF THE HIGH COST OF TRANSFERENCE CHARGES.
GREAT. WHY'S DYING ALWAYS CHEAPER?
WHOEVER FLOODED THIS ROD POOL, COMMISSIONER GORDON, SAVED TWO CITY BLOCKS FROM BEING CONTAMINATED TONIGHT. ANY IDEAS?
YEAH. A FEW.

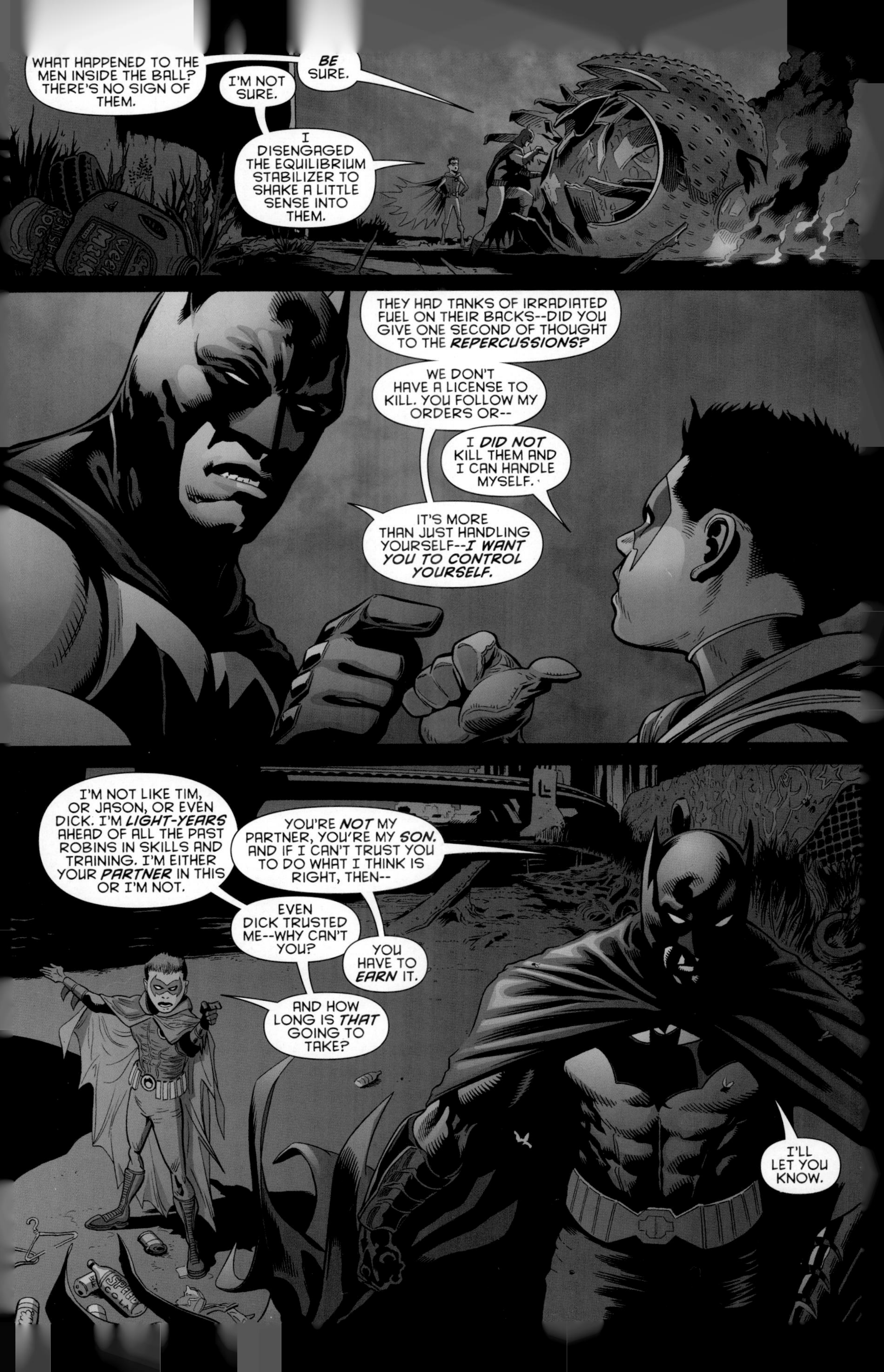
WHAT HAPPENED TO THE MEN INSIDE THE BALL? THERE'S NO SIGN OF THEM.
I'M NOT SURE.
I DISENGAGED THE EQUILIBRIUM STABILIZER TO SHAKE A LITTLE SENSE INTO THEM.
BE SURE.
THEY HAD TANKS OF IRRADIATED FUEL ON THEIR BACKS--DID YOU GIVE ONE SECOND OF THOUGHT TO THE REPERCUSSIONS?
WE DON'T HAVE A LICENSE TO KILL. YOU FOLLOW MY ORDERS OR--
I DID NOT KILL THEM AND I CAN HANDLE MYSELF.
IT'S MORE THAN JUST HANDLING YOURSELF--I WANT YOU TO CONTROL YOURSELF.
I'M NOT LIKE TIM, OR JASON, OR EVEN DICK. I'M LIGHT-YEARS AHEAD OF ALL THE PAST ROBINS IN SKILLS AND TRAINING. I'M EITHER YOUR PARTNER IN THIS OR I'M NOT.
YOU'RE NOT MY PARTNER, YOU'RE MY SON. AND IF I CAN'T TRUST YOU TO DO WHAT I THINK IS RIGHT, THEN--
EVEN DICK TRUSTED ME--WHY CAN'T YOU?
YOU HAVE TO EARN IT.
AND HOW LONG IS THAT GOING TO TAKE?
I'LL LET YOU KNOW.

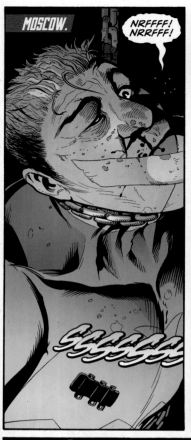

MOSCOW.
NRFFFF! NRFFFF!
SSSSSSS
RRRGFFF! RRRGFF!
MY APOLOGIES, I EXPECTED YOU TO REMAIN UNCONSCIOUS FOR THIS. YOU MUST COME FROM HARDY STOCK.
SSSSSSS
SSSSSSS
NAARR! RRAFFF!
I'M ERASING YOU.
NRRRRRRR!
IT'LL BE LIKE YOU NEVER EXISTED AT ALL.
SSSSSSS
THIS NEW GLOBAL CIRCUS ACT OF HIS HAS TO END.
IT'S TIME TO PAY BRUCE WAYNE A VISIT.

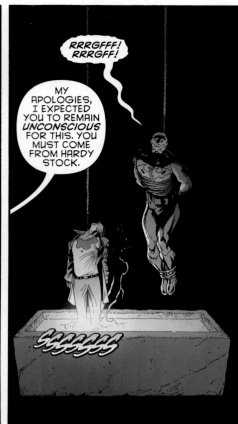

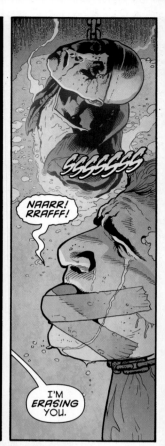

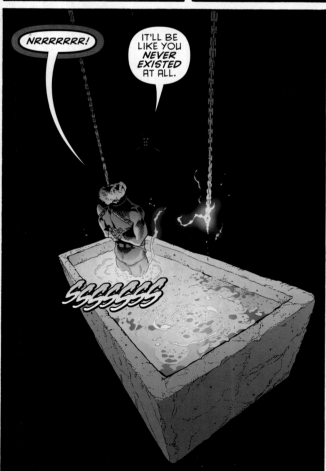

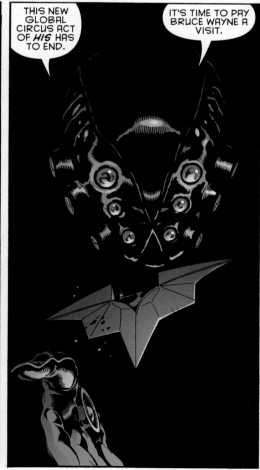

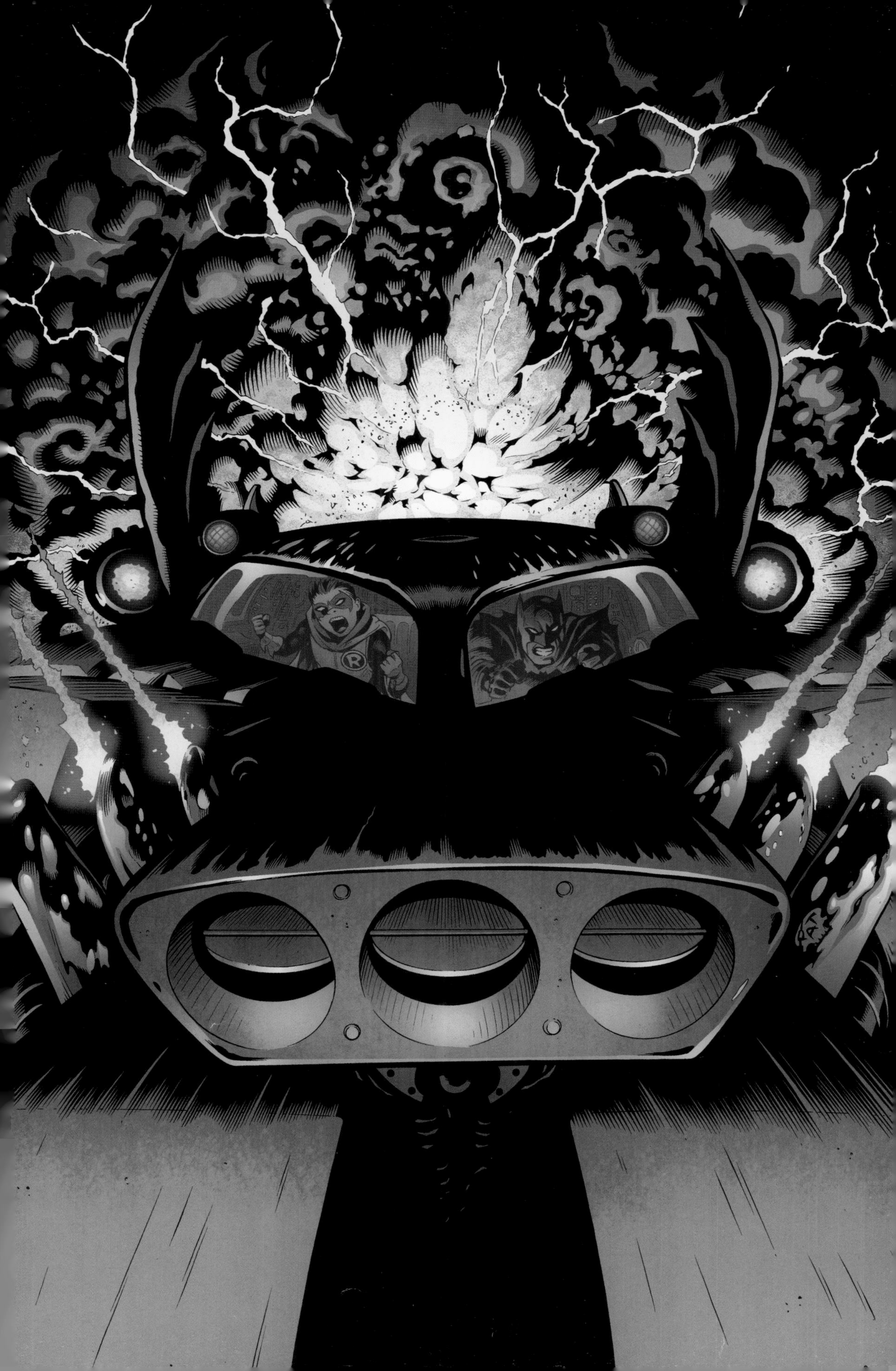

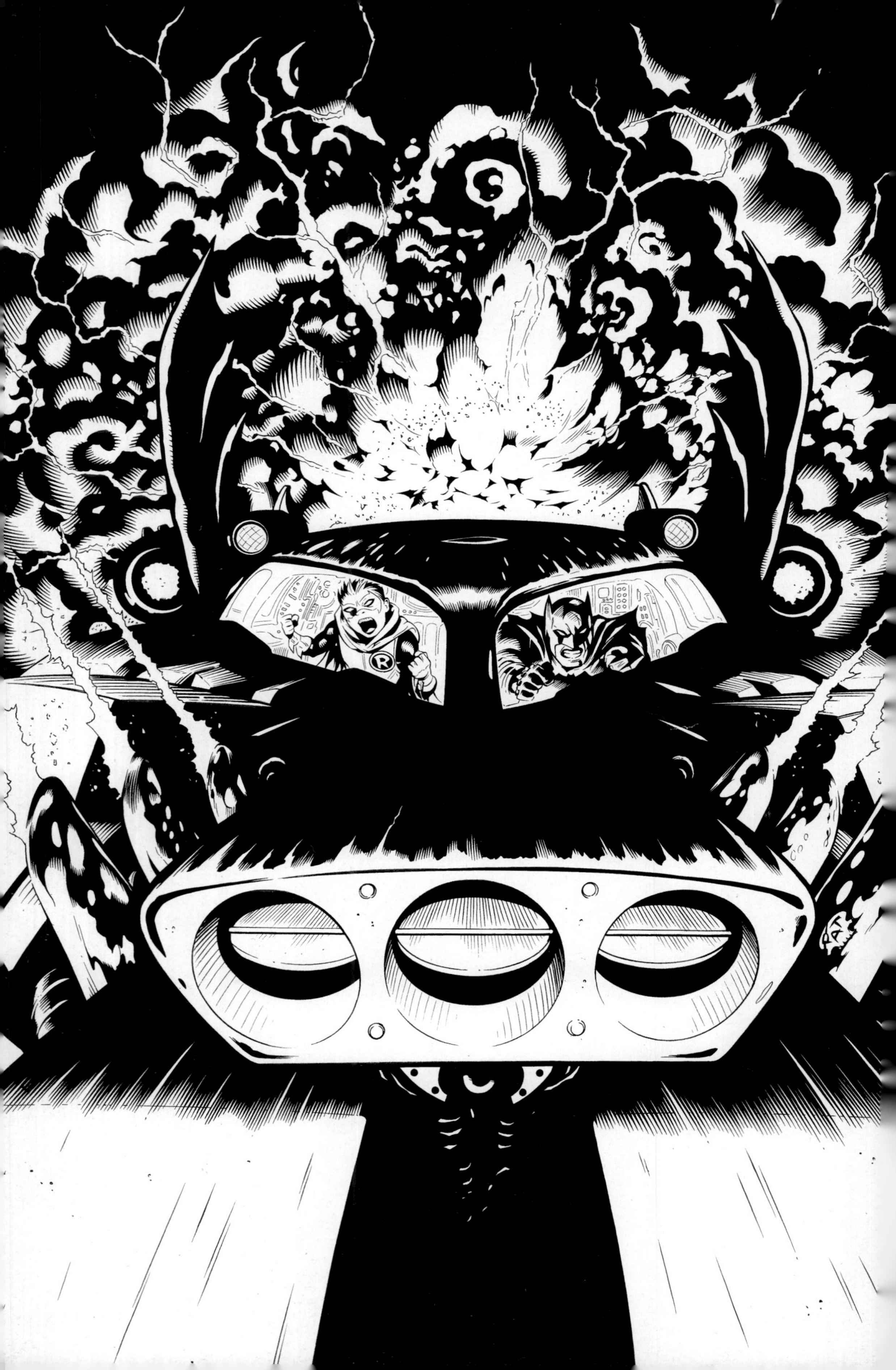

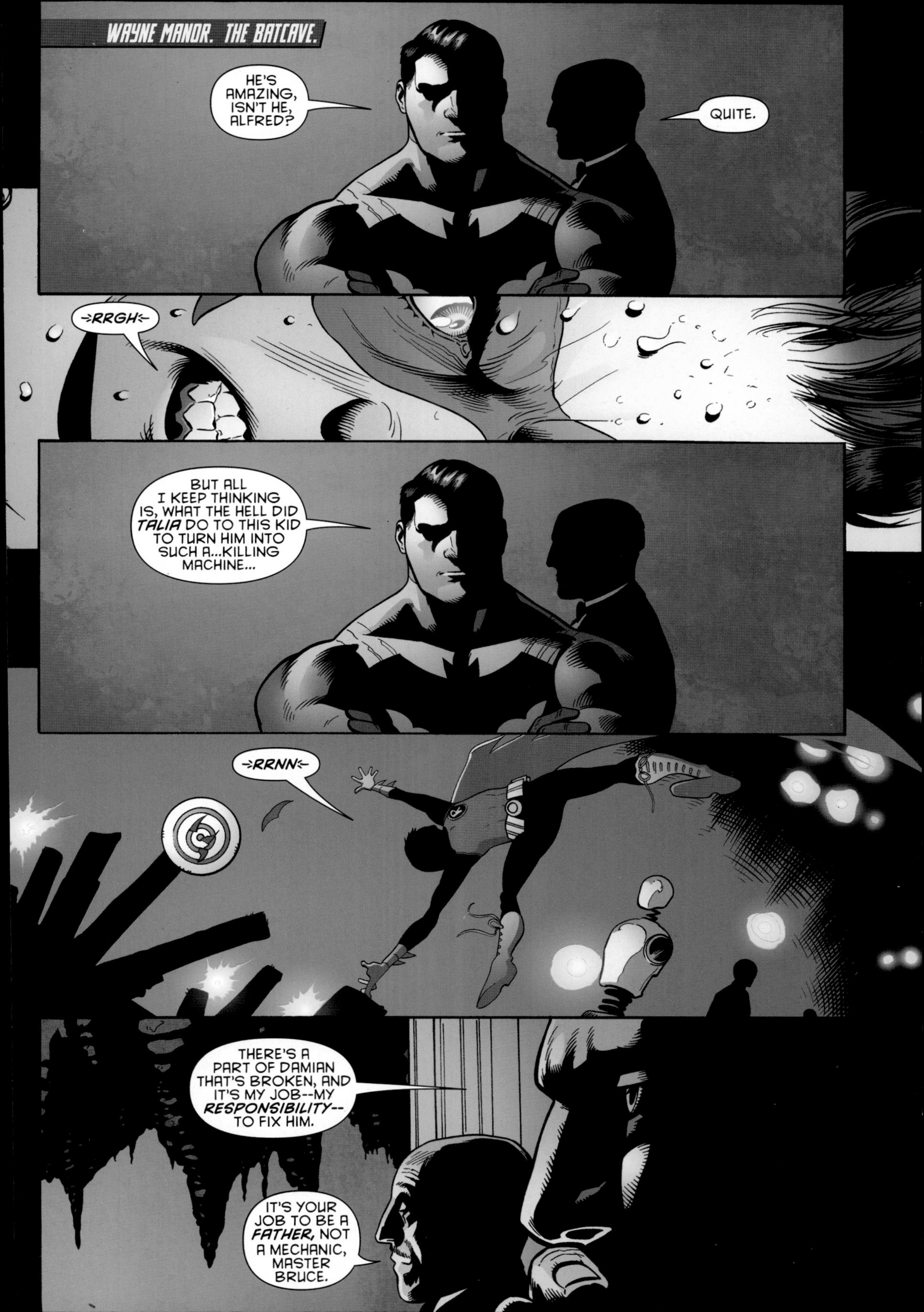
WAYNE MANOR. THE BATCAVE.
HE'S AMAZING, ISN'T HE, ALFRED?
QUITE.
-RRGH-
BUT ALL I KEEP THINKING IS, WHAT THE HELL DID *TALIA* DO TO THIS KID TO TURN HIM INTO SUCH A...KILLING MACHINE...
-RRNN-
THERE'S A PART OF DAMIAN THAT'S BROKEN, AND IT'S MY JOB--MY *RESPONSIBILITY*-- TO FIX HIM.
IT'S YOUR JOB TO BE A *FATHER,* NOT A MECHANIC, MASTER BRUCE.

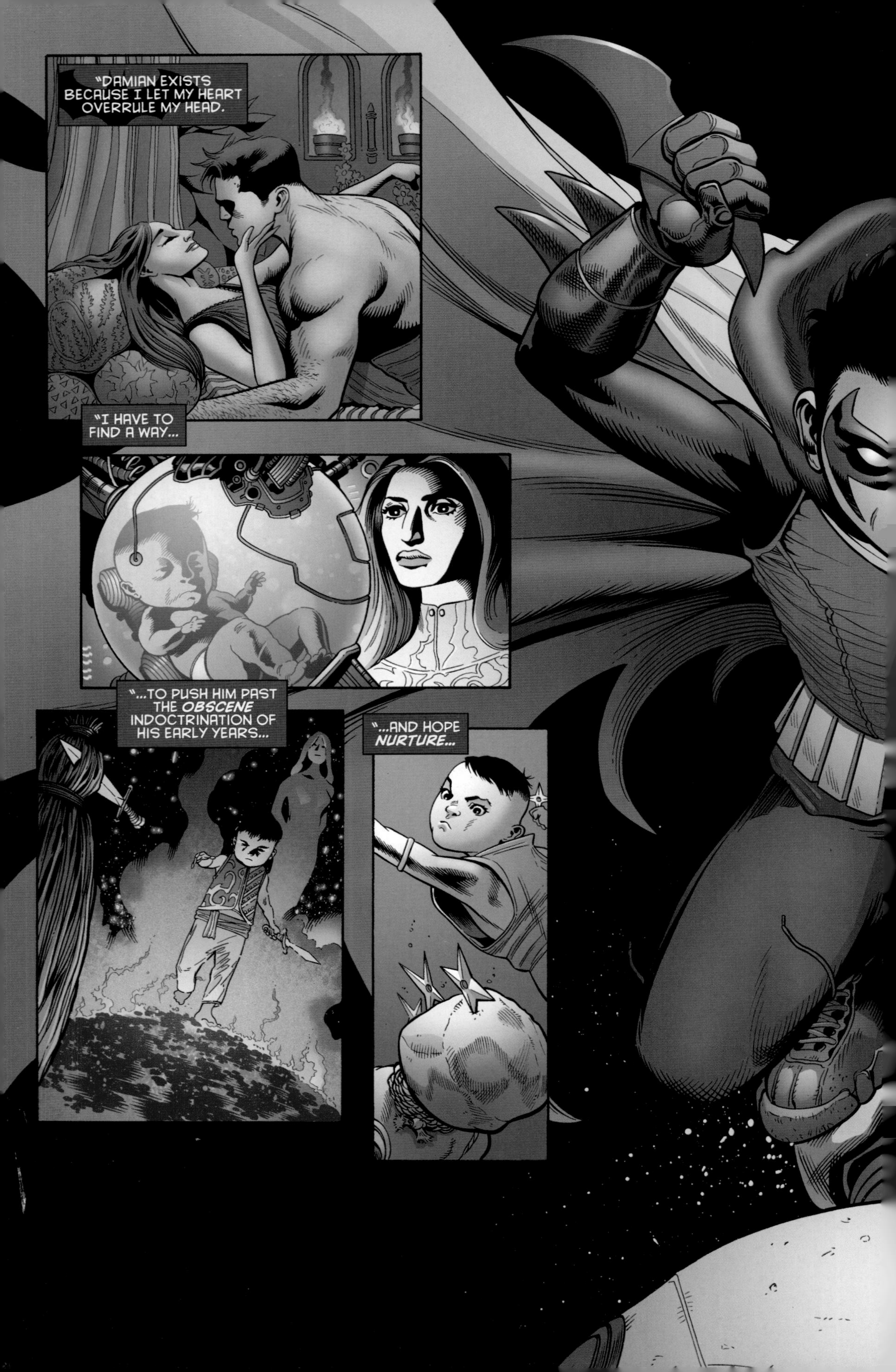
"DAMIAN EXISTS BECAUSE I LET MY HEART OVERRULE MY HEAD.
"I HAVE TO FIND A WAY...
"...TO PUSH HIM PAST THE OBSCENE INDOCTRINATION OF HIS EARLY YEARS...
"...AND HOPE NURTURE...

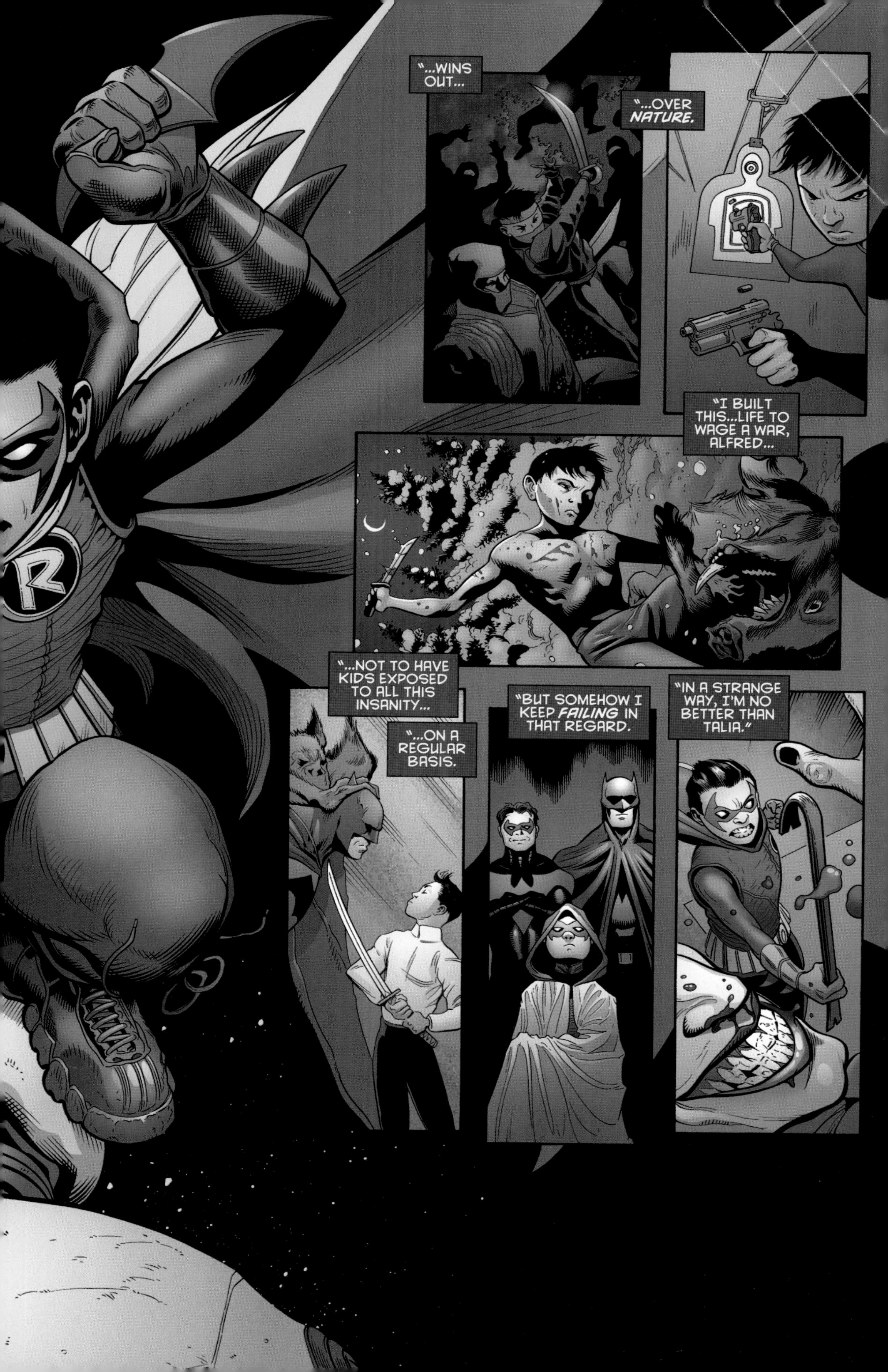
"...WINS OUT...
"...OVER NATURE.
"I BUILT THIS...LIFE TO WAGE A WAR, ALFRED...
"...NOT TO HAVE KIDS EXPOSED TO ALL THIS INSANITY...
"...ON A REGULAR BASIS.
"BUT SOMEHOW I KEEP FAILING IN THAT REGARD.
"IN A STRANGE WAY, I'M NO BETTER THAN TALIA."

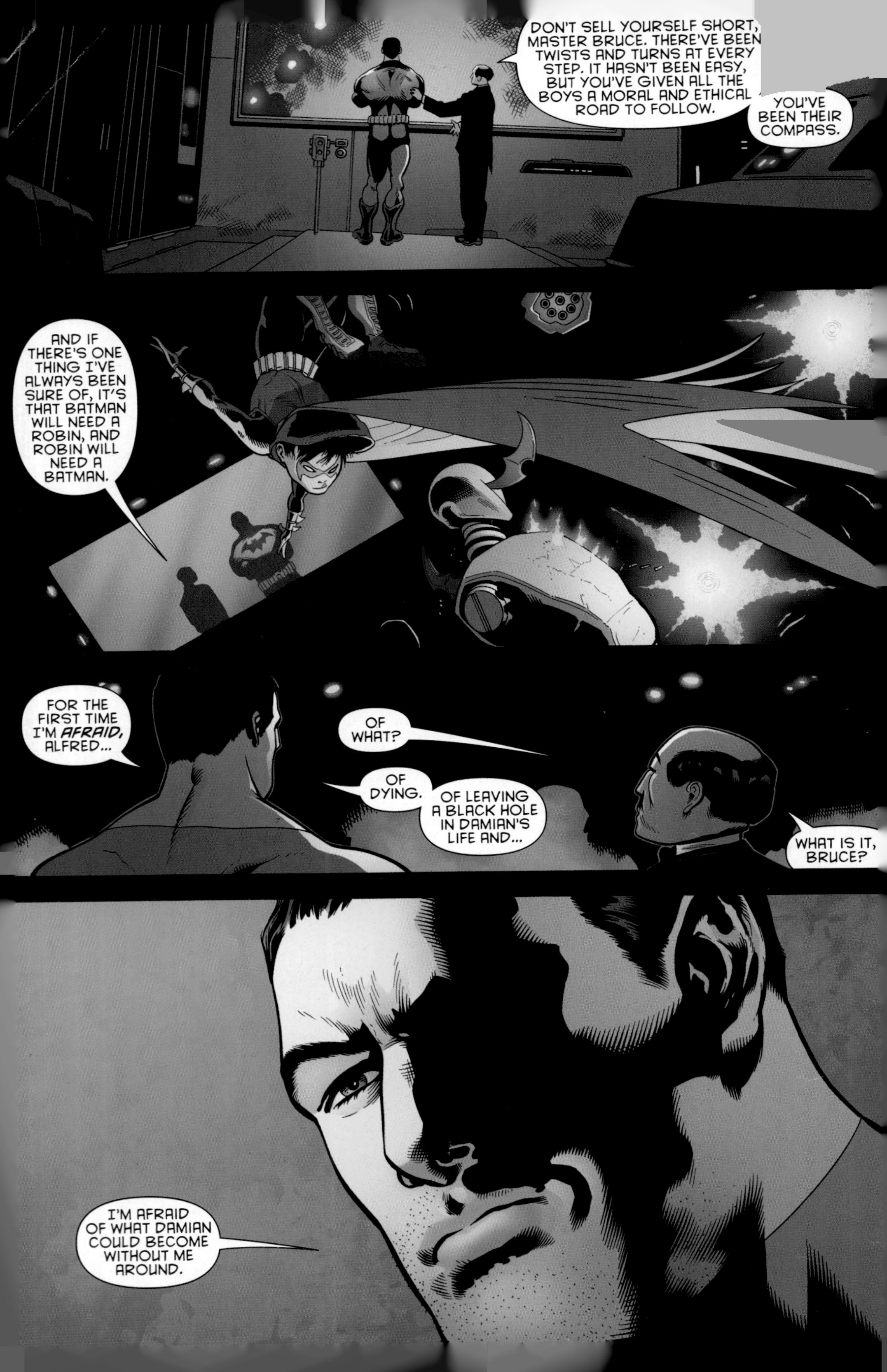
DON'T SELL YOURSELF SHORT, MASTER BRUCE. THERE'VE BEEN TWISTS AND TURNS AT EVERY STEP. IT HASN'T BEEN EASY, BUT YOU'VE GIVEN ALL THE BOYS A MORAL AND ETHICAL ROAD TO FOLLOW.
YOU'VE BEEN THEIR COMPASS.
AND IF THERE'S ONE THING I'VE ALWAYS BEEN SURE OF, IT'S THAT BATMAN WILL NEED A ROBIN, AND ROBIN WILL NEED A BATMAN.
FOR THE FIRST TIME I'M AFRAID, ALFRED...
OF WHAT?
OF DYING.
OF LEAVING A BLACK HOLE IN DAMIAN'S LIFE AND...
WHAT IS IT, BRUCE?
I'M AFRAID OF WHAT DAMIAN COULD BECOME WITHOUT ME AROUND.

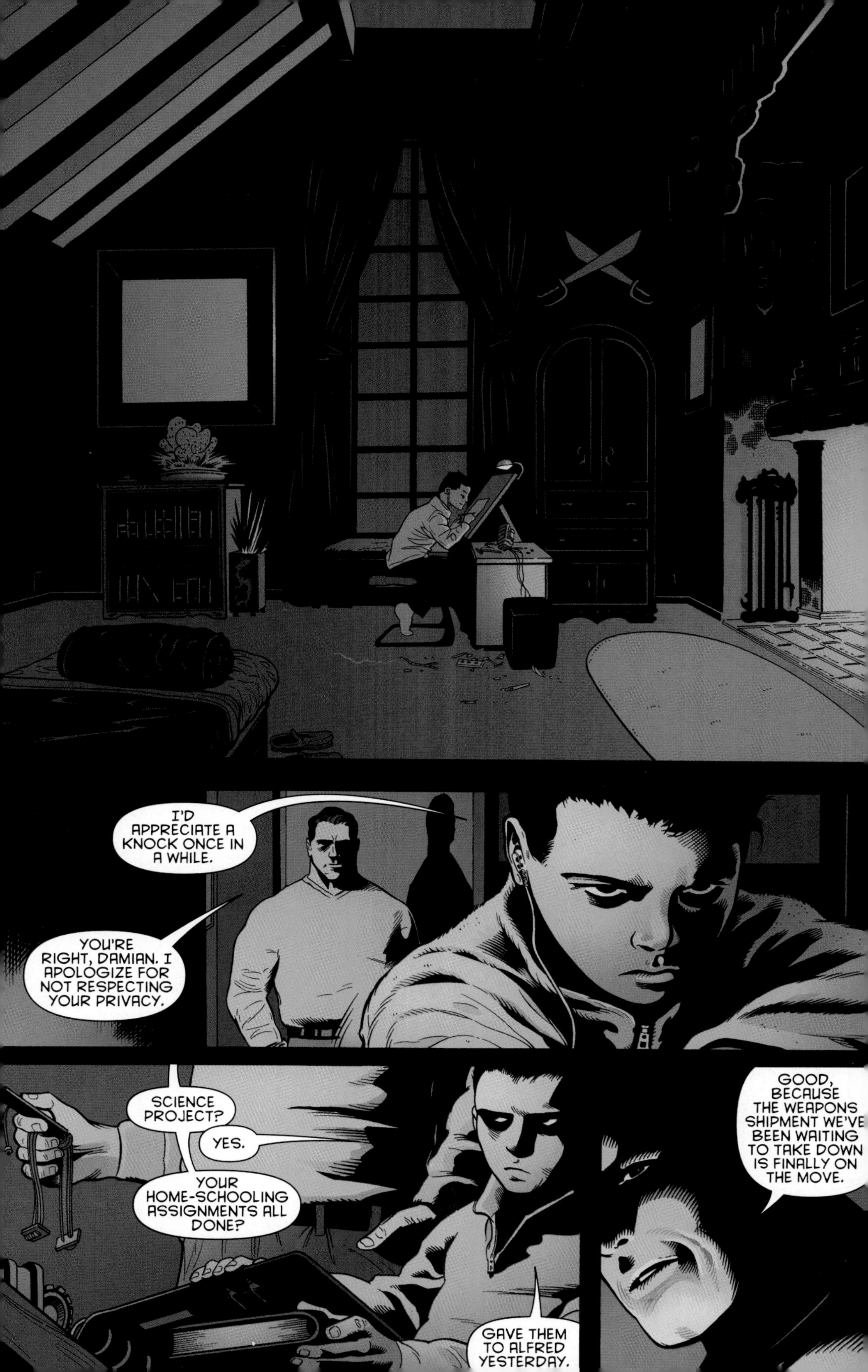
I'D APPRECIATE A KNOCK ONCE IN A WHILE.
YOU'RE RIGHT, DAMIAN. I APOLOGIZE FOR NOT RESPECTING YOUR PRIVACY.
SCIENCE PROJECT?
YES.
YOUR HOME-SCHOOLING ASSIGNMENTS ALL DONE?
GAVE THEM TO ALFRED YESTERDAY.
GOOD, BECAUSE THE WEAPONS SHIPMENT WE'VE BEEN WAITING TO TAKE DOWN IS FINALLY ON THE MOVE.

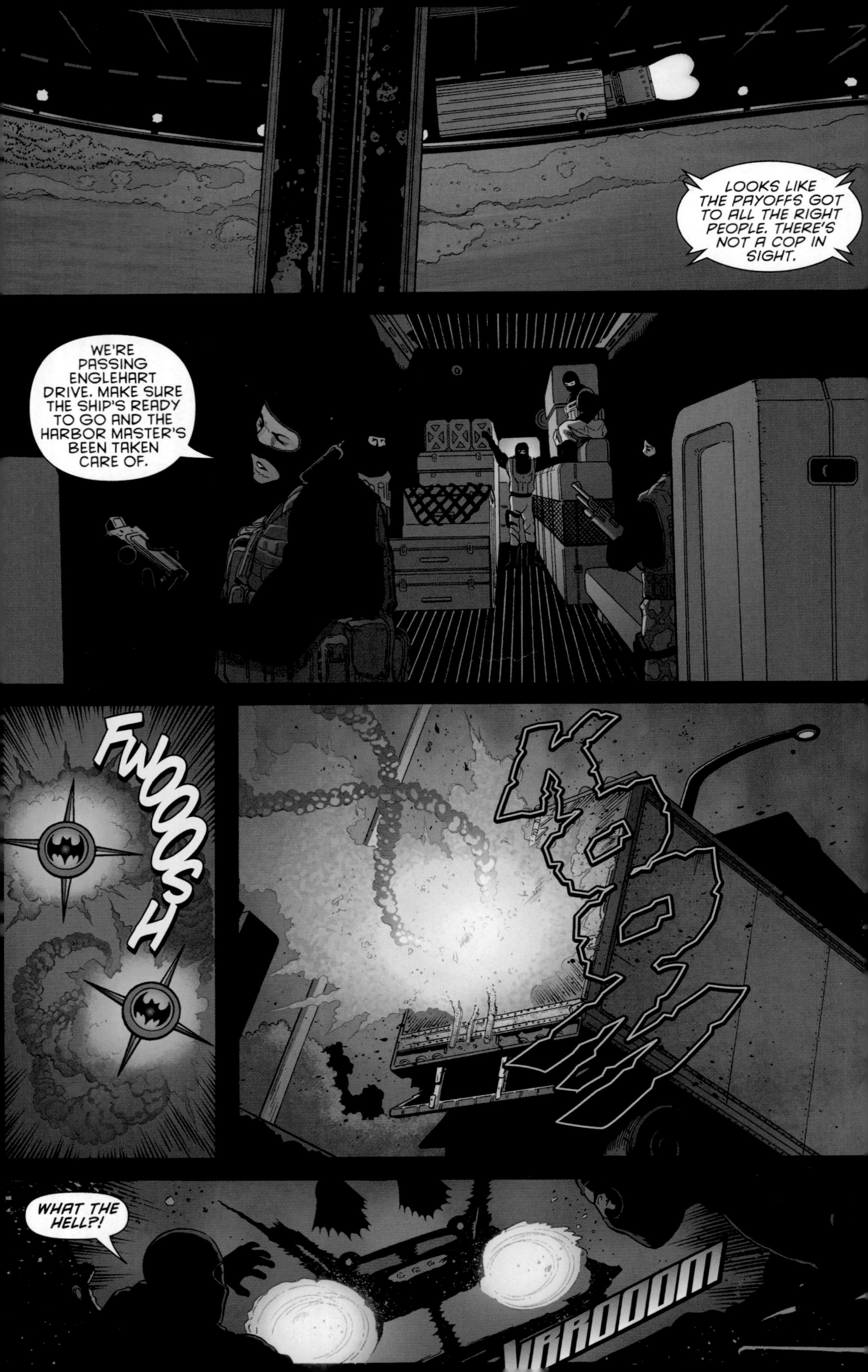
LOOKS LIKE THE PAYOFFS GOT TO ALL THE RIGHT PEOPLE. THERE'S NOT A COP IN SIGHT.
WE'RE PASSING ENGLEHART DRIVE. MAKE SURE THE SHIP'S READY TO GO AND THE HARBOR MASTER'S BEEN TAKEN CARE OF.
FWOOOOSH
WHAT THE HELL?!
VRROOOM

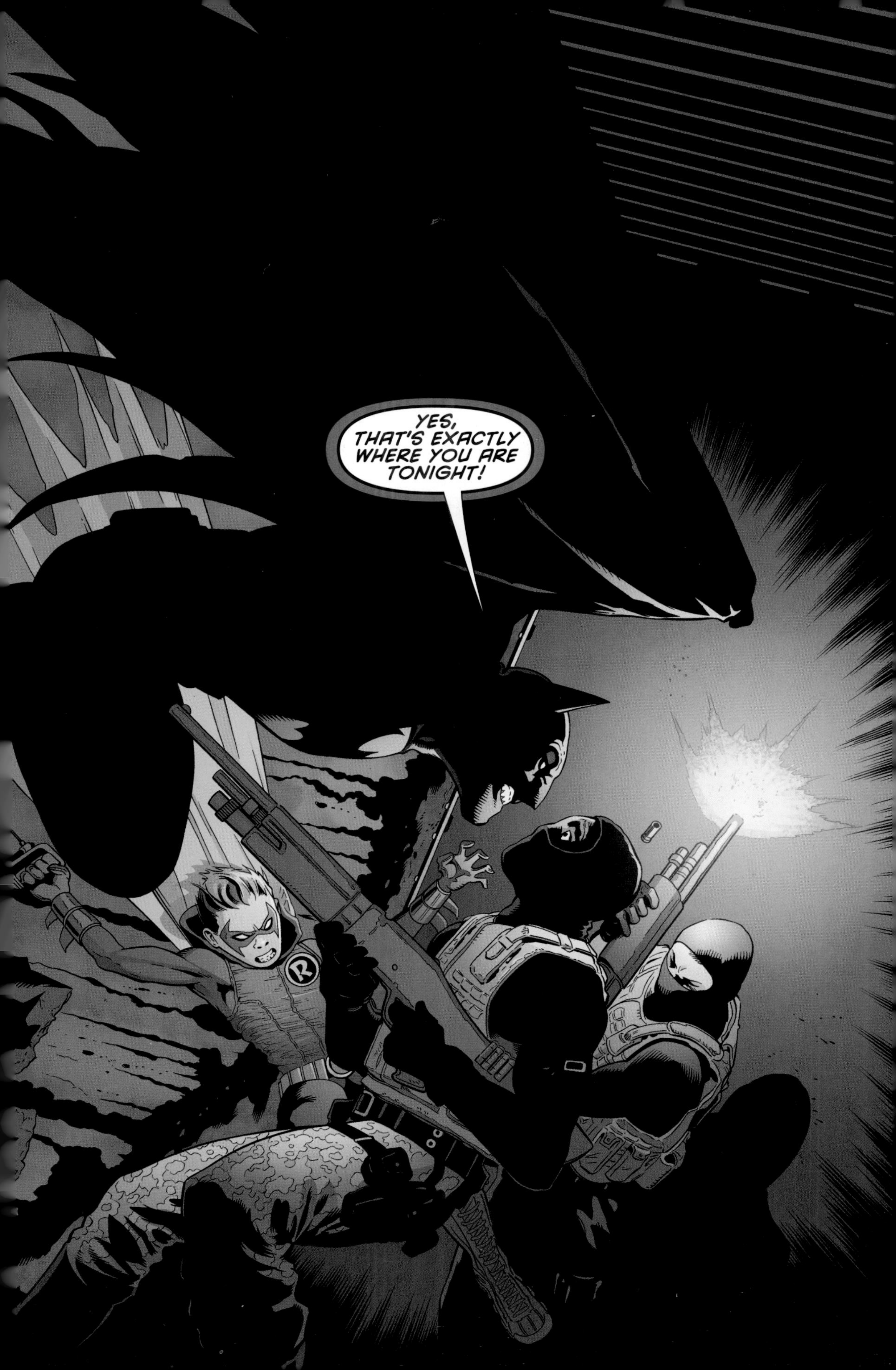
YES, THAT'S EXACTLY WHERE YOU ARE TONIGHT!

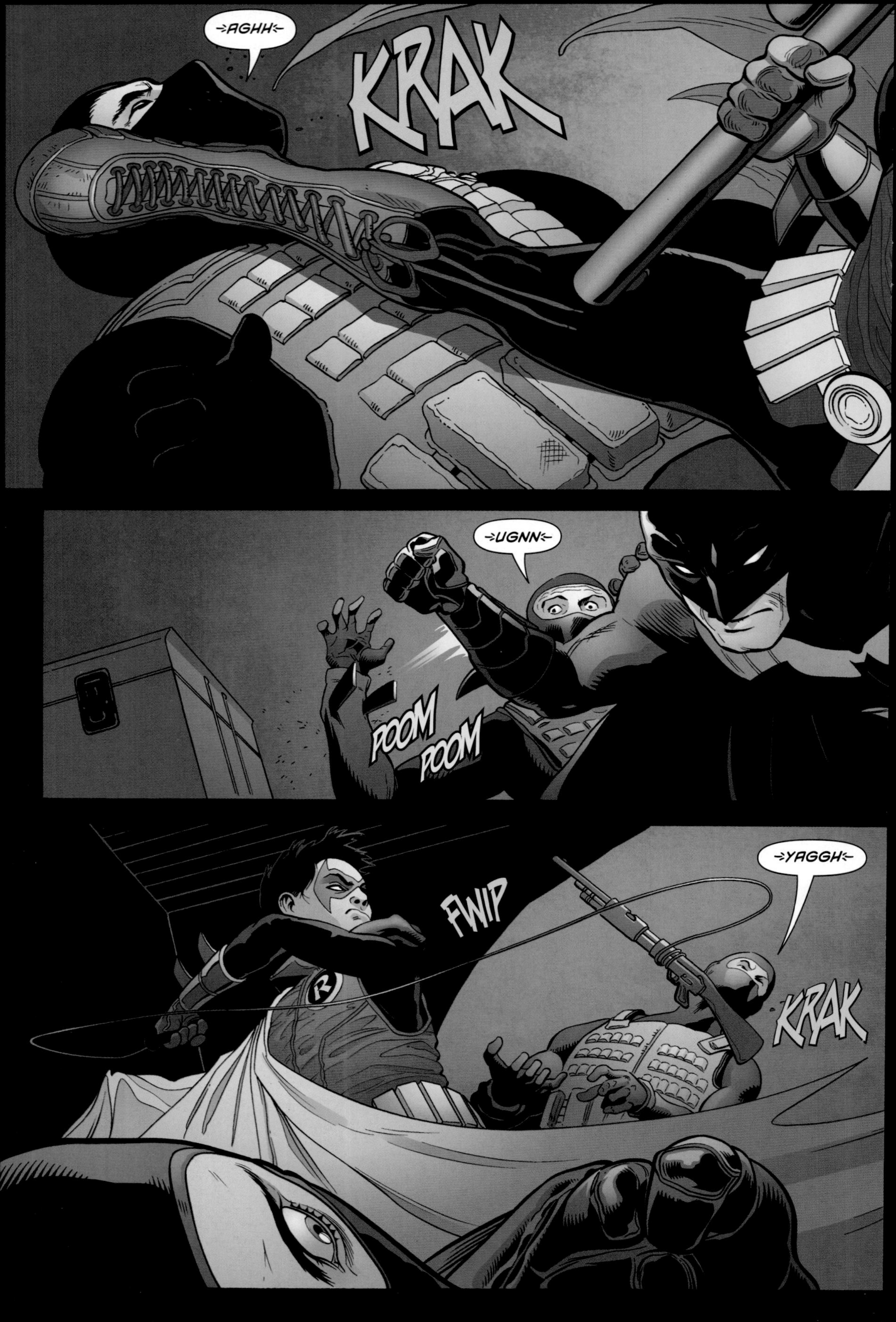

-AGHH-
KRAK
-UGNN-
POOM
POOM
FWIP
-YAGGH-
KRAK

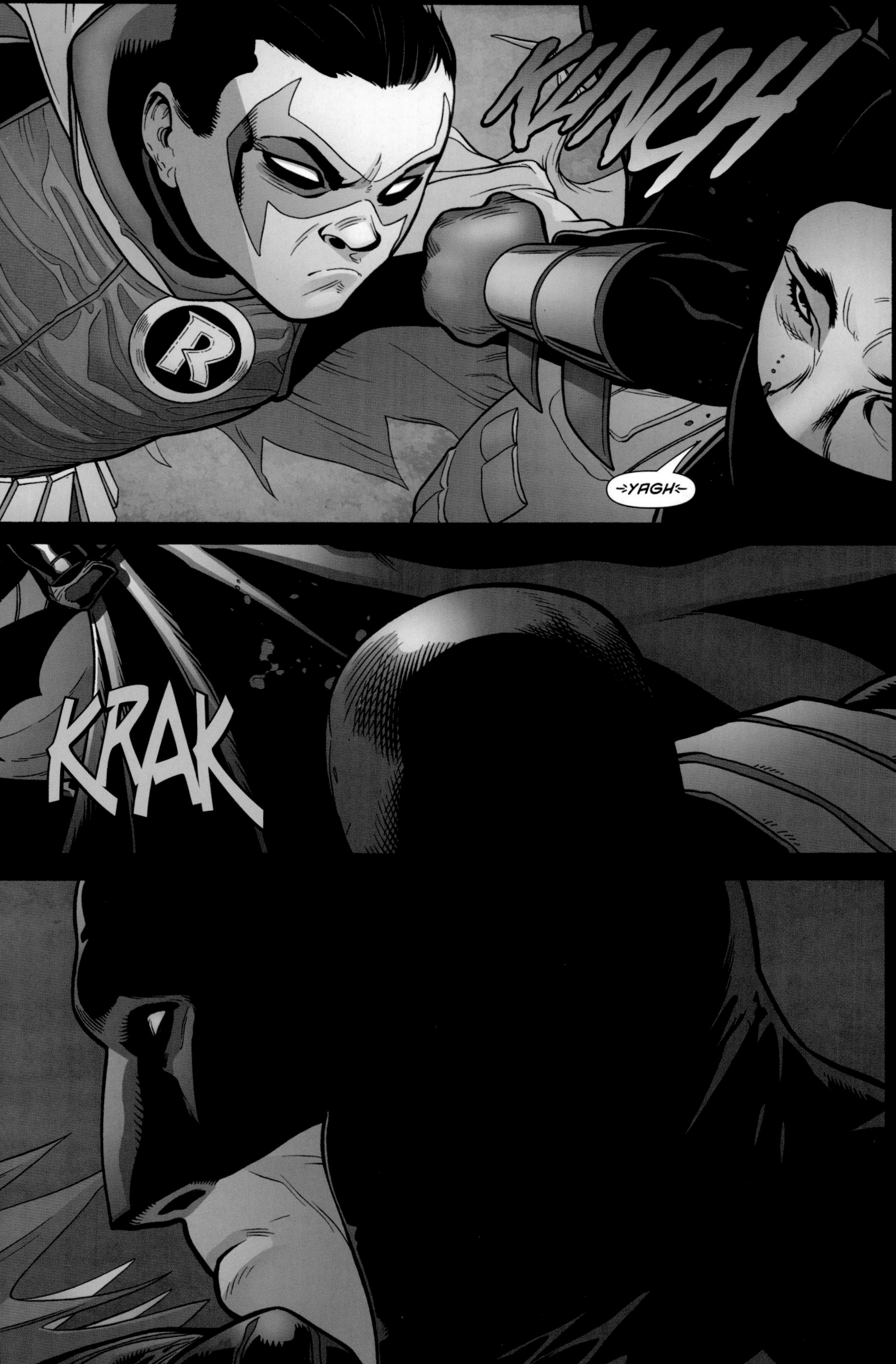
YAGH
KRAK

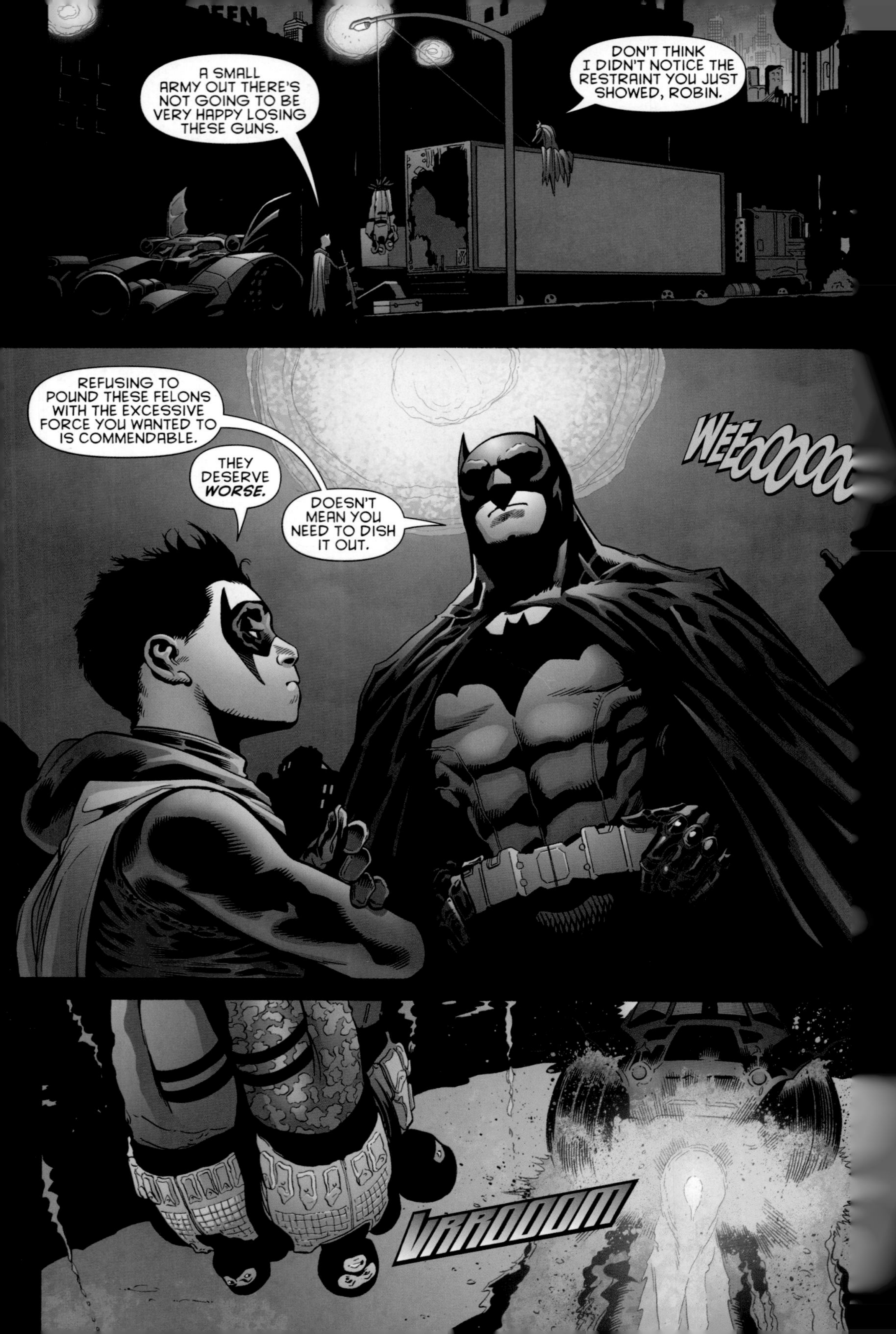
A SMALL ARMY OUT THERE'S NOT GOING TO BE VERY HAPPY LOSING THESE GUNS.
DON'T THINK I DIDN'T NOTICE THE RESTRAINT YOU JUST SHOWED, ROBIN.
REFUSING TO POUND THESE FELONS WITH THE EXCESSIVE FORCE YOU WANTED TO IS COMMENDABLE.
THEY DESERVE *WORSE.*
DOESN'T MEAN YOU NEED TO DISH IT OUT.
WEEOOOOO
VRROOOM

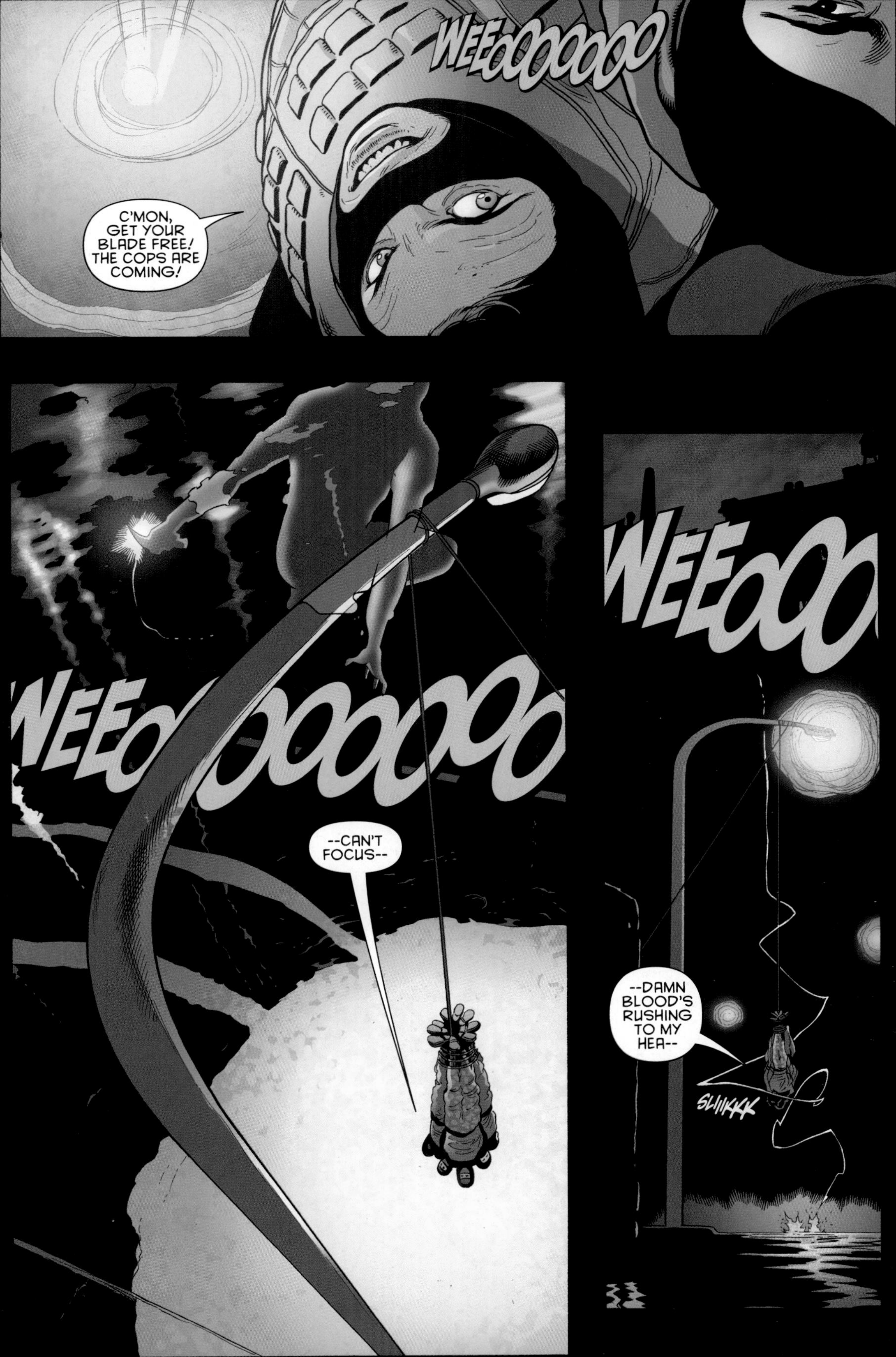
WEEOOOOOOO
C'MON, GET YOUR BLADE FREE! THE COPS ARE COMING!
WEEOOOOOOOO
--CAN'T FOCUS--
WEEOOO
--DAMN BLOOD'S RUSHING TO MY HEA--
SLIIIKKK

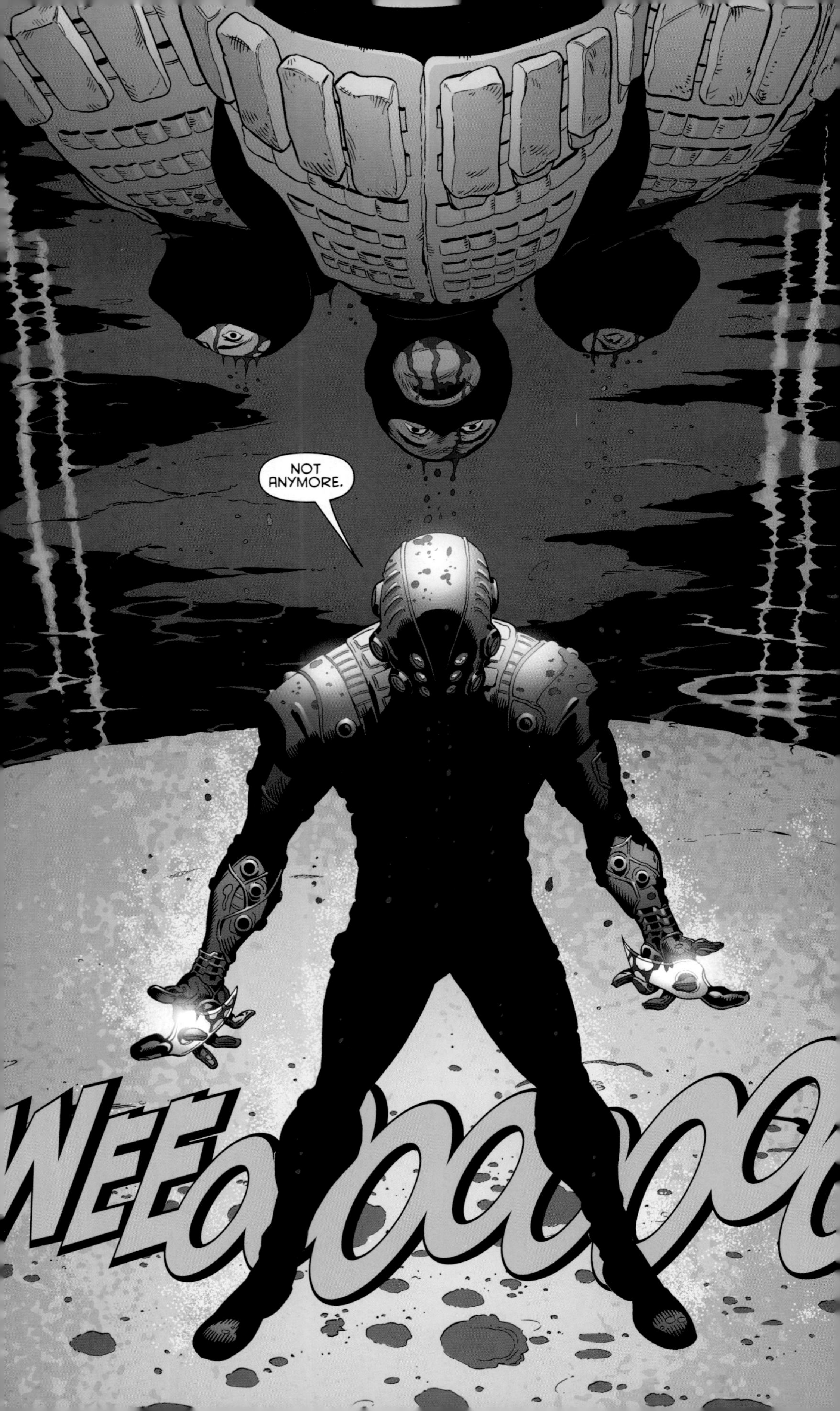
NOT ANYMORE.
WEEaaaaa

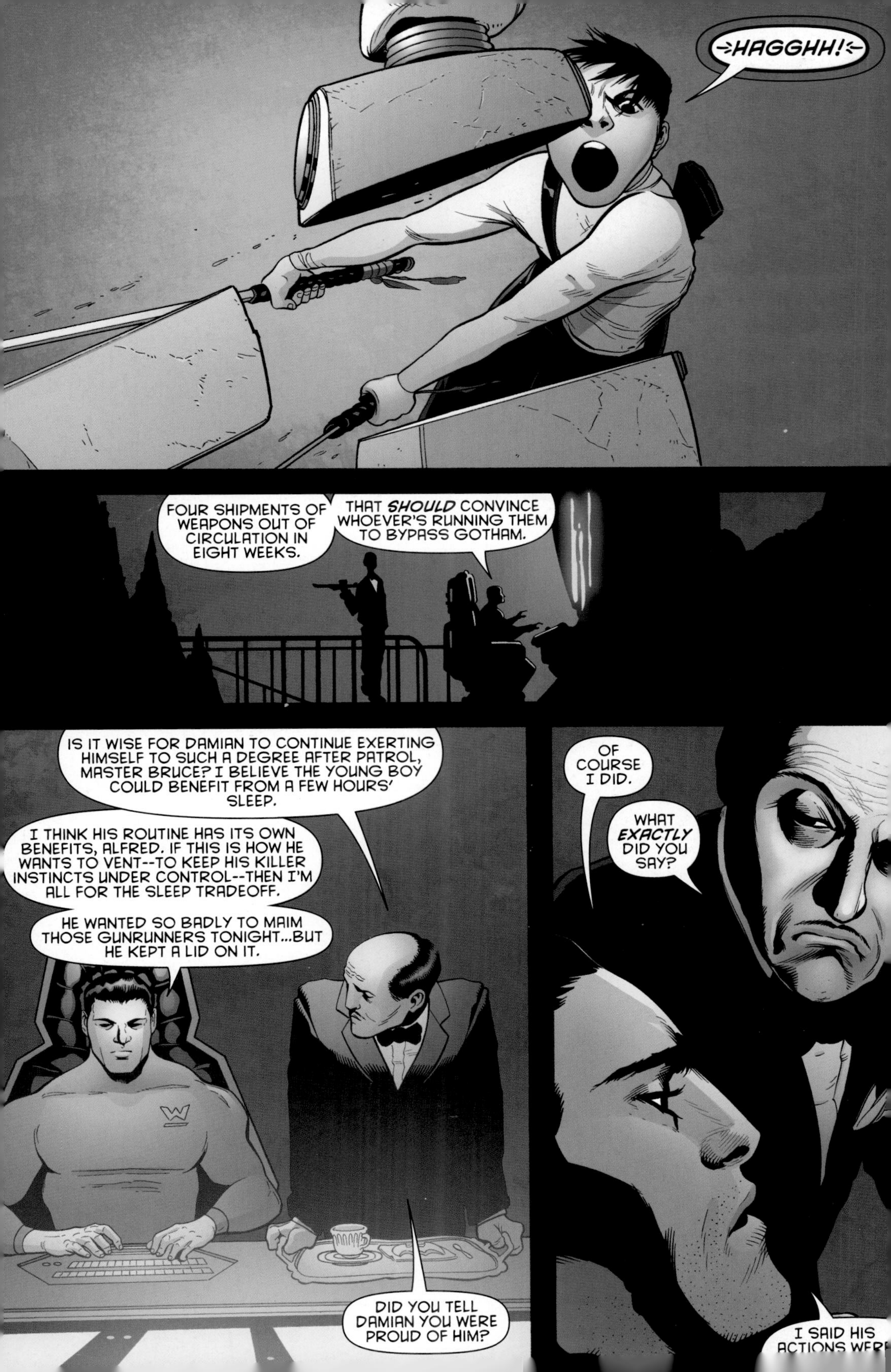

HAGGHH!
FOUR SHIPMENTS OF WEAPONS OUT OF CIRCULATION IN EIGHT WEEKS.
THAT SHOULD CONVINCE WHOEVER'S RUNNING THEM TO BYPASS GOTHAM.
IS IT WISE FOR DAMIAN TO CONTINUE EXERTING HIMSELF TO SUCH A DEGREE AFTER PATROL, MASTER BRUCE? I BELIEVE THE YOUNG BOY COULD BENEFIT FROM A FEW HOURS' SLEEP.
I THINK HIS ROUTINE HAS ITS OWN BENEFITS, ALFRED. IF THIS IS HOW HE WANTS TO VENT--TO KEEP HIS KILLER INSTINCTS UNDER CONTROL--THEN I'M ALL FOR THE SLEEP TRADEOFF.
HE WANTED SO BADLY TO MAIM THOSE GUNRUNNERS TONIGHT...BUT HE KEPT A LID ON IT.
DID YOU TELL DAMIAN YOU WERE PROUD OF HIM?
OF COURSE I DID.
WHAT EXACTLY DID YOU SAY?
I SAID HIS ACTIONS WERE

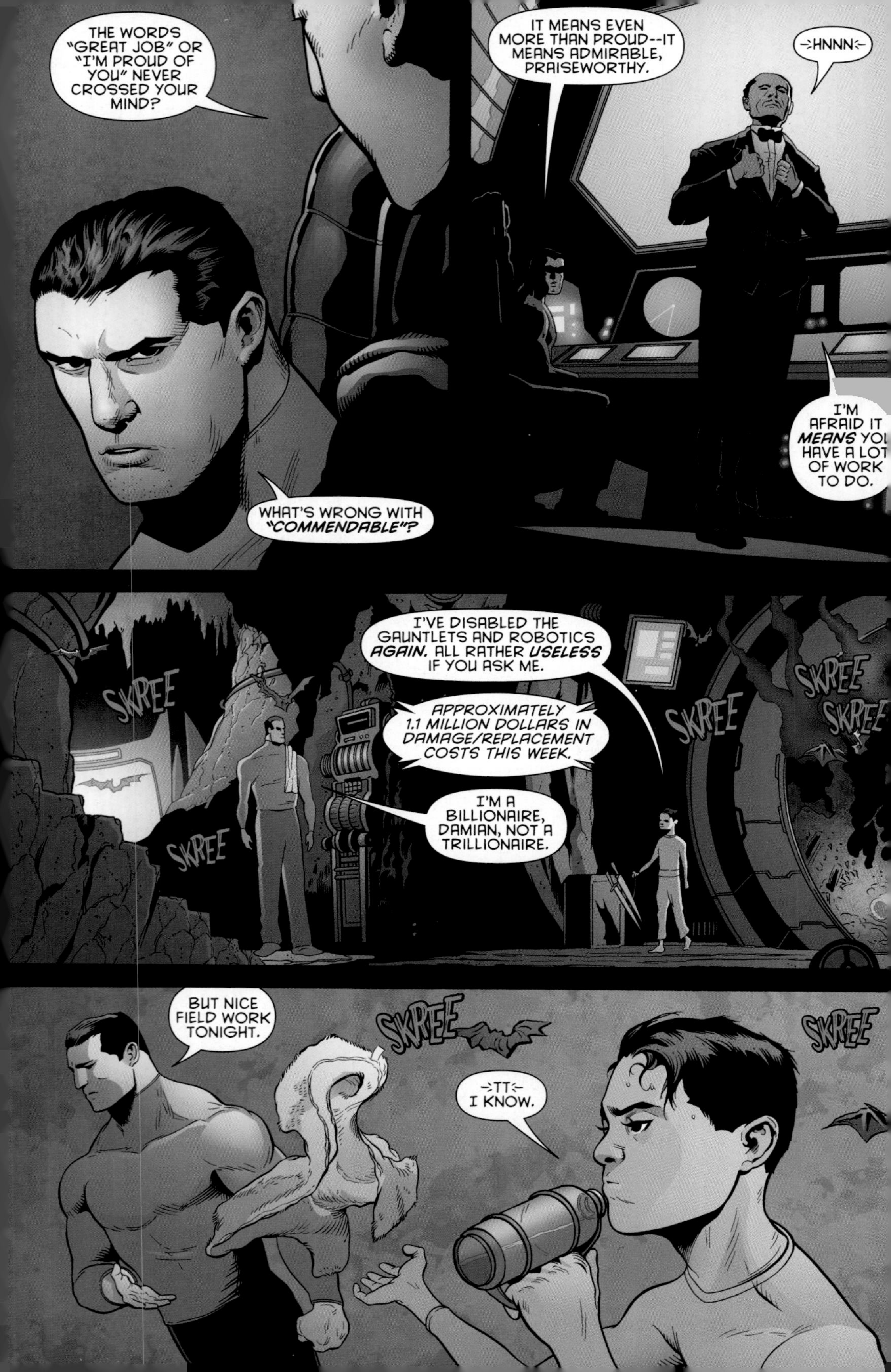
THE WORDS "GREAT JOB" OR "I'M PROUD OF YOU" NEVER CROSSED YOUR MIND?
IT MEANS EVEN MORE THAN PROUD--IT MEANS ADMIRABLE, PRAISEWORTHY.
WHAT'S WRONG WITH "COMMENDABLE"?
HNNN
I'M AFRAID IT MEANS YOU HAVE A LOT OF WORK TO DO.
SKREE
SKREE
I'VE DISABLED THE GAUNTLETS AND ROBOTICS AGAIN. ALL RATHER USELESS IF YOU ASK ME.
APPROXIMATELY 1.1 MILLION DOLLARS IN DAMAGE/REPLACEMENT COSTS THIS WEEK.
I'M A BILLIONAIRE, DAMIAN, NOT A TRILLIONAIRE.
SKREE
SKREE
SKREE
BUT NICE FIELD WORK TONIGHT.
SKREE
SKREE
TT
I KNOW.

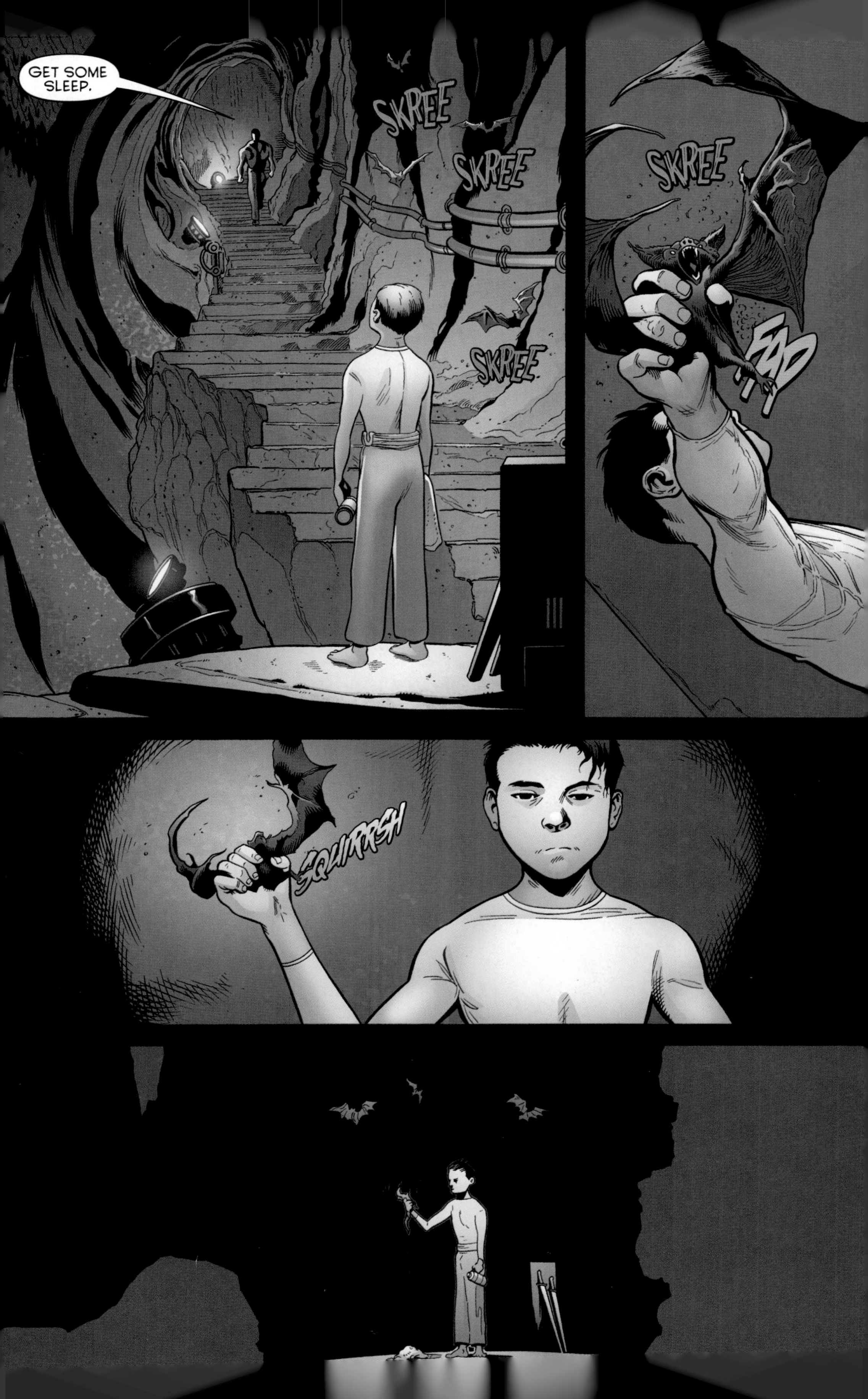
GET SOME SLEEP.
SKREE
SKREE
SKREE
SKREE
SQUIRRSH

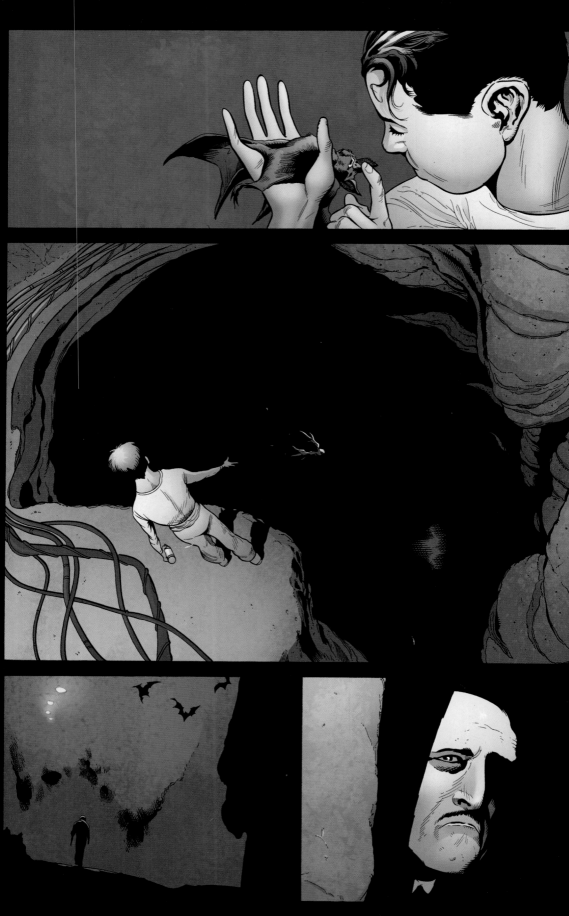

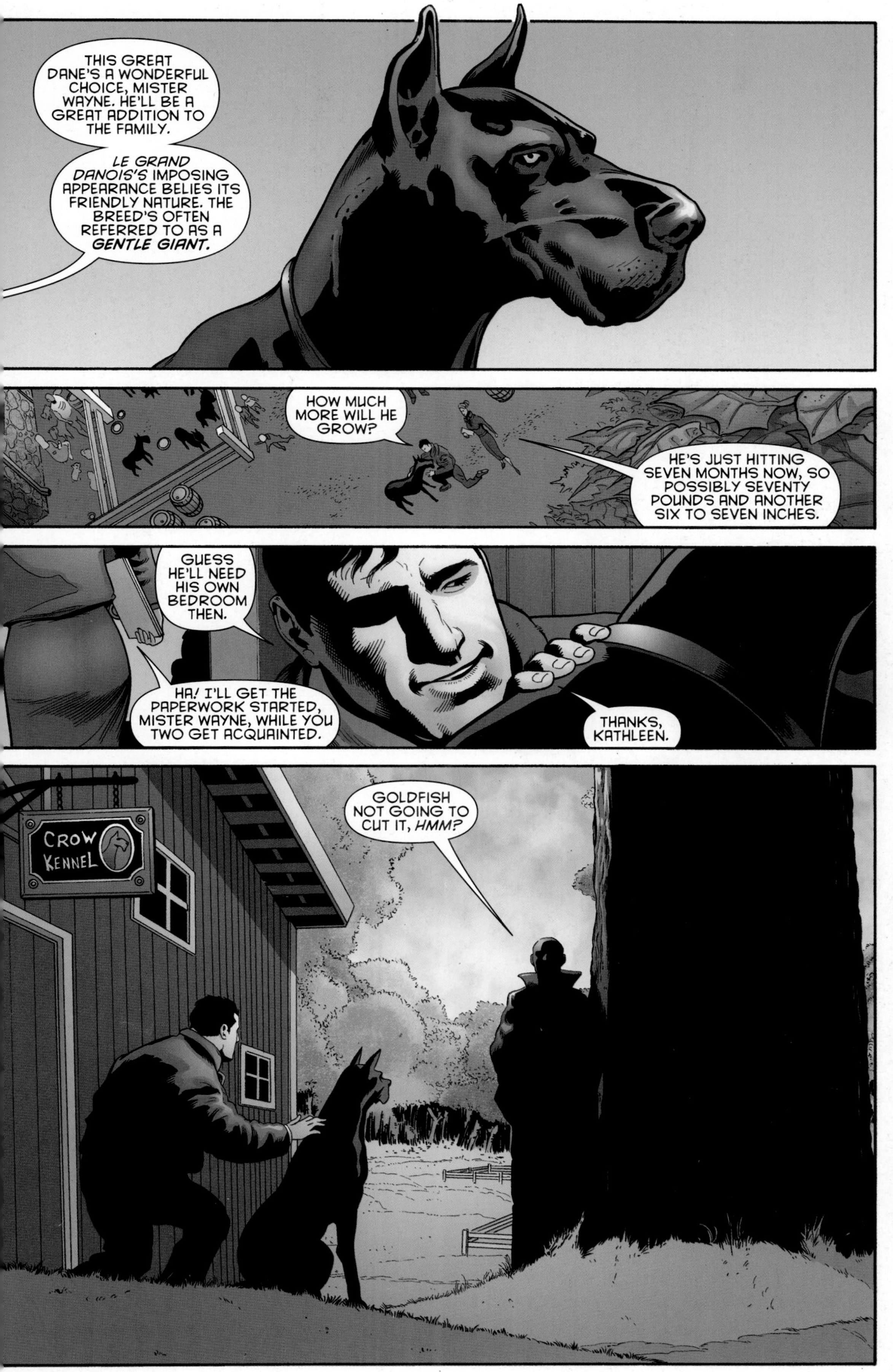
THIS GREAT DANE'S A WONDERFUL CHOICE, MISTER WAYNE. HE'LL BE A GREAT ADDITION TO THE FAMILY.
LE GRAND DANOIS'S IMPOSING APPEARANCE BELIES ITS FRIENDLY NATURE. THE BREED'S OFTEN REFERRED TO AS A GENTLE GIANT.
HOW MUCH MORE WILL HE GROW?
HE'S JUST HITTING SEVEN MONTHS NOW, SO POSSIBLY SEVENTY POUNDS AND ANOTHER SIX TO SEVEN INCHES.
GUESS HE'LL NEED HIS OWN BEDROOM THEN.
HA! I'LL GET THE PAPERWORK STARTED, MISTER WAYNE, WHILE YOU TWO GET ACQUAINTED.
THANKS, KATHLEEN.
CROW KENNEL
GOLDFISH NOT GOING TO CUT IT, HMM?

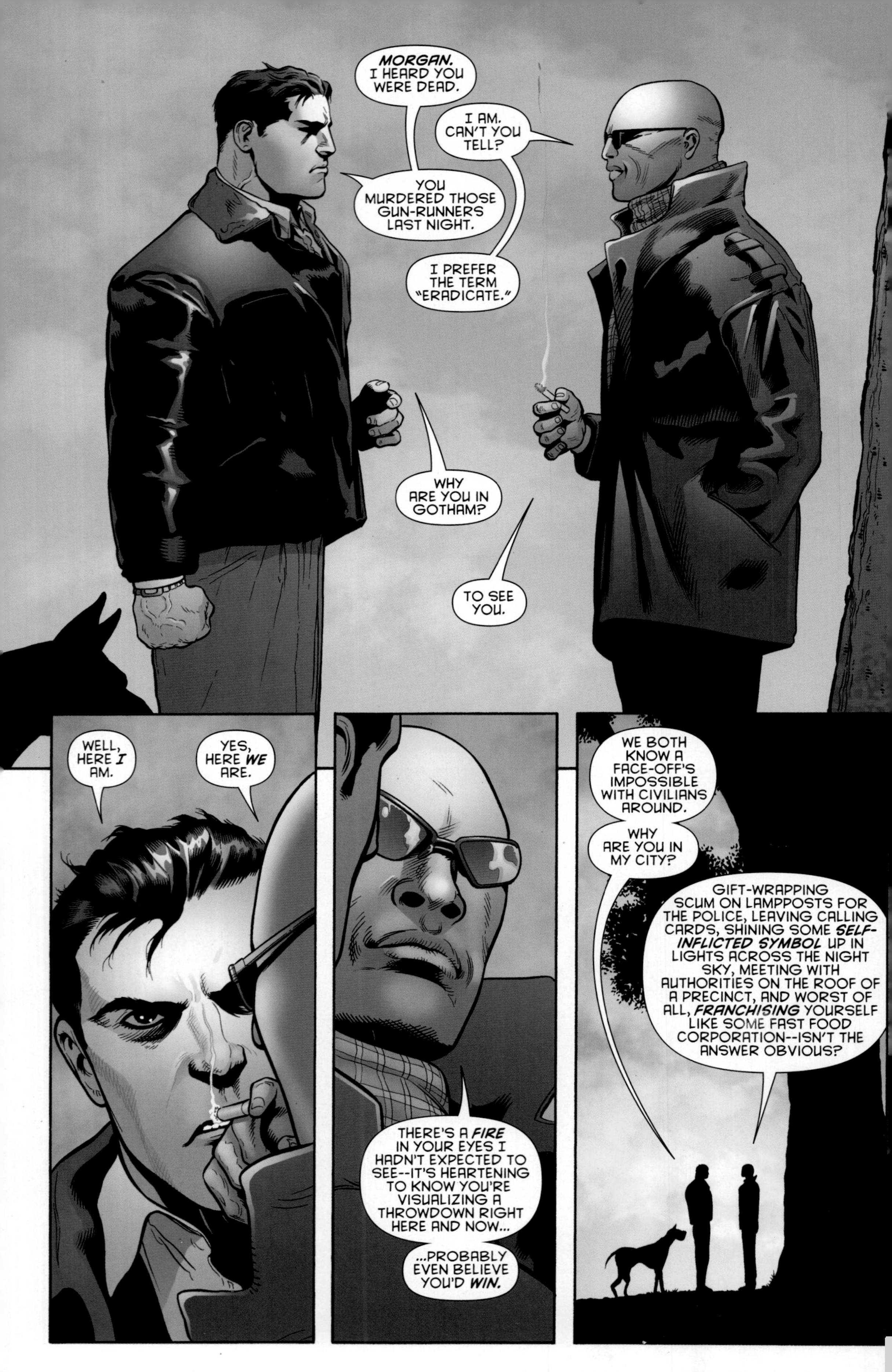

MORGAN. I HEARD YOU WERE DEAD.
I AM. CAN'T YOU TELL?
YOU MURDERED THOSE GUN-RUNNERS LAST NIGHT.
I PREFER THE TERM "ERADICATE."
WHY ARE YOU IN GOTHAM?
TO SEE YOU.
WELL, HERE I AM.
YES, HERE WE ARE.
THERE'S A FIRE IN YOUR EYES I HADN'T EXPECTED TO SEE--IT'S HEARTENING TO KNOW YOU'RE VISUALIZING A THROWDOWN RIGHT HERE AND NOW...
...PROBABLY EVEN BELIEVE YOU'D WIN.
WE BOTH KNOW A FACE-OFF'S IMPOSSIBLE WITH CIVILIANS AROUND.
WHY ARE YOU IN MY CITY?
GIFT-WRAPPING SCUM ON LAMPPOSTS FOR THE POLICE, LEAVING CALLING CARDS, SHINING SOME SELF-INFLICTED SYMBOL UP IN LIGHTS ACROSS THE NIGHT SKY, MEETING WITH AUTHORITIES ON THE ROOF OF A PRECINCT, AND WORST OF ALL, FRANCHISING YOURSELF LIKE SOME FAST FOOD CORPORATION--ISN'T THE ANSWER OBVIOUS?

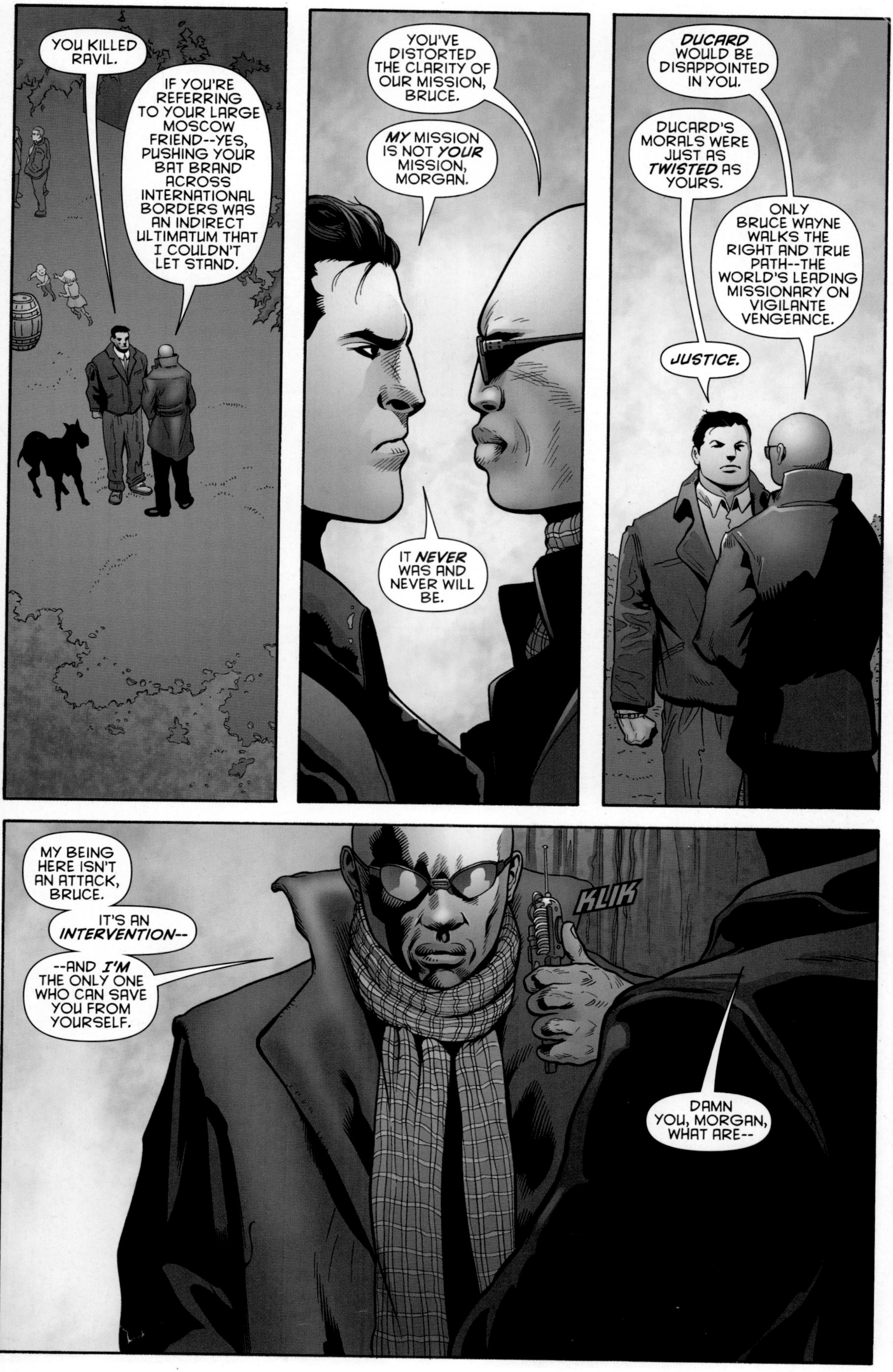
YOU KILLED RAVIL.
IF YOU'RE REFERRING TO YOUR LARGE MOSCOW FRIEND--YES, PUSHING YOUR BAT BRAND ACROSS INTERNATIONAL BORDERS WAS AN INDIRECT ULTIMATUM THAT I COULDN'T LET STAND.
YOU'VE DISTORTED THE CLARITY OF OUR MISSION, BRUCE.
MY MISSION IS NOT YOUR MISSION, MORGAN.
IT NEVER WAS AND NEVER WILL BE.
DUCARD WOULD BE DISAPPOINTED IN YOU.
DUCARD'S MORALS WERE JUST AS TWISTED AS YOURS.
ONLY BRUCE WAYNE WALKS THE RIGHT AND TRUE PATH--THE WORLD'S LEADING MISSIONARY ON VIGILANTE VENGEANCE.
JUSTICE.
MY BEING HERE ISN'T AN ATTACK, BRUCE.
IT'S AN INTERVENTION--
--AND I'M THE ONLY ONE WHO CAN SAVE YOU FROM YOURSELF.
KLIK
DAMN YOU, MORGAN, WHAT ARE--

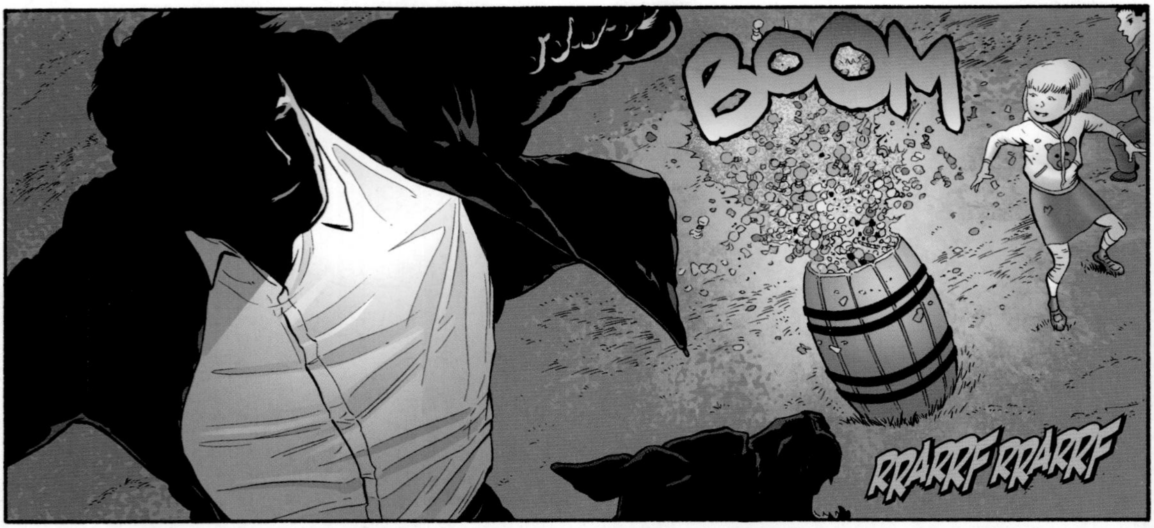
BOOM
RRARRF RRARRF

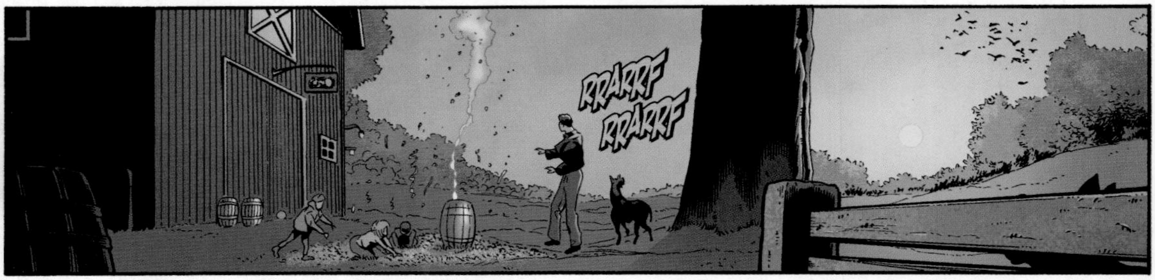
RRARRF
RRARRF

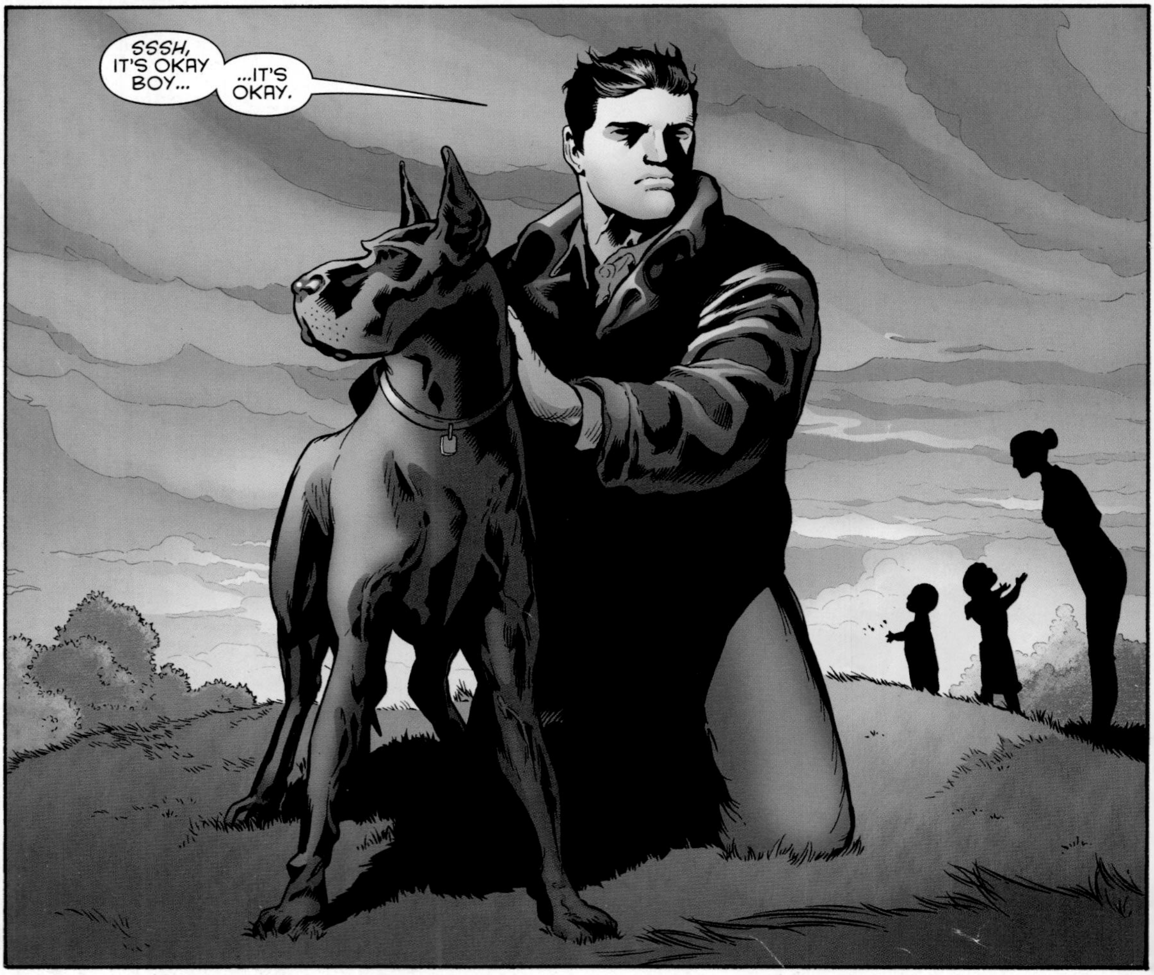
SSSH, IT'S OKAY BOY...
...IT'S OKAY.

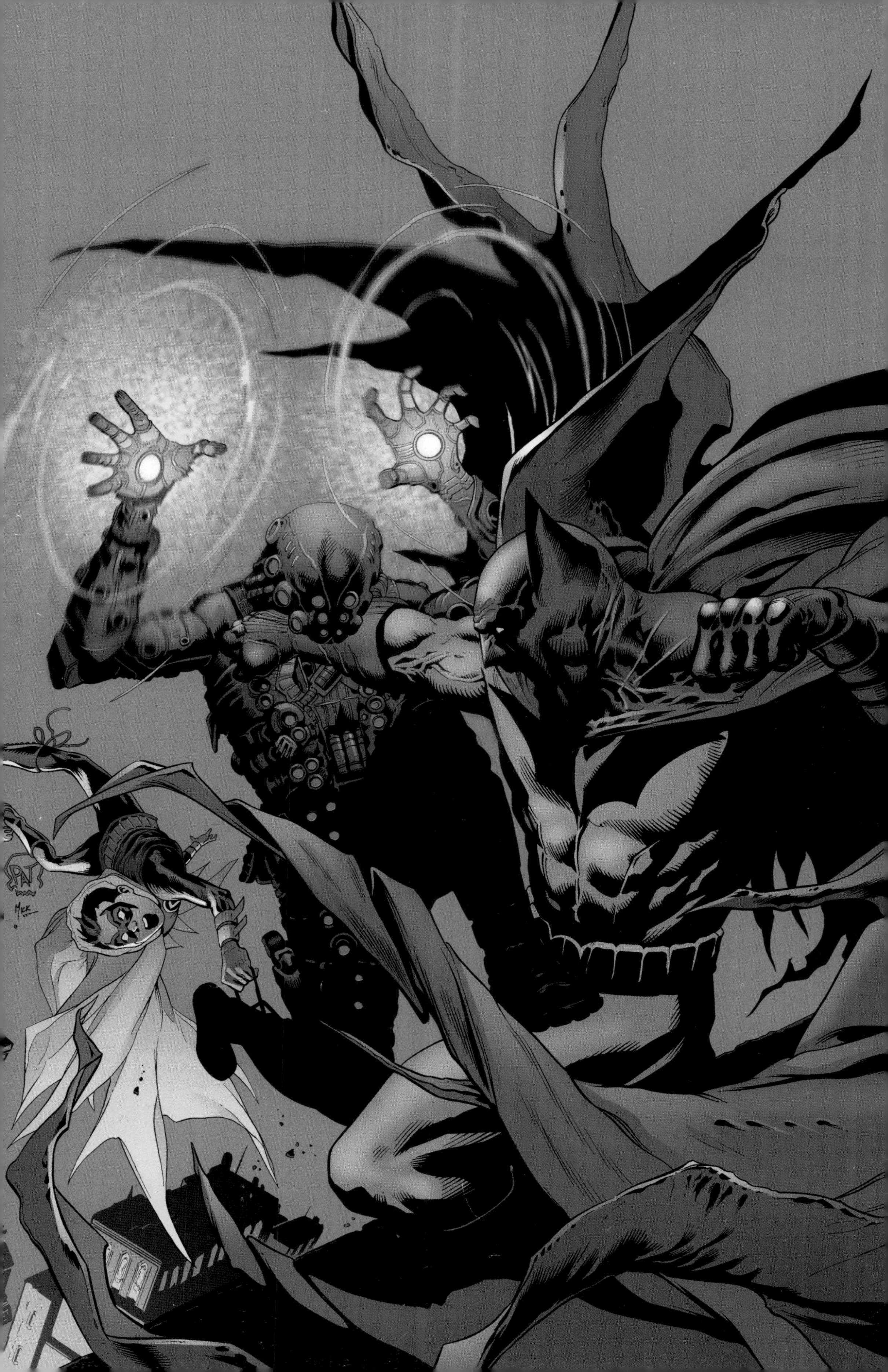

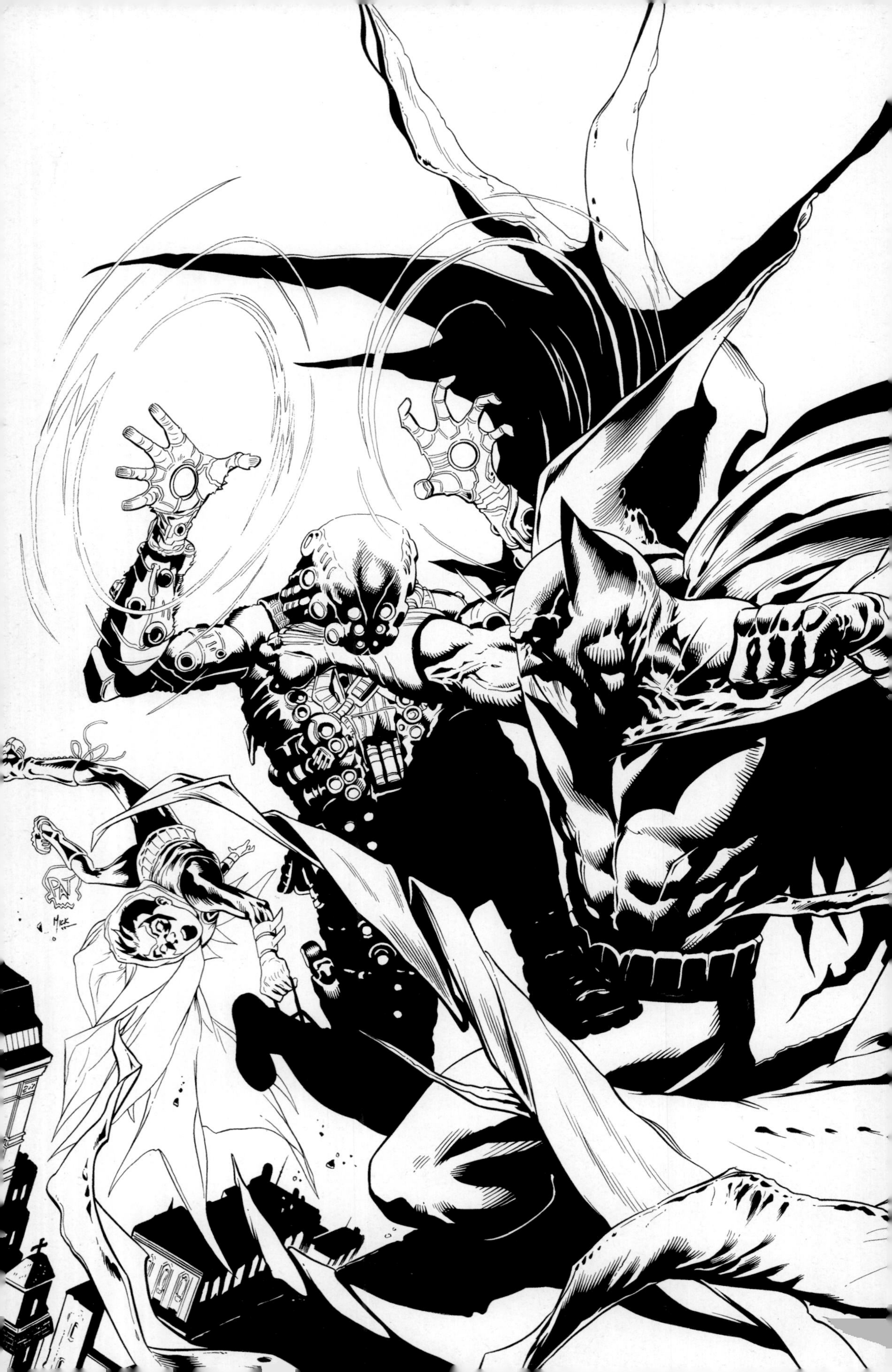
PAT
MICK

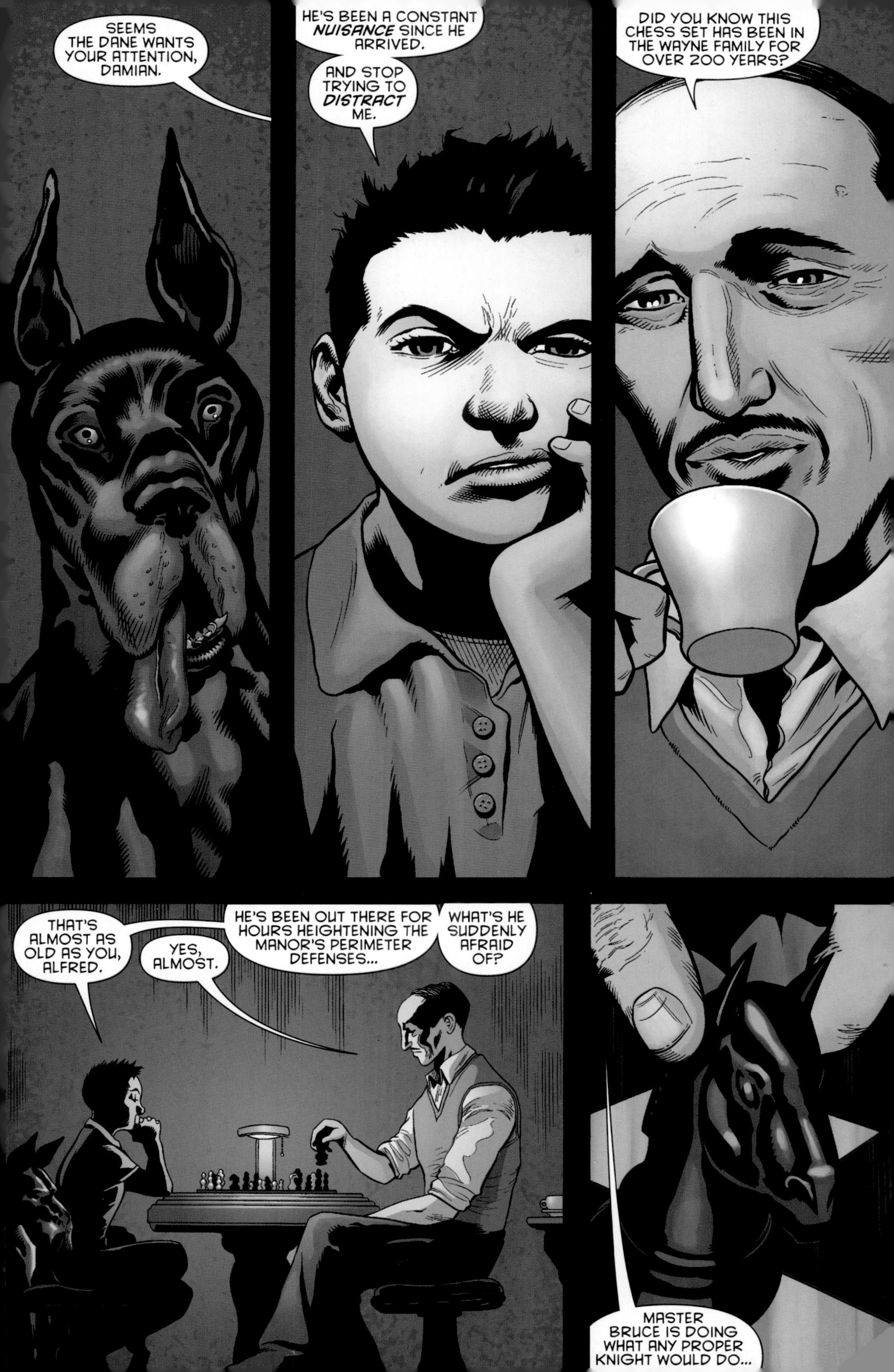
SEEMS THE DANE WANTS YOUR ATTENTION, DAMIAN.
HE'S BEEN A CONSTANT *NUISANCE* SINCE HE ARRIVED.
AND STOP TRYING TO *DISTRACT* ME.
DID YOU KNOW THIS CHESS SET HAS BEEN IN THE WAYNE FAMILY FOR OVER 200 YEARS?
THAT'S ALMOST AS OLD AS YOU, ALFRED.
YES, ALMOST.
HE'S BEEN OUT THERE FOR HOURS HEIGHTENING THE MANOR'S PERIMETER DEFENSES...
WHAT'S HE SUDDENLY AFRAID OF?
MASTER BRUCE IS DOING WHAT ANY PROPER KNIGHT WOULD DO...

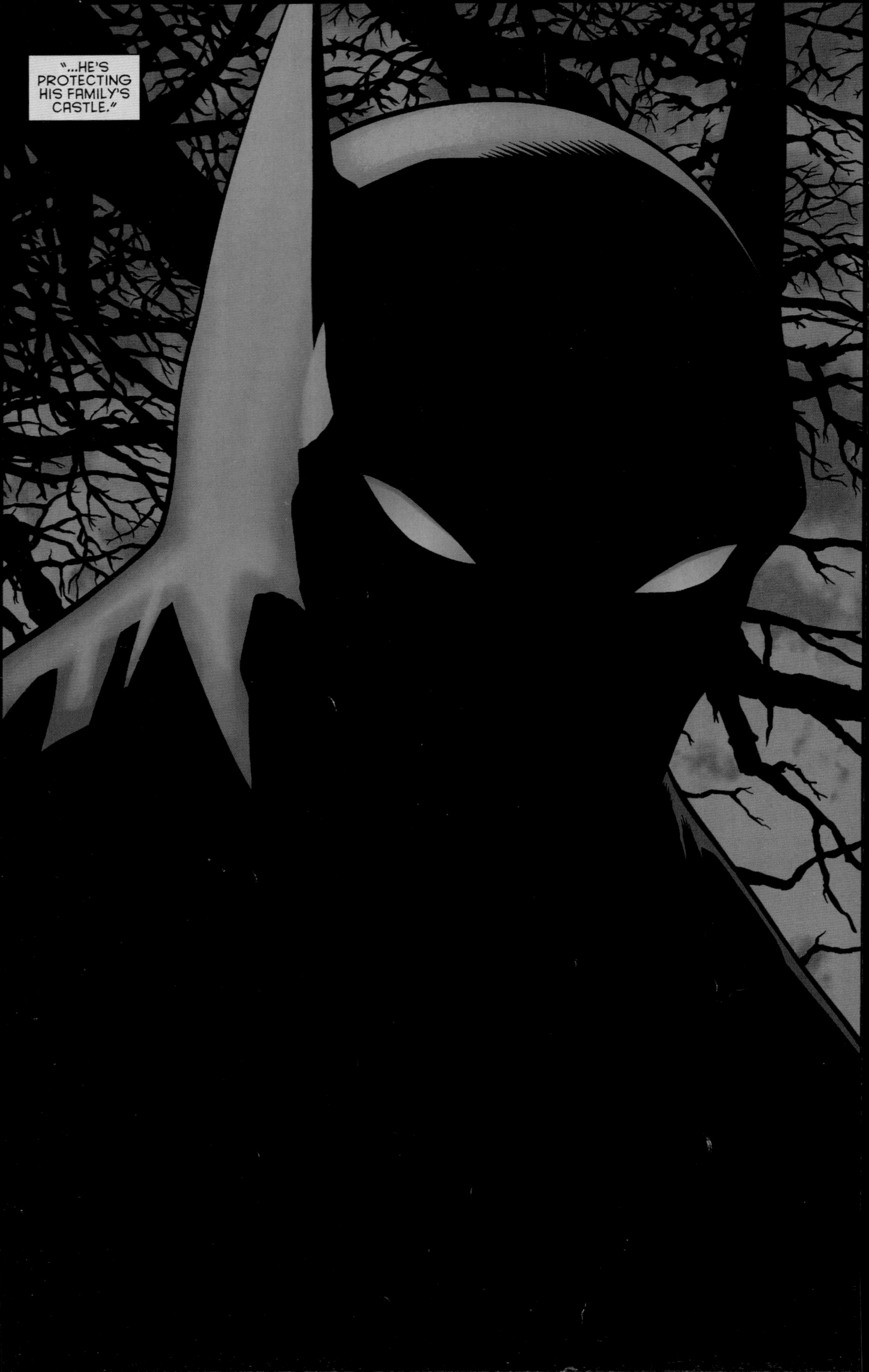
"...HE'S PROTECTING HIS FAMILY'S CASTLE."

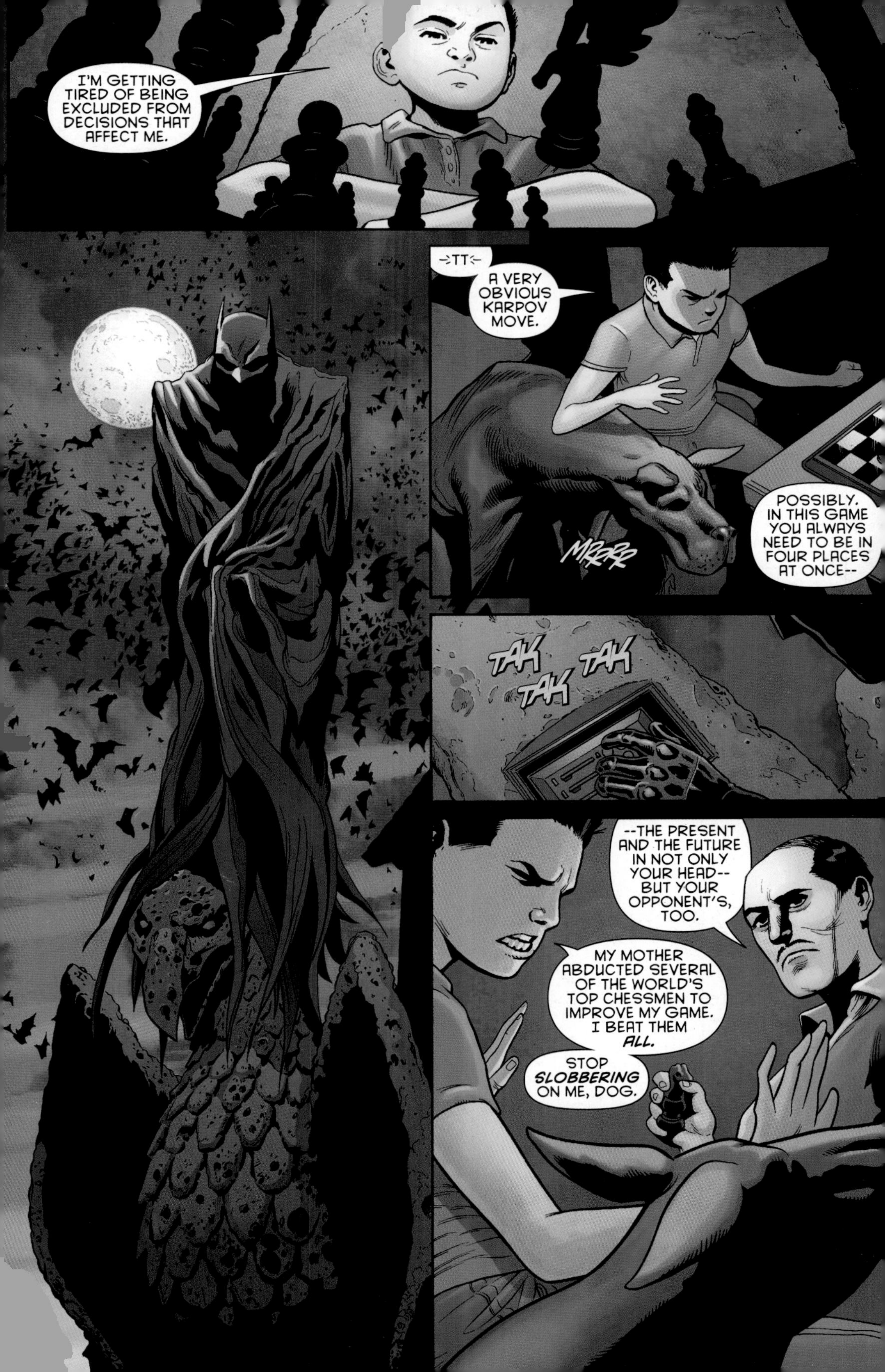
I'M GETTING TIRED OF BEING EXCLUDED FROM DECISIONS THAT AFFECT ME.
-TT-
A VERY OBVIOUS KARPOV MOVE.
MRRRR
POSSIBLY. IN THIS GAME YOU ALWAYS NEED TO BE IN FOUR PLACES AT ONCE--
TAK TAK TAK
--THE PRESENT AND THE FUTURE IN NOT ONLY YOUR HEAD--BUT YOUR OPPONENT'S, TOO.
MY MOTHER ABDUCTED SEVERAL OF THE WORLD'S TOP CHESSMEN TO IMPROVE MY GAME. I BEAT THEM ALL.
STOP SLOBBERING ON ME, DOG.

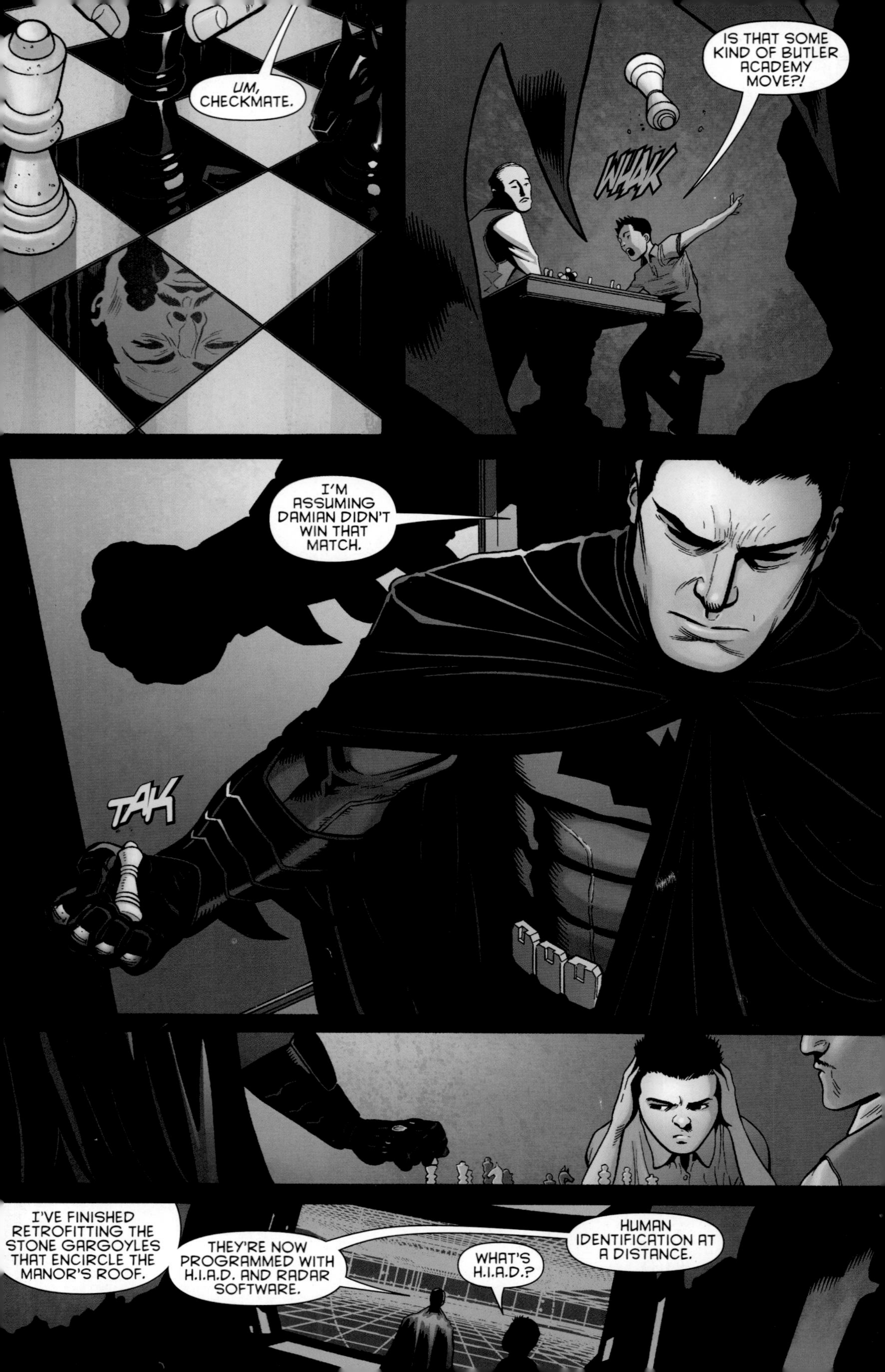
UM, CHECKMATE.
IS THAT SOME KIND OF BUTLER ACADEMY MOVE?!
WHAK
I'M ASSUMING DAMIAN DIDN'T WIN THAT MATCH.
TAK
I'VE FINISHED RETROFITTING THE STONE GARGOYLES THAT ENCIRCLE THE MANOR'S ROOF.
THEY'RE NOW PROGRAMMED WITH H.I.A.D. AND RADAR SOFTWARE.
WHAT'S H.I.A.D.?
HUMAN IDENTIFICATION AT A DISTANCE.

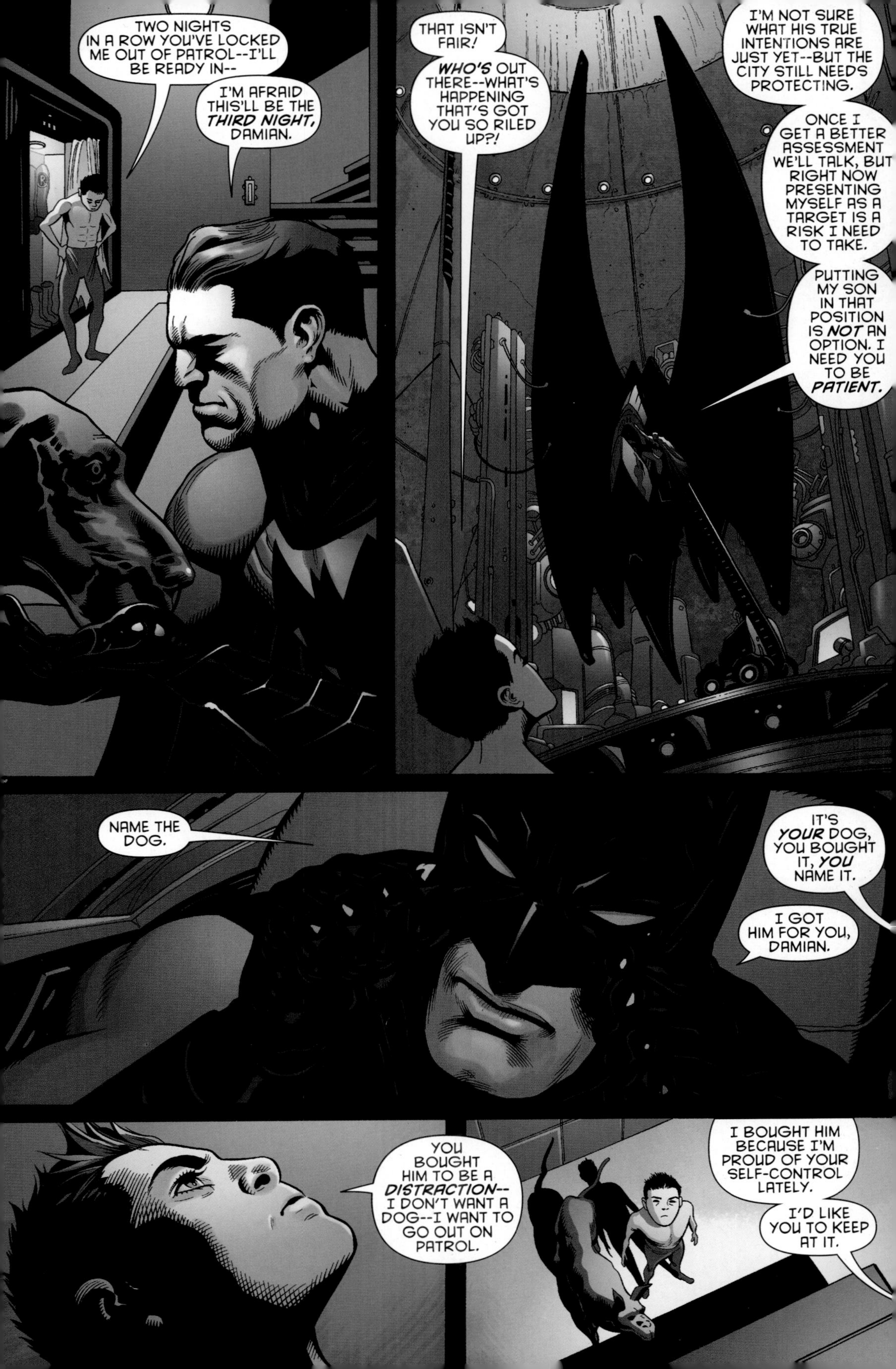
TWO NIGHTS IN A ROW YOU'VE LOCKED ME OUT OF PATROL--I'LL BE READY IN--
I'M AFRAID THIS'LL BE THE *THIRD NIGHT,* DAMIAN.
THAT ISN'T FAIR!
WHO'S OUT THERE--WHAT'S HAPPENING THAT'S GOT YOU SO RILED UP?!
I'M NOT SURE WHAT HIS TRUE INTENTIONS ARE JUST YET--BUT THE CITY STILL NEEDS PROTECTING.
ONCE I GET A BETTER ASSESSMENT WE'LL TALK, BUT RIGHT NOW PRESENTING MYSELF AS A TARGET IS A RISK I NEED TO TAKE.
PUTTING MY SON IN THAT POSITION IS *NOT* AN OPTION. I NEED YOU TO BE *PATIENT.*
NAME THE DOG.
IT'S *YOUR* DOG, YOU BOUGHT IT, *YOU* NAME IT.
I GOT HIM FOR YOU, DAMIAN.
YOU BOUGHT HIM TO BE A *DISTRACTION*--I DON'T WANT A DOG--I WANT TO GO OUT ON PATROL.
I BOUGHT HIM BECAUSE I'M PROUD OF YOUR SELF-CONTROL LATELY.
I'D LIKE YOU TO KEEP AT IT.

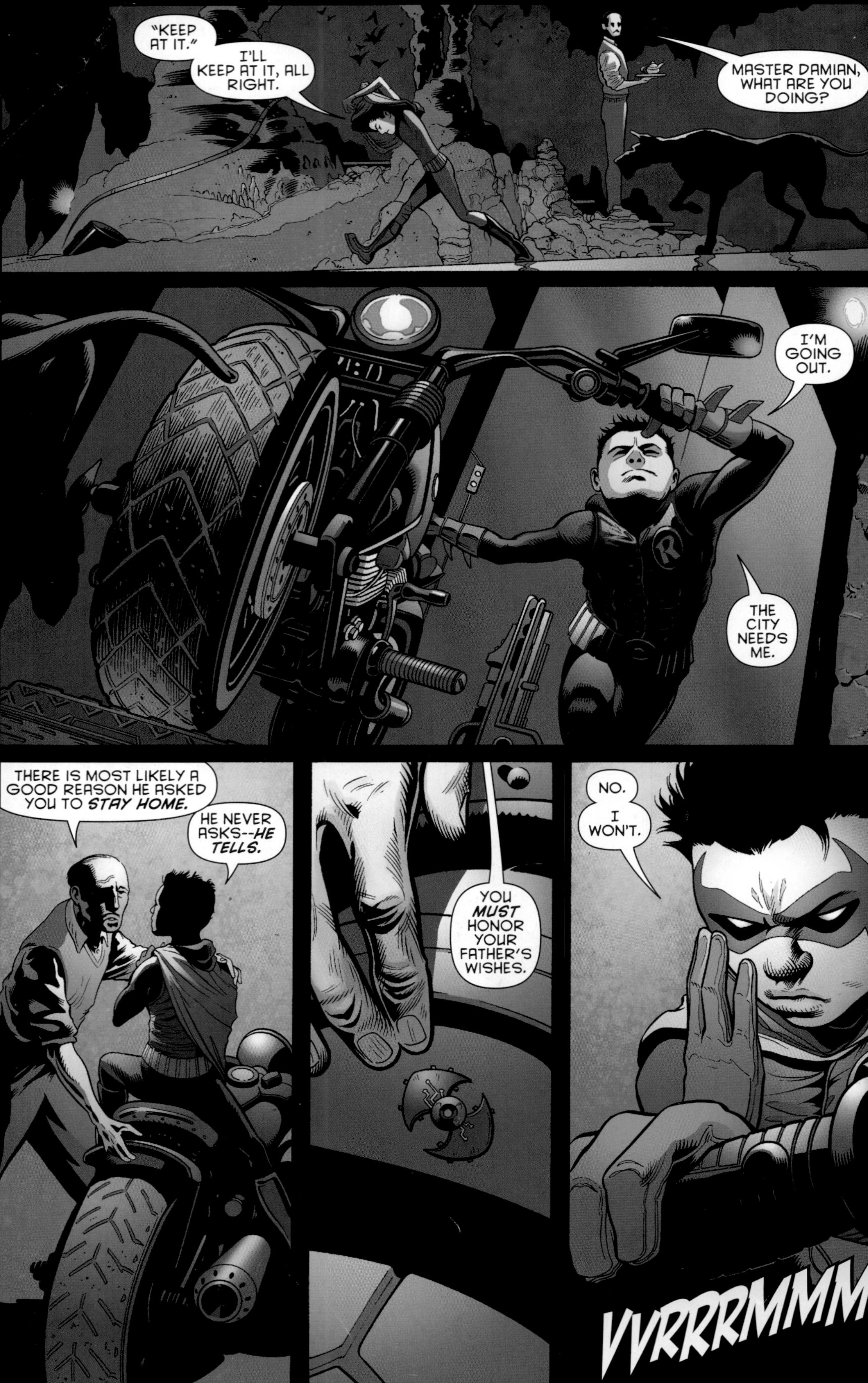

"KEEP AT IT."
I'LL KEEP AT IT, ALL RIGHT.
MASTER DAMIAN, WHAT ARE YOU DOING?
I'M GOING OUT.
THE CITY NEEDS ME.
THERE IS MOST LIKELY A GOOD REASON HE ASKED YOU TO STAY HOME.
HE NEVER ASKS--HE TELLS.
YOU MUST HONOR YOUR FATHER'S WISHES.
NO.
I WON'T.
VVRRRMMM

AND BY THE WAY...

...NICE SLEIGHT OF HAND THERE, ALFRED.

VVROOOMMM

FLIK

DON'T GIVE UP YOUR DAY JOB.

SCREEEEE

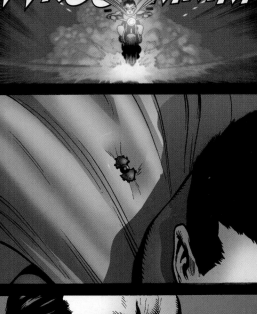

VVROOOMMM

DON'T WORRY, DAMIAN, I WON'T.

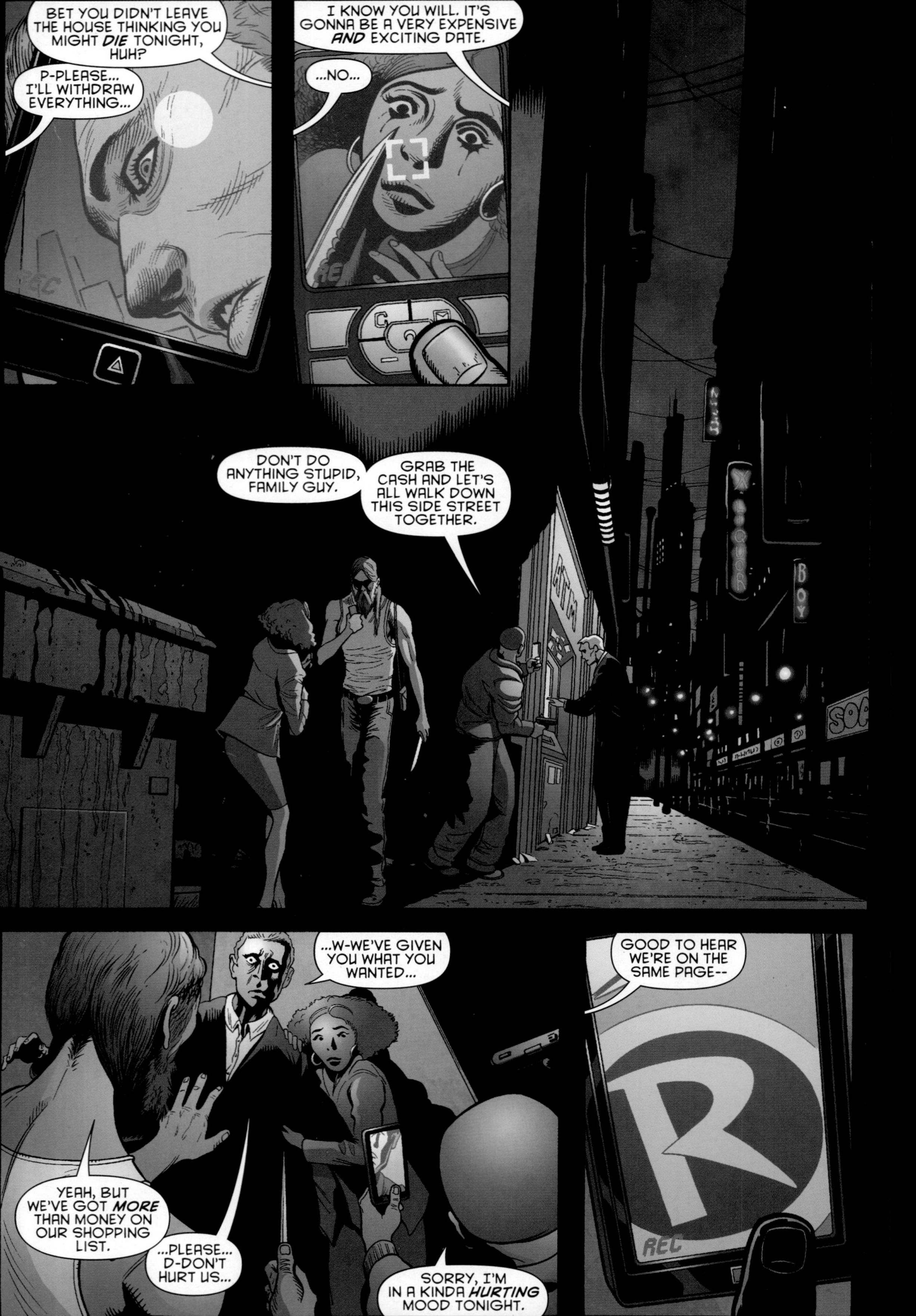

BET YOU DIDN'T LEAVE THE HOUSE THINKING YOU MIGHT *DIE* TONIGHT, HUH?
P-PLEASE... I'LL WITHDRAW EVERYTHING...
I KNOW YOU WILL. IT'S GONNA BE A VERY EXPENSIVE *AND* EXCITING DATE.
...NO...
REC
DON'T DO ANYTHING STUPID, FAMILY GUY.
GRAB THE CASH AND LET'S ALL WALK DOWN THIS SIDE STREET TOGETHER.
ATM
LIQUOR
BOY
...W-WE'VE GIVEN YOU WHAT YOU WANTED...
YEAH, BUT WE'VE GOT *MORE* THAN MONEY ON OUR SHOPPING LIST.
...PLEASE... D-DON'T HURT US...
SORRY, I'M IN A KINDA *HURTING* MOOD TONIGHT.
GOOD TO HEAR WE'RE ON THE SAME PAGE--
REC

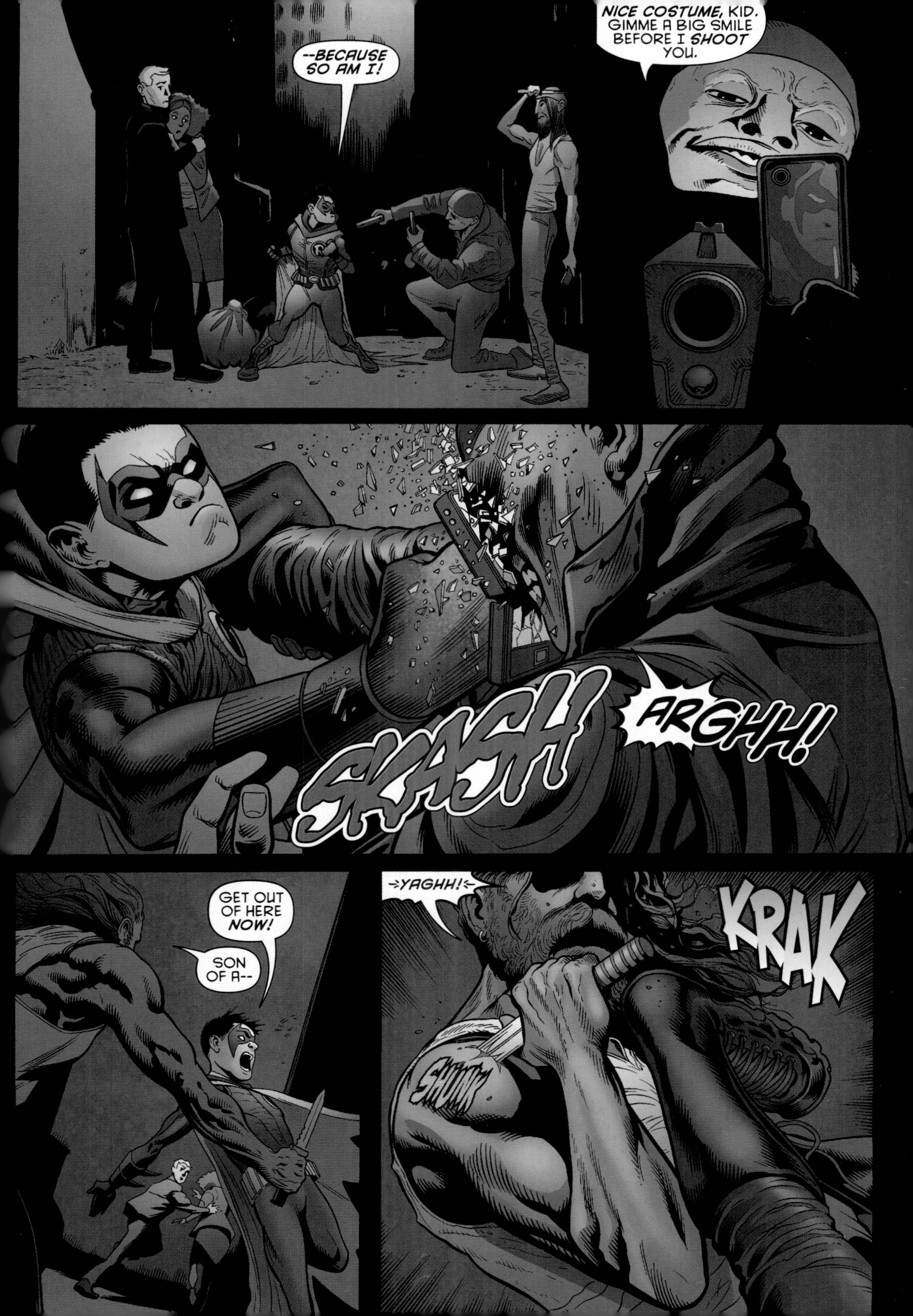
--BECAUSE SO AM I!
NICE COSTUME, KID. GIMME A BIG SMILE BEFORE I SHOOT YOU.
SKASH
ARGHH!
GET OUT OF HERE NOW!
SON OF A--
-YAGHH!-
KRAK
SHUNK

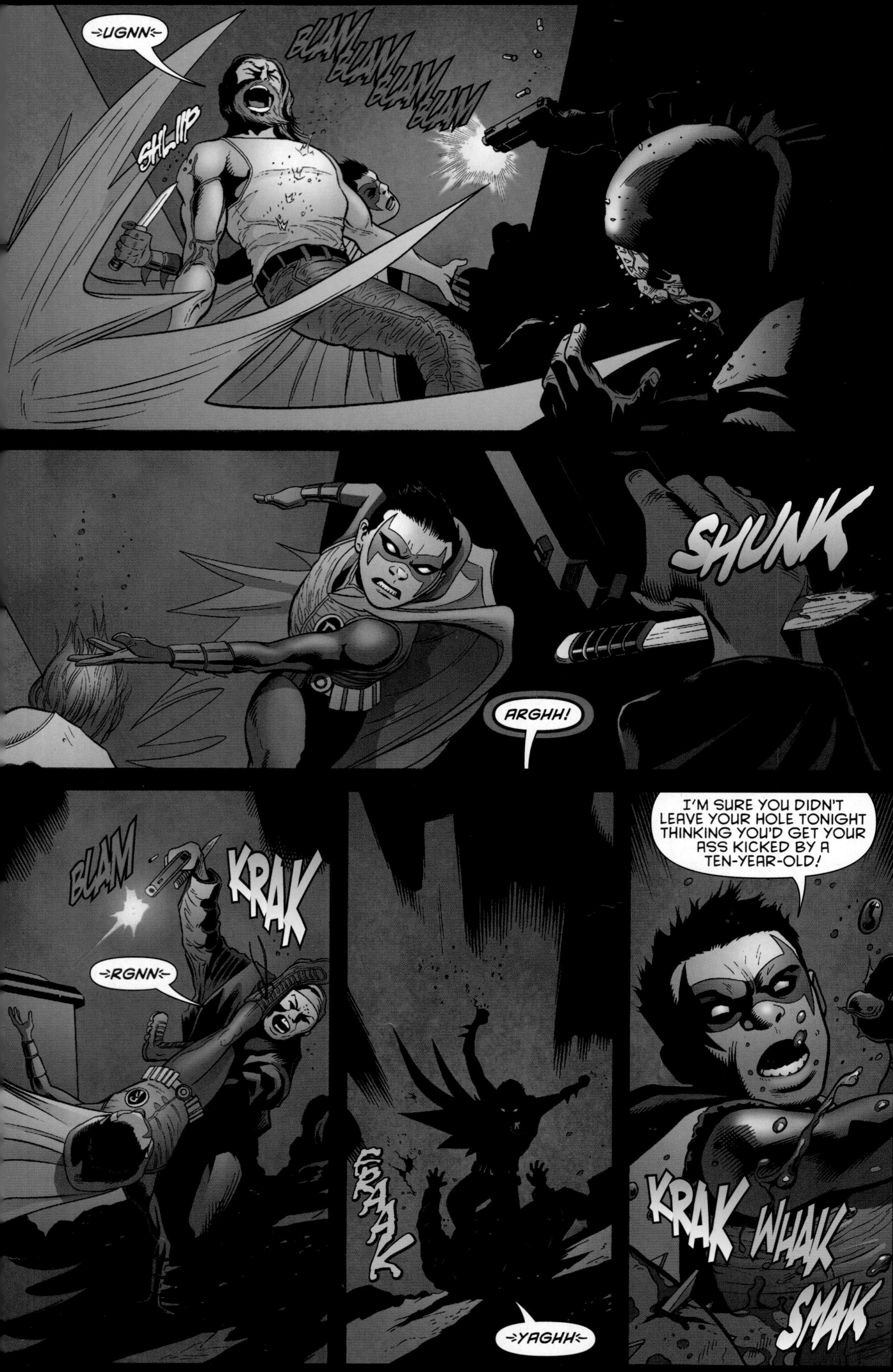
UGNN
BLAM BLAM BLAM BLAM
SHLIIP
SHUNK
ARGHH!
BLAM
KRAK
RGNN
FRAAK
YAGHH
I'M SURE YOU DIDN'T LEAVE YOUR HOLE TONIGHT THINKING YOU'D GET YOUR ASS KICKED BY A TEN-YEAR-OLD!
KRAK WHAK
SMAK

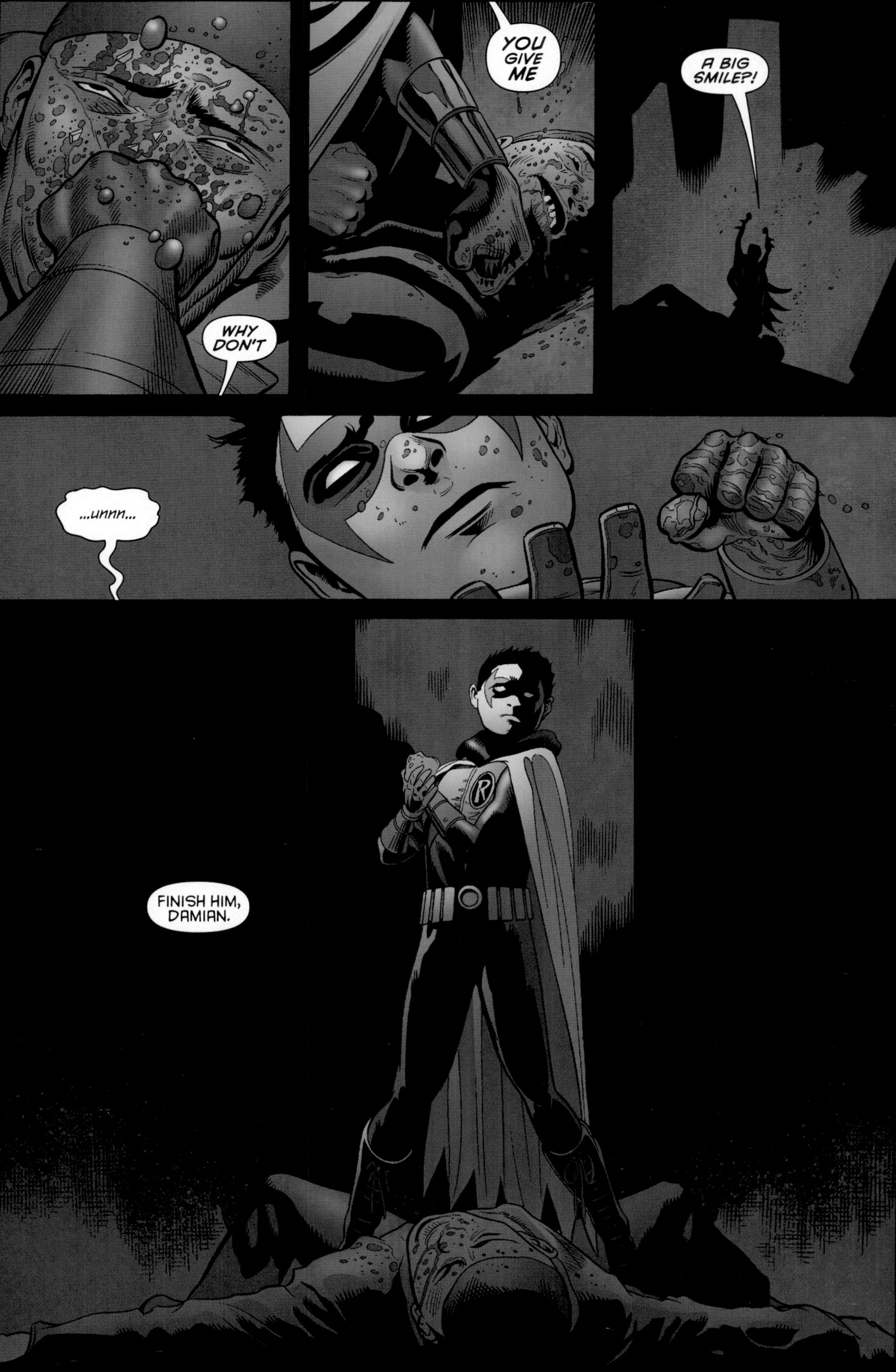
WHY DON'T
YOU GIVE ME
A BIG SMILE?!
...unnn...
FINISH HIM, DAMIAN.

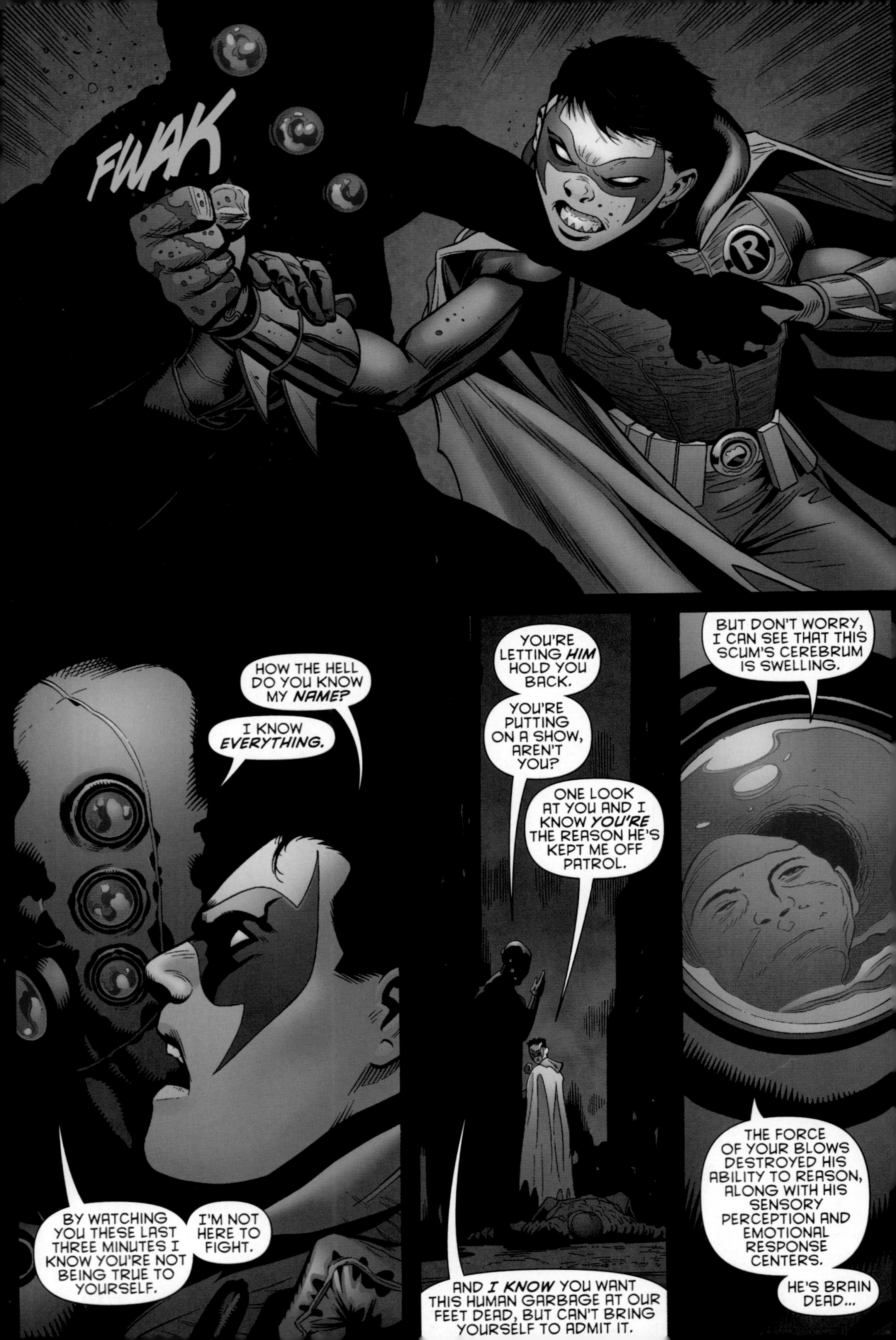
FWAK
HOW THE HELL DO YOU KNOW MY NAME?
I KNOW EVERYTHING.
BY WATCHING YOU THESE LAST THREE MINUTES I KNOW YOU'RE NOT BEING TRUE TO YOURSELF.
I'M NOT HERE TO FIGHT.
YOU'RE LETTING HIM HOLD YOU BACK.
YOU'RE PUTTING ON A SHOW, AREN'T YOU?
ONE LOOK AT YOU AND I KNOW YOU'RE THE REASON HE'S KEPT ME OFF PATROL.
AND I KNOW YOU WANT THIS HUMAN GARBAGE AT OUR FEET DEAD, BUT CAN'T BRING YOURSELF TO ADMIT IT.
BUT DON'T WORRY, I CAN SEE THAT THIS SCUM'S CEREBRUM IS SWELLING.
THE FORCE OF YOUR BLOWS DESTROYED HIS ABILITY TO REASON, ALONG WITH HIS SENSORY PERCEPTION AND EMOTIONAL RESPONSE CENTERS.
HE'S BRAIN DEAD...

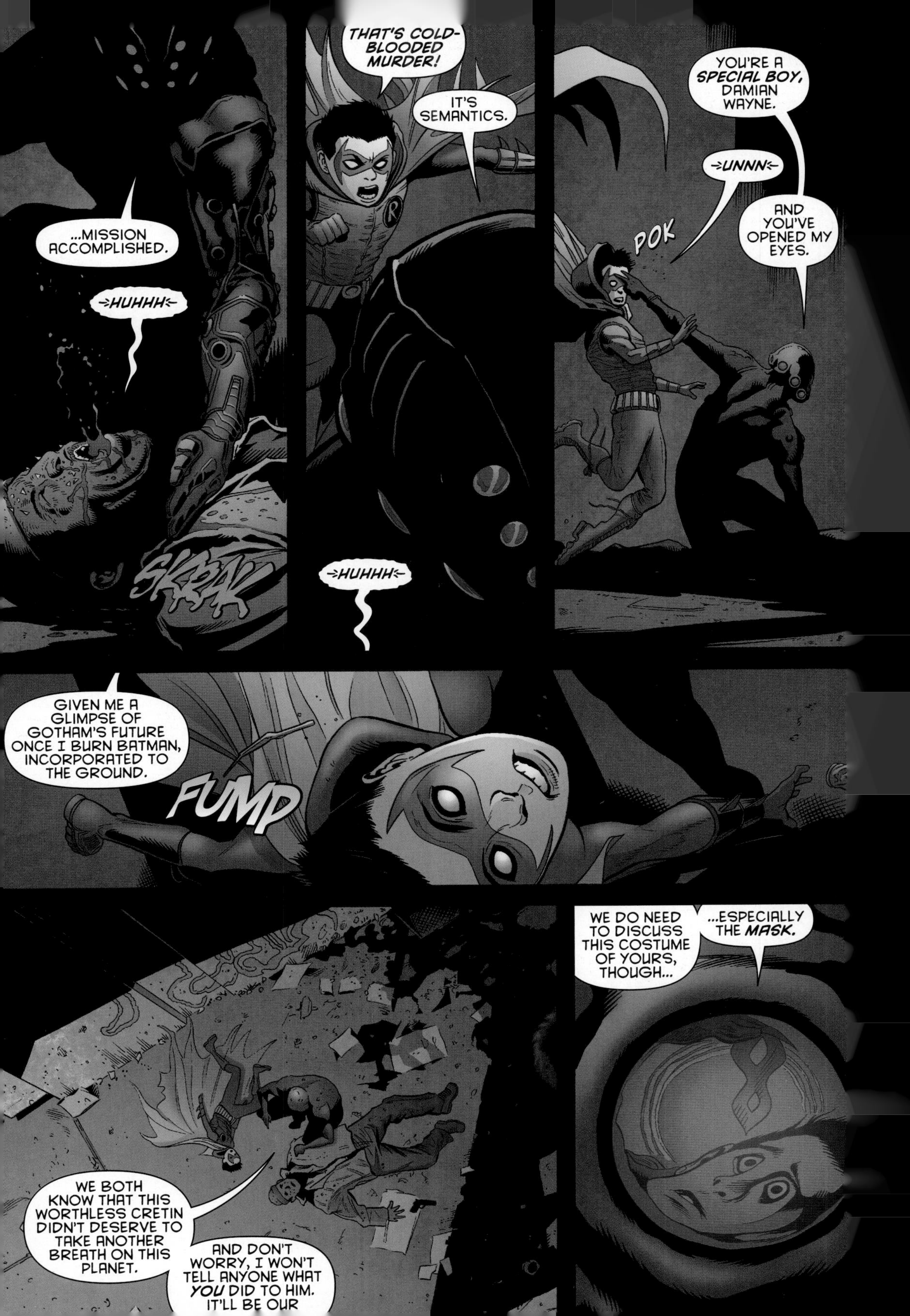

...MISSION ACCOMPLISHED.
HUHHH
SKRAK
THAT'S COLD-BLOODED MURDER!
IT'S SEMANTICS.
HUHHH
YOU'RE A SPECIAL BOY, DAMIAN WAYNE.
UNNN
POK
AND YOU'VE OPENED MY EYES.
GIVEN ME A GLIMPSE OF GOTHAM'S FUTURE ONCE I BURN BATMAN, INCORPORATED TO THE GROUND.
FUMP
WE BOTH KNOW THAT THIS WORTHLESS CRETIN DIDN'T DESERVE TO TAKE ANOTHER BREATH ON THIS PLANET.
AND DON'T WORRY, I WON'T TELL ANYONE WHAT YOU DID TO HIM. IT'LL BE OUR
WE DO NEED TO DISCUSS THIS COSTUME OF YOURS, THOUGH...
...ESPECIALLY THE MASK.

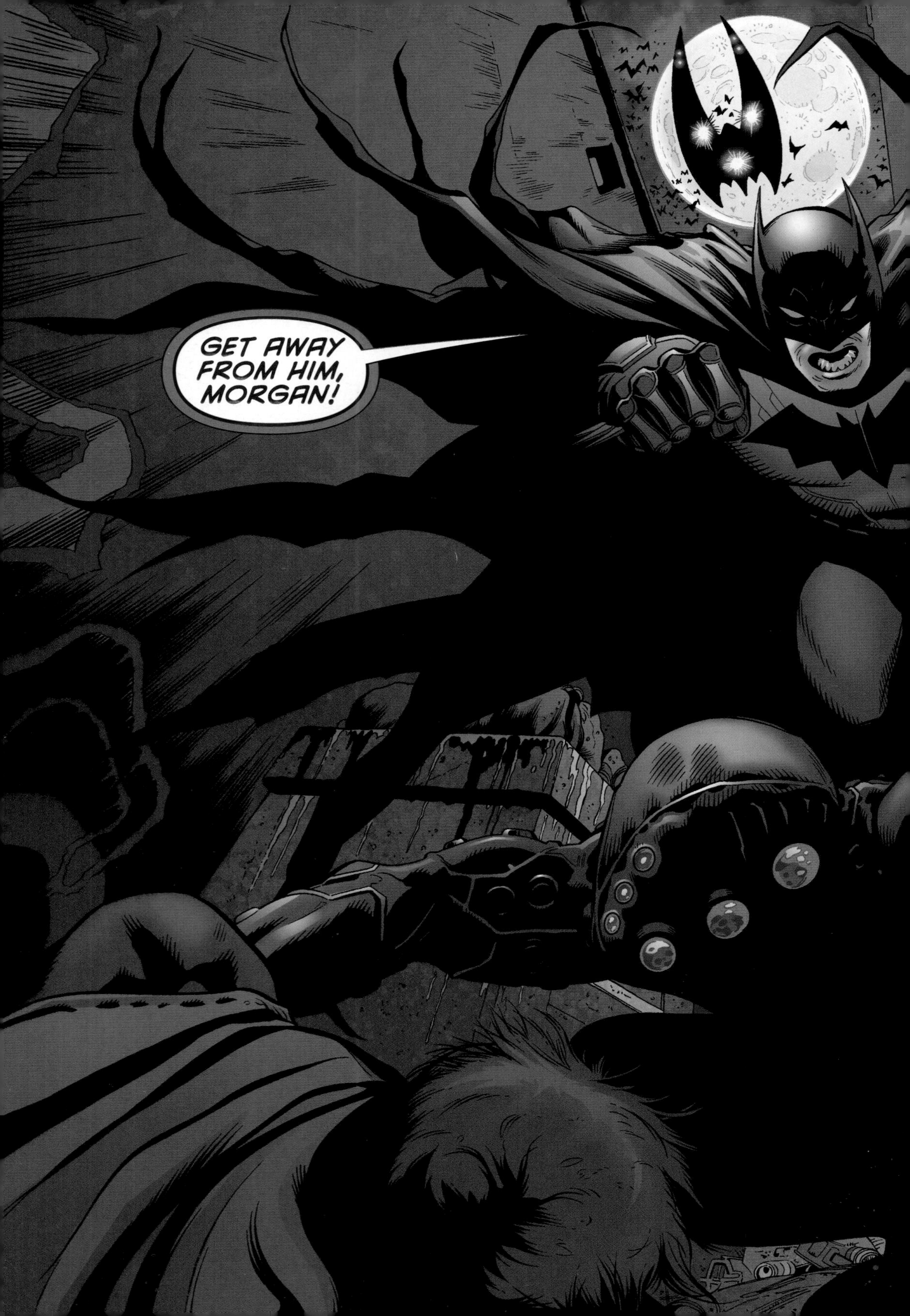
GET AWAY FROM HIM, MORGAN!

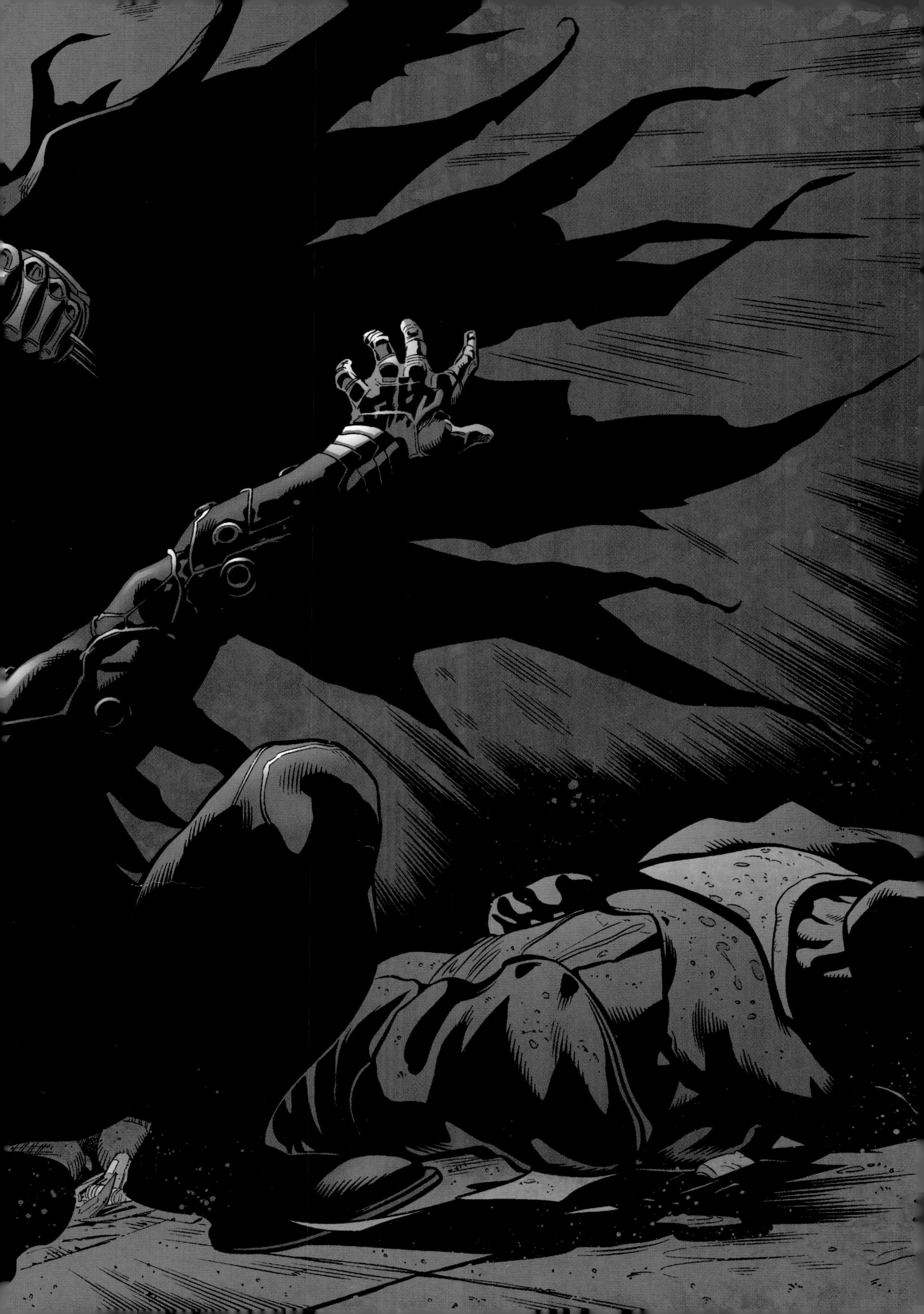

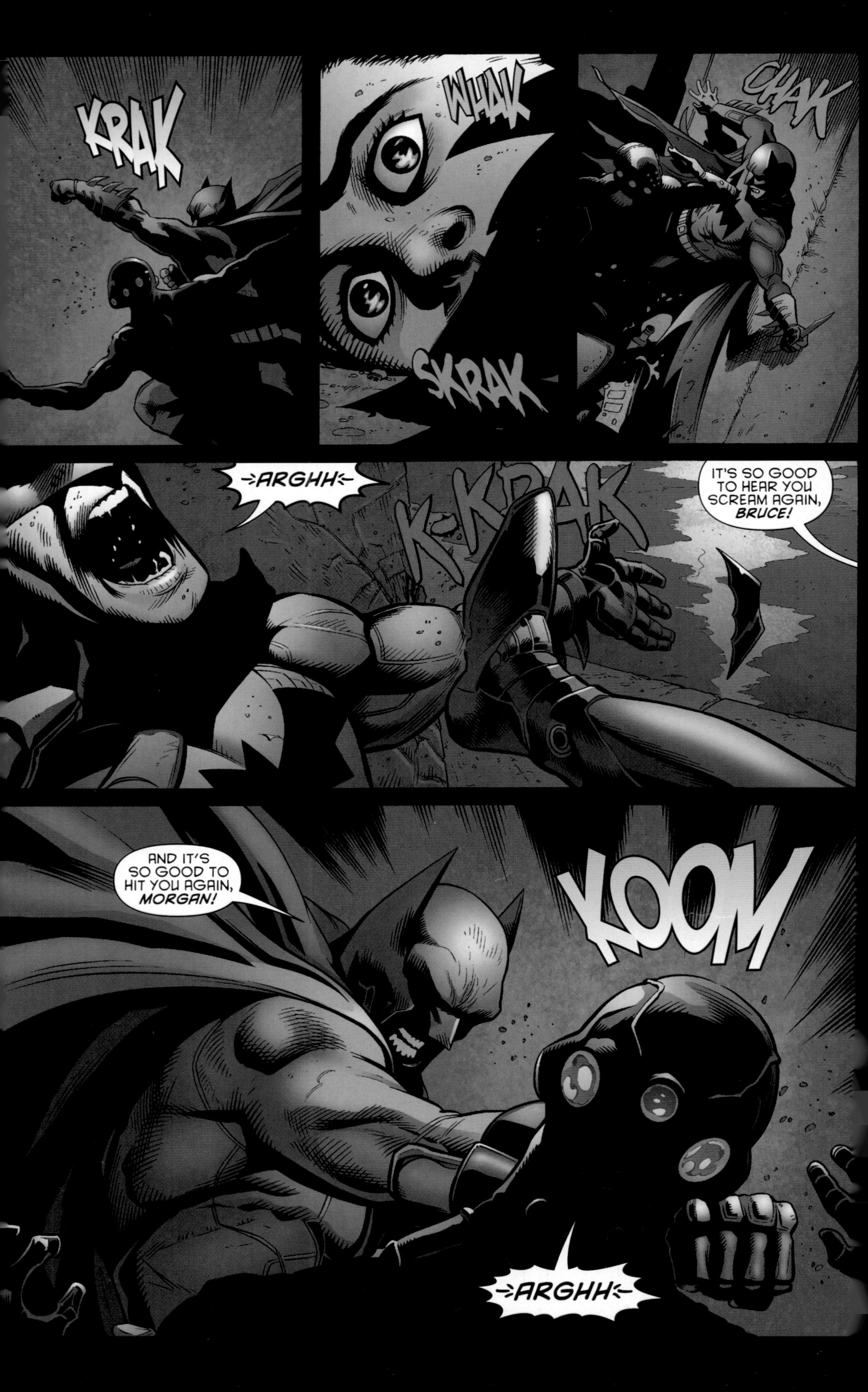
KRAK
WHAK
SKRAK
CHAK
ARGHH
K-KRAK
IT'S SO GOOD TO HEAR YOU SCREAM AGAIN, BRUCE!
AND IT'S SO GOOD TO HIT YOU AGAIN, MORGAN!
KOOM
ARGHH

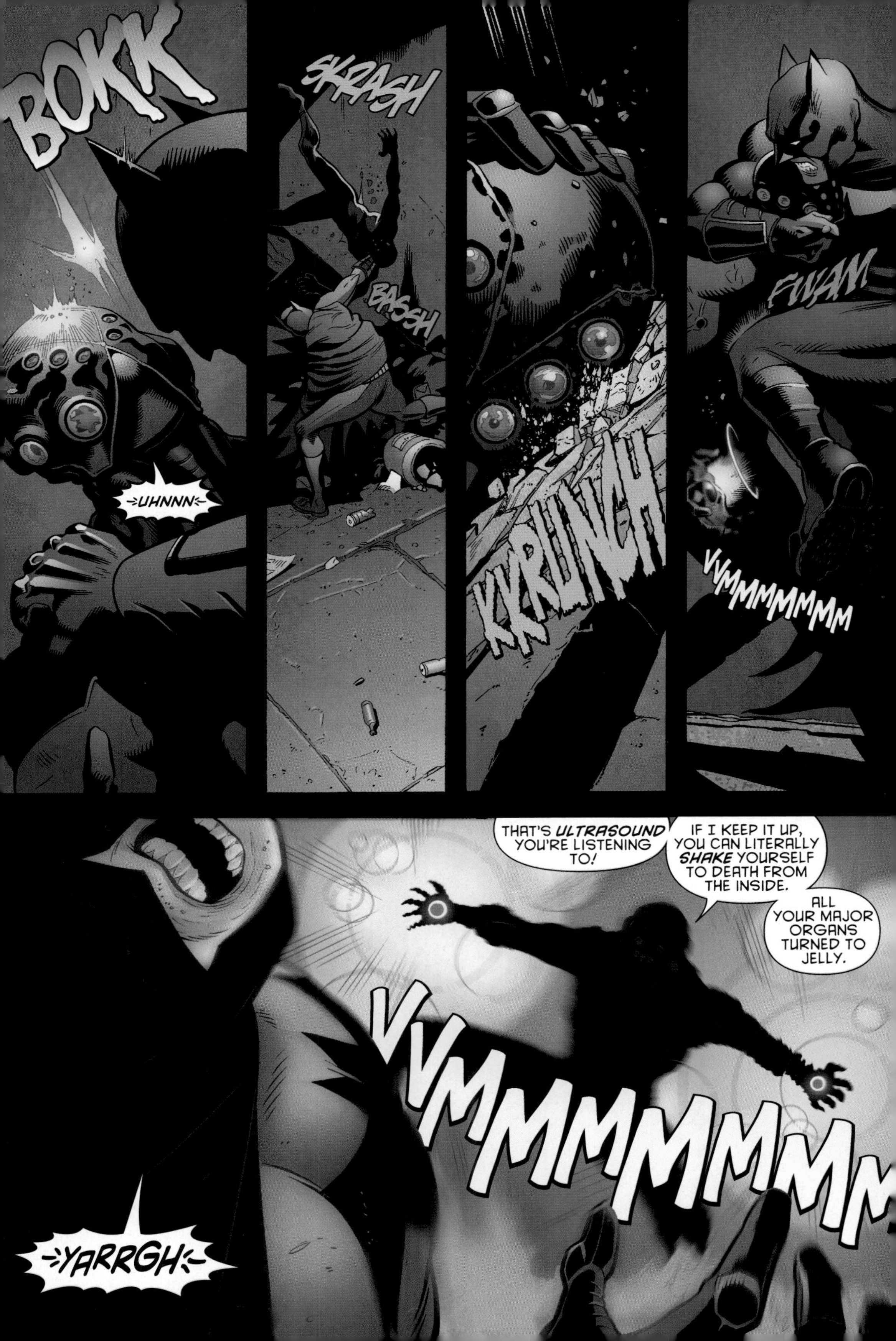
BOKK
UHNNN
SKRASH
BASSH
KKRUNCH
FWAM
VVMMMMMMMM
THAT'S *ULTRASOUND* YOU'RE LISTENING TO!
IF I KEEP IT UP, YOU CAN LITERALLY *SHAKE* YOURSELF TO DEATH FROM THE INSIDE.
ALL YOUR MAJOR ORGANS TURNED TO JELLY.
YARRGH
VVMMMMMMMM

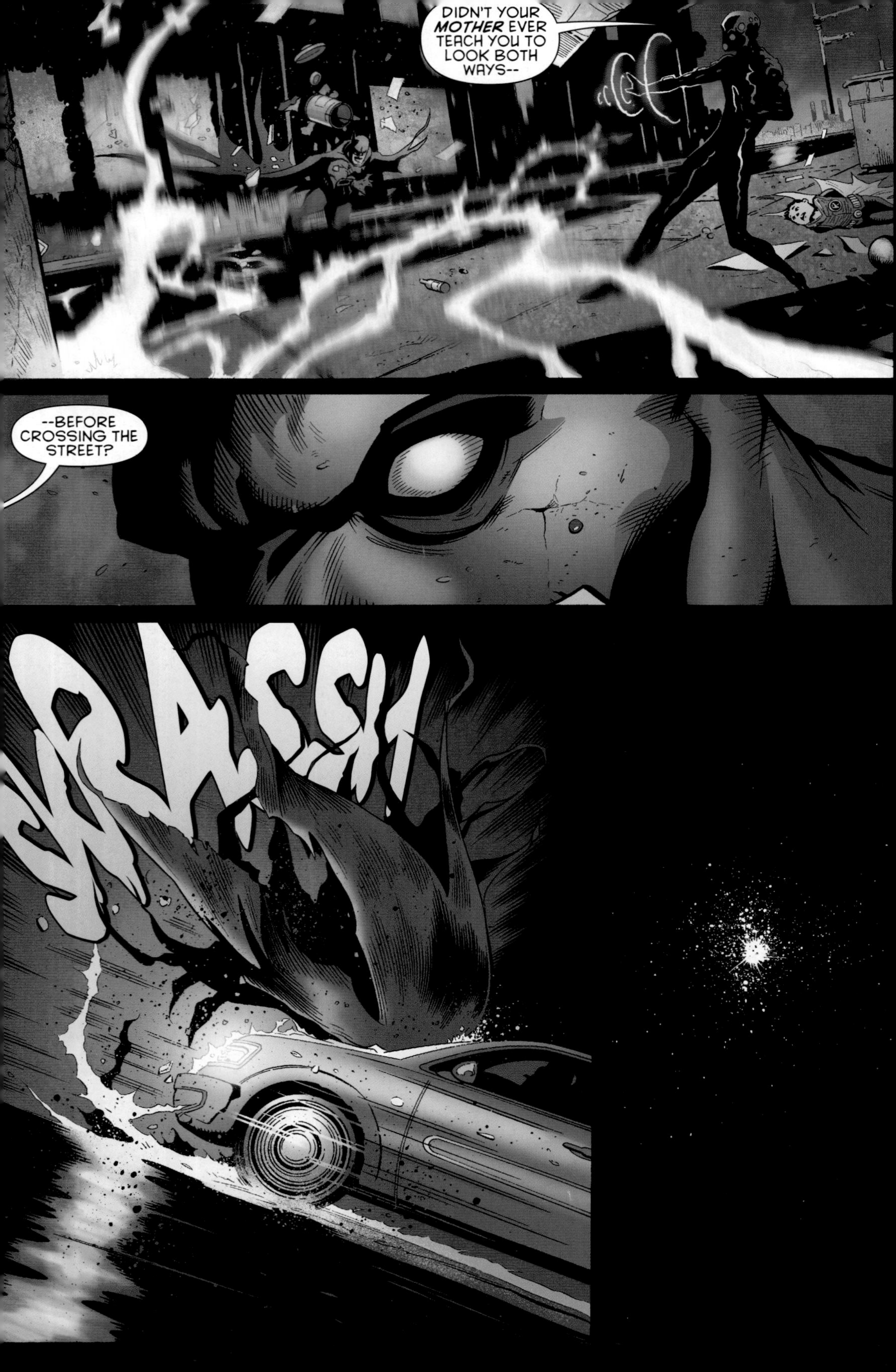
DIDN'T YOUR *MOTHER* EVER TEACH YOU TO LOOK BOTH WAYS--
--BEFORE CROSSING THE STREET?

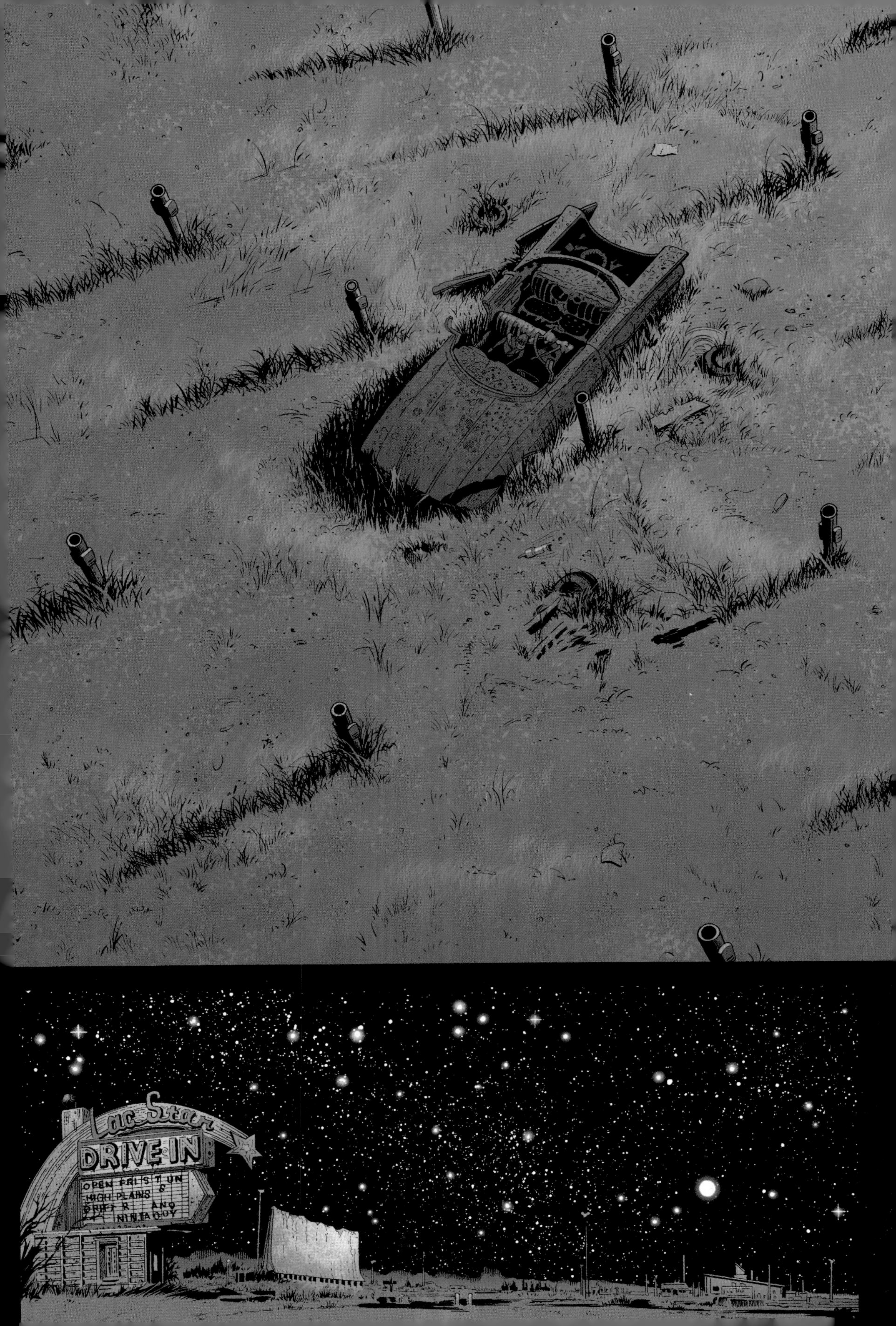
Lac Star
DRIVE-IN
OPEN FRI S T UN
HIGH PLAINS
R AND
NINJA GUY

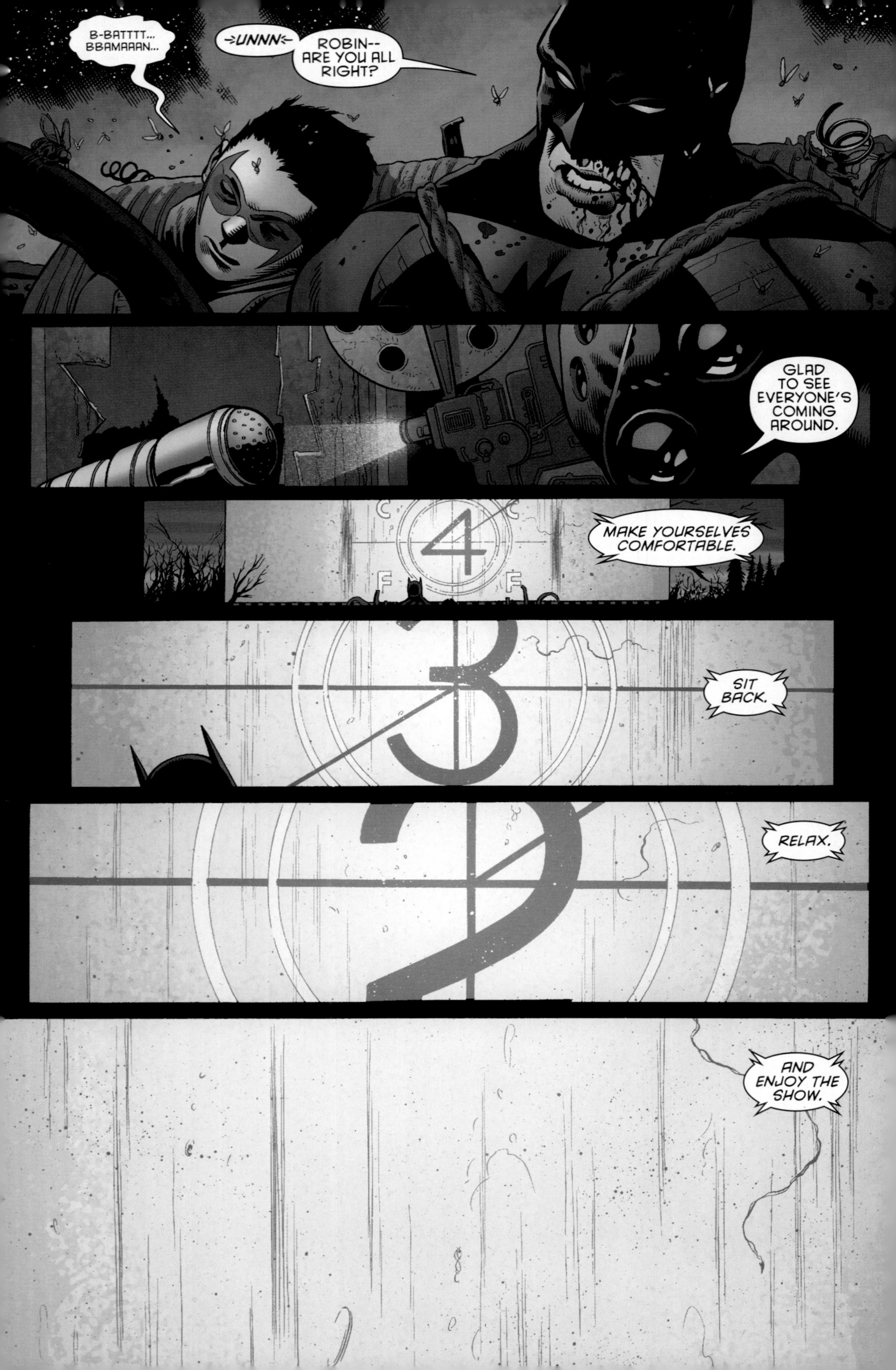
B-BATTTT... BBAMAAAN...
UNNN
ROBIN-- ARE YOU ALL RIGHT?
GLAD TO SEE EVERYONE'S COMING AROUND.
MAKE YOURSELVES COMFORTABLE.
SIT BACK.
RELAX.
AND ENJOY THE SHOW.

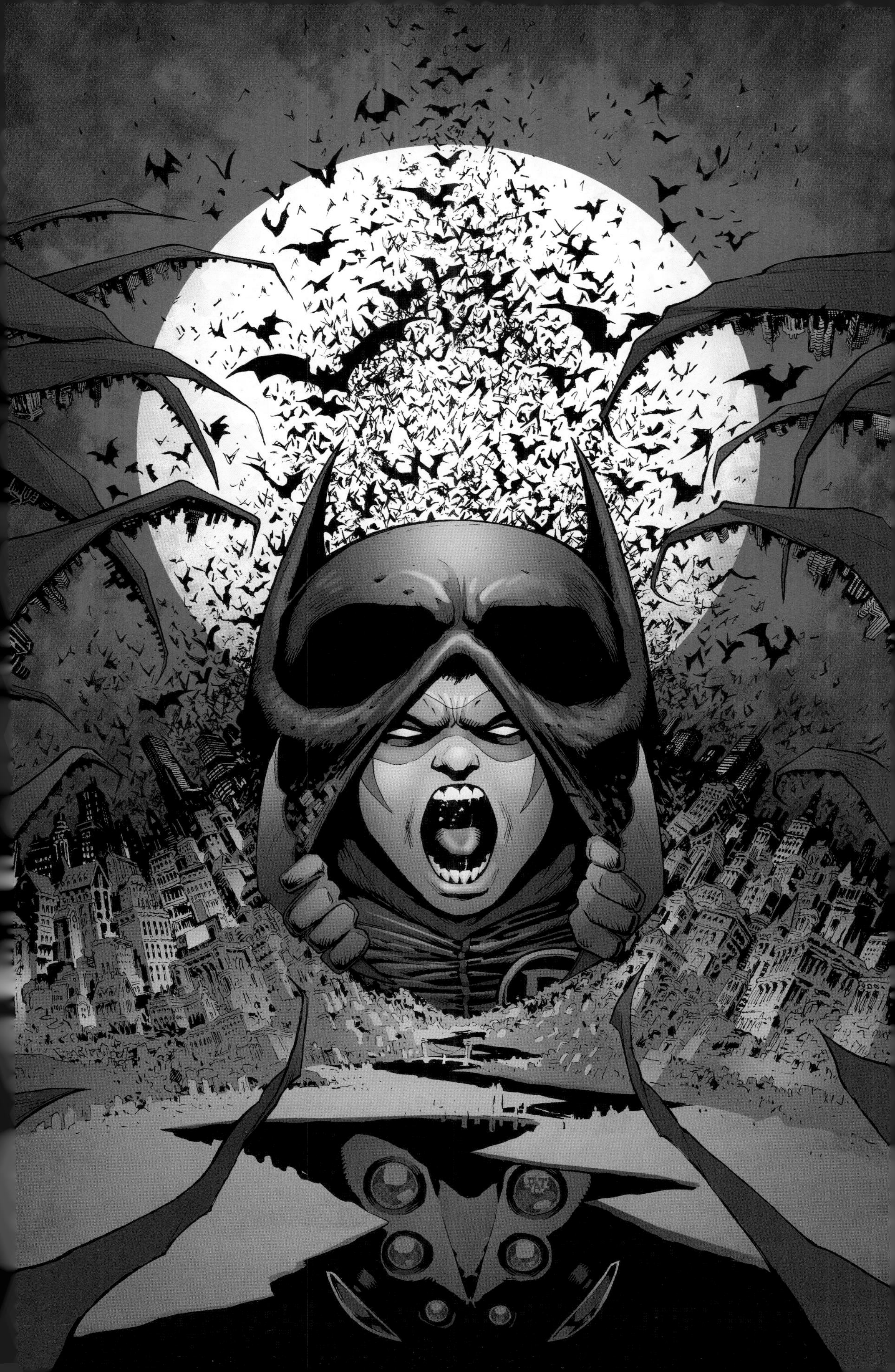

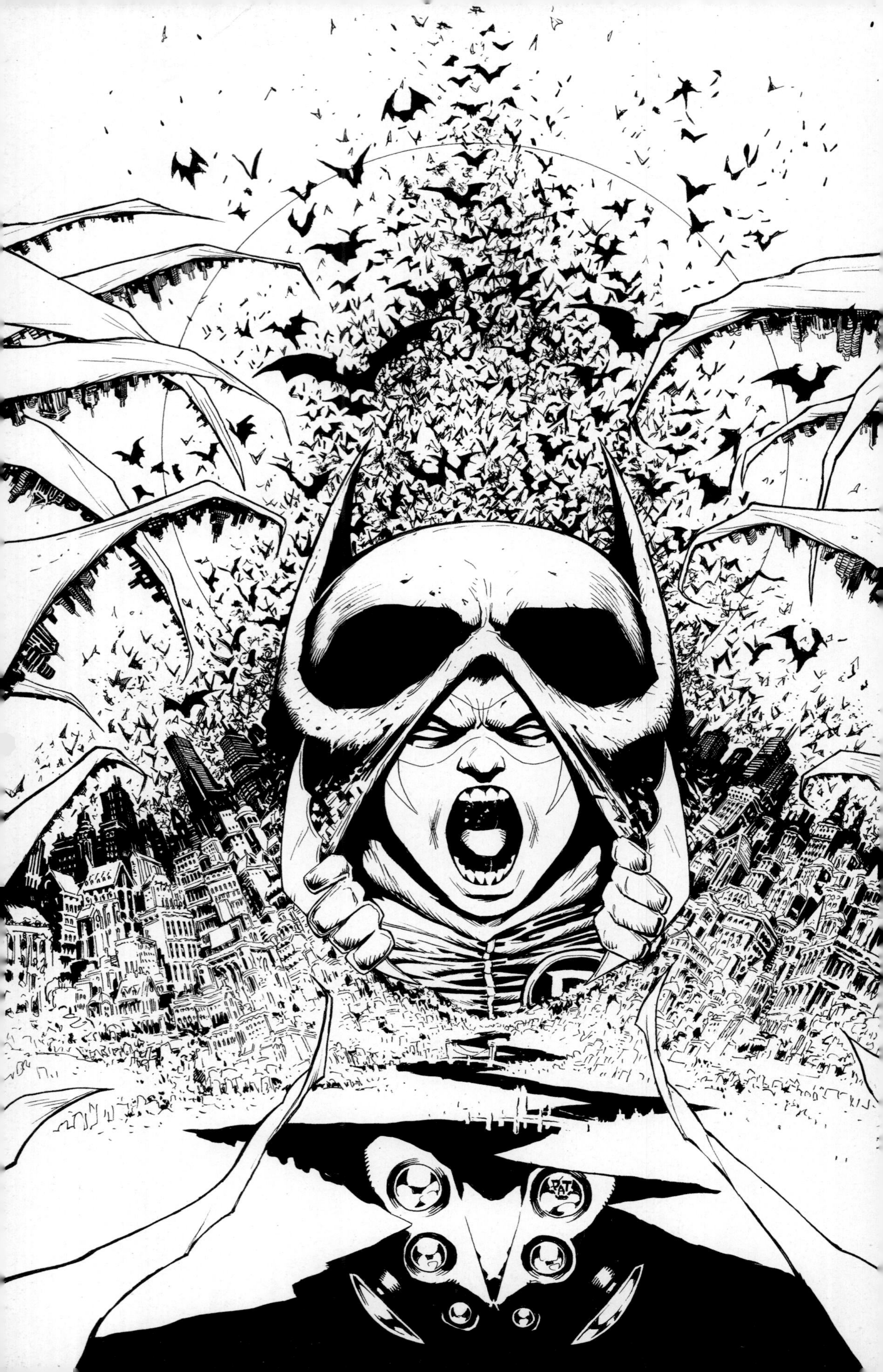

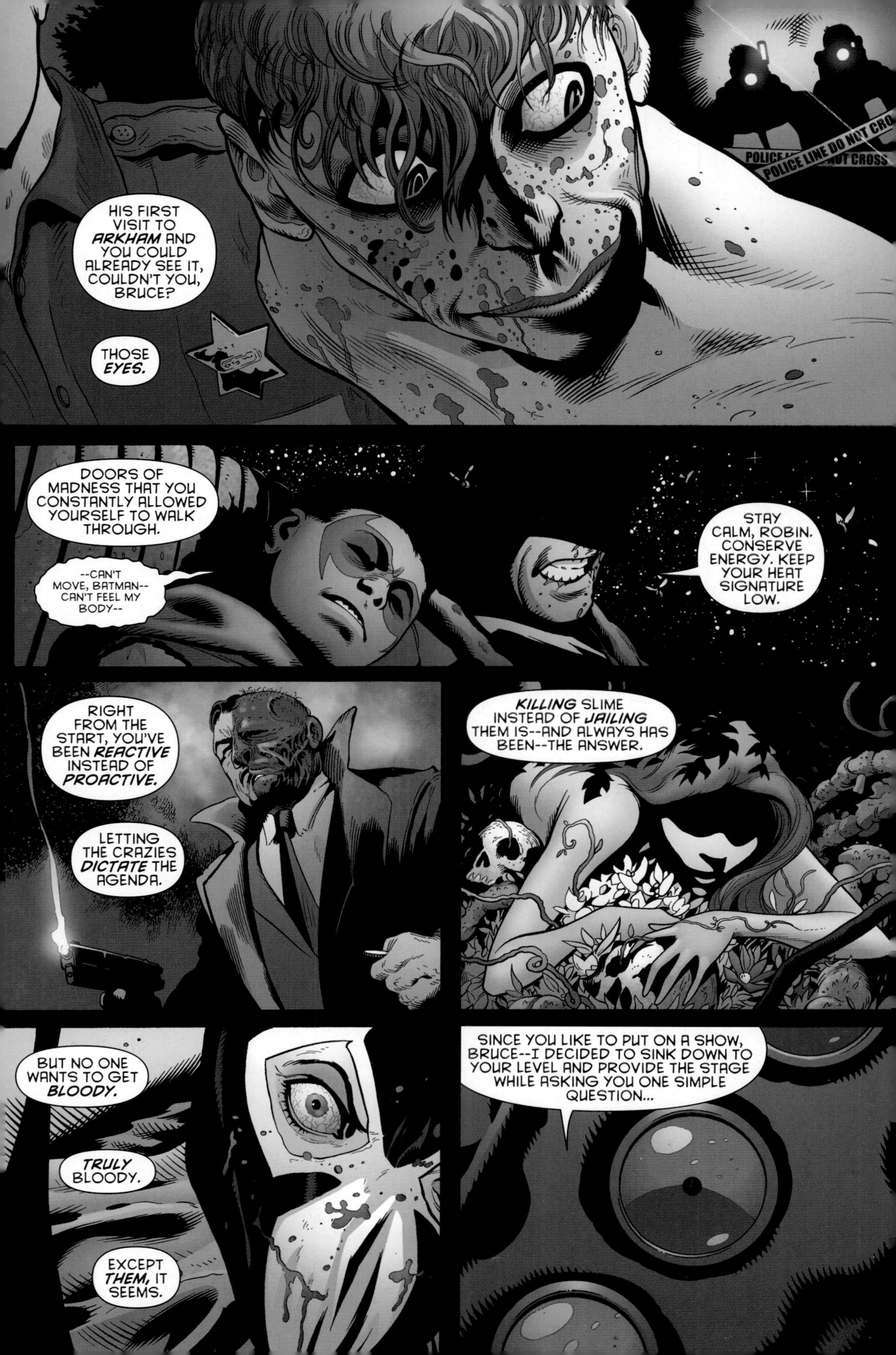
POLICE LINE DO NOT CROSS
HIS FIRST VISIT TO *ARKHAM* AND YOU COULD ALREADY SEE IT, COULDN'T YOU, BRUCE?
THOSE *EYES.*
DOORS OF MADNESS THAT YOU CONSTANTLY ALLOWED YOURSELF TO WALK THROUGH.
--CAN'T MOVE, BATMAN-- CAN'T FEEL MY BODY--
STAY CALM, ROBIN. CONSERVE ENERGY. KEEP YOUR HEAT SIGNATURE LOW.
RIGHT FROM THE START, YOU'VE BEEN *REACTIVE* INSTEAD OF *PROACTIVE.*
LETTING THE CRAZIES *DICTATE* THE AGENDA.
KILLING SLIME INSTEAD OF *JAILING* THEM IS--AND ALWAYS HAS BEEN--THE ANSWER.
BUT NO ONE WANTS TO GET *BLOODY.*
TRULY BLOODY.
EXCEPT *THEM,* IT SEEMS.
SINCE YOU LIKE TO PUT ON A SHOW, BRUCE--I DECIDED TO SINK DOWN TO YOUR LEVEL AND PROVIDE THE STAGE WHILE ASKING YOU ONE SIMPLE QUESTION...

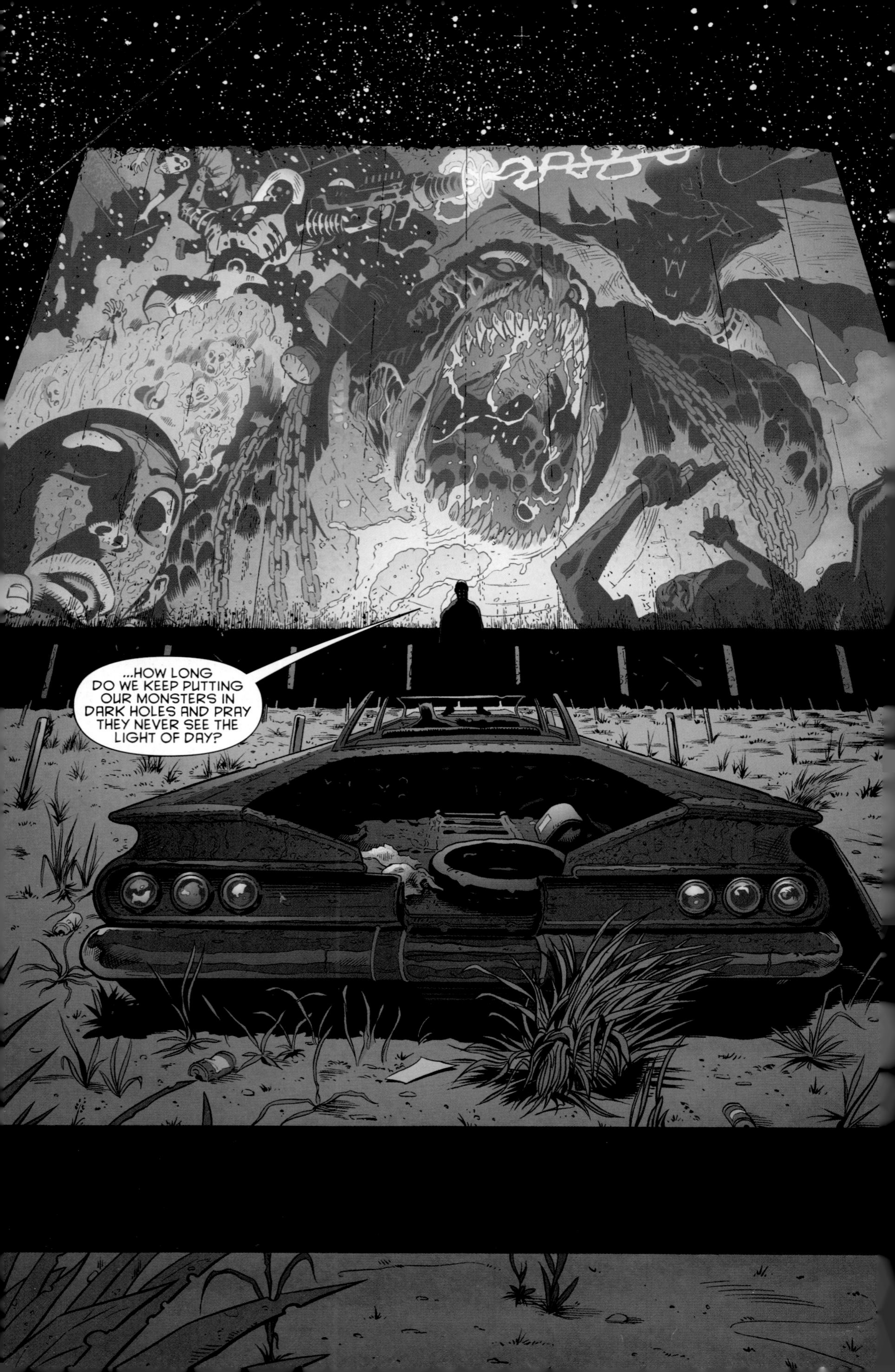
...HOW LONG DO WE KEEP PUTTING OUR MONSTERS IN DARK HOLES AND PRAY THEY NEVER SEE THE LIGHT OF DAY?

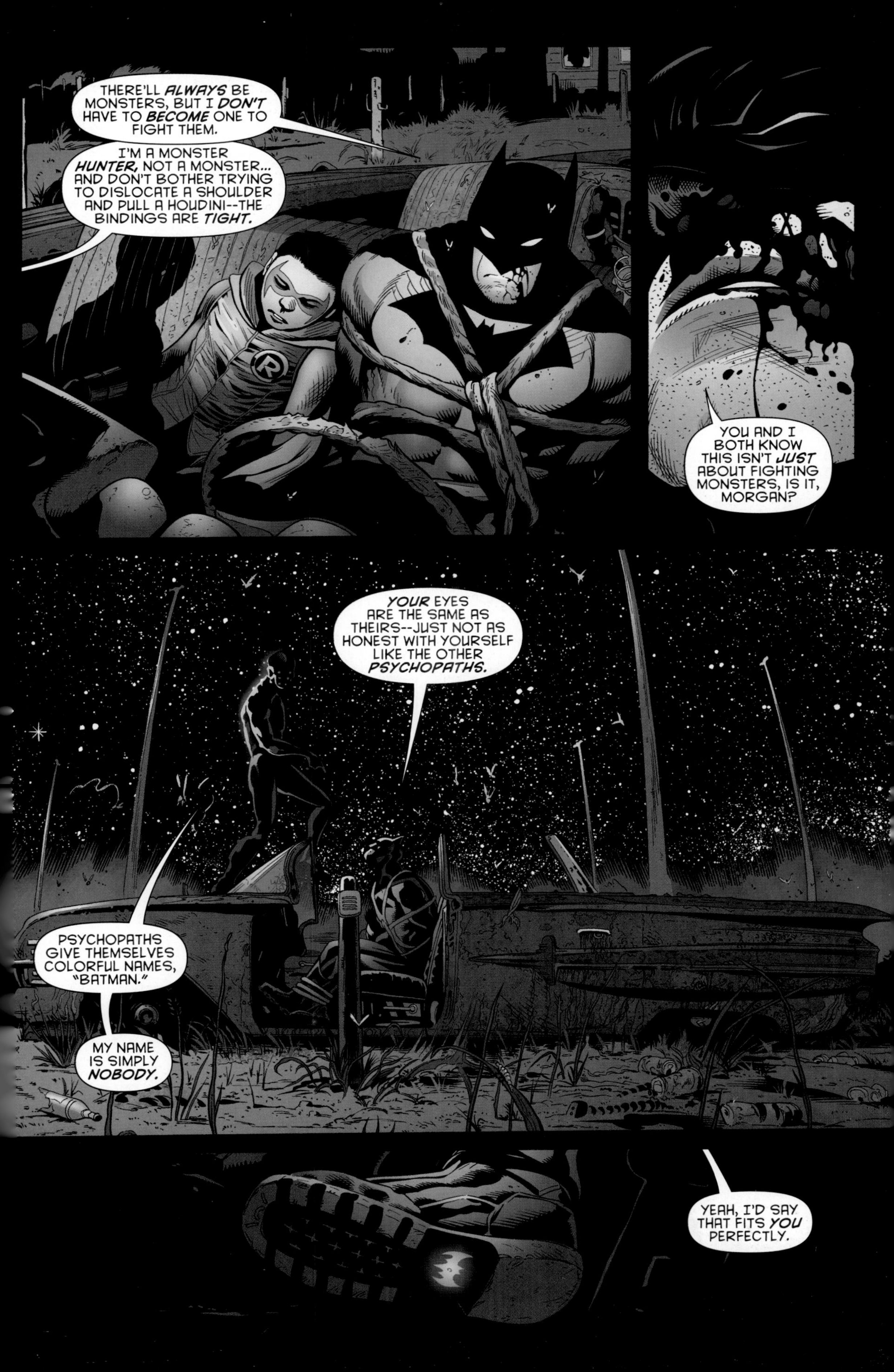
THERE'LL ALWAYS BE MONSTERS, BUT I DON'T HAVE TO BECOME ONE TO FIGHT THEM.
I'M A MONSTER HUNTER, NOT A MONSTER... AND DON'T BOTHER TRYING TO DISLOCATE A SHOULDER AND PULL A HOUDINI--THE BINDINGS ARE TIGHT.
YOU AND I BOTH KNOW THIS ISN'T JUST ABOUT FIGHTING MONSTERS, IS IT, MORGAN?
YOUR EYES ARE THE SAME AS THEIRS--JUST NOT AS HONEST WITH YOURSELF LIKE THE OTHER PSYCHOPATHS.
PSYCHOPATHS GIVE THEMSELVES COLORFUL NAMES, "BATMAN."
MY NAME IS SIMPLY NOBODY.
YEAH, I'D SAY THAT FITS YOU PERFECTLY.

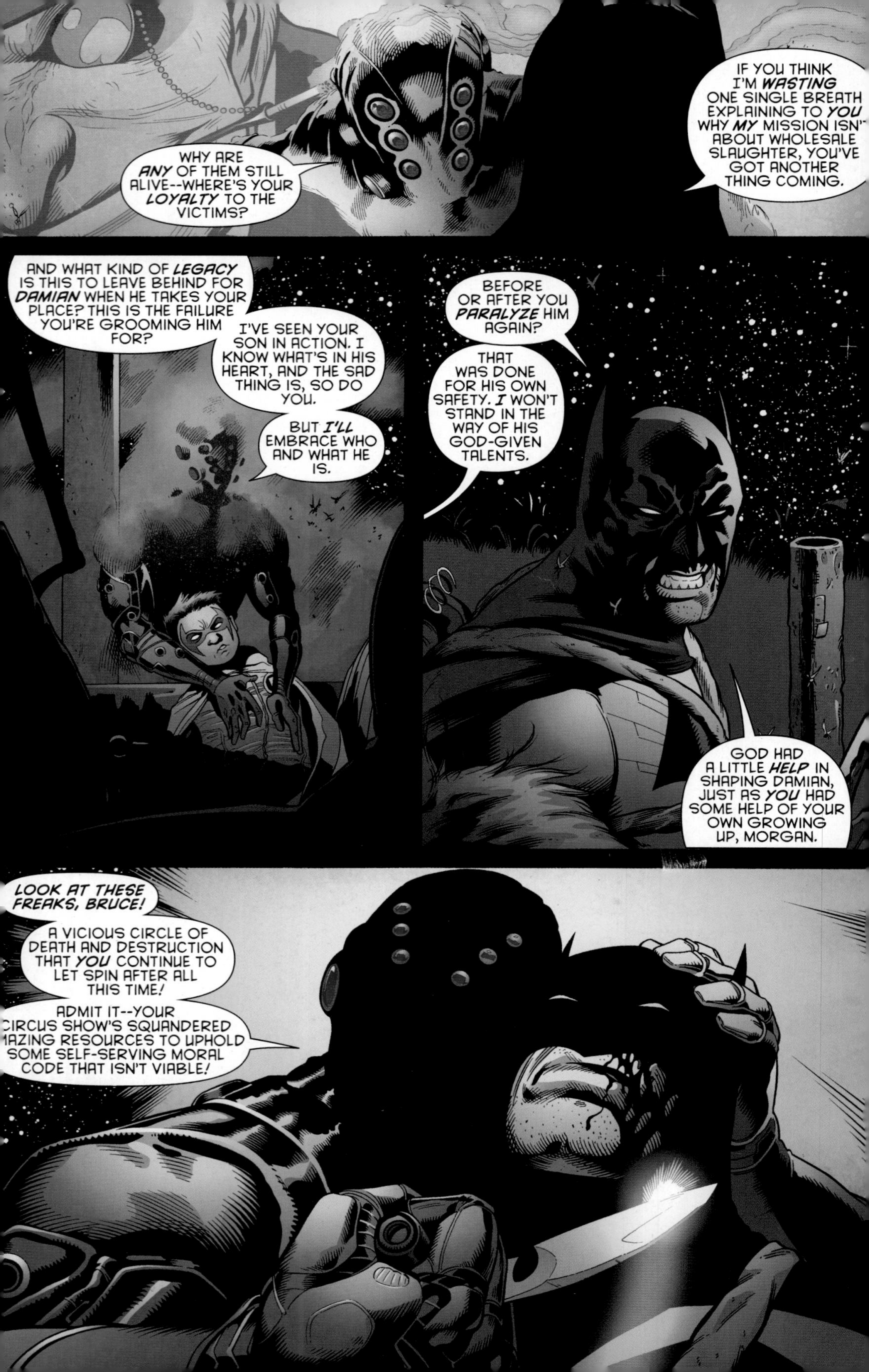
WHY ARE ANY OF THEM STILL ALIVE--WHERE'S YOUR LOYALTY TO THE VICTIMS?
IF YOU THINK I'M WASTING ONE SINGLE BREATH EXPLAINING TO YOU WHY MY MISSION ISN'T ABOUT WHOLESALE SLAUGHTER, YOU'VE GOT ANOTHER THING COMING.
AND WHAT KIND OF LEGACY IS THIS TO LEAVE BEHIND FOR DAMIAN WHEN HE TAKES YOUR PLACE? THIS IS THE FAILURE YOU'RE GROOMING HIM FOR?
I'VE SEEN YOUR SON IN ACTION. I KNOW WHAT'S IN HIS HEART, AND THE SAD THING IS, SO DO YOU.
BUT I'LL EMBRACE WHO AND WHAT HE IS.
BEFORE OR AFTER YOU PARALYZE HIM AGAIN?
THAT WAS DONE FOR HIS OWN SAFETY. I WON'T STAND IN THE WAY OF HIS GOD-GIVEN TALENTS.
GOD HAD A LITTLE HELP IN SHAPING DAMIAN, JUST AS YOU HAD SOME HELP OF YOUR OWN GROWING UP, MORGAN.
LOOK AT THESE FREAKS, BRUCE!
A VICIOUS CIRCLE OF DEATH AND DESTRUCTION THAT YOU CONTINUE TO LET SPIN AFTER ALL THIS TIME!
ADMIT IT--YOUR CIRCUS SHOW'S SQUANDERED AMAZING RESOURCES TO UPHOLD SOME SELF-SERVING MORAL CODE THAT ISN'T VIABLE!

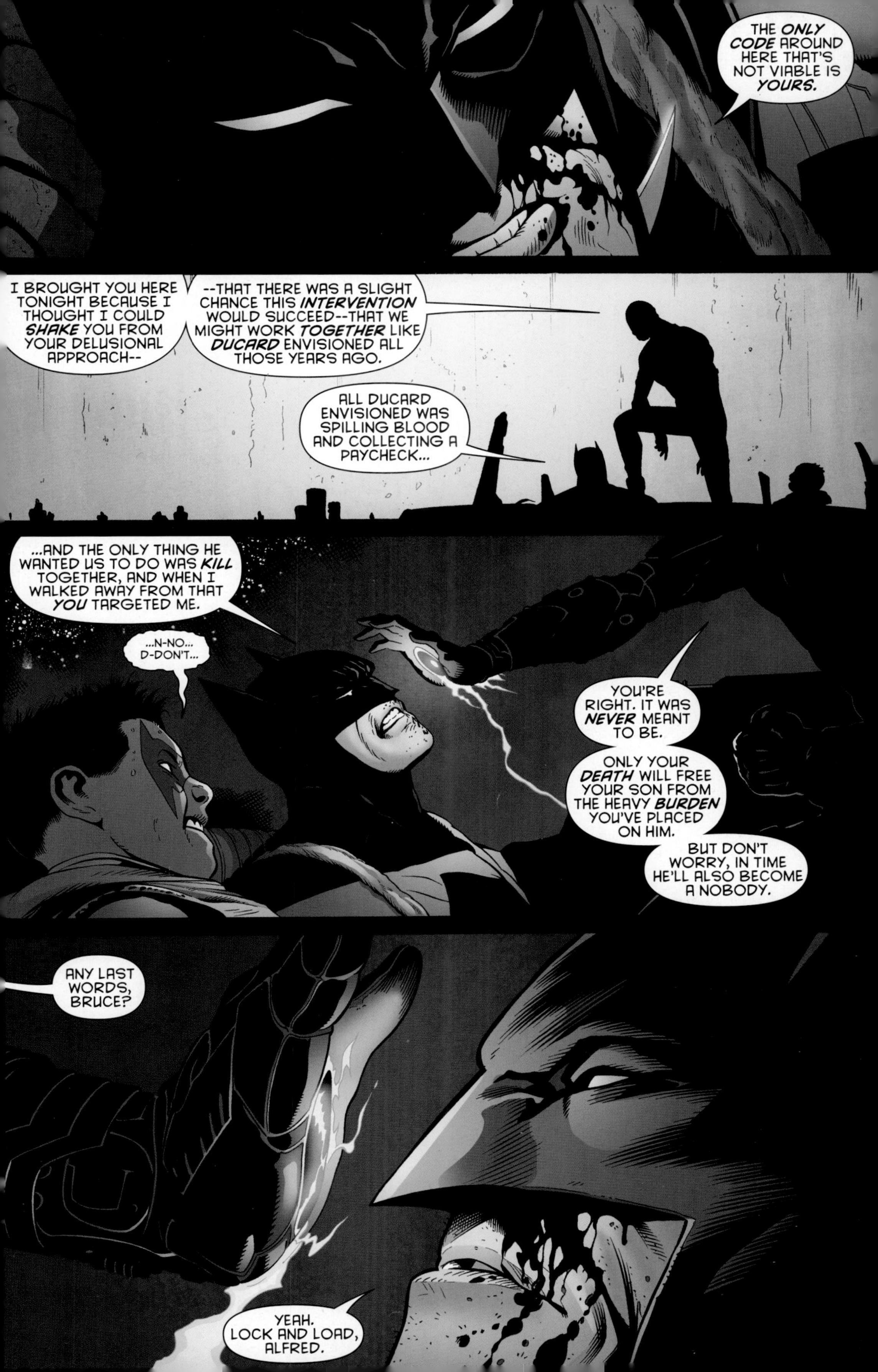
THE ONLY CODE AROUND HERE THAT'S NOT VIABLE IS YOURS.
I BROUGHT YOU HERE TONIGHT BECAUSE I THOUGHT I COULD SHAKE YOU FROM YOUR DELUSIONAL APPROACH--
--THAT THERE WAS A SLIGHT CHANCE THIS INTERVENTION WOULD SUCCEED--THAT WE MIGHT WORK TOGETHER LIKE DUCARD ENVISIONED ALL THOSE YEARS AGO.
ALL DUCARD ENVISIONED WAS SPILLING BLOOD AND COLLECTING A PAYCHECK...
...AND THE ONLY THING HE WANTED US TO DO WAS KILL TOGETHER, AND WHEN I WALKED AWAY FROM THAT YOU TARGETED ME.
...N-NO... D-DON'T...
YOU'RE RIGHT. IT WAS NEVER MEANT TO BE.
ONLY YOUR DEATH WILL FREE YOUR SON FROM THE HEAVY BURDEN YOU'VE PLACED ON HIM.
BUT DON'T WORRY, IN TIME HE'LL ALSO BECOME A NOBODY.
ANY LAST WORDS, BRUCE?
YEAH. LOCK AND LOAD, ALFRED.

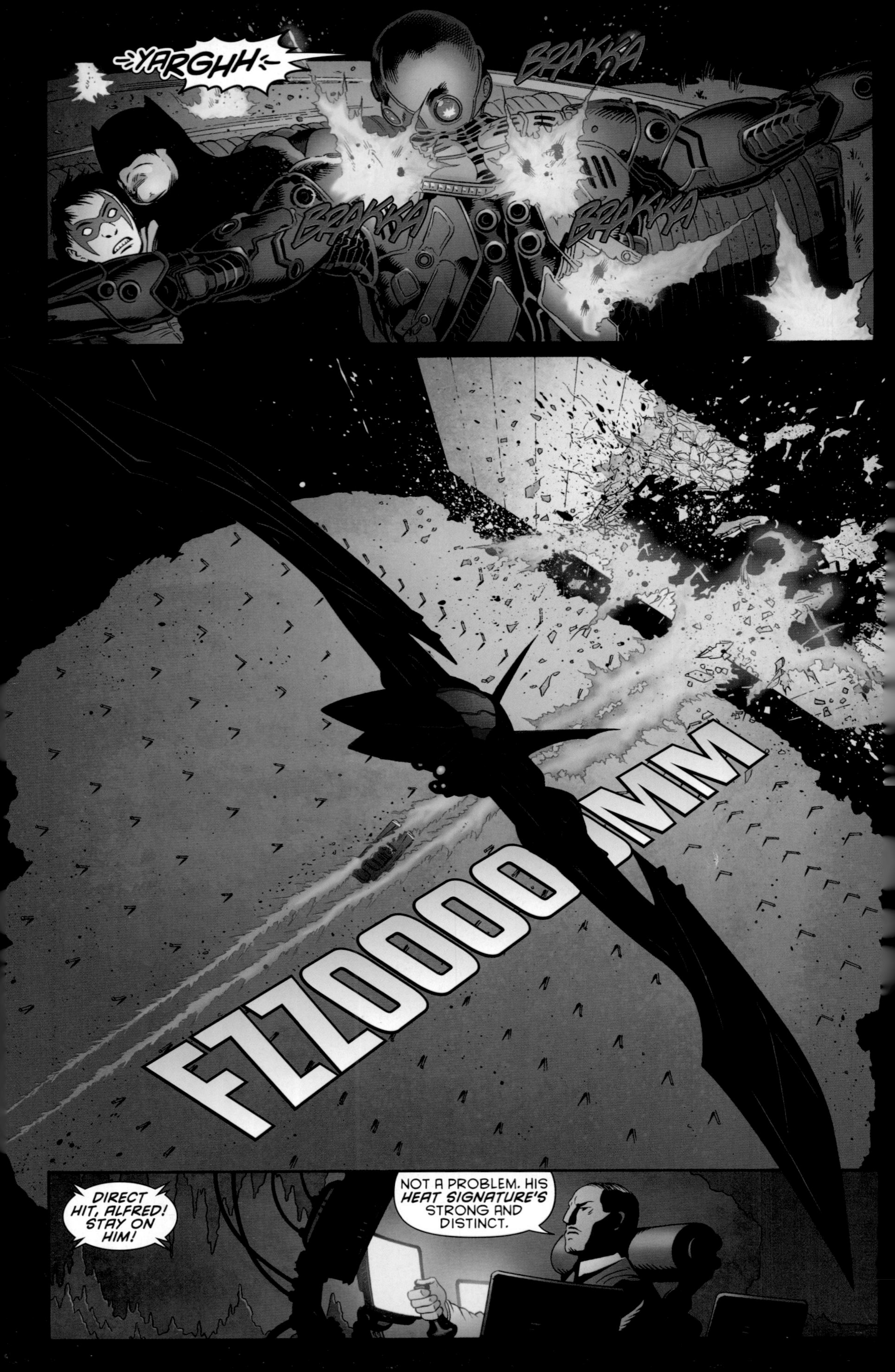
YARGHH
BRAKKA
BRAKKA
BRAKKA
FZZOOOOMM
DIRECT HIT, ALFRED! STAY ON HIM!
NOT A PROBLEM. HIS HEAT SIGNATURE'S STRONG AND DISTINCT.

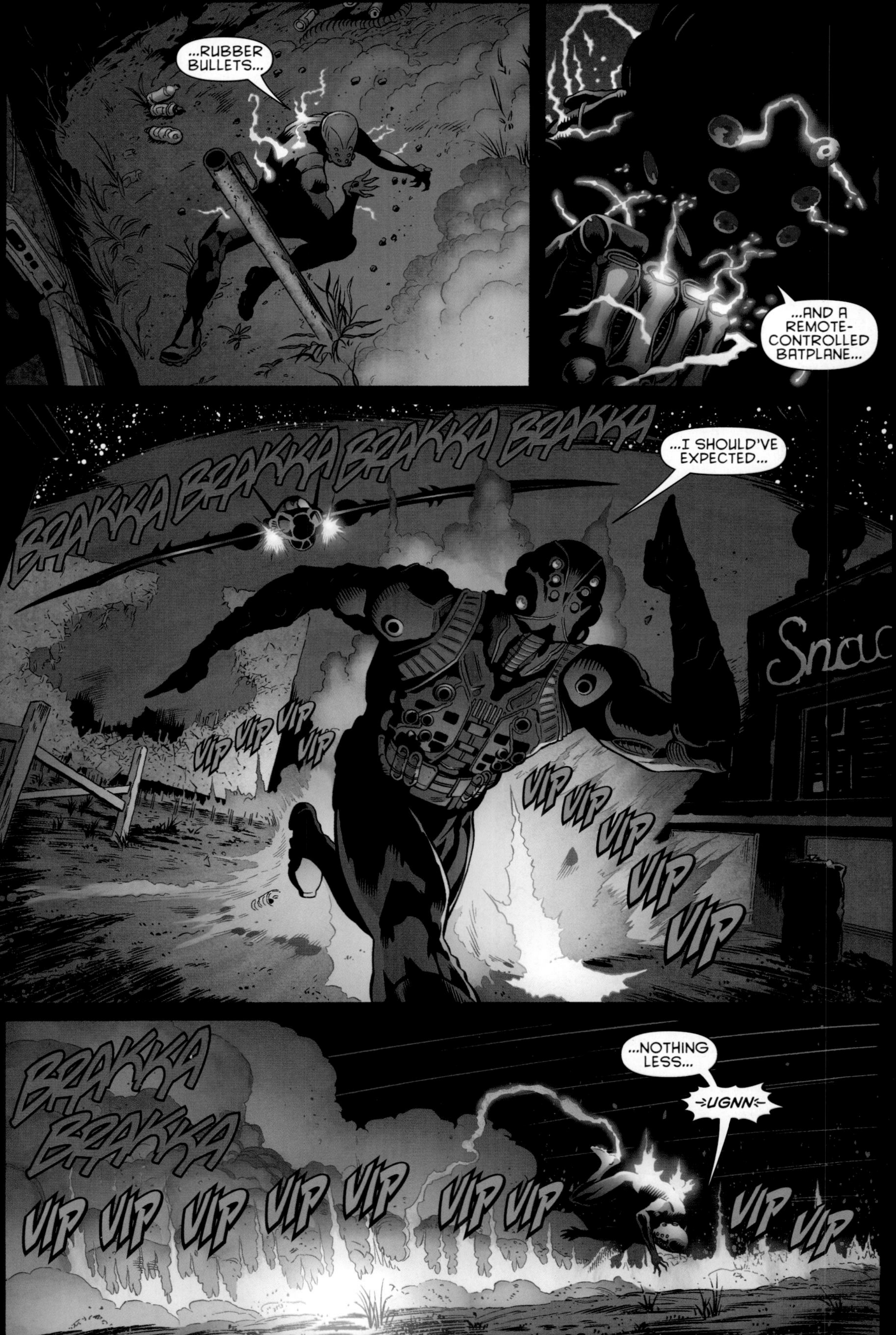
...RUBBER BULLETS...
...AND A REMOTE-CONTROLLED BATPLANE...
BRAKKA BRAKKA BRAKKA BRAKKA
...I SHOULD'VE EXPECTED...
VIP VIP VIP VIP
VIP VIP VIP VIP VIP
Snac
BRAKKA BRAKKA
VIP VIP VIP VIP VIP VIP VIP VIP VIP
...NOTHING LESS...
UGNN

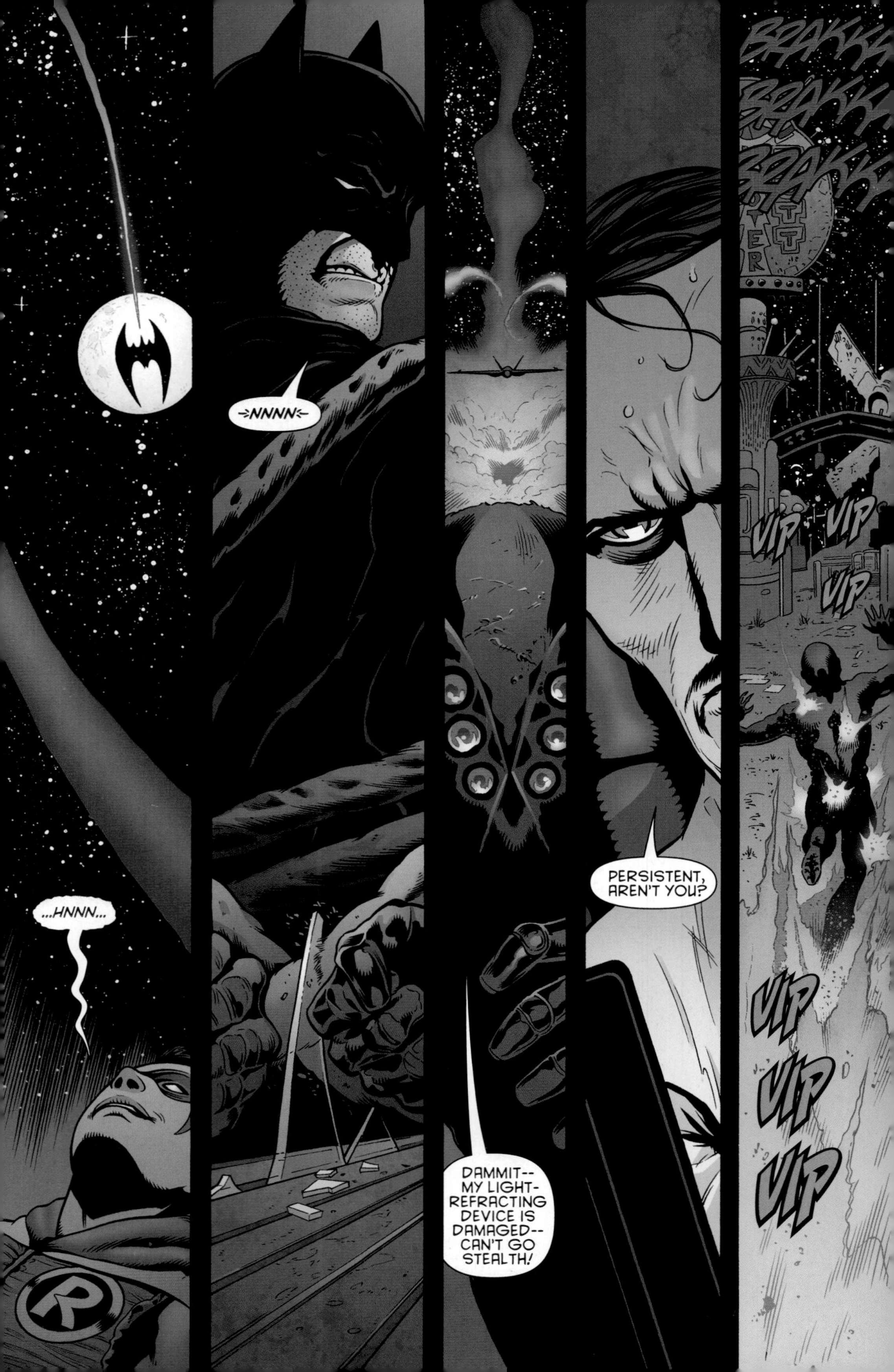
...HNNN...
-NNNN-
PERSISTENT, AREN'T YOU?
DAMMIT-- MY LIGHT-REFRACTING DEVICE IS DAMAGED-- CAN'T GO STEALTH!
BRAKKA
BRAKKA
BRAKKA
VIP VIP
VIP
VIP
VIP
VIP

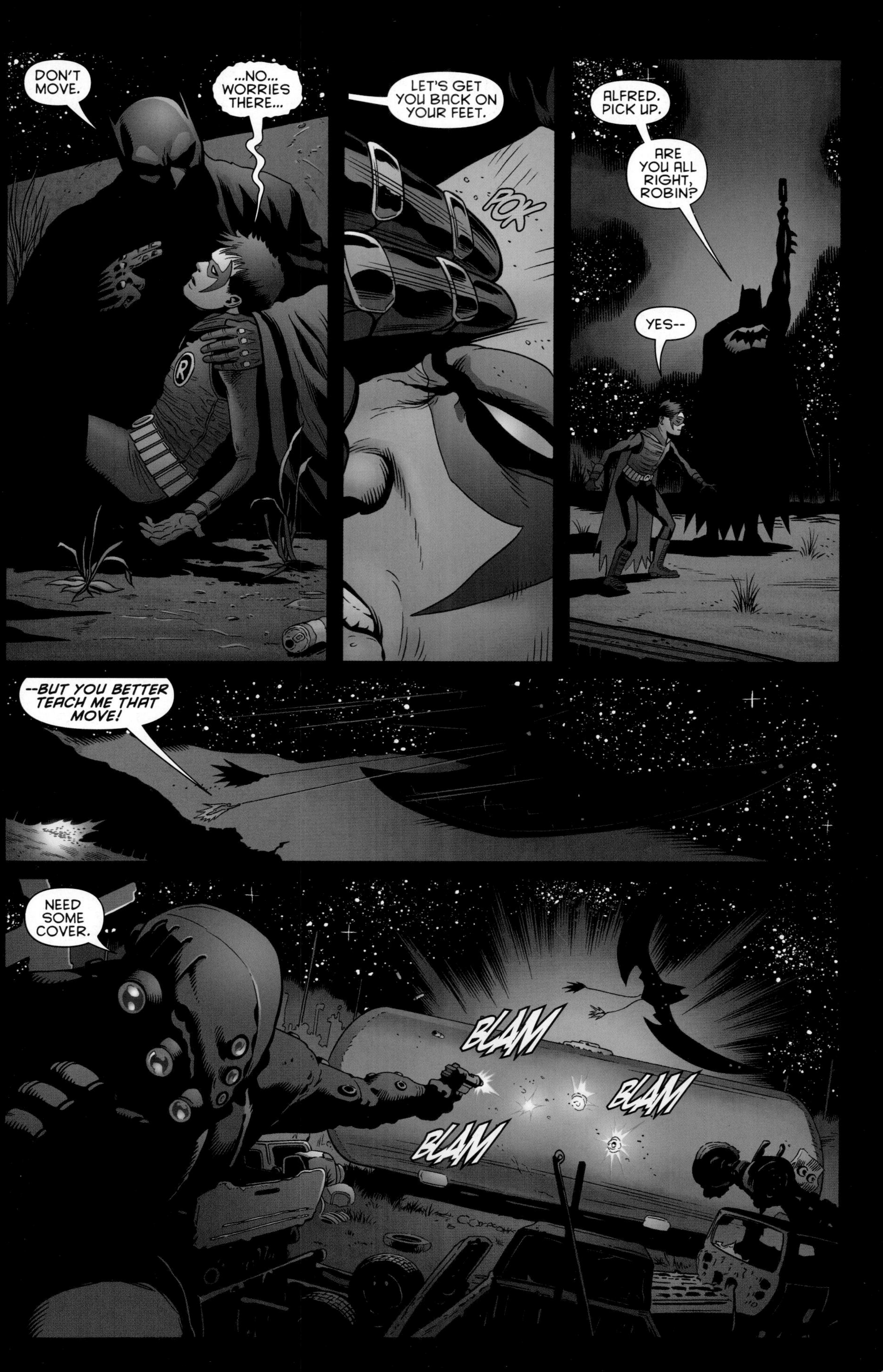
DON'T MOVE.
...NO... WORRIES THERE...
LET'S GET YOU BACK ON YOUR FEET.
POK
ALFRED. PICK UP.
ARE YOU ALL RIGHT, ROBIN?
YES--
--BUT YOU BETTER TEACH ME THAT MOVE!
NEED SOME COVER.
BLAM
BLAM
BLAM

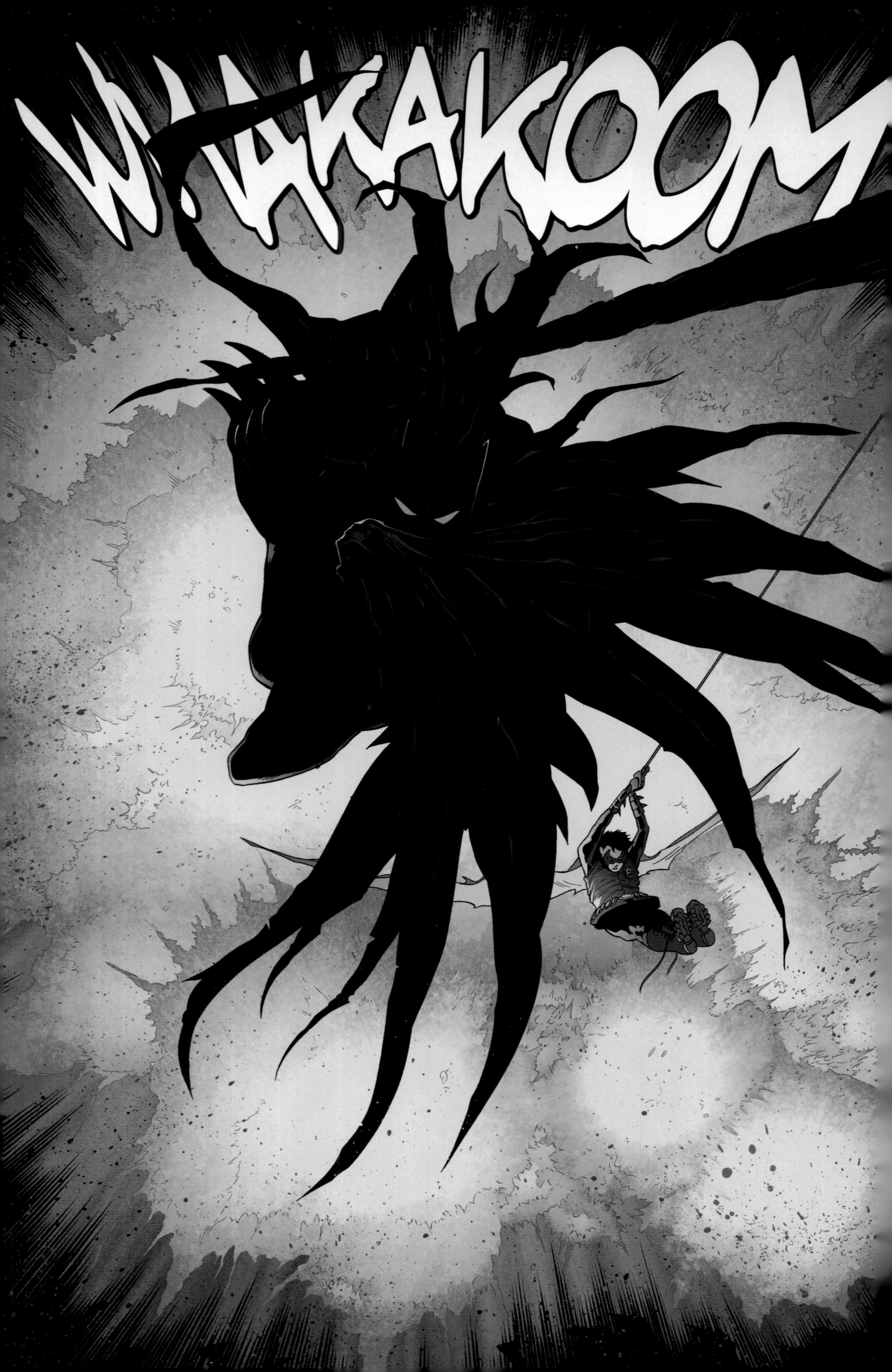
WHAKOOM

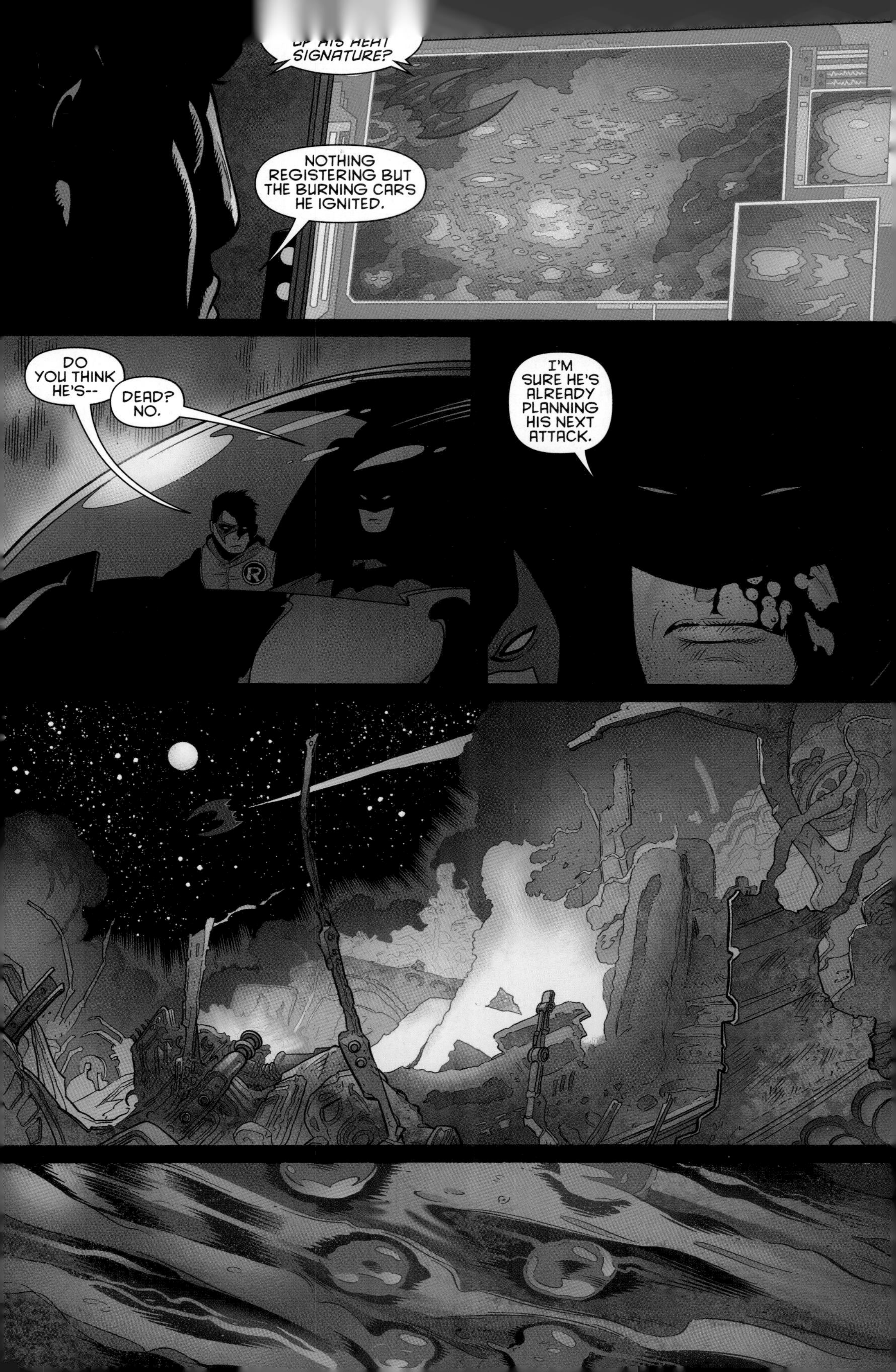
SIGNATURE?
NOTHING REGISTERING BUT THE BURNING CARS HE IGNITED.
DO YOU THINK HE'S--
DEAD? NO.
I'M SURE HE'S ALREADY PLANNING HIS NEXT ATTACK.

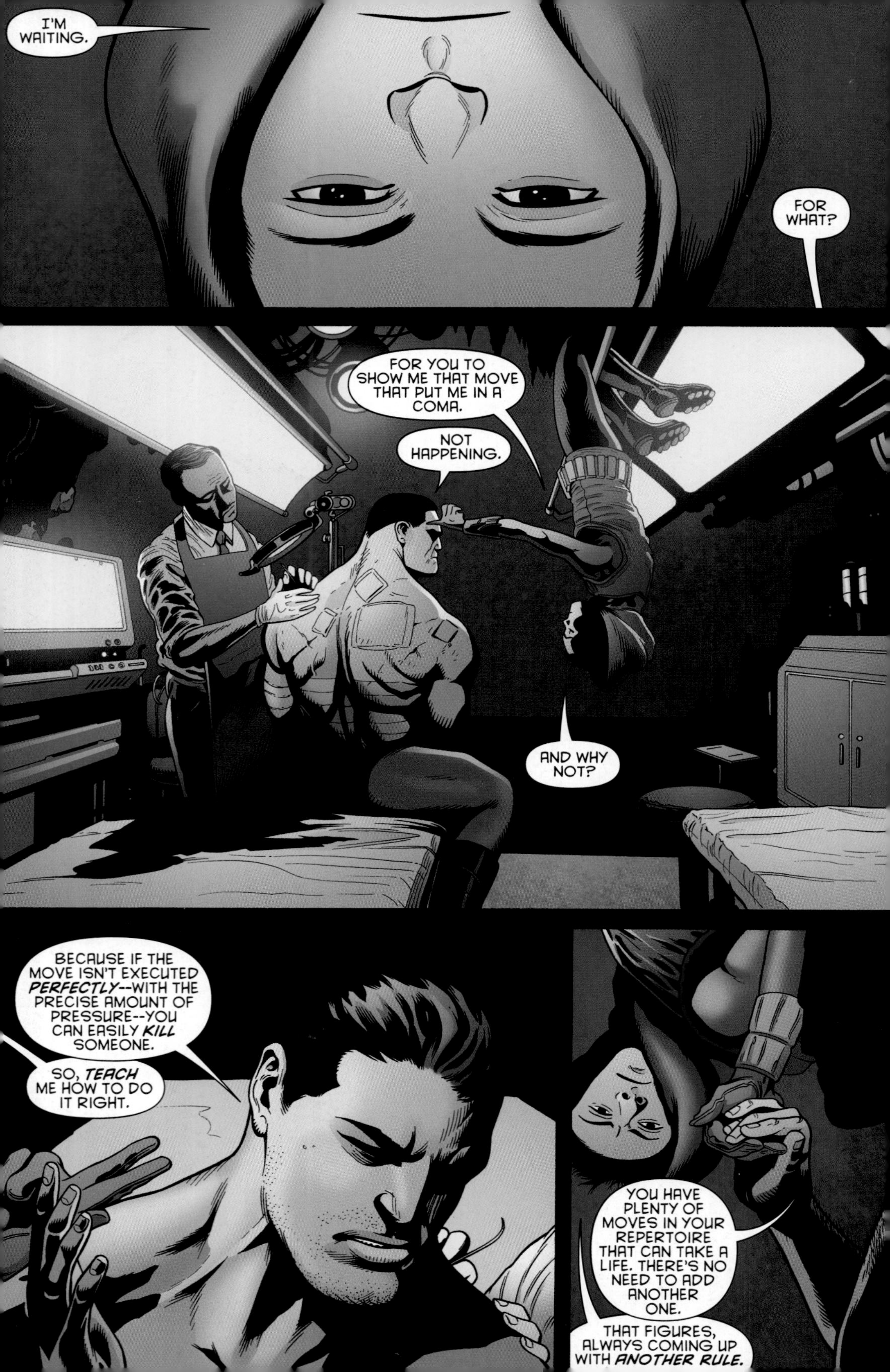
I'M WAITING.
FOR WHAT?
FOR YOU TO SHOW ME THAT MOVE THAT PUT ME IN A COMA.
NOT HAPPENING.
AND WHY NOT?
BECAUSE IF THE MOVE ISN'T EXECUTED *PERFECTLY*--WITH THE PRECISE AMOUNT OF PRESSURE--YOU CAN EASILY *KILL* SOMEONE.
SO, *TEACH* ME HOW TO DO IT RIGHT.
YOU HAVE PLENTY OF MOVES IN YOUR REPERTOIRE THAT CAN TAKE A LIFE. THERE'S NO NEED TO ADD ANOTHER ONE.
THAT FIGURES, ALWAYS COMING UP WITH *ANOTHER RULE*.

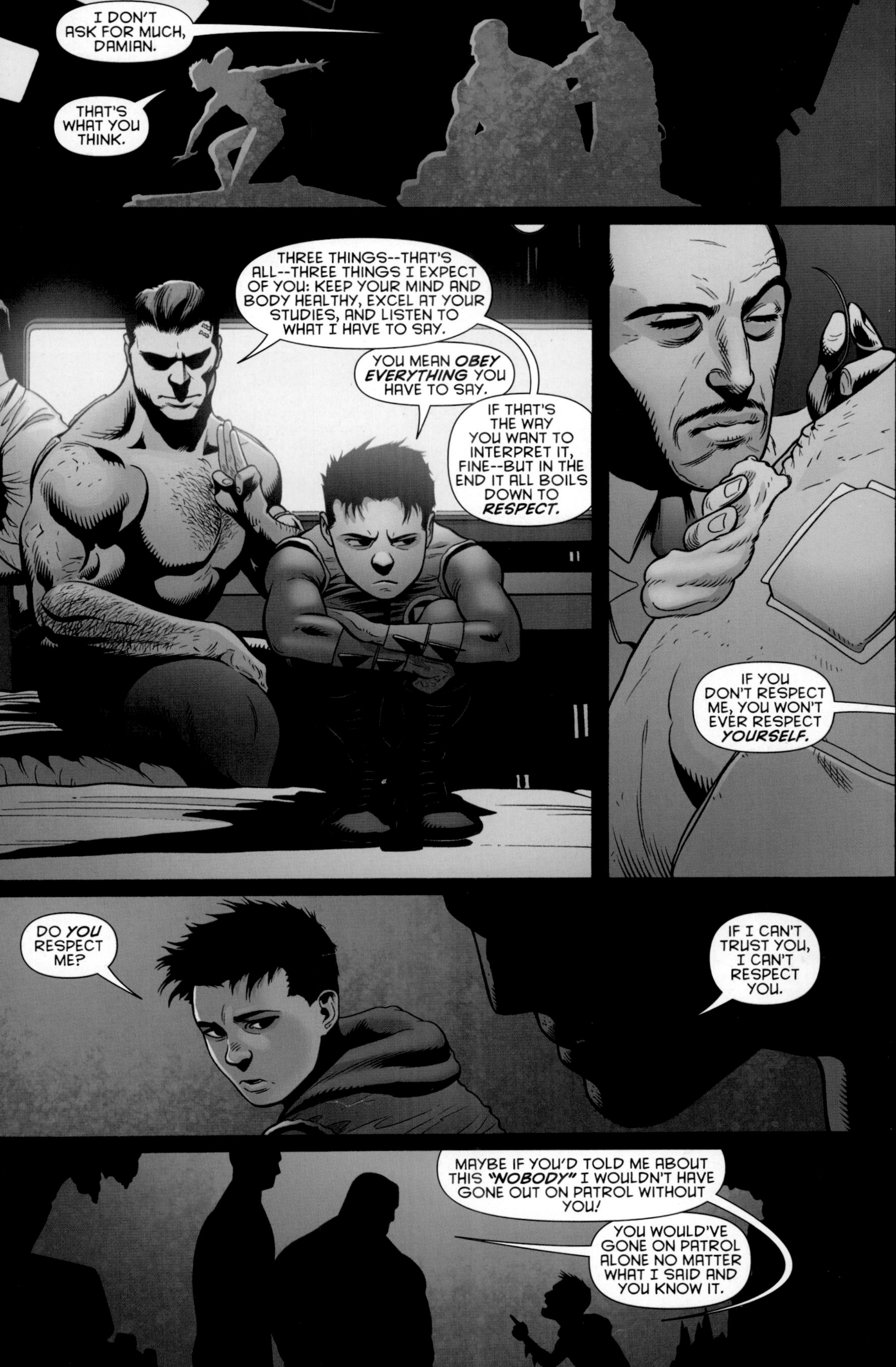
I DON'T ASK FOR MUCH, DAMIAN.
THAT'S WHAT YOU THINK.
THREE THINGS--THAT'S ALL--THREE THINGS I EXPECT OF YOU: KEEP YOUR MIND AND BODY HEALTHY, EXCEL AT YOUR STUDIES, AND LISTEN TO WHAT I HAVE TO SAY.
YOU MEAN OBEY EVERYTHING YOU HAVE TO SAY.
IF THAT'S THE WAY YOU WANT TO INTERPRET IT, FINE--BUT IN THE END IT ALL BOILS DOWN TO RESPECT.
IF YOU DON'T RESPECT ME, YOU WON'T EVER RESPECT YOURSELF.
DO YOU RESPECT ME?
IF I CAN'T TRUST YOU, I CAN'T RESPECT YOU.
MAYBE IF YOU'D TOLD ME ABOUT THIS "NOBODY" I WOULDN'T HAVE GONE OUT ON PATROL WITHOUT YOU!
YOU WOULD'VE GONE ON PATROL ALONE NO MATTER WHAT I SAID AND YOU KNOW IT.

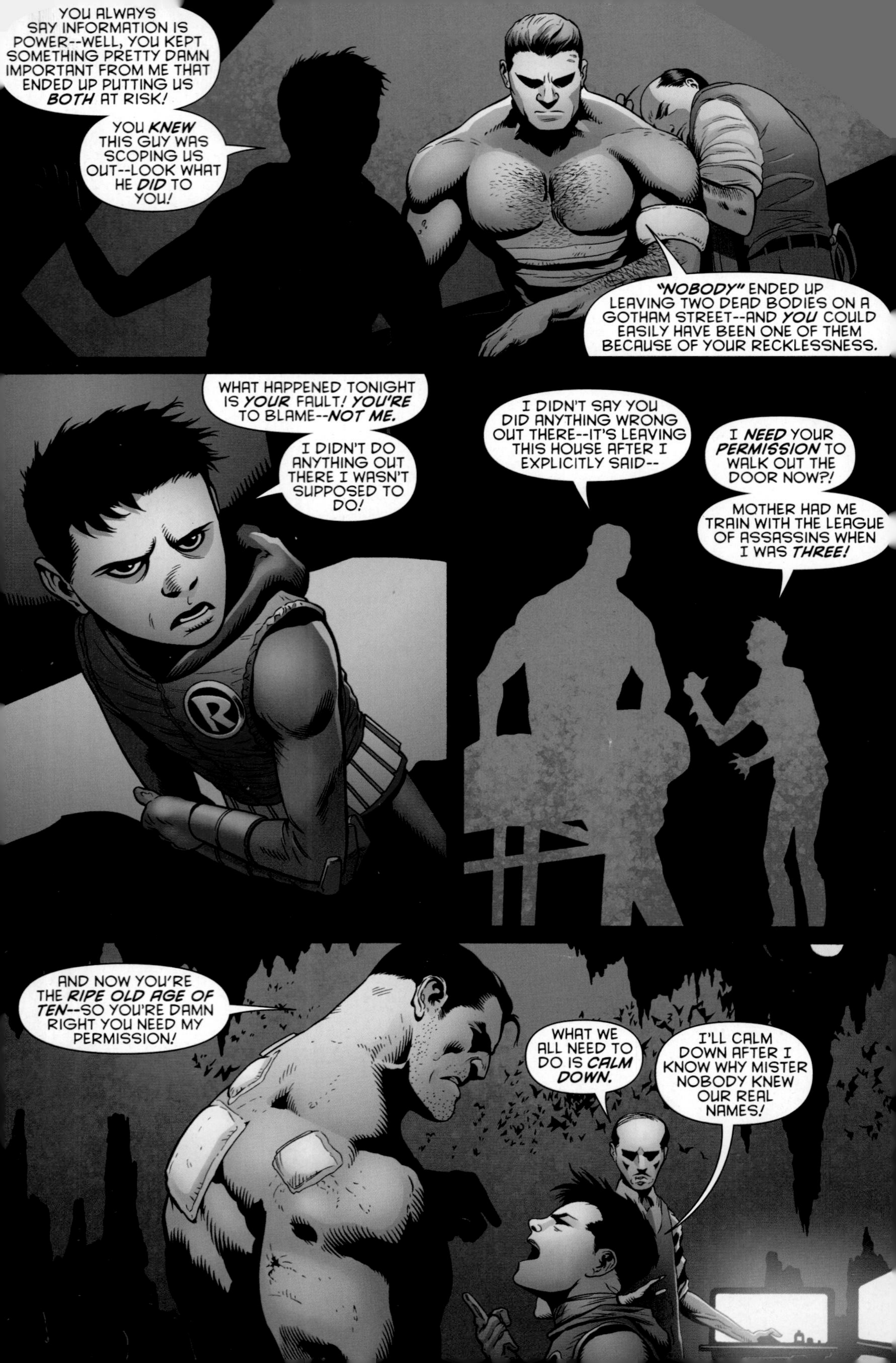
YOU ALWAYS SAY INFORMATION IS POWER--WELL, YOU KEPT SOMETHING PRETTY DAMN IMPORTANT FROM ME THAT ENDED UP PUTTING US BOTH AT RISK!
YOU KNEW THIS GUY WAS SCOPING US OUT--LOOK WHAT HE DID TO YOU!
"NOBODY" ENDED UP LEAVING TWO DEAD BODIES ON A GOTHAM STREET--AND YOU COULD EASILY HAVE BEEN ONE OF THEM BECAUSE OF YOUR RECKLESSNESS.
WHAT HAPPENED TONIGHT IS YOUR FAULT! YOU'RE TO BLAME--NOT ME.
I DIDN'T DO ANYTHING OUT THERE I WASN'T SUPPOSED TO DO!
I DIDN'T SAY YOU DID ANYTHING WRONG OUT THERE--IT'S LEAVING THIS HOUSE AFTER I EXPLICITLY SAID--
I NEED YOUR PERMISSION TO WALK OUT THE DOOR NOW?!
MOTHER HAD ME TRAIN WITH THE LEAGUE OF ASSASSINS WHEN I WAS THREE!
AND NOW YOU'RE THE RIPE OLD AGE OF TEN--SO YOU'RE DAMN RIGHT YOU NEED MY PERMISSION!
WHAT WE ALL NEED TO DO IS CALM DOWN.
I'LL CALM DOWN AFTER I KNOW WHY MISTER NOBODY KNEW OUR REAL NAMES!

NOBODY'S NAME IS *MORGAN DUCARD*, HE'S THE SON OF HENRI DUCARD.

ISN'T HENRI DUCARD ONE OF THE FOUR WHO ORIGINALLY TRAINED YOU?

YES, BUT THERE WERE ACTUALLY *SIX* PEOPLE WHO TRAINED ME.

HENRI DUCARD WAS MY LAST STOP ON THE LIST. HE WAS A SPECIAL INVESTIGATOR WHO WORKED FOR INTERPOL AND OTHER GOVERNMENT AGENCIES TRACKING DOWN THE MOST DANGEROUS CRIMINALS AROUND THE WORLD.

WHEN ANYONE WANTED SOMEONE FOUND, IT WAS HENRI DUCARD THEY WENT TO SEE. HE WAS ONE OF THE GREATEST MAN-HUNTERS THAT EVER LIVED.

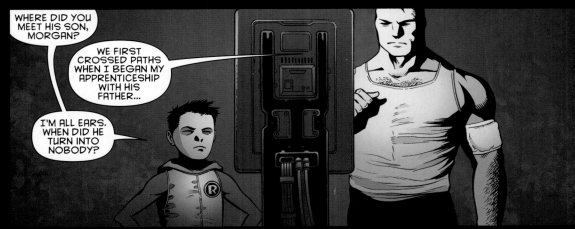
WHERE DID YOU MEET HIS SON, MORGAN?

WE FIRST CROSSED PATHS WHEN I BEGAN MY APPRENTICESHIP WITH HIS FATHER...

I'M ALL EARS. WHEN DID HE TURN INTO NOBODY?

IT'S *NOT* A STORY I CAN SHARE WITH YOU RIGHT NOW, BUT THE APPLE DIDN'T FALL FAR FROM THE TREE. MORGAN IS *VERY* MUCH HIS FATHER'S SON.

AND THAT'S IT?

IF I THOUGHT THERE WAS MORE YOU NEEDED TO KNOW, YOU'D KNOW IT.

YOU WANT *ME* TO BE HONEST ALL THE TIME, BUT *YOU* GET TO PICK AND CHOOSE WHEN YOU WANT TO BE.

I DON'T EXPECT YOU TO UNDERSTAND THIS, BUT AS A FATHER THERE ARE SOME THINGS I...

HAVE TO LIE ABOUT.

CAN'T *DISCUSS* WITH YOU YET. THERE'S A DIFFERENCE.

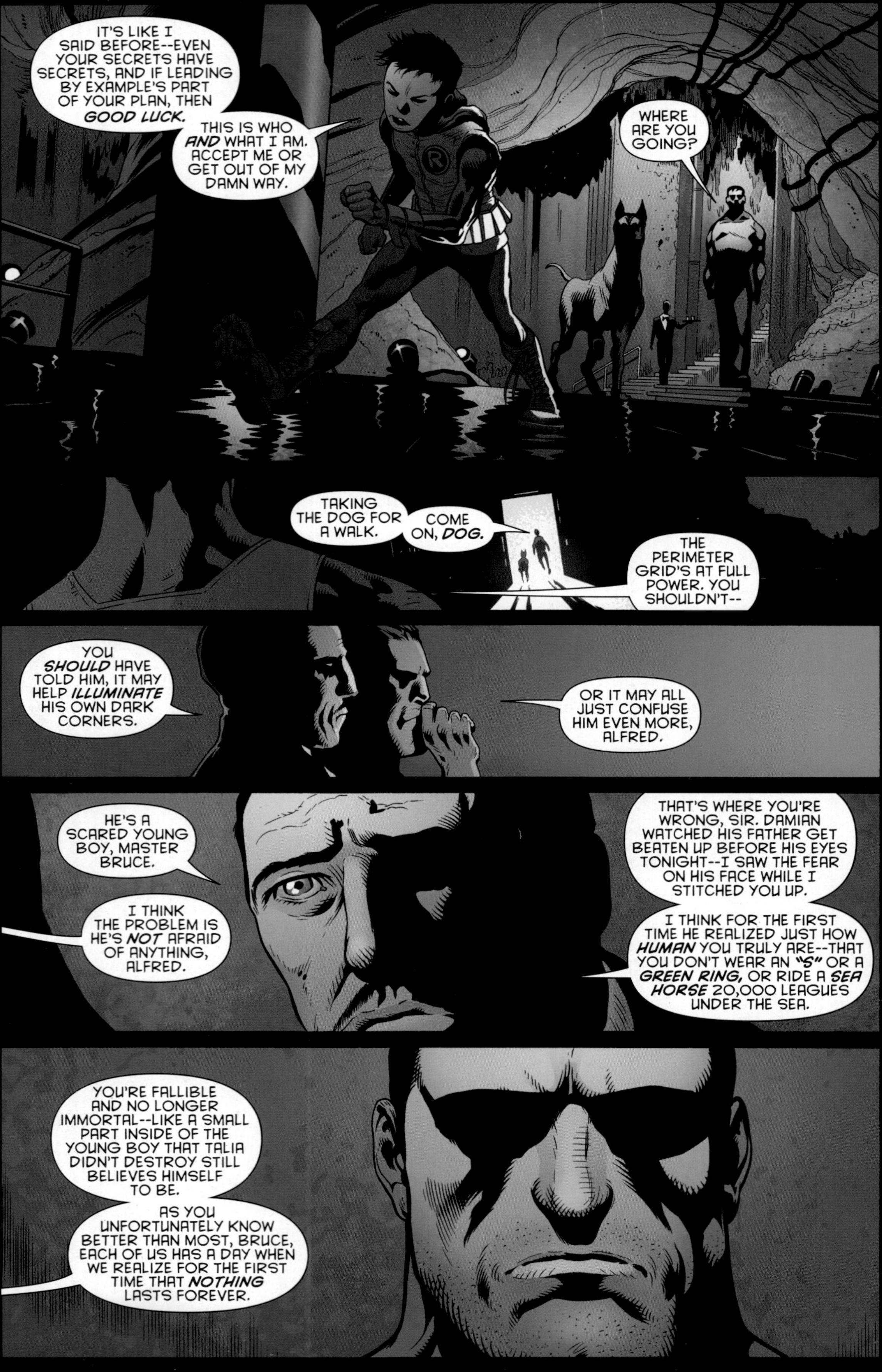
IT'S LIKE I SAID BEFORE--EVEN YOUR SECRETS HAVE SECRETS, AND IF LEADING BY EXAMPLE'S PART OF YOUR PLAN, THEN GOOD LUCK.
THIS IS WHO AND WHAT I AM. ACCEPT ME OR GET OUT OF MY DAMN WAY.
WHERE ARE YOU GOING?
TAKING THE DOG FOR A WALK.
COME ON, DOG.
THE PERIMETER GRID'S AT FULL POWER. YOU SHOULDN'T--
YOU SHOULD HAVE TOLD HIM, IT MAY HELP ILLUMINATE HIS OWN DARK CORNERS.
OR IT MAY ALL JUST CONFUSE HIM EVEN MORE, ALFRED.
HE'S A SCARED YOUNG BOY, MASTER BRUCE.
I THINK THE PROBLEM IS HE'S NOT AFRAID OF ANYTHING, ALFRED.
THAT'S WHERE YOU'RE WRONG, SIR. DAMIAN WATCHED HIS FATHER GET BEATEN UP BEFORE HIS EYES TONIGHT--I SAW THE FEAR ON HIS FACE WHILE I STITCHED YOU UP.
I THINK FOR THE FIRST TIME HE REALIZED JUST HOW HUMAN YOU TRULY ARE--THAT YOU DON'T WEAR AN "S" OR A GREEN RING, OR RIDE A SEA HORSE 20,000 LEAGUES UNDER THE SEA.
YOU'RE FALLIBLE AND NO LONGER IMMORTAL--LIKE A SMALL PART INSIDE OF THE YOUNG BOY THAT TALIA DIDN'T DESTROY STILL BELIEVES HIMSELF TO BE.
AS YOU UNFORTUNATELY KNOW BETTER THAN MOST, BRUCE, EACH OF US HAS A DAY WHEN WE REALIZE FOR THE FIRST TIME THAT NOTHING LASTS FOREVER.

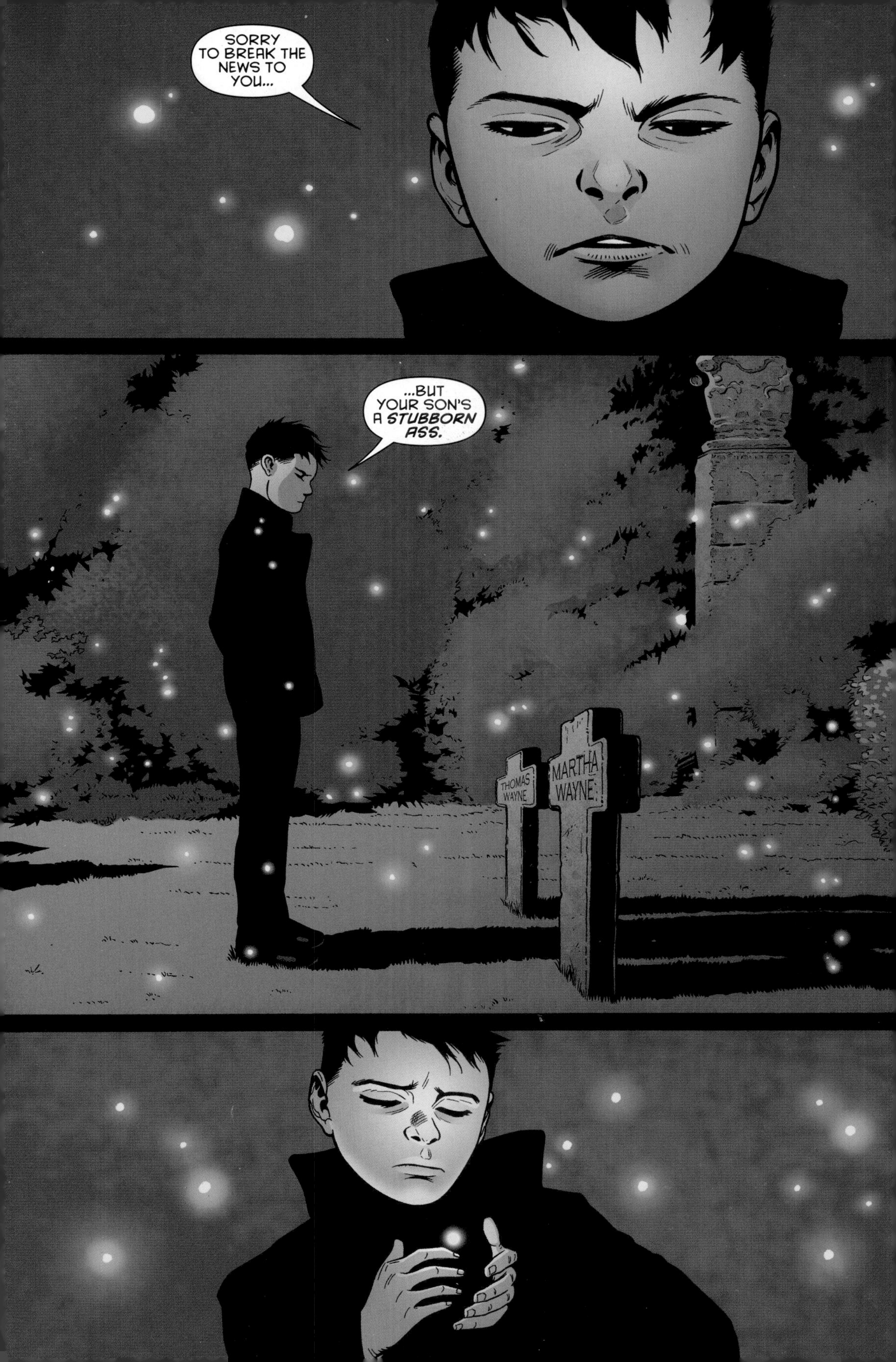
SORRY TO BREAK THE NEWS TO YOU...
...BUT YOUR SON'S A STUBBORN ASS.
THOMAS WAYNE
MARTHA WAYNE

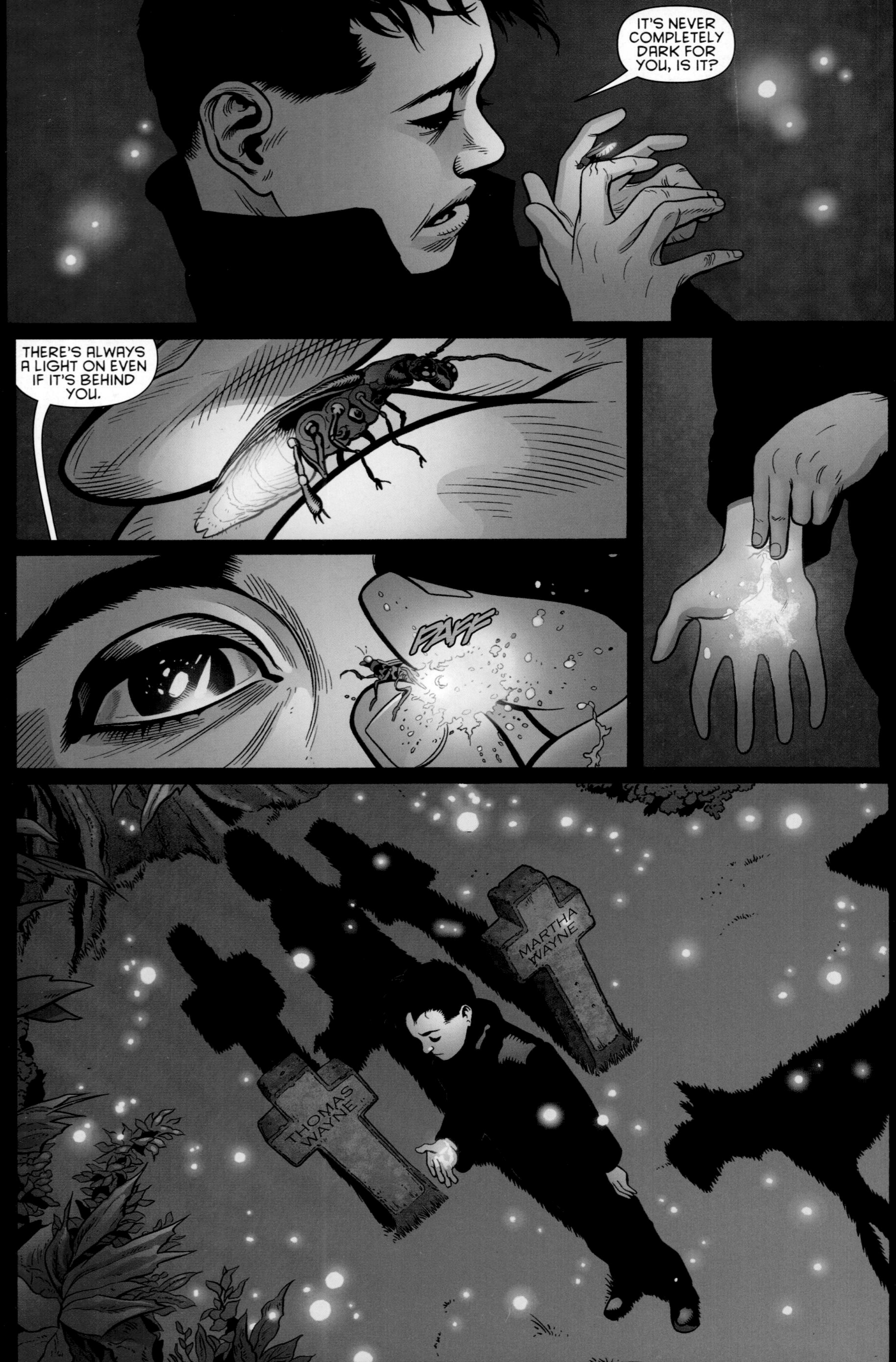

IT'S NEVER COMPLETELY DARK FOR YOU, IS IT?
THERE'S ALWAYS A LIGHT ON EVEN IF IT'S BEHIND YOU.
FAFF
MARTHA WAYNE
THOMAS WAYNE

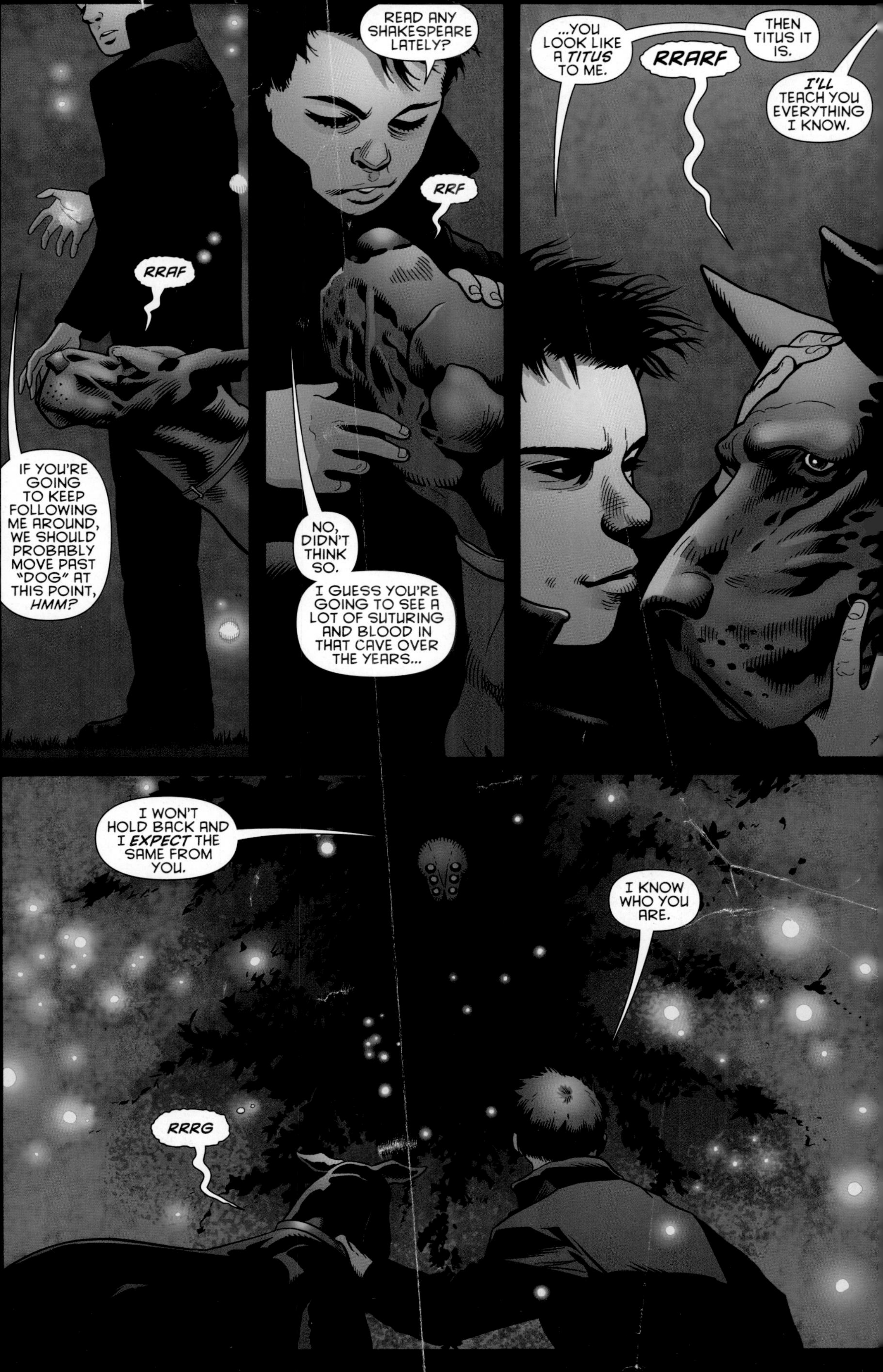
RRAF
IF YOU'RE GOING TO KEEP FOLLOWING ME AROUND, WE SHOULD PROBABLY MOVE PAST "DOG" AT THIS POINT, HMM?
READ ANY SHAKESPEARE LATELY?
RRF
NO, DIDN'T THINK SO.
I GUESS YOU'RE GOING TO SEE A LOT OF SUTURING AND BLOOD IN THAT CAVE OVER THE YEARS...
...YOU LOOK LIKE A TITUS TO ME.
RRARF
THEN TITUS IT IS.
I'LL TEACH YOU EVERYTHING I KNOW.
I WON'T HOLD BACK AND I EXPECT THE SAME FROM YOU.
I KNOW WHO YOU ARE.
RRRG

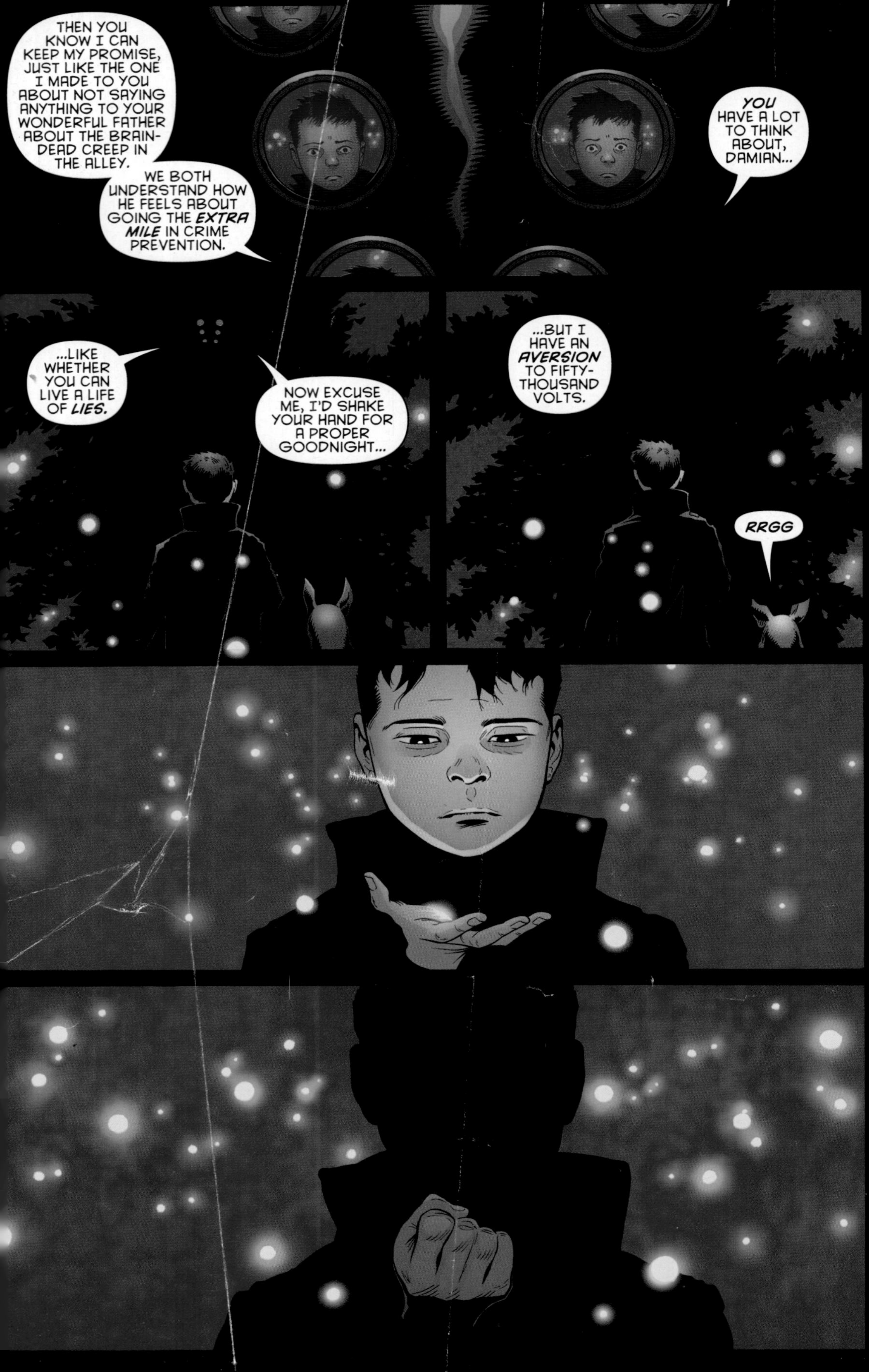
THEN YOU KNOW I CAN KEEP MY PROMISE, JUST LIKE THE ONE I MADE TO YOU ABOUT NOT SAYING ANYTHING TO YOUR WONDERFUL FATHER ABOUT THE BRAIN-DEAD CREEP IN THE ALLEY.
WE BOTH UNDERSTAND HOW HE FEELS ABOUT GOING THE EXTRA MILE IN CRIME PREVENTION.
YOU HAVE A LOT TO THINK ABOUT, DAMIAN...
...LIKE WHETHER YOU CAN LIVE A LIFE OF LIES.
NOW EXCUSE ME, I'D SHAKE YOUR HAND FOR A PROPER GOODNIGHT...
...BUT I HAVE AN AVERSION TO FIFTY-THOUSAND VOLTS.
RRGG

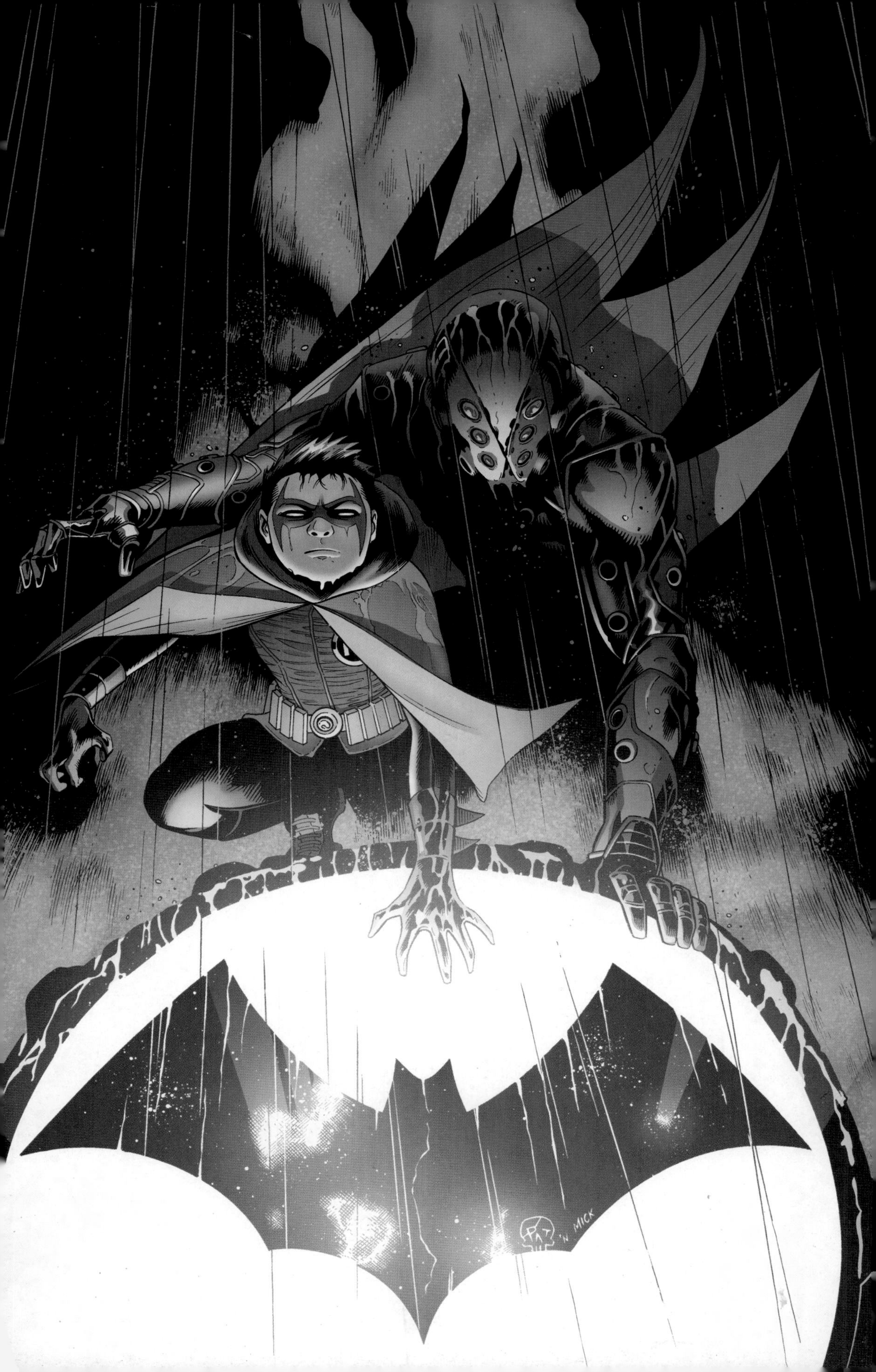
PAT 'N MICK

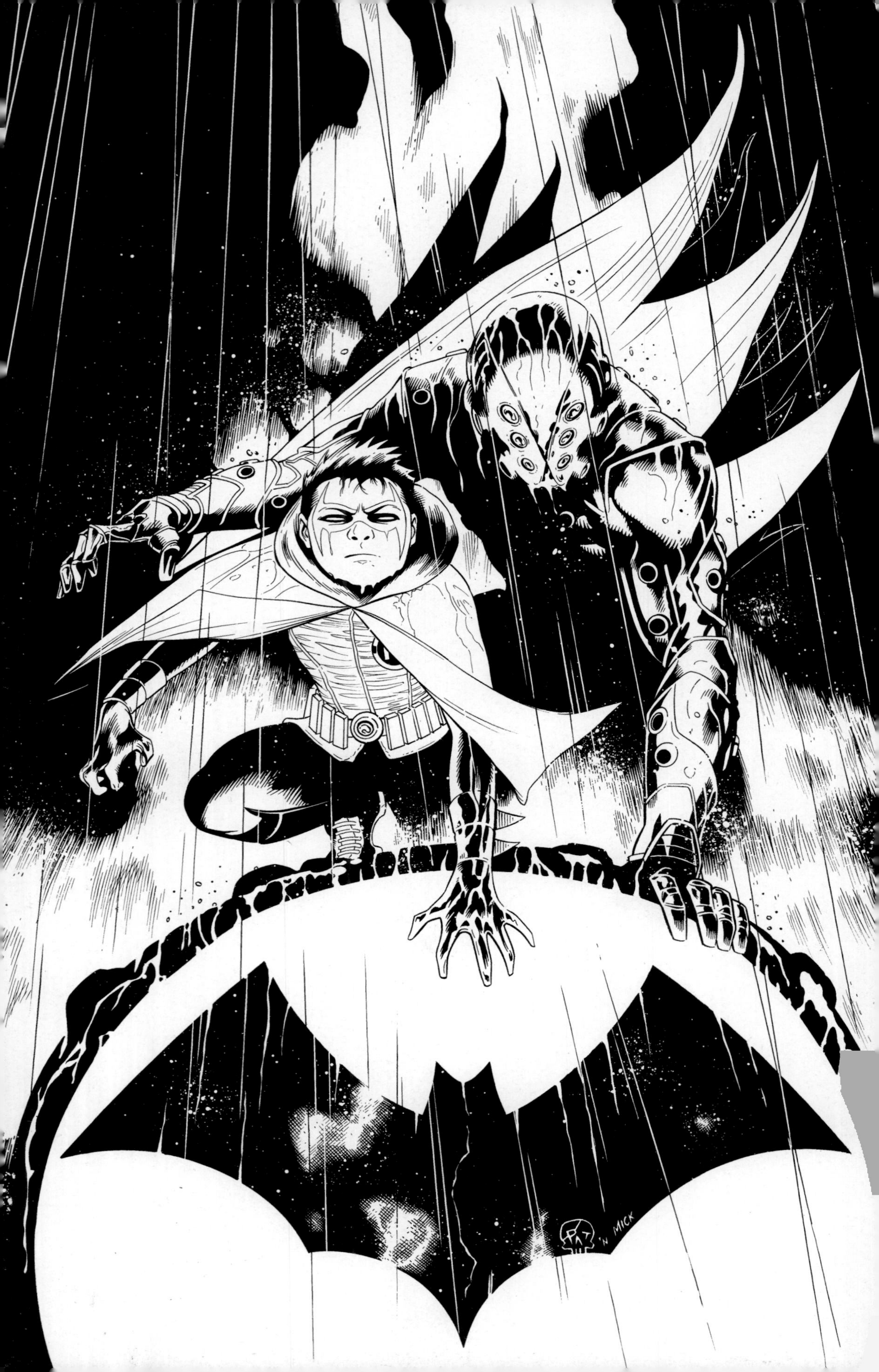
PAT 'N MICK

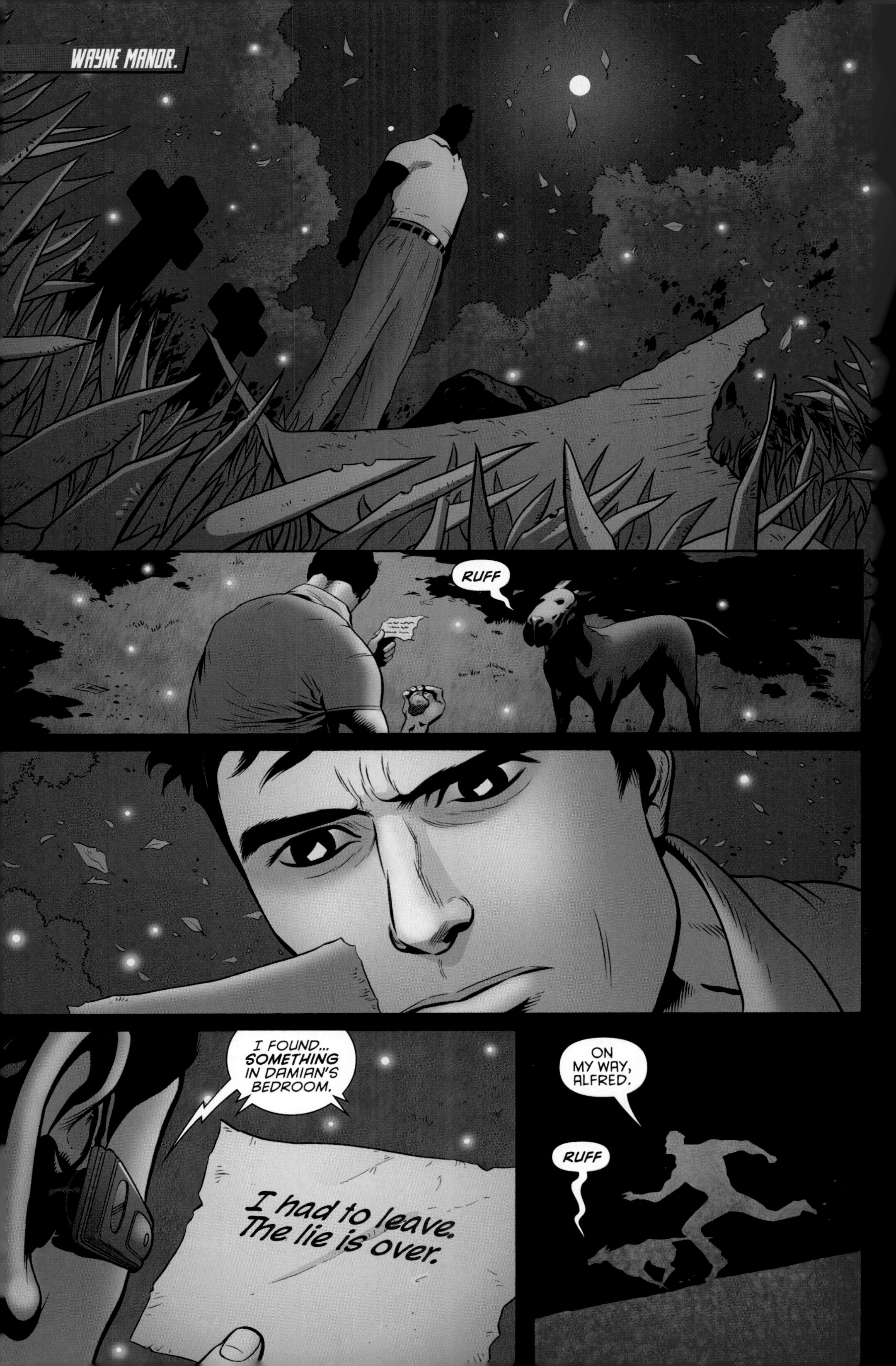
WAYNE MANOR.
RUFF
I FOUND... SOMETHING IN DAMIAN'S BEDROOM.
I had to leave. The lie is over.
ON MY WAY, ALFRED.
RUFF

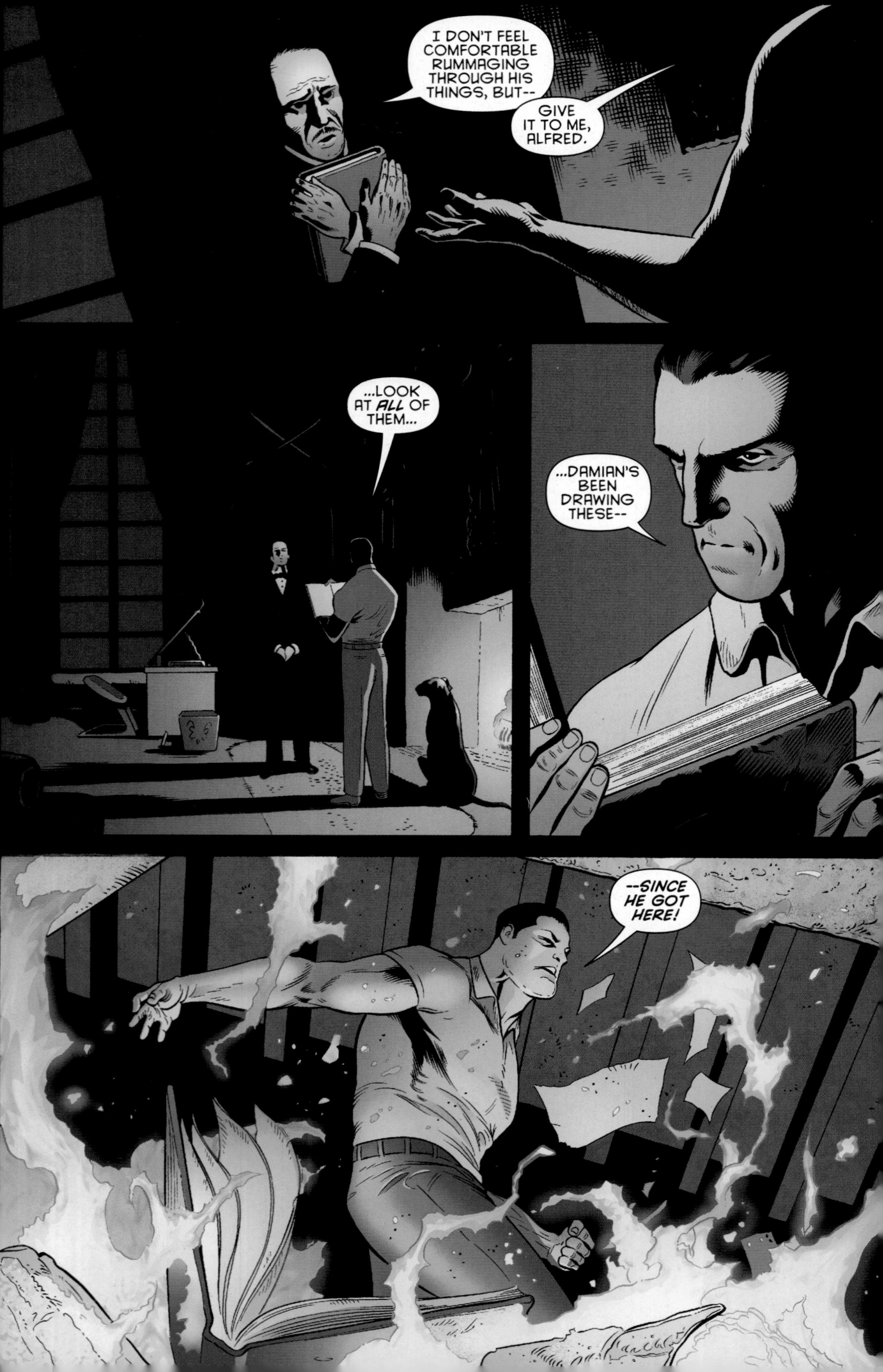
I DON'T FEEL COMFORTABLE RUMMAGING THROUGH HIS THINGS, BUT--
GIVE IT TO ME, ALFRED.
...LOOK AT ALL OF THEM...
...DAMIAN'S BEEN DRAWING THESE--
--SINCE HE GOT HERE!

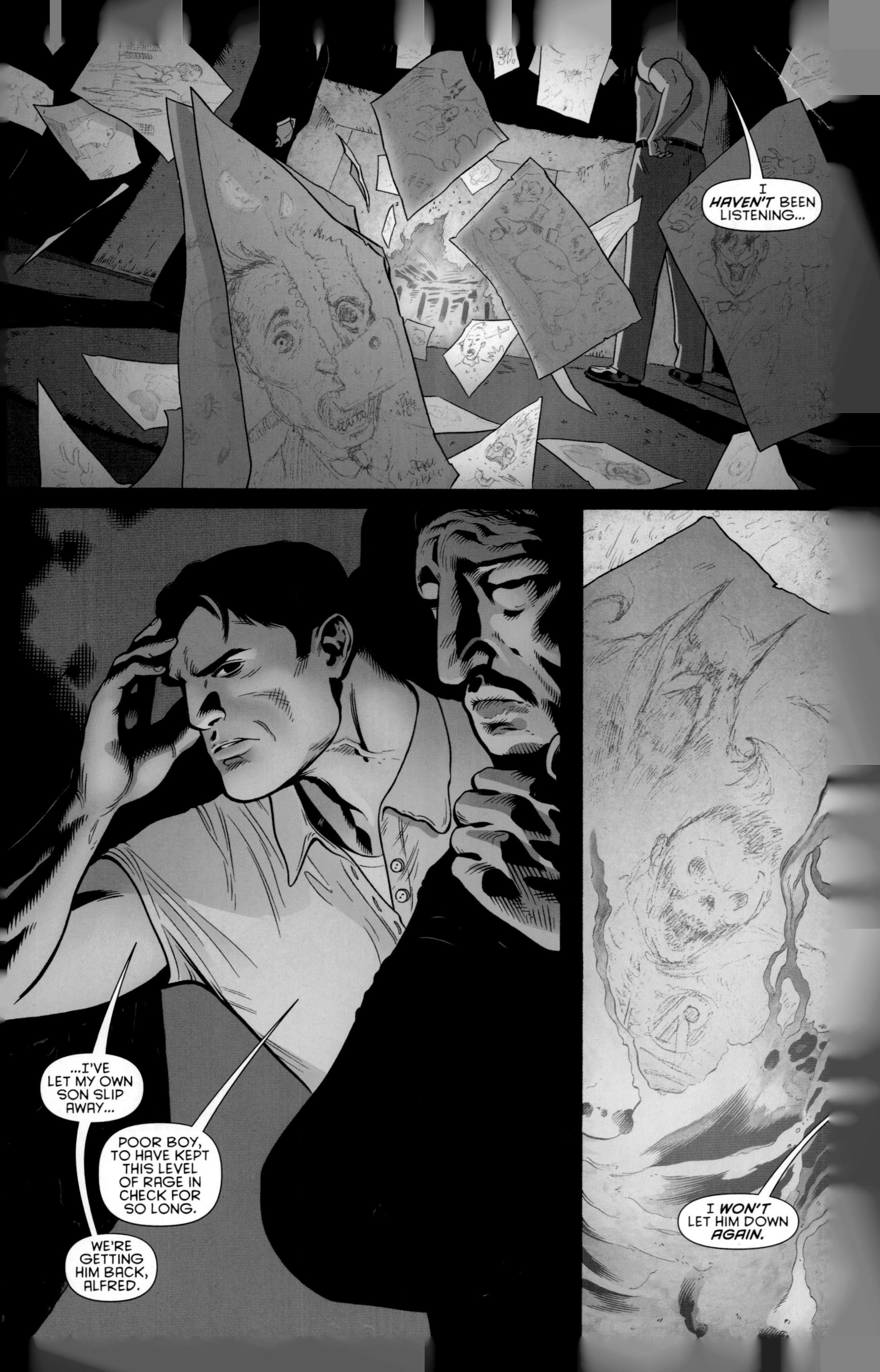

I HAVEN'T BEEN LISTENING...
...I'VE LET MY OWN SON SLIP AWAY...
POOR BOY, TO HAVE KEPT THIS LEVEL OF RAGE IN CHECK FOR SO LONG.
WE'RE GETTING HIM BACK, ALFRED.
I WON'T LET HIM DOWN AGAIN.

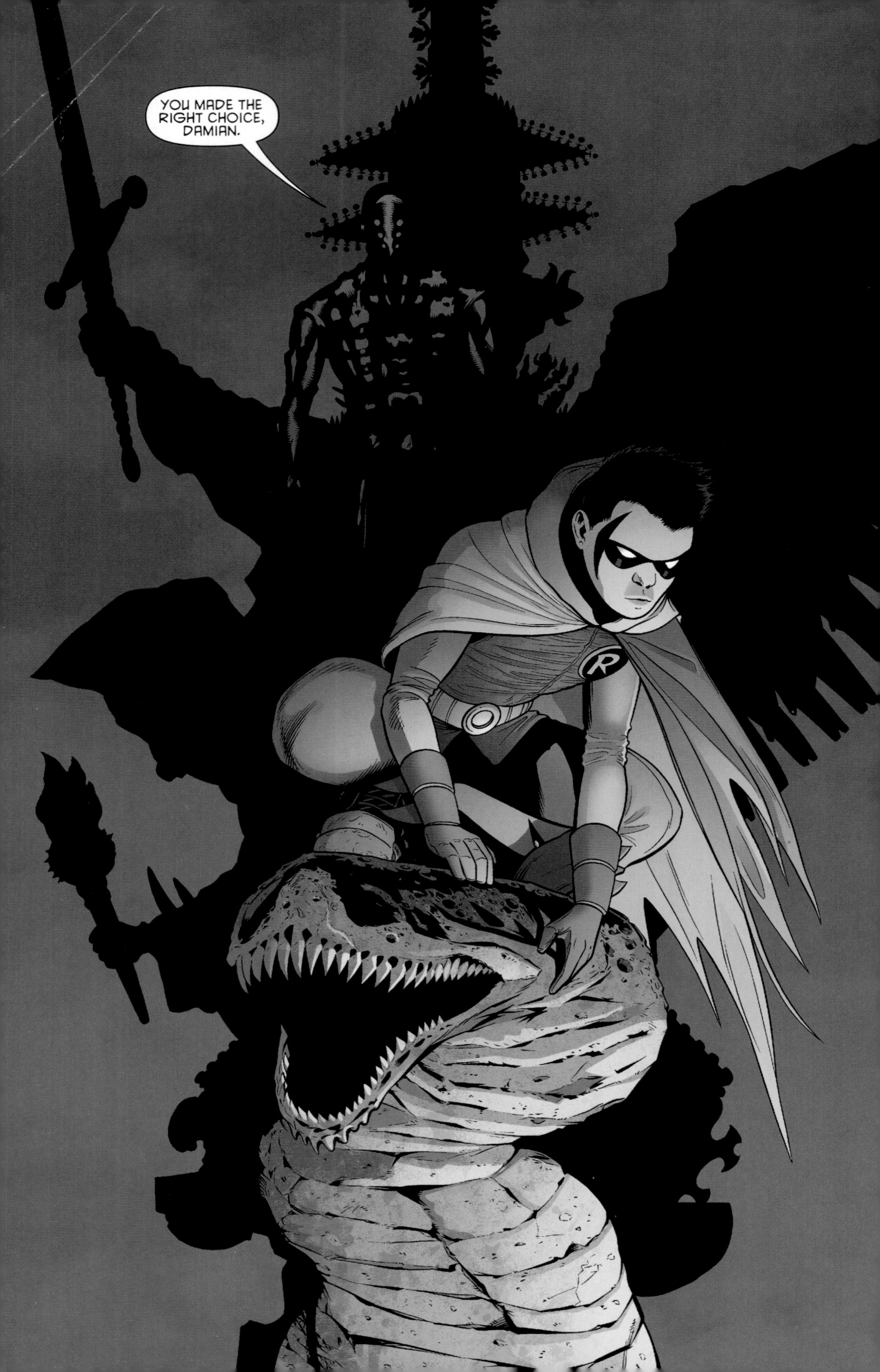
YOU MADE THE RIGHT CHOICE, DAMIAN.

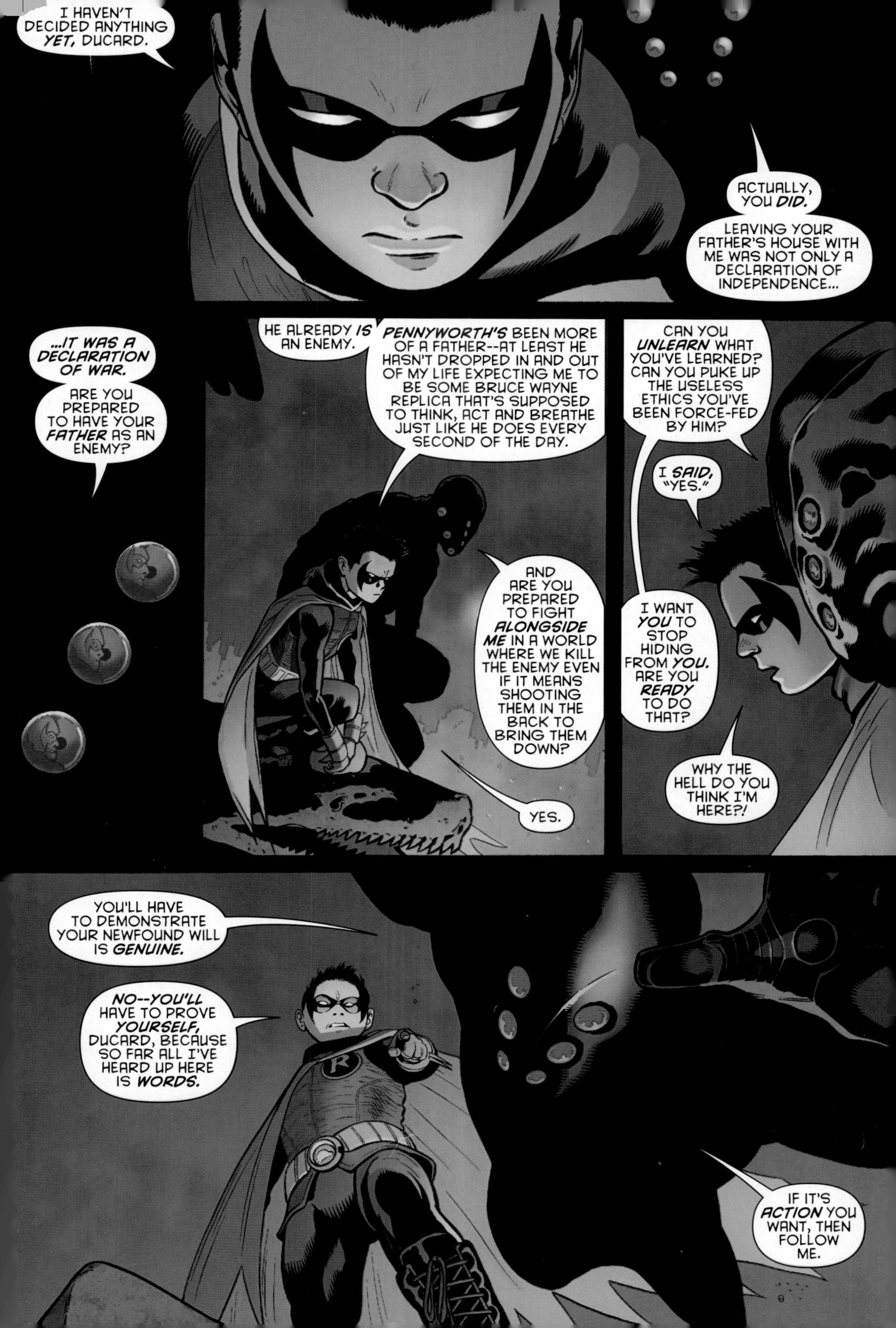

I HAVEN'T DECIDED ANYTHING *YET,* DUCARD.
ACTUALLY, YOU *DID.*
LEAVING YOUR FATHER'S HOUSE WITH ME WAS NOT ONLY A DECLARATION OF INDEPENDENCE...
...IT WAS A DECLARATION OF WAR.
ARE YOU PREPARED TO HAVE YOUR *FATHER* AS AN ENEMY?
HE ALREADY *IS* AN ENEMY.
PENNYWORTH'S BEEN MORE OF A FATHER--AT LEAST HE HASN'T DROPPED IN AND OUT OF MY LIFE EXPECTING ME TO BE SOME BRUCE WAYNE REPLICA THAT'S SUPPOSED TO THINK, ACT AND BREATHE JUST LIKE HE DOES EVERY SECOND OF THE DAY.
AND ARE YOU PREPARED TO FIGHT *ALONGSIDE ME* IN A WORLD WHERE WE KILL THE ENEMY EVEN IF IT MEANS SHOOTING THEM IN THE BACK TO BRING THEM DOWN?
YES.
CAN YOU *UNLEARN* WHAT YOU'VE LEARNED? CAN YOU PUKE UP THE USELESS ETHICS YOU'VE BEEN FORCE-FED BY HIM?
I *SAID,* "YES."
I WANT *YOU* TO STOP HIDING FROM *YOU.* ARE YOU *READY* TO DO THAT?
WHY THE HELL DO YOU THINK I'M HERE?!
YOU'LL HAVE TO DEMONSTRATE YOUR NEWFOUND WILL IS *GENUINE.*
NO--YOU'LL HAVE TO PROVE *YOURSELF,* DUCARD, BECAUSE SO FAR ALL I'VE HEARD UP HERE IS *WORDS.*
IF IT'S *ACTION* YOU WANT, THEN FOLLOW ME.

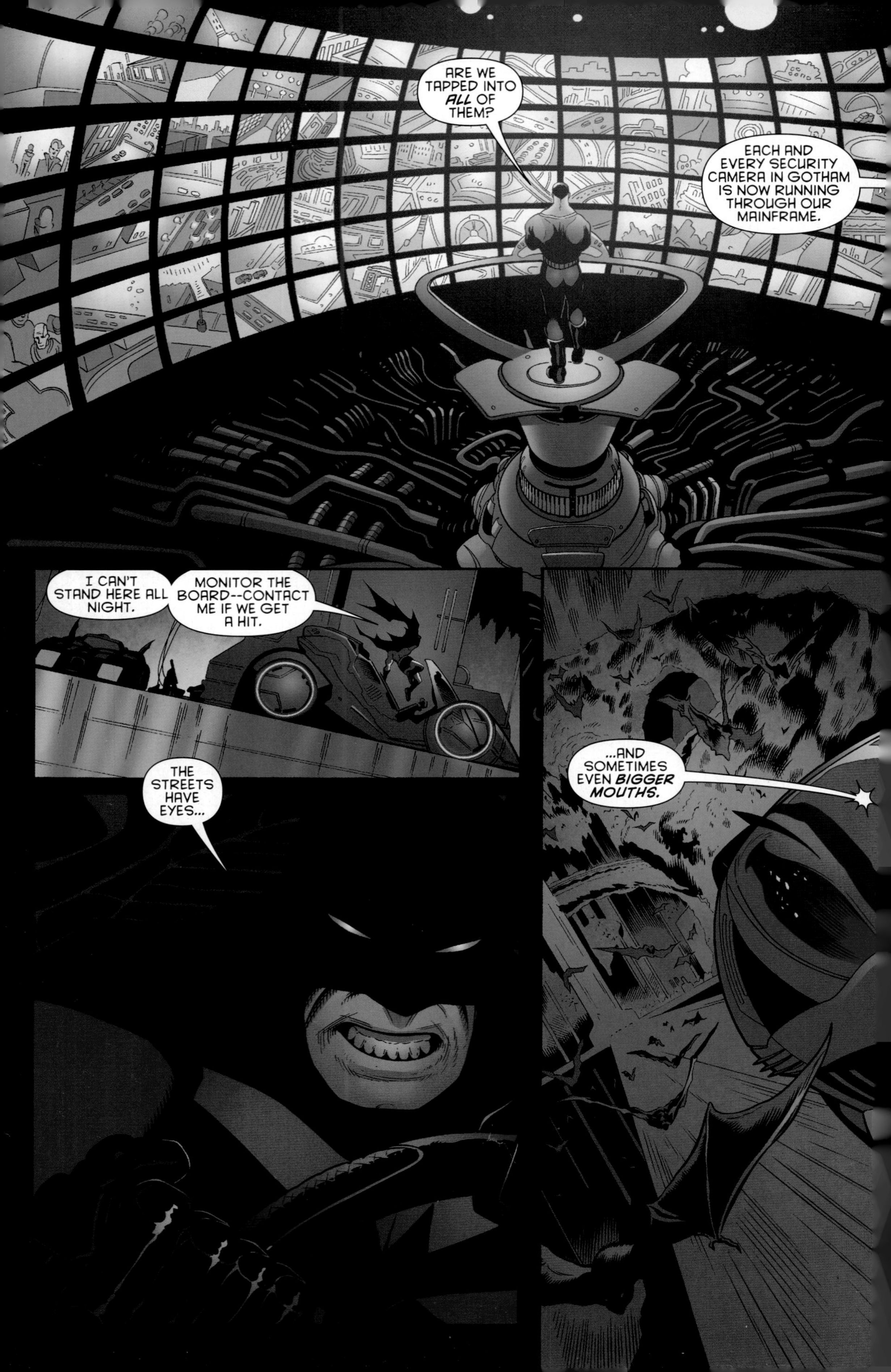
ARE WE TAPPED INTO ALL OF THEM?
EACH AND EVERY SECURITY CAMERA IN GOTHAM IS NOW RUNNING THROUGH OUR MAINFRAME.
I CAN'T STAND HERE ALL NIGHT.
MONITOR THE BOARD--CONTACT ME IF WE GET A HIT.
THE STREETS HAVE EYES...
...AND SOMETIMES EVEN BIGGER MOUTHS.

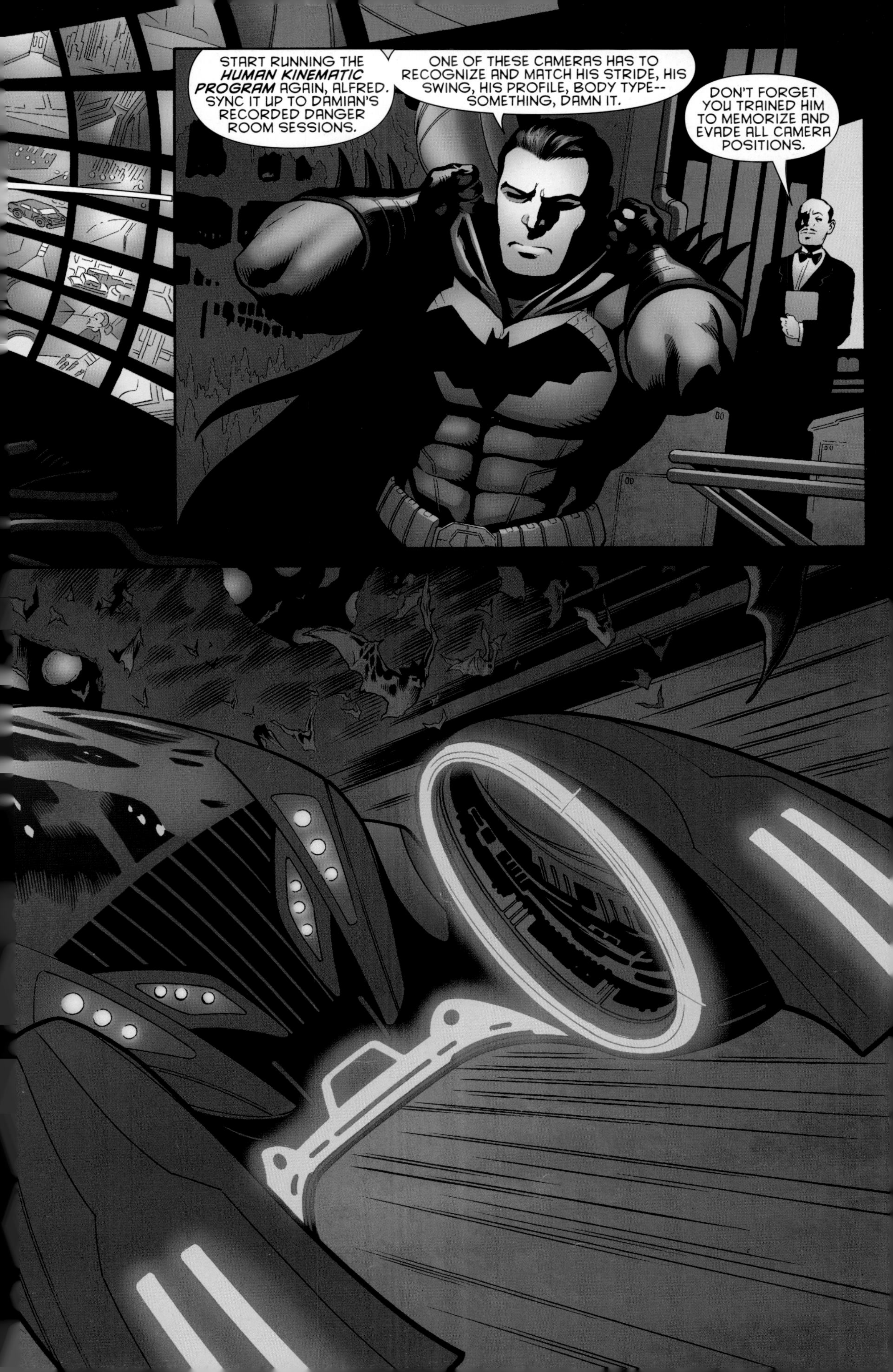
START RUNNING THE *HUMAN KINEMATIC PROGRAM* AGAIN, ALFRED. SYNC IT UP TO DAMIAN'S RECORDED DANGER ROOM SESSIONS.
ONE OF THESE CAMERAS HAS TO RECOGNIZE AND MATCH HIS STRIDE, HIS SWING, HIS PROFILE, BODY TYPE-- SOMETHING, DAMN IT.
DON'T FORGET YOU TRAINED HIM TO MEMORIZE AND EVADE ALL CAMERA POSITIONS.

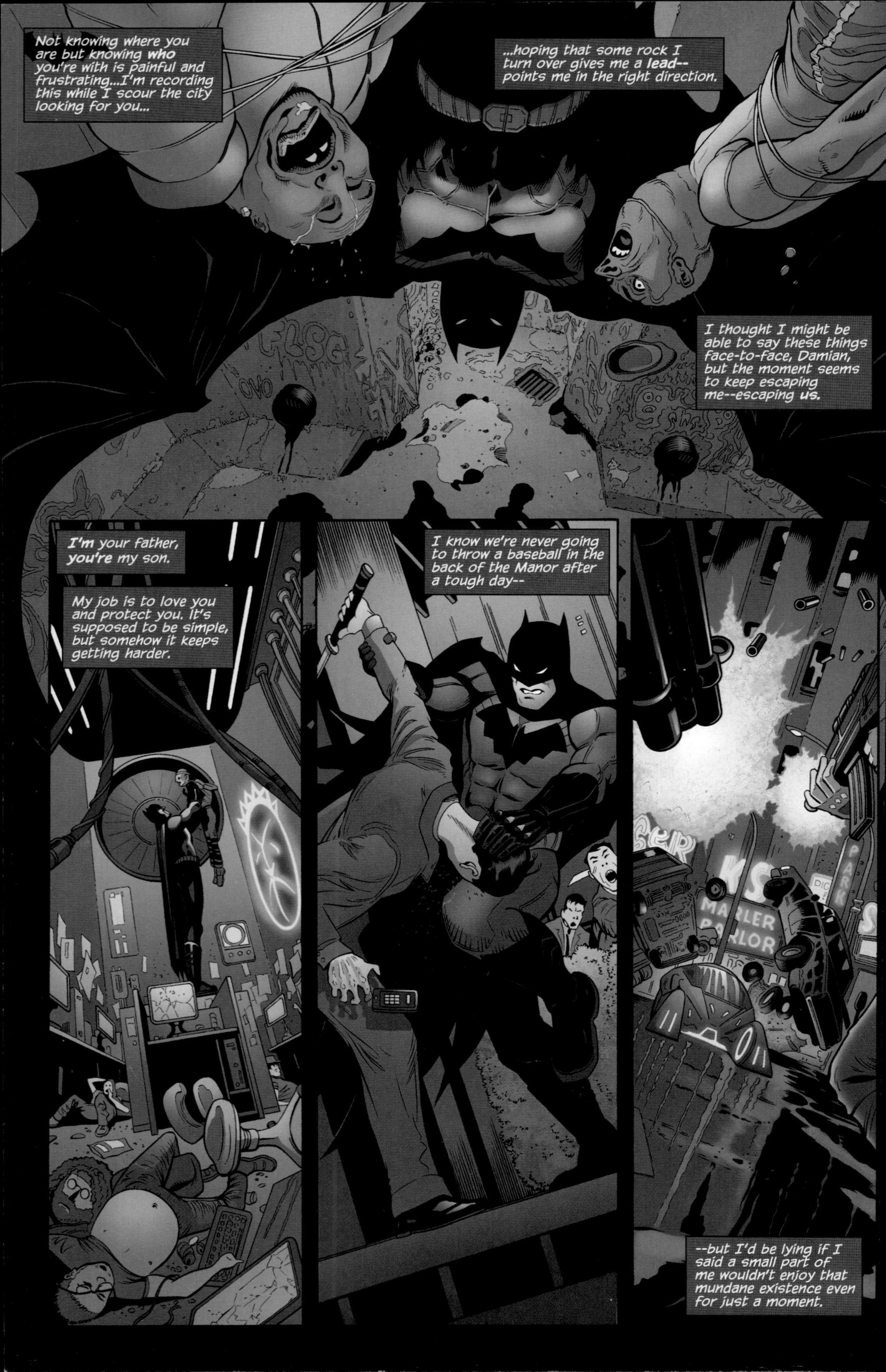

Not knowing where you are but knowing **who** you're with is painful and frustrating...I'm recording this while I scour the city looking for you...
...hoping that some rock I turn over gives me a **lead**-- points me in the right direction.
I thought I might be able to say these things face-to-face, Damian, but the moment seems to keep escaping me--escaping **us**.
I'm your father, **you're** my son.
My job is to love you and protect you. It's supposed to be simple, but somehow it keeps getting harder.
I know we're never going to throw a baseball in the back of the Manor after a tough day--
--but I'd be lying if I said a small part of me wouldn't enjoy that mundane existence even for just a moment.
MARLER
PARLOR
PARK

Right now I'm at one of our emergency uniform sites. Your suit and utility belt are gone.

And you've turned **off** the tracking device inside the belt.

Only one word keeps pounding in my brain.

Why?

Why would you step into the darkness so fast?

But who am I kidding? I know the answer to that.

If I'm going to be honest with you, Damian, I'll need to be honest with myself.

It's not just the **upbringing** that your mother forced on you that made you who you are...

...I'm also to blame.

I **didn't** tell you everything about Morgan Ducard at the Batcave earlier because of what happened between us years ago in **France**.

I took a long hard look at **myself** for the first time because of him and his father, and I didn't like what I saw.

But before I tell you how my story intersects with the Ducards, I need to start at the beginning of theirs...

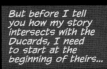

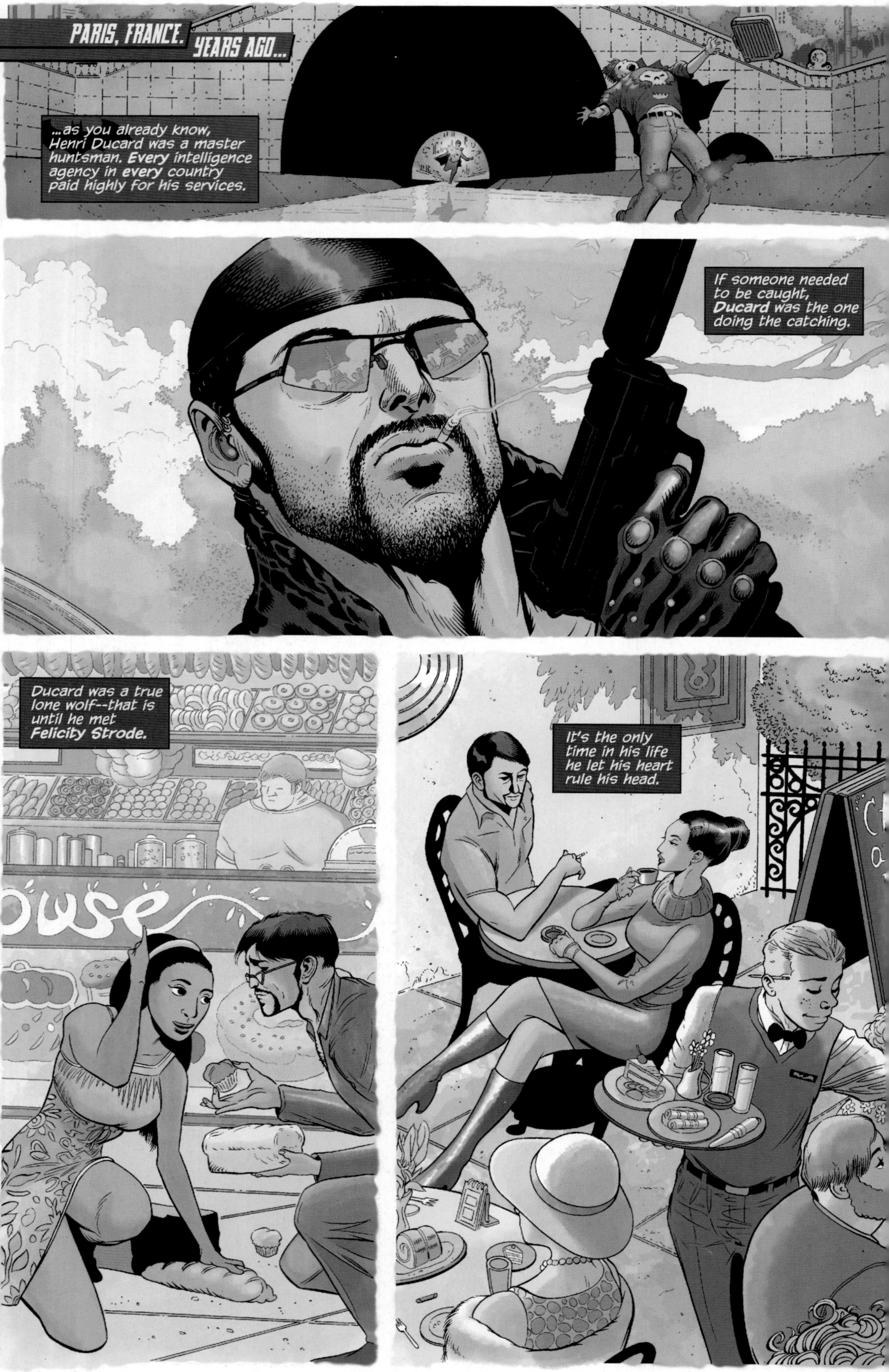
PARIS, FRANCE.
YEARS AGO...
...as you already know, Henri Ducard was a master huntsman. Every intelligence agency in every country paid highly for his services.
If someone needed to be caught, Ducard was the one doing the catching.
Ducard was a true lone wolf--that is until he met Felicity Strode.
It's the only time in his life he let his heart rule his head.

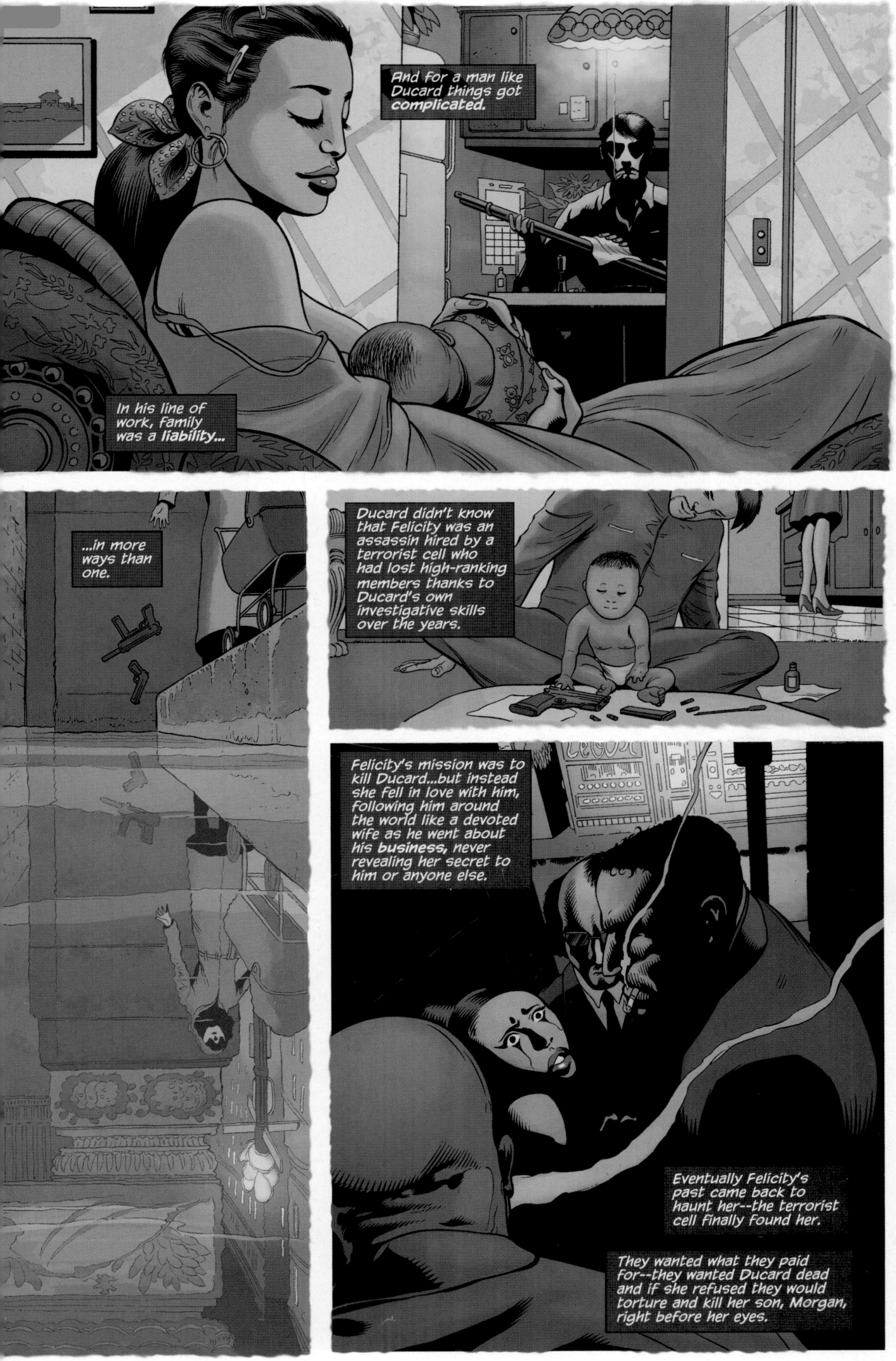
And for a man like Ducard things got complicated.
In his line of work, family was a liability...
...in more ways than one.
Ducard didn't know that Felicity was an assassin hired by a terrorist cell who had lost high-ranking members thanks to Ducard's own investigative skills over the years.
Felicity's mission was to kill Ducard...but instead she fell in love with him, following him around the world like a devoted wife as he went about his business, never revealing her secret to him or anyone else.
Eventually Felicity's past came back to haunt her--the terrorist cell finally found her.
They wanted what they paid for--they wanted Ducard dead and if she refused they would torture and kill her son, Morgan, right before her eyes.

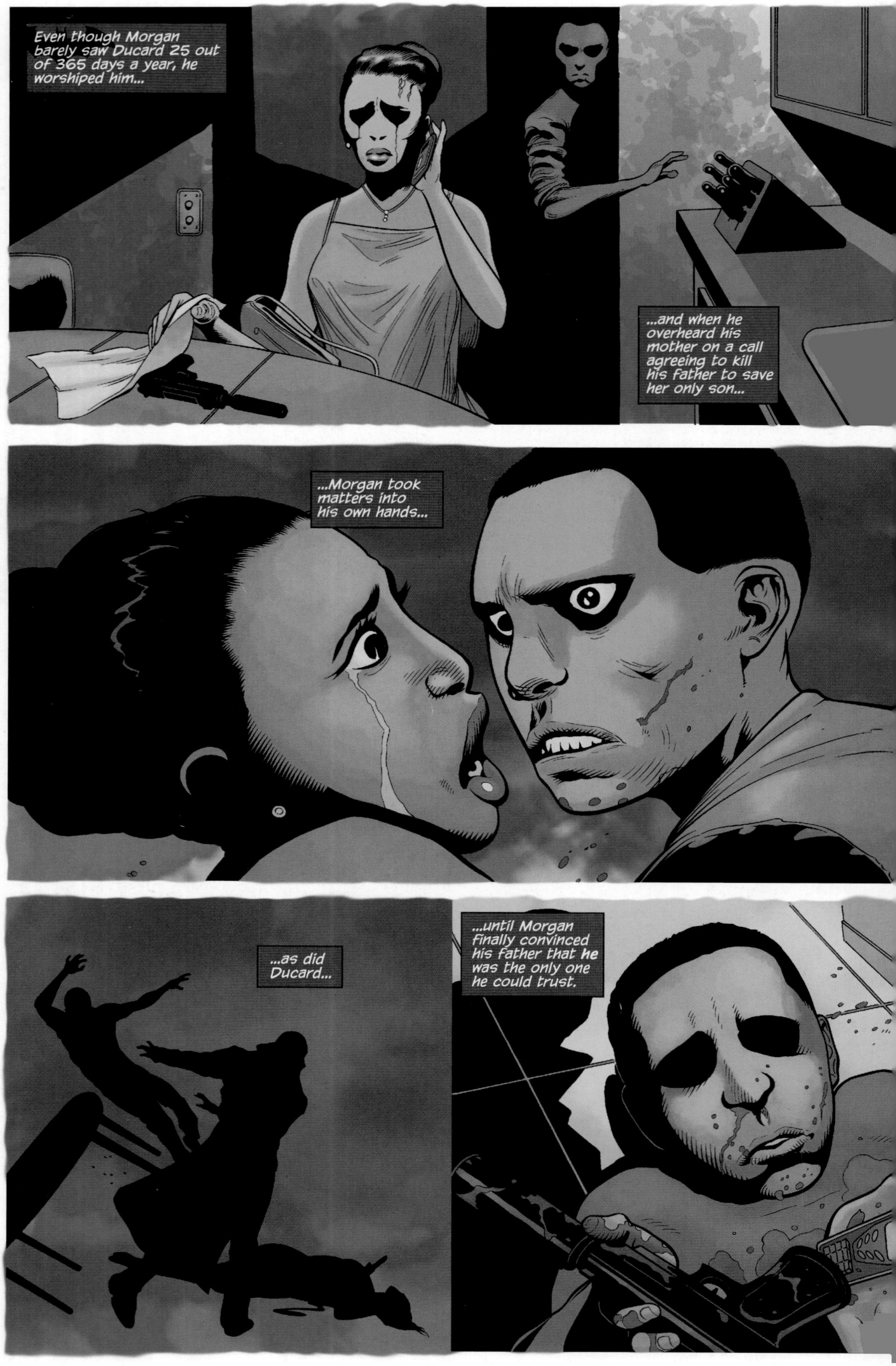
Even though Morgan barely saw Ducard 25 out of 365 days a year, he worshiped him...
...and when he overheard his mother on a call agreeing to kill his father to save her only son...
...Morgan took matters into his own hands...
...as did Ducard...
...until Morgan finally convinced his father that he was the only one he could trust.

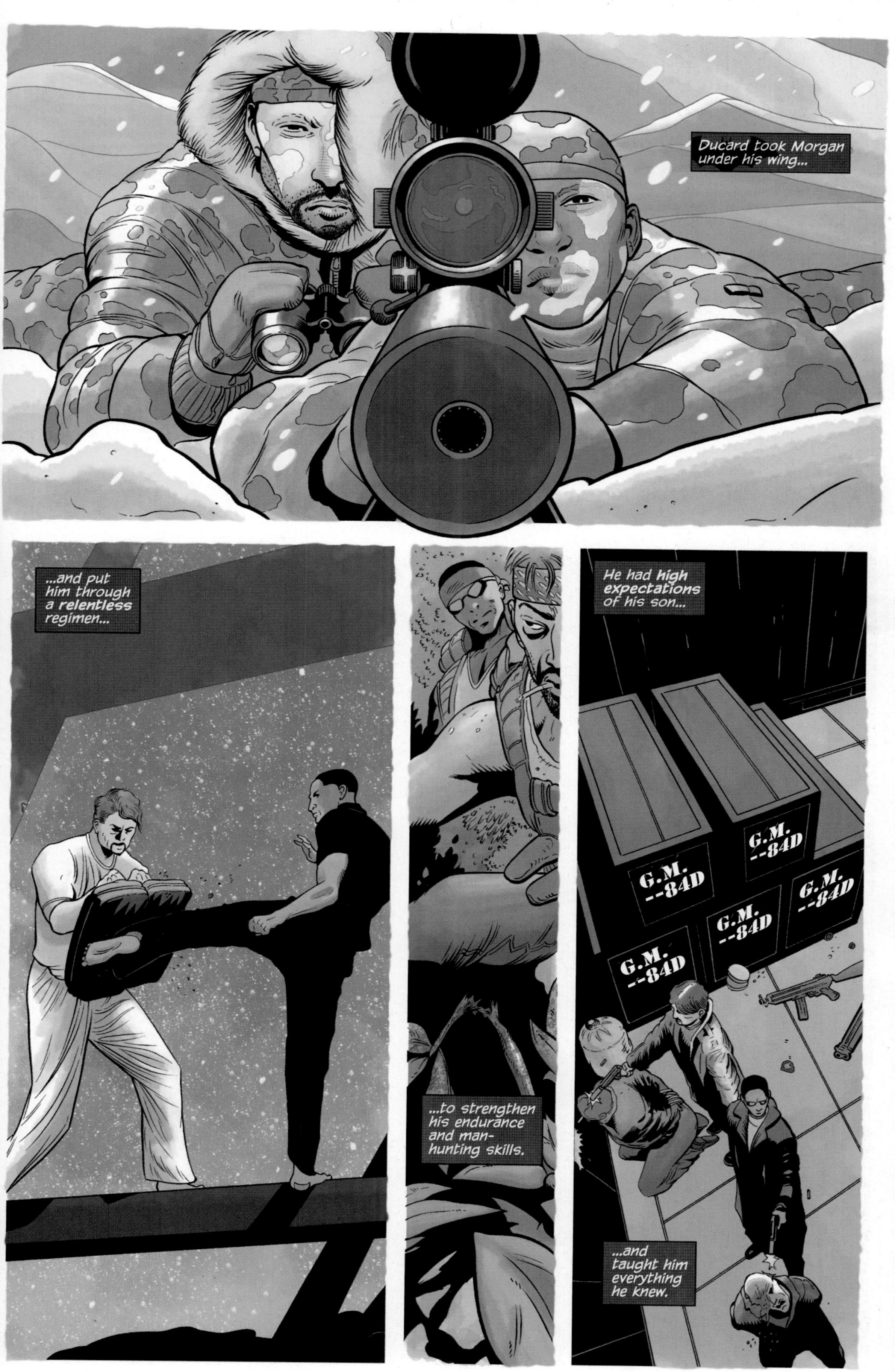
Ducard took Morgan under his wing...
...and put him through a relentless regimen...
...to strengthen his endurance and man-hunting skills.
He had high expectations of his son...
G.M. --84D
G.M. --84D
G.M. --84D
G.M. --84D
G.M. --84D
...and taught him everything he knew.

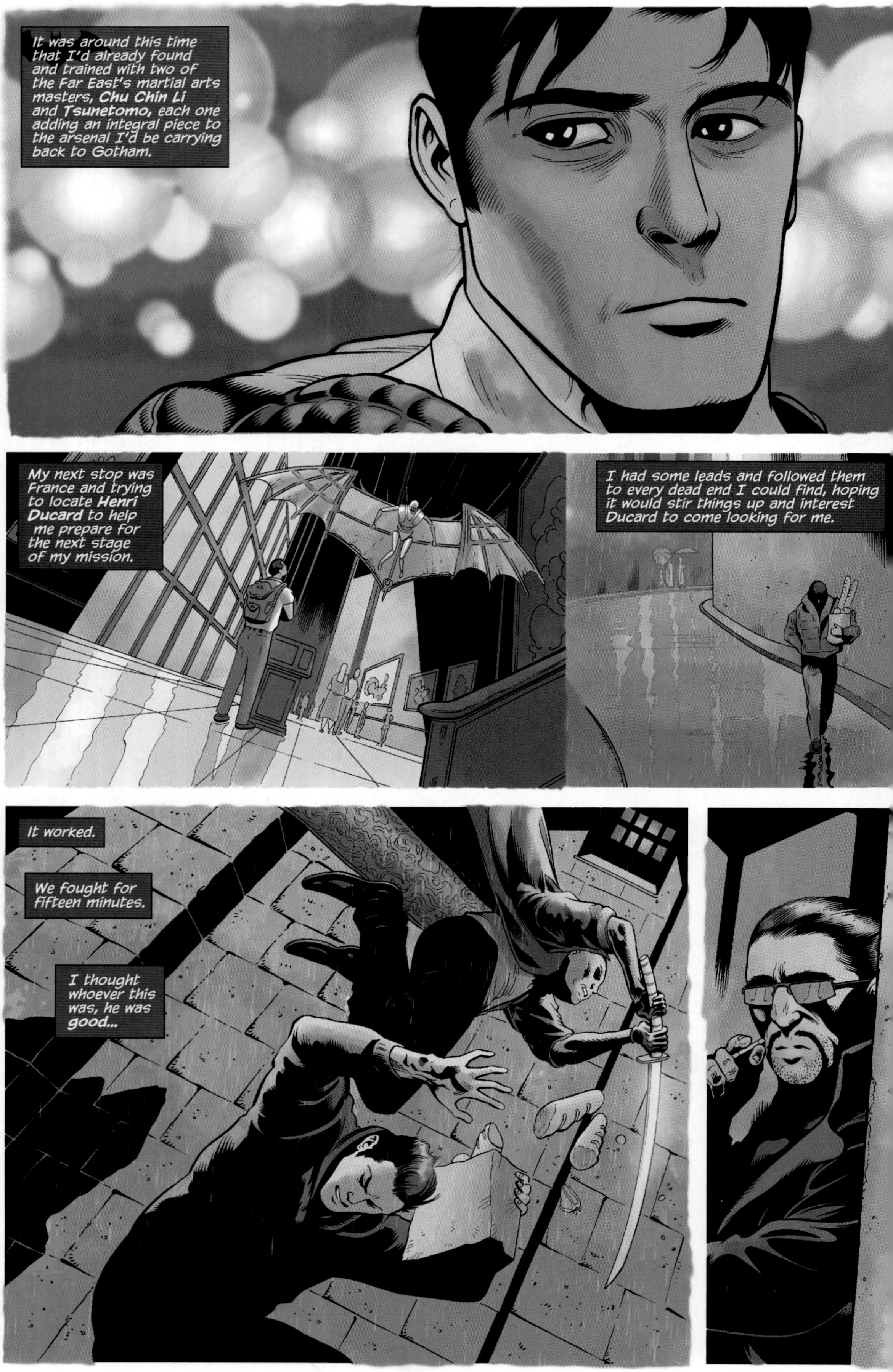
It was around this time that I'd already found and trained with two of the Far East's martial arts masters, **Chu Chin Li** and **Tsunetomo,** each one adding an integral piece to the arsenal I'd be carrying back to Gotham.
My next stop was France and trying to locate **Henri Ducard** to help me prepare for the next stage of my mission.
I had some leads and followed them to every dead end I could find, hoping it would stir things up and interest Ducard to come looking for me.
It worked.
We fought for fifteen minutes.
I thought whoever this was, he was **good...**

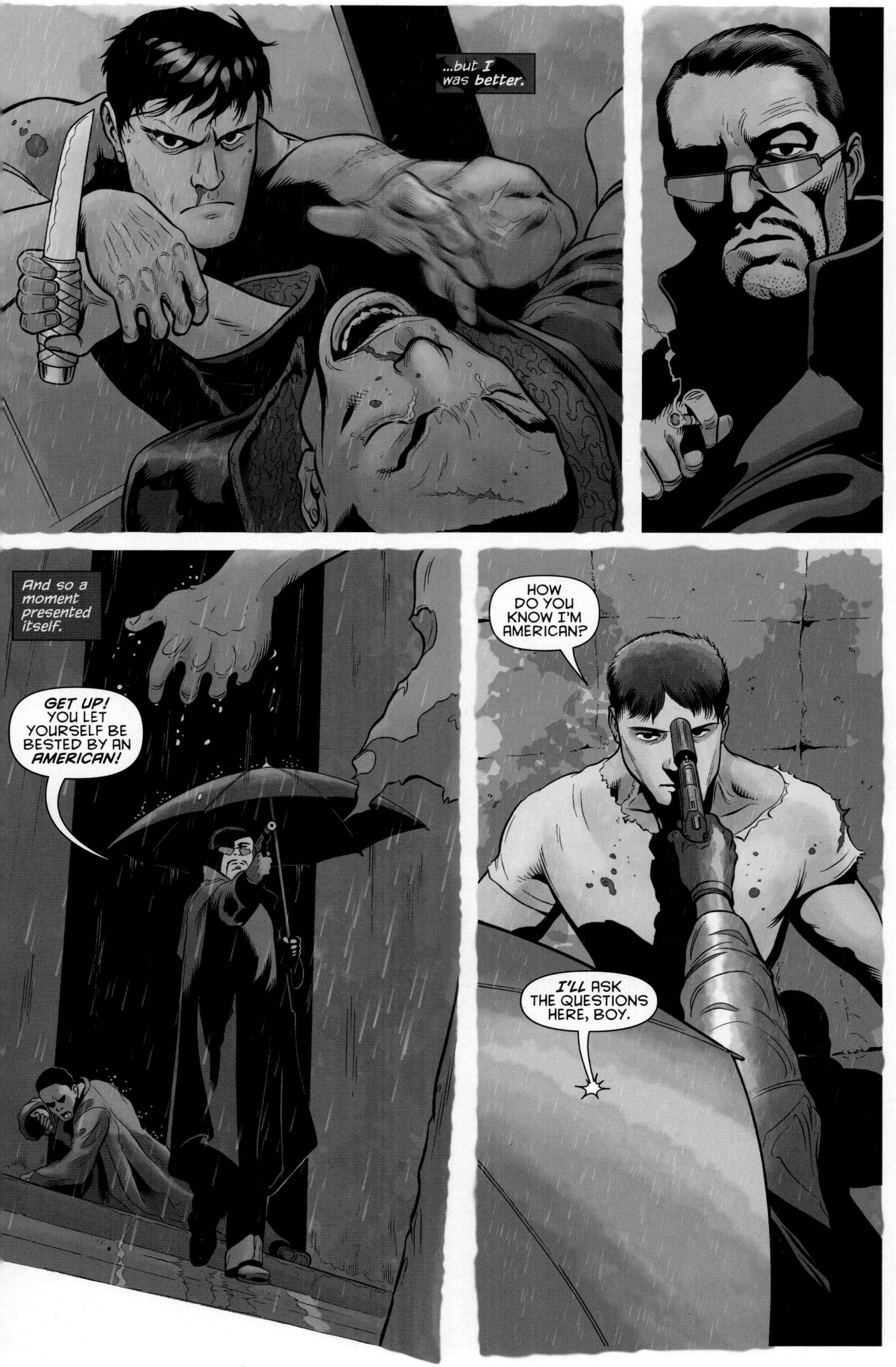

...but I was better.
And so a moment presented itself.
GET UP! YOU LET YOURSELF BE BESTED BY AN AMERICAN!
HOW DO YOU KNOW I'M AMERICAN?
I'LL ASK THE QUESTIONS HERE, BOY.

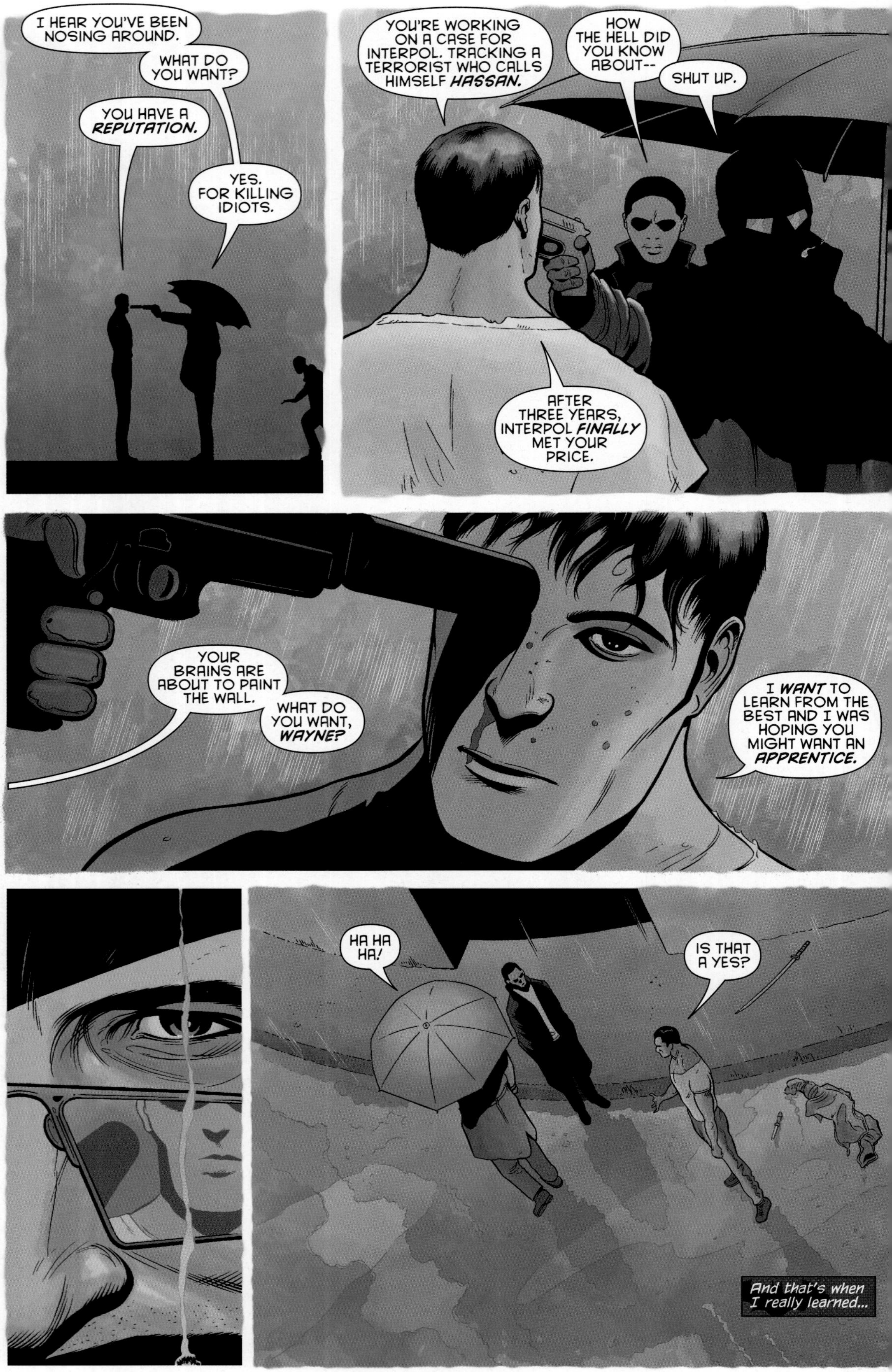
I HEAR YOU'VE BEEN NOSING AROUND.
WHAT DO YOU WANT?
YOU HAVE A *REPUTATION.*
YES. FOR KILLING IDIOTS.
YOU'RE WORKING ON A CASE FOR INTERPOL. TRACKING A TERRORIST WHO CALLS HIMSELF *HASSAN.*
HOW THE HELL DID YOU KNOW ABOUT--
SHUT UP.
AFTER THREE YEARS, INTERPOL *FINALLY* MET YOUR PRICE.
YOUR BRAINS ARE ABOUT TO PAINT THE WALL.
WHAT DO YOU WANT, *WAYNE?*
I *WANT* TO LEARN FROM THE BEST AND I WAS HOPING YOU MIGHT WANT AN *APPRENTICE.*
HA HA HA!
IS THAT A YES?
And that's when I really learned...

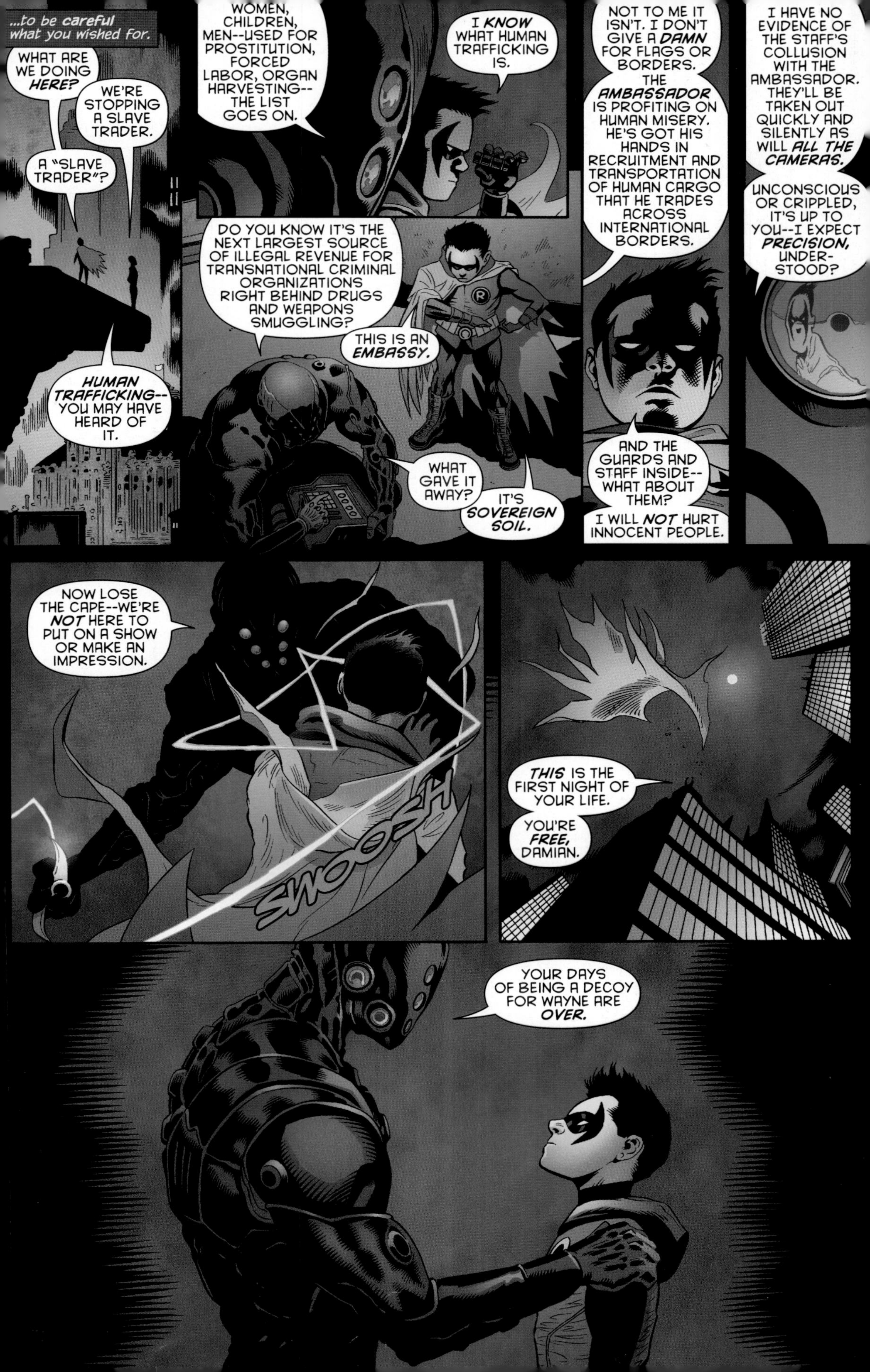
...to be careful what you wished for.
WHAT ARE WE DOING HERE?
WE'RE STOPPING A SLAVE TRADER.
A "SLAVE TRADER"?
HUMAN TRAFFICKING--YOU MAY HAVE HEARD OF IT.
WOMEN, CHILDREN, MEN--USED FOR PROSTITUTION, FORCED LABOR, ORGAN HARVESTING--THE LIST GOES ON.
I KNOW WHAT HUMAN TRAFFICKING IS.
DO YOU KNOW IT'S THE NEXT LARGEST SOURCE OF ILLEGAL REVENUE FOR TRANSNATIONAL CRIMINAL ORGANIZATIONS RIGHT BEHIND DRUGS AND WEAPONS SMUGGLING?
THIS IS AN EMBASSY.
WHAT GAVE IT AWAY?
IT'S SOVEREIGN SOIL.
NOT TO ME IT ISN'T. I DON'T GIVE A DAMN FOR FLAGS OR BORDERS.
THE AMBASSADOR IS PROFITING ON HUMAN MISERY. HE'S GOT HIS HANDS IN RECRUITMENT AND TRANSPORTATION OF HUMAN CARGO THAT HE TRADES ACROSS INTERNATIONAL BORDERS.
AND THE GUARDS AND STAFF INSIDE--WHAT ABOUT THEM?
I WILL NOT HURT INNOCENT PEOPLE.
I HAVE NO EVIDENCE OF THE STAFF'S COLLUSION WITH THE AMBASSADOR. THEY'LL BE TAKEN OUT QUICKLY AND SILENTLY AS WILL ALL THE CAMERAS.
UNCONSCIOUS OR CRIPPLED, IT'S UP TO YOU--I EXPECT PRECISION, UNDERSTOOD?
NOW LOSE THE CAPE--WE'RE NOT HERE TO PUT ON A SHOW OR MAKE AN IMPRESSION.
SWOOSH
THIS IS THE FIRST NIGHT OF YOUR LIFE.
YOU'RE FREE, DAMIAN.
YOUR DAYS OF BEING A DECOY FOR WAYNE ARE OVER.

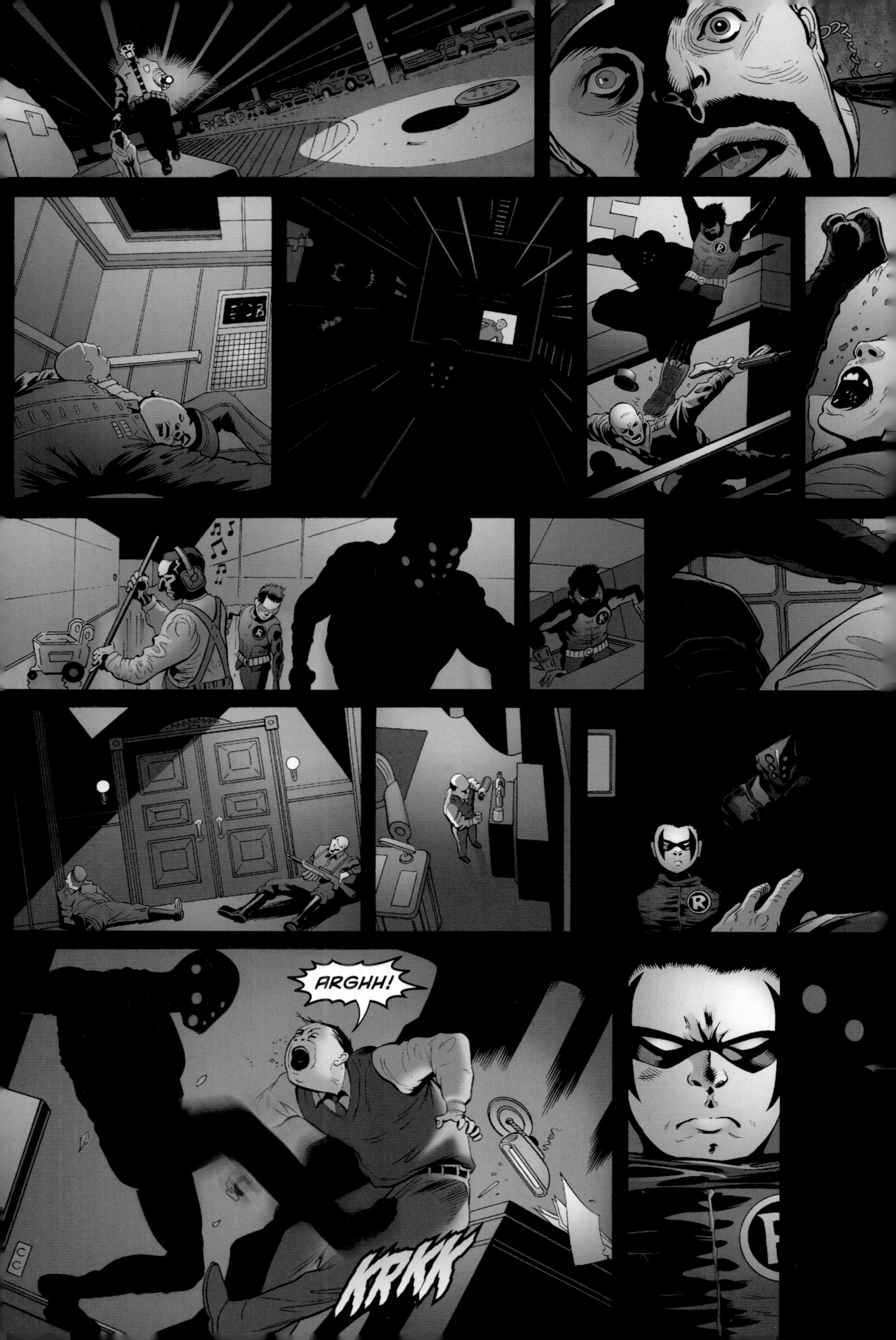

ARGHH!
KRKK

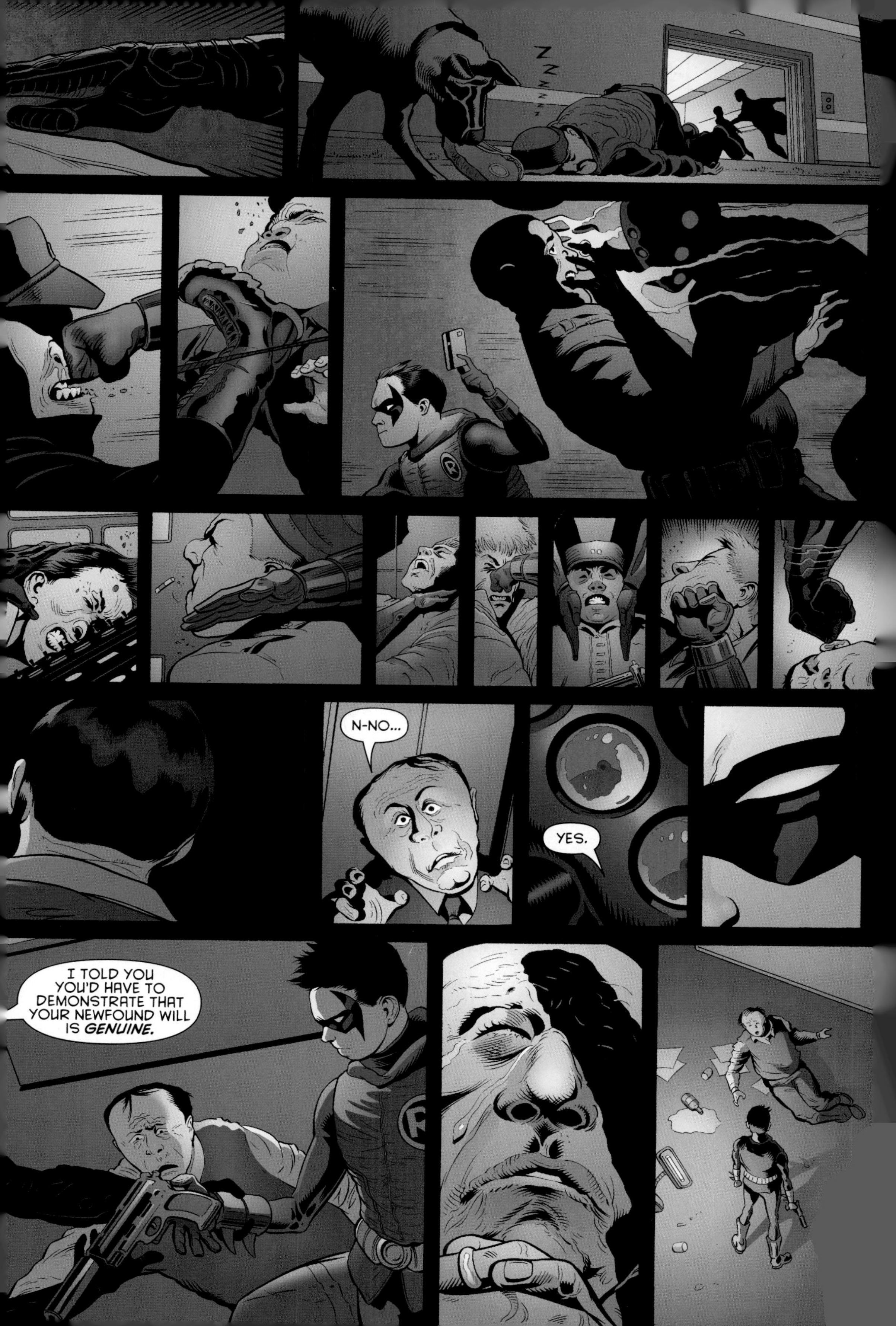
ZZZZ
N-NO...
YES.
I TOLD YOU YOU'D HAVE TO DEMONSTRATE THAT YOUR NEWFOUND WILL IS *GENUINE.*

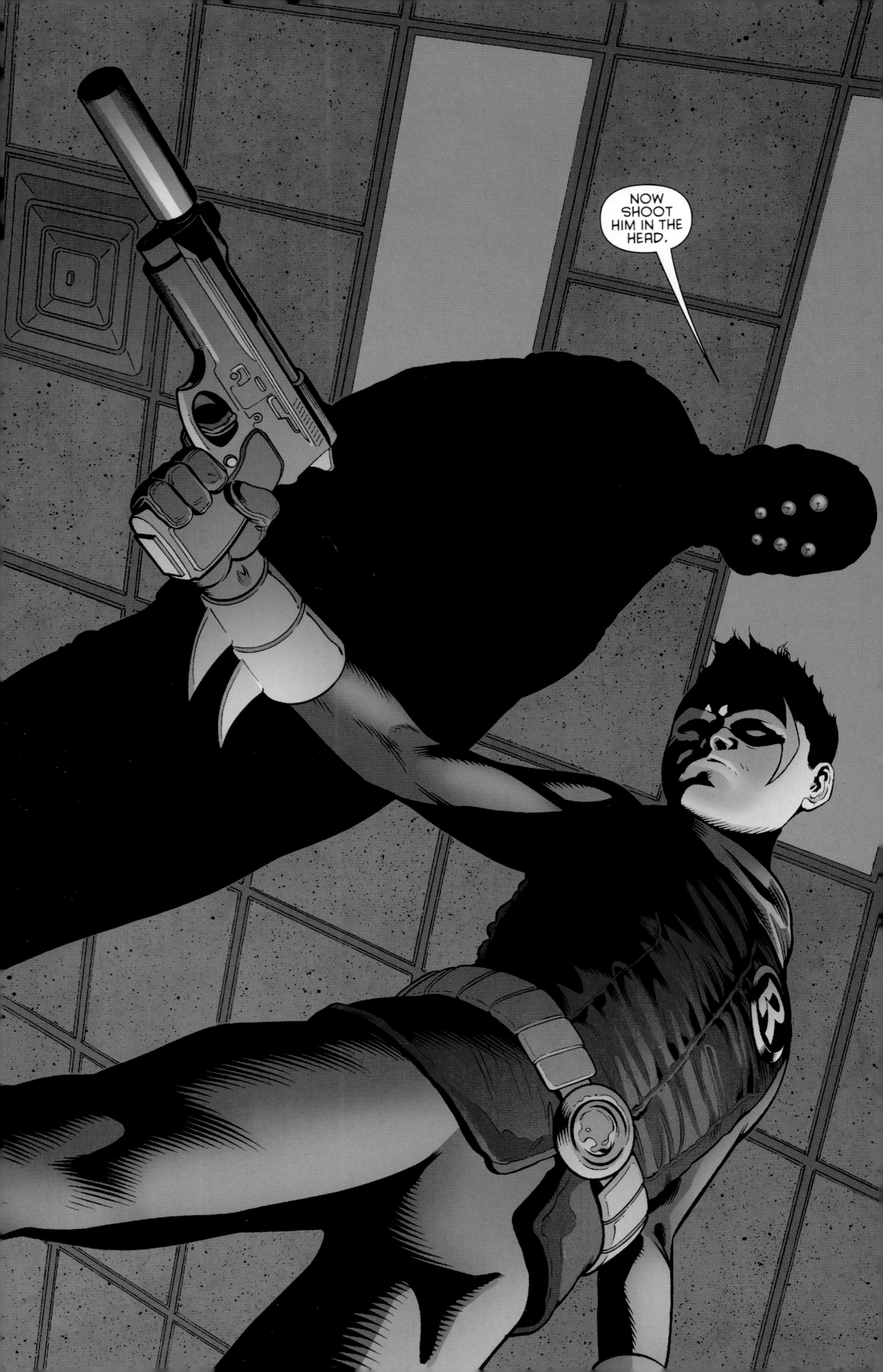
NOW SHOOT HIM IN THE HEAD.

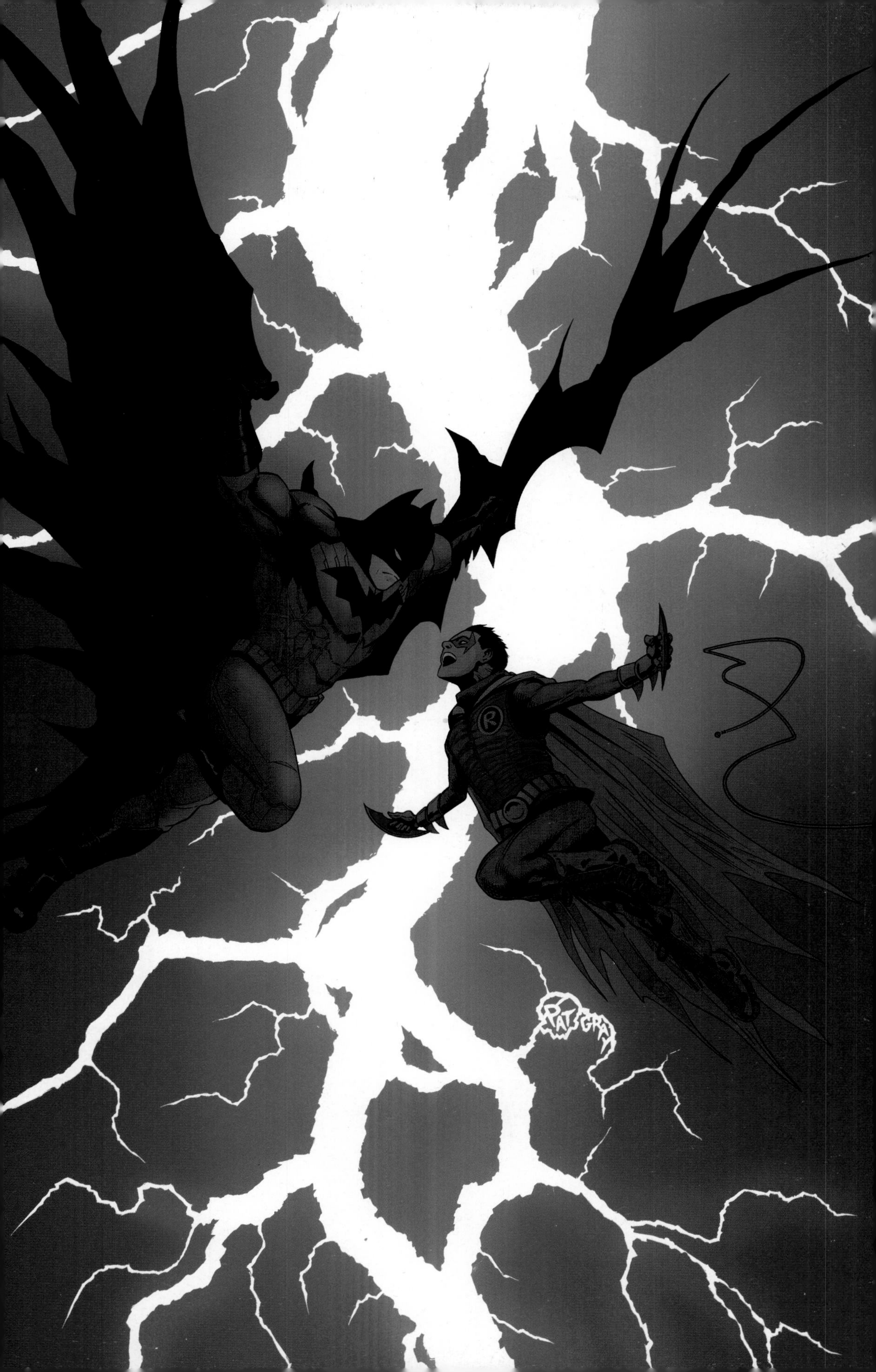

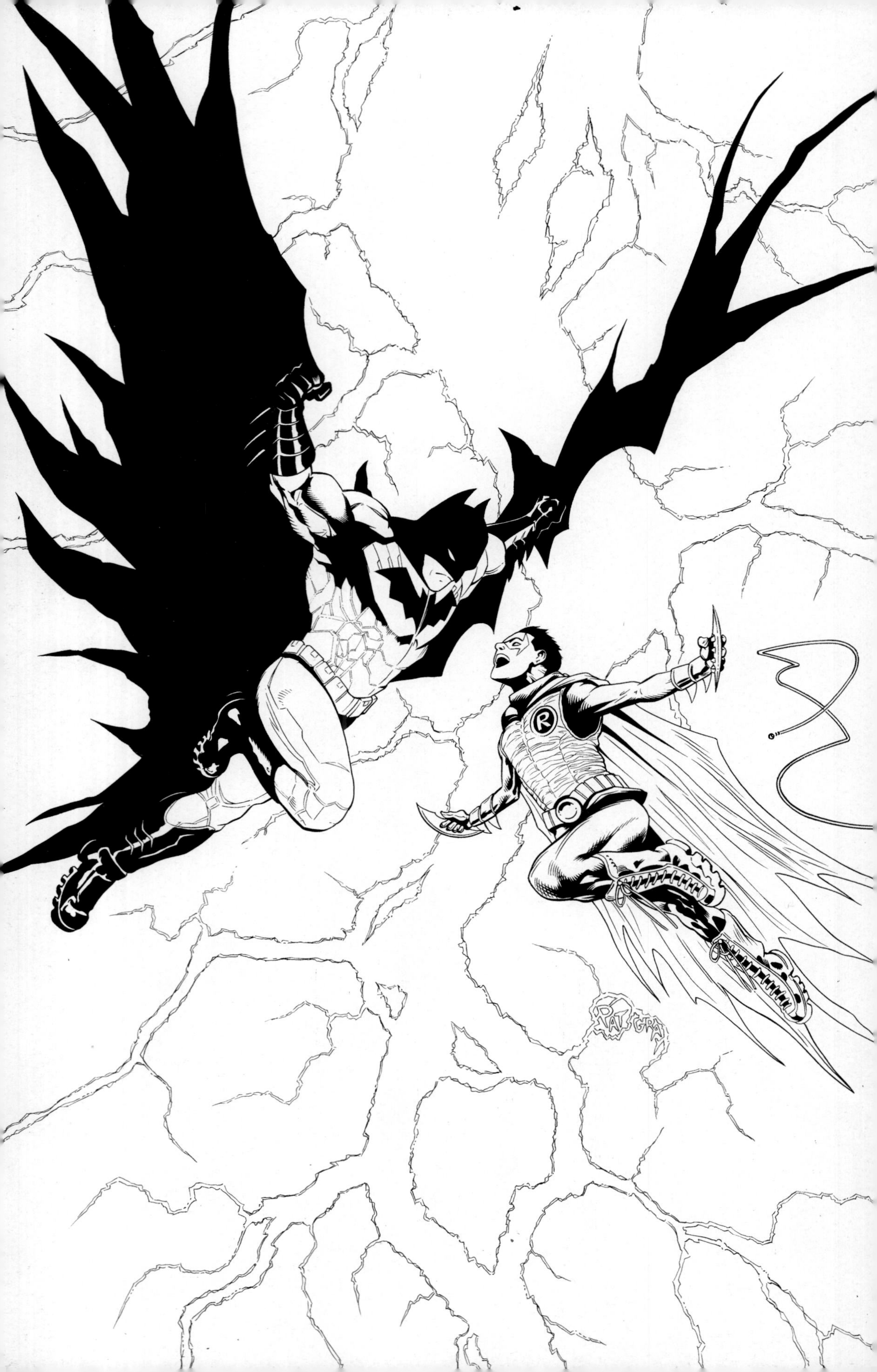

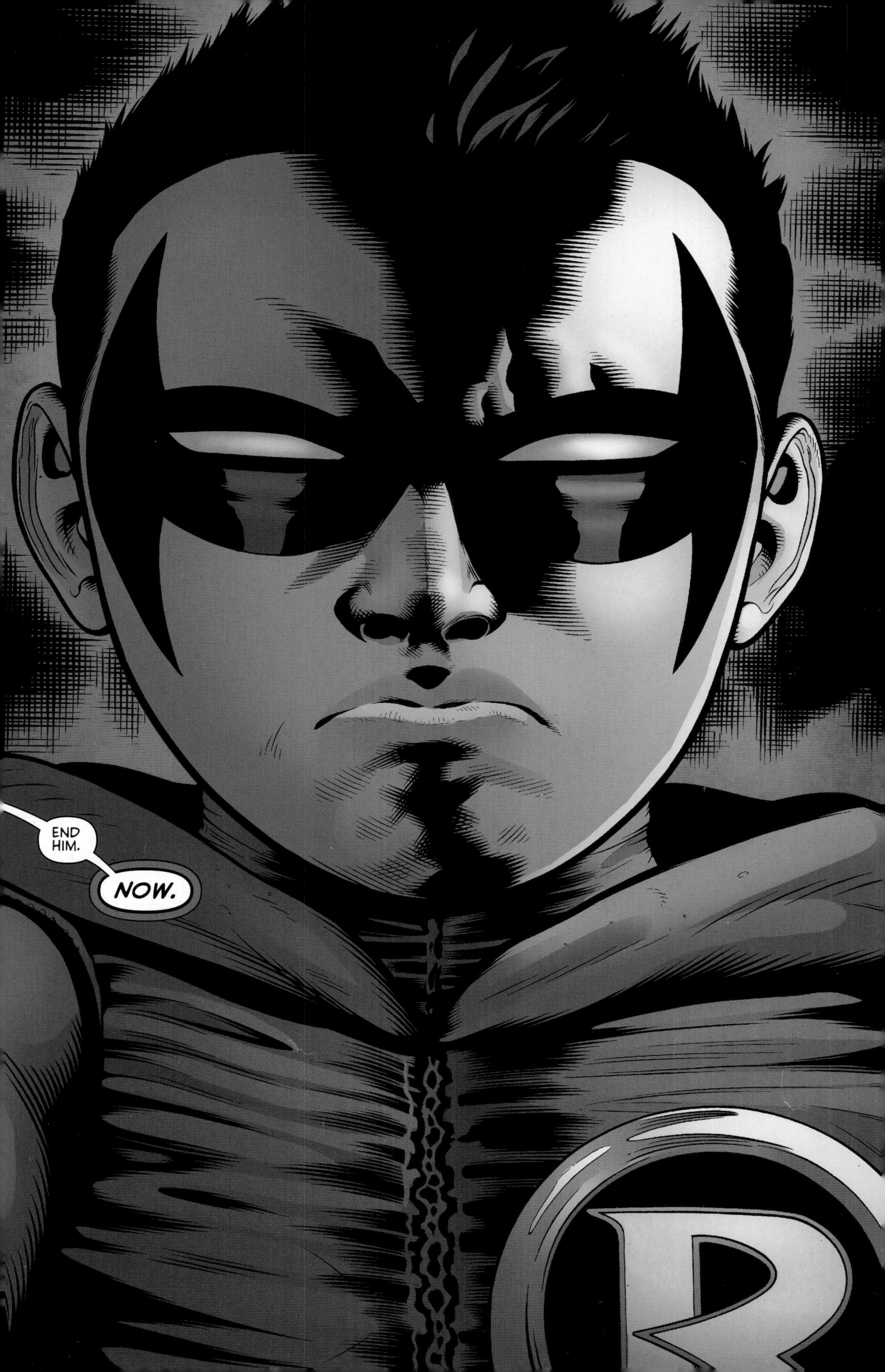
END HIM.
NOW.

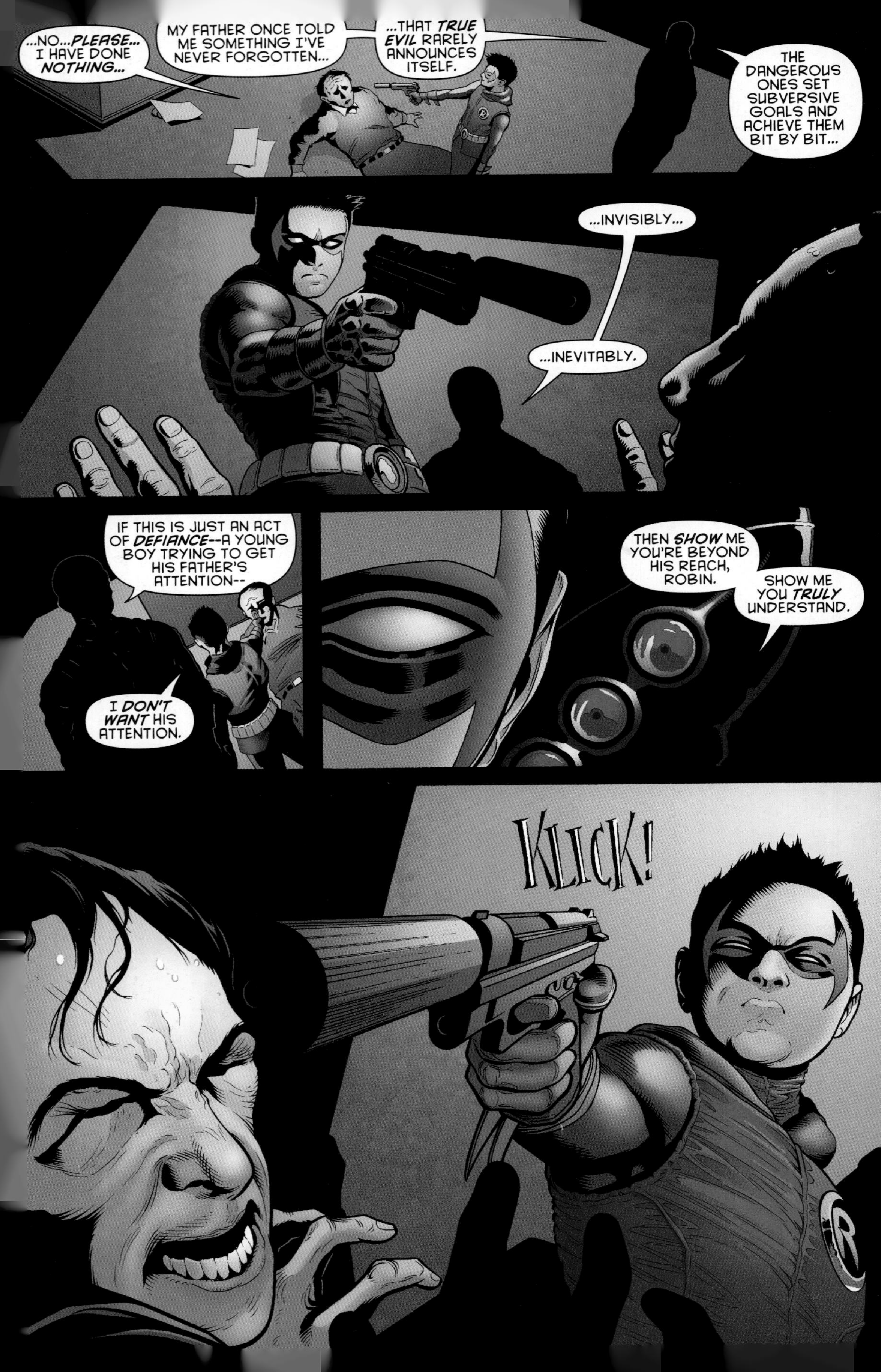
...NO...PLEASE... I HAVE DONE NOTHING...
MY FATHER ONCE TOLD ME SOMETHING I'VE NEVER FORGOTTEN...
...THAT TRUE EVIL RARELY ANNOUNCES ITSELF.
THE DANGEROUS ONES SET SUBVERSIVE GOALS AND ACHIEVE THEM BIT BY BIT...
...INVISIBLY...
...INEVITABLY.
IF THIS IS JUST AN ACT OF DEFIANCE--A YOUNG BOY TRYING TO GET HIS FATHER'S ATTENTION--
I DON'T WANT HIS ATTENTION.
THEN SHOW ME YOU'RE BEYOND HIS REACH, ROBIN.
SHOW ME YOU TRULY UNDERSTAND.
KLICK!

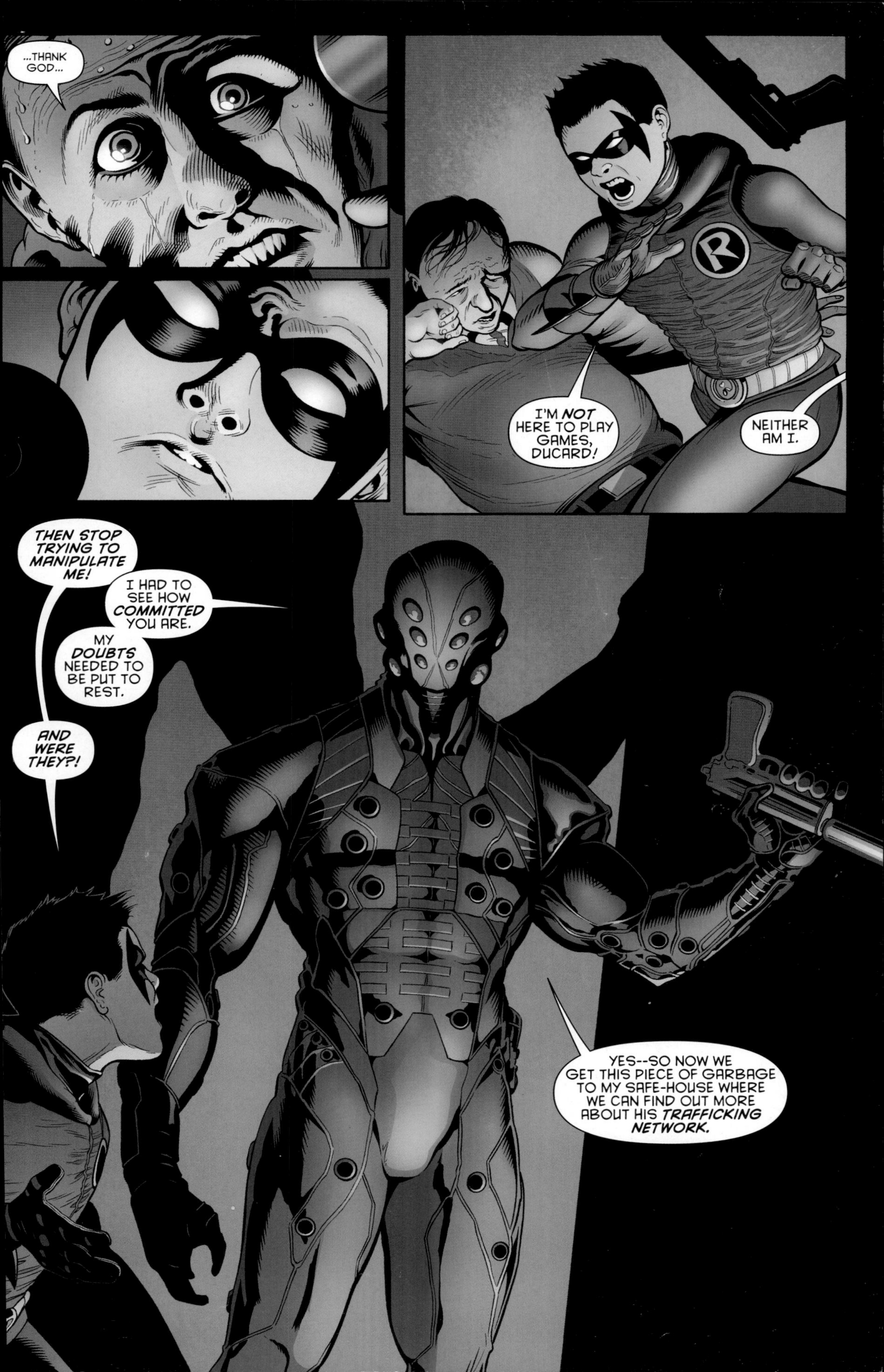
...THANK GOD...
I'M NOT HERE TO PLAY GAMES, DUCARD!
NEITHER AM I.
THEN STOP TRYING TO MANIPULATE ME!
I HAD TO SEE HOW COMMITTED YOU ARE.
MY DOUBTS NEEDED TO BE PUT TO REST.
AND WERE THEY?!
YES--SO NOW WE GET THIS PIECE OF GARBAGE TO MY SAFE-HOUSE WHERE WE CAN FIND OUT MORE ABOUT HIS TRAFFICKING NETWORK.

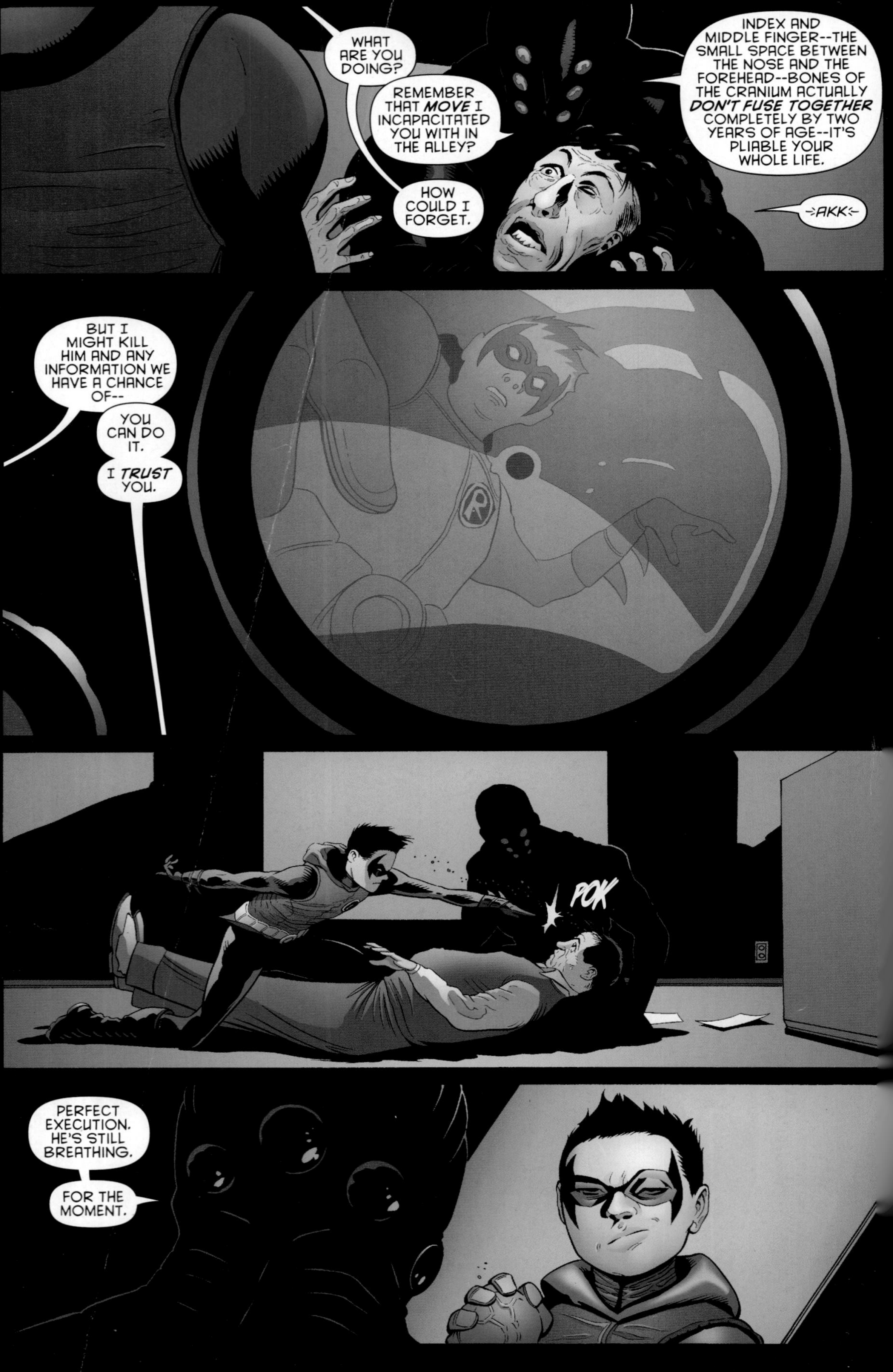
WHAT ARE YOU DOING?
REMEMBER THAT MOVE I INCAPACITATED YOU WITH IN THE ALLEY?
HOW COULD I FORGET.
INDEX AND MIDDLE FINGER--THE SMALL SPACE BETWEEN THE NOSE AND THE FOREHEAD--BONES OF THE CRANIUM ACTUALLY DON'T FUSE TOGETHER COMPLETELY BY TWO YEARS OF AGE--IT'S PLIABLE YOUR WHOLE LIFE.
AKK
BUT I MIGHT KILL HIM AND ANY INFORMATION WE HAVE A CHANCE OF--
YOU CAN DO IT.
I TRUST YOU.
POK
PERFECT EXECUTION. HE'S STILL BREATHING.
FOR THE MOMENT.

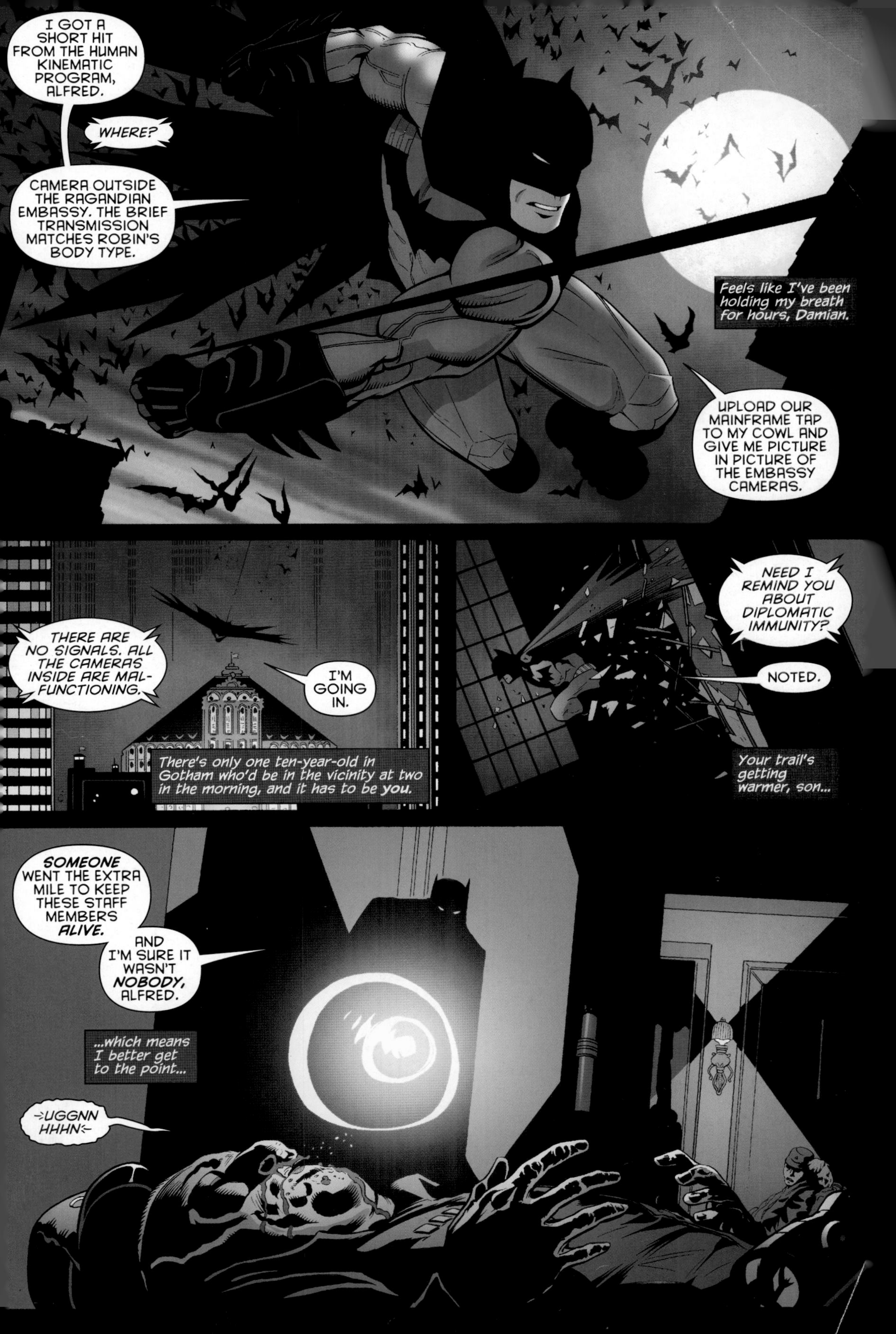
I GOT A SHORT HIT FROM THE HUMAN KINEMATIC PROGRAM, ALFRED.
WHERE?
CAMERA OUTSIDE THE RAGANDIAN EMBASSY. THE BRIEF TRANSMISSION MATCHES ROBIN'S BODY TYPE.
Feels like I've been holding my breath for hours, Damian.
UPLOAD OUR MAINFRAME TAP TO MY COWL AND GIVE ME PICTURE IN PICTURE OF THE EMBASSY CAMERAS.
THERE ARE NO SIGNALS. ALL THE CAMERAS INSIDE ARE MAL-FUNCTIONING.
I'M GOING IN.
There's only one ten-year-old in Gotham who'd be in the vicinity at two in the morning, and it has to be you.
NEED I REMIND YOU ABOUT DIPLOMATIC IMMUNITY?
NOTED.
Your trail's getting warmer, son...
SOMEONE WENT THE EXTRA MILE TO KEEP THESE STAFF MEMBERS ALIVE.
AND I'M SURE IT WASN'T NOBODY, ALFRED.
...which means I better get to the point...
UGGNN HHHN

...of why I'm telling you this story to begin with, Damian.

NO HARD FEELINGS, RIGHT? I'M HERE TO *LEARN*, NOT TO GET IN THE WAY, MORGAN.

SURE, BRUCE, I THINK WE CAN TEACH EACH OTHER A LOT IF YOU'RE GAME.

LET'S BE CLEAR HERE, BOYS-- IT *COSTS* A LOT TO PLAY IN *MY GAME*, BUT THAT SHOULDN'T BE A PROBLEM FOR A WAYNE FROM GOTHAM CITY, HMM?

I wasn't that *naïve* to think that Ducard would take me under his wing for *nothing*.

WATCH THE SHOULDER, MORGAN, YOU'RE TELEGRAPHING YOUR MOVE.

OKAY, GOT IT.

Ducard knew I was prepared to pay for the *privilege* of being a student in his master class.

YOU'LL NEED TO MOVE *FASTER*, BRUCE.

It was no secret we all wanted *something* from each other. it was the perfect storm...

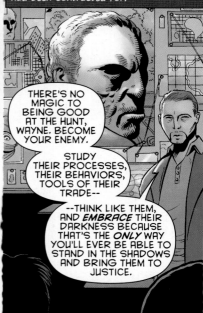

...and inside the eye of this storm was our syllabus for tracking and capturing the elusive terrorist *Hassan* that Ducard had been contracted for.

THERE'S NO MAGIC TO BEING GOOD AT THE HUNT, WAYNE. BECOME YOUR ENEMY.

STUDY THEIR PROCESSES, THEIR BEHAVIORS, TOOLS OF THEIR TRADE--

--THINK LIKE THEM, AND *EMBRACE* THEIR DARKNESS BECAUSE THAT'S THE *ONLY* WAY YOU'LL EVER BE ABLE TO STAND IN THE SHADOWS AND BRING THEM TO JUSTICE.

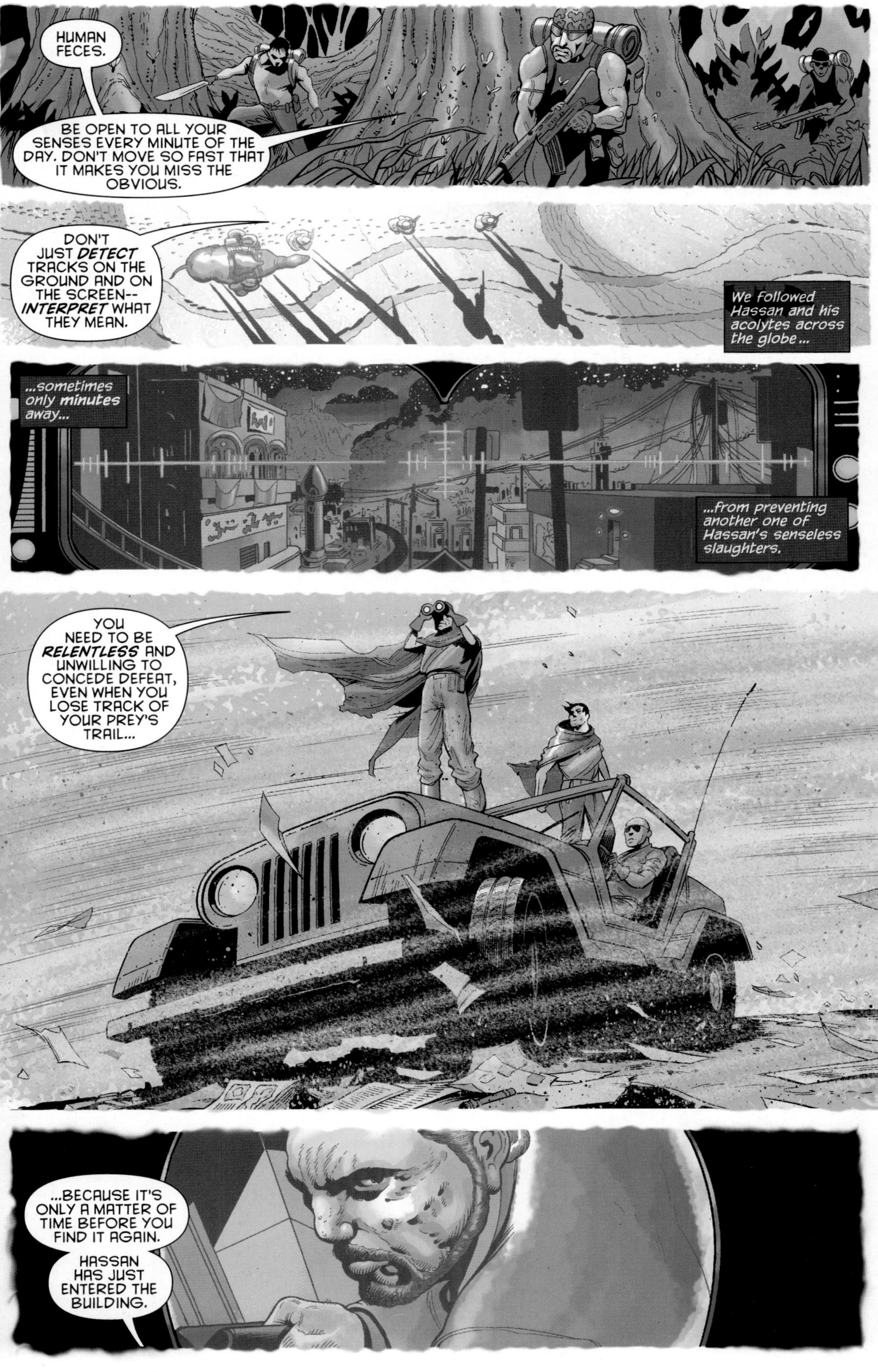
HUMAN FECES.
BE OPEN TO ALL YOUR SENSES EVERY MINUTE OF THE DAY. DON'T MOVE SO FAST THAT IT MAKES YOU MISS THE OBVIOUS.
DON'T JUST *DETECT* TRACKS ON THE GROUND AND ON THE SCREEN-- *INTERPRET* WHAT THEY MEAN.
We followed Hassan and his acolytes across the globe...
...sometimes only **minutes** away...
...from preventing another one of Hassan's senseless slaughters.
YOU NEED TO BE *RELENTLESS* AND UNWILLING TO CONCEDE DEFEAT, EVEN WHEN YOU LOSE TRACK OF YOUR PREY'S TRAIL...
...BECAUSE IT'S ONLY A MATTER OF TIME BEFORE YOU FIND IT AGAIN.
HASSAN HAS JUST ENTERED THE BUILDING.

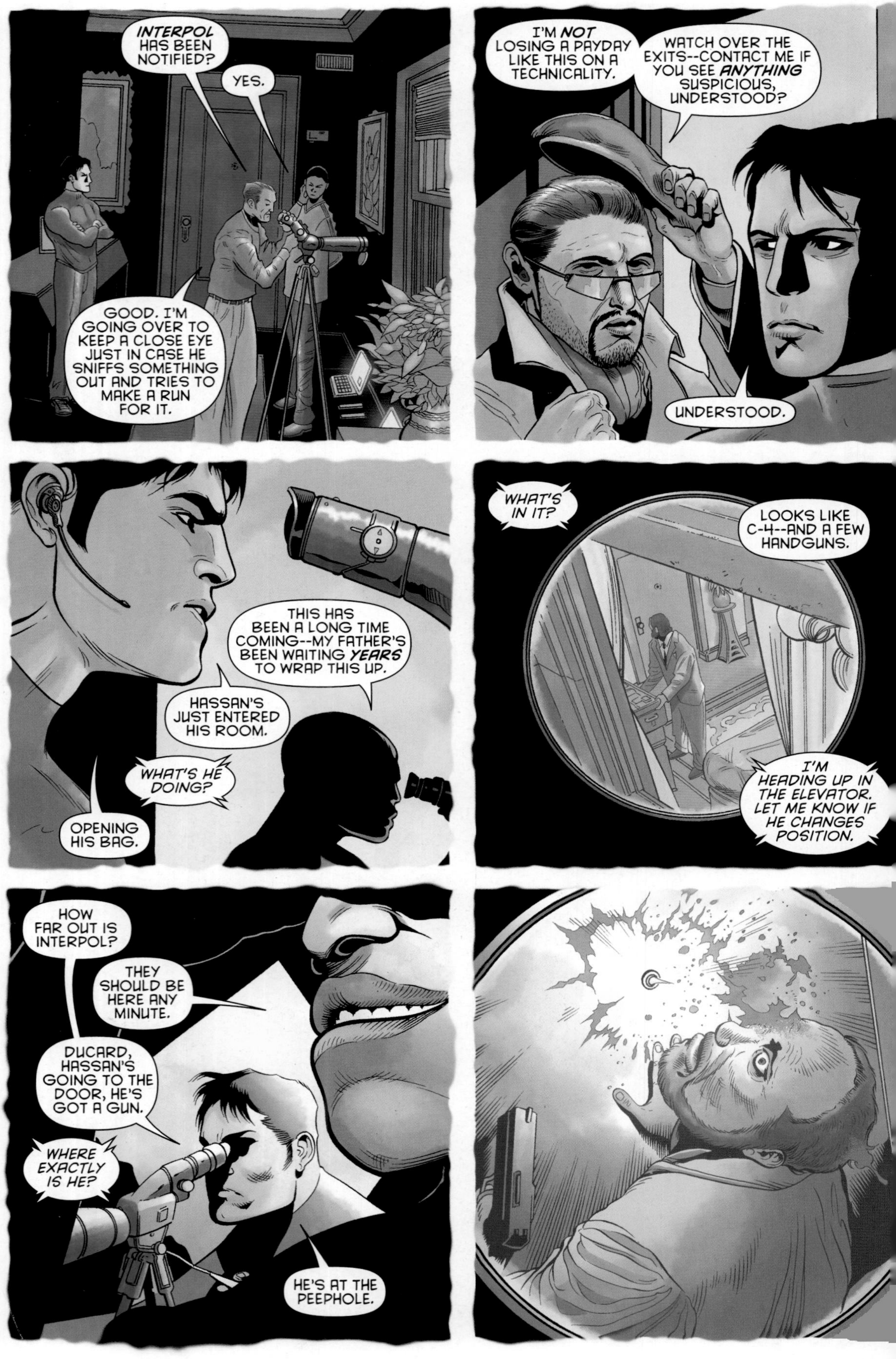
INTERPOL HAS BEEN NOTIFIED?
YES.
GOOD. I'M GOING OVER TO KEEP A CLOSE EYE JUST IN CASE HE SNIFFS SOMETHING OUT AND TRIES TO MAKE A RUN FOR IT.
I'M *NOT* LOSING A PAYDAY LIKE THIS ON A TECHNICALITY.
WATCH OVER THE EXITS--CONTACT ME IF YOU SEE *ANYTHING* SUSPICIOUS, UNDERSTOOD?
UNDERSTOOD.
THIS HAS BEEN A LONG TIME COMING--MY FATHER'S BEEN WAITING *YEARS* TO WRAP THIS UP.
HASSAN'S JUST ENTERED HIS ROOM.
WHAT'S HE DOING?
OPENING HIS BAG.
WHAT'S IN IT?
LOOKS LIKE C-4--AND A FEW HANDGUNS.
I'M HEADING UP IN THE ELEVATOR. LET ME KNOW IF HE CHANGES POSITION.
HOW FAR OUT IS INTERPOL?
THEY SHOULD BE HERE ANY MINUTE.
DUCARD, HASSAN'S GOING TO THE DOOR, HE'S GOT A GUN.
WHERE EXACTLY IS HE?
HE'S AT THE PEEPHOLE.

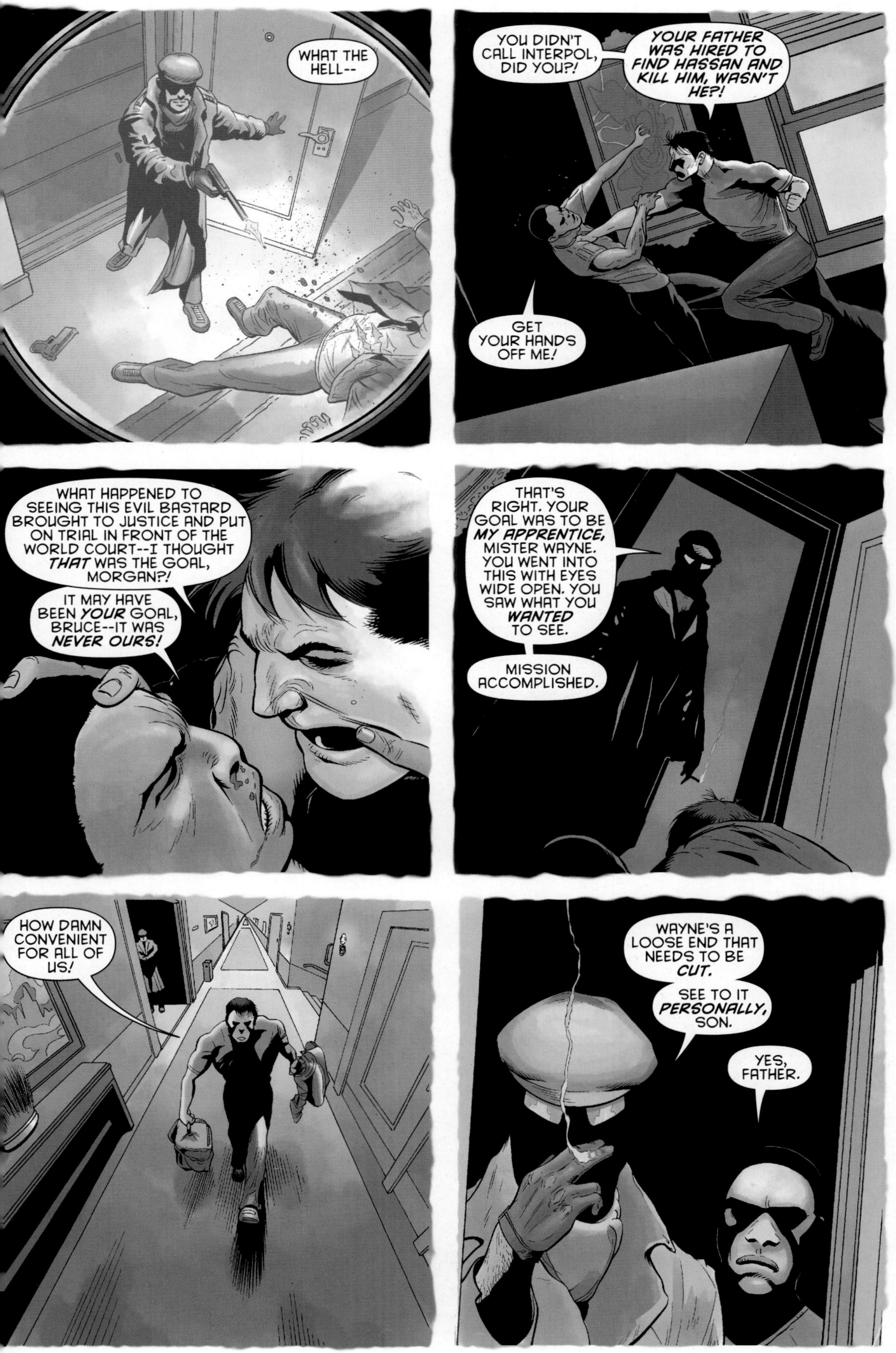
WHAT THE HELL--
YOU DIDN'T CALL INTERPOL, DID YOU?!
YOUR FATHER WAS HIRED TO FIND HASSAN AND KILL HIM, WASN'T HE?!
GET YOUR HANDS OFF ME!
WHAT HAPPENED TO SEEING THIS EVIL BASTARD BROUGHT TO JUSTICE AND PUT ON TRIAL IN FRONT OF THE WORLD COURT--I THOUGHT THAT WAS THE GOAL, MORGAN?!
IT MAY HAVE BEEN YOUR GOAL, BRUCE--IT WAS NEVER OURS!
THAT'S RIGHT. YOUR GOAL WAS TO BE MY APPRENTICE, MISTER WAYNE. YOU WENT INTO THIS WITH EYES WIDE OPEN. YOU SAW WHAT YOU WANTED TO SEE.
MISSION ACCOMPLISHED.
HOW DAMN CONVENIENT FOR ALL OF US!
WAYNE'S A LOOSE END THAT NEEDS TO BE CUT.
SEE TO IT PERSONALLY, SON.
YES, FATHER.

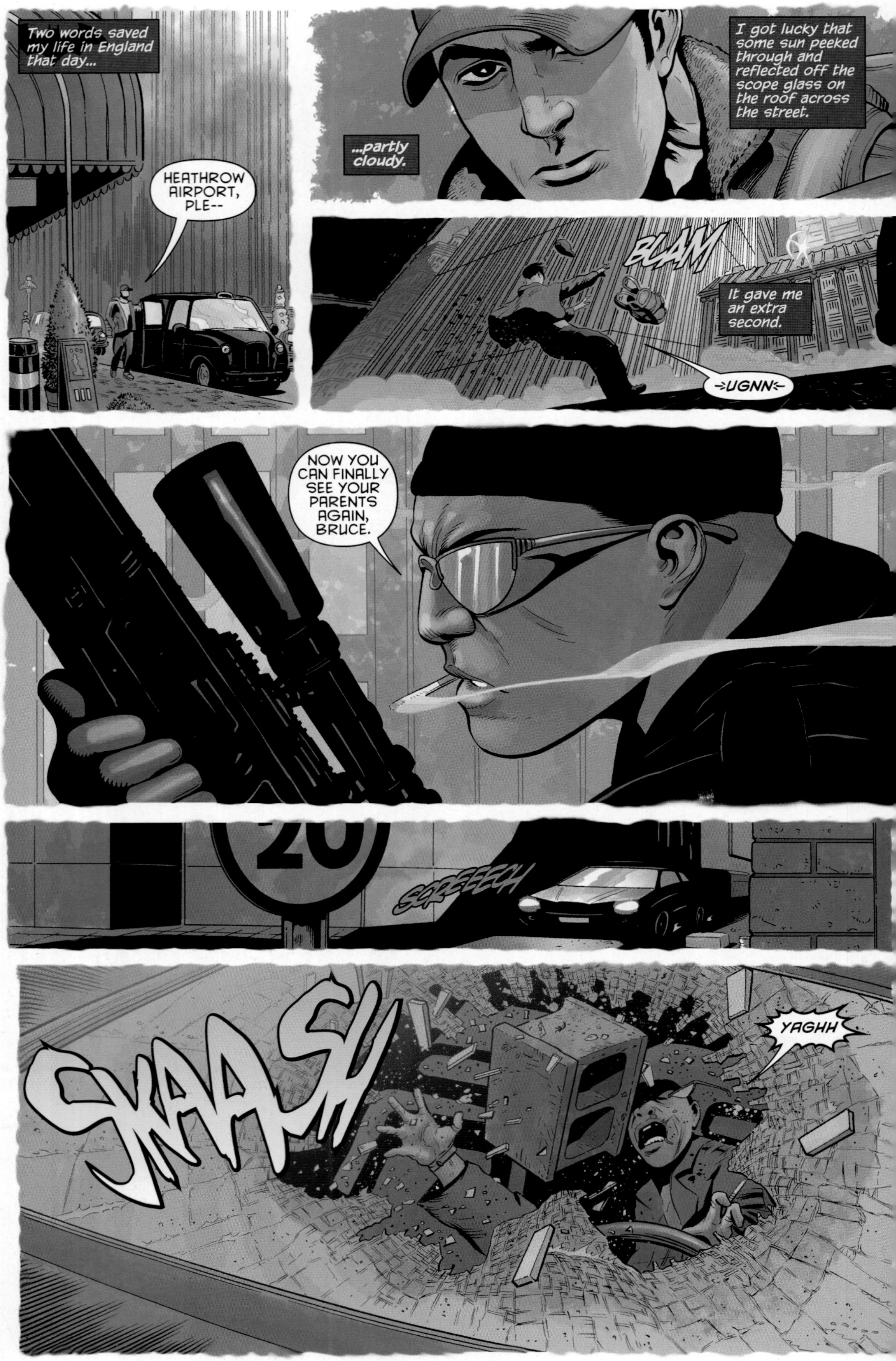
Two words saved my life in England that day...
HEATHROW AIRPORT, PLE--
...partly cloudy.
I got lucky that some sun peeked through and reflected off the scope glass on the roof across the street.
BLAM
It gave me an extra second.
UGNN
NOW YOU CAN FINALLY SEE YOUR PARENTS AGAIN, BRUCE.
20
SCREEECH
SKRASH
YAGHH

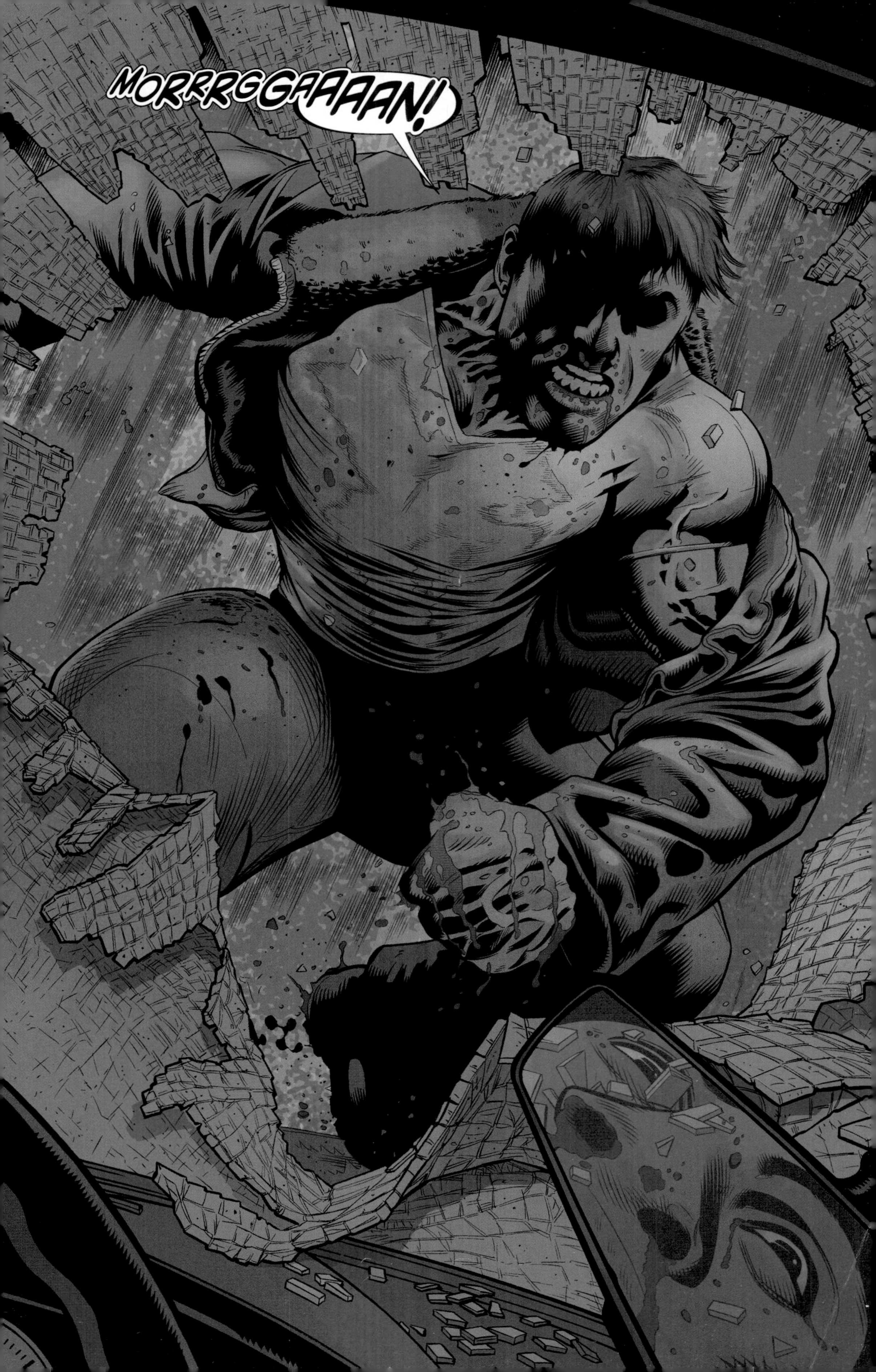
MORRRGGAAAAAN!

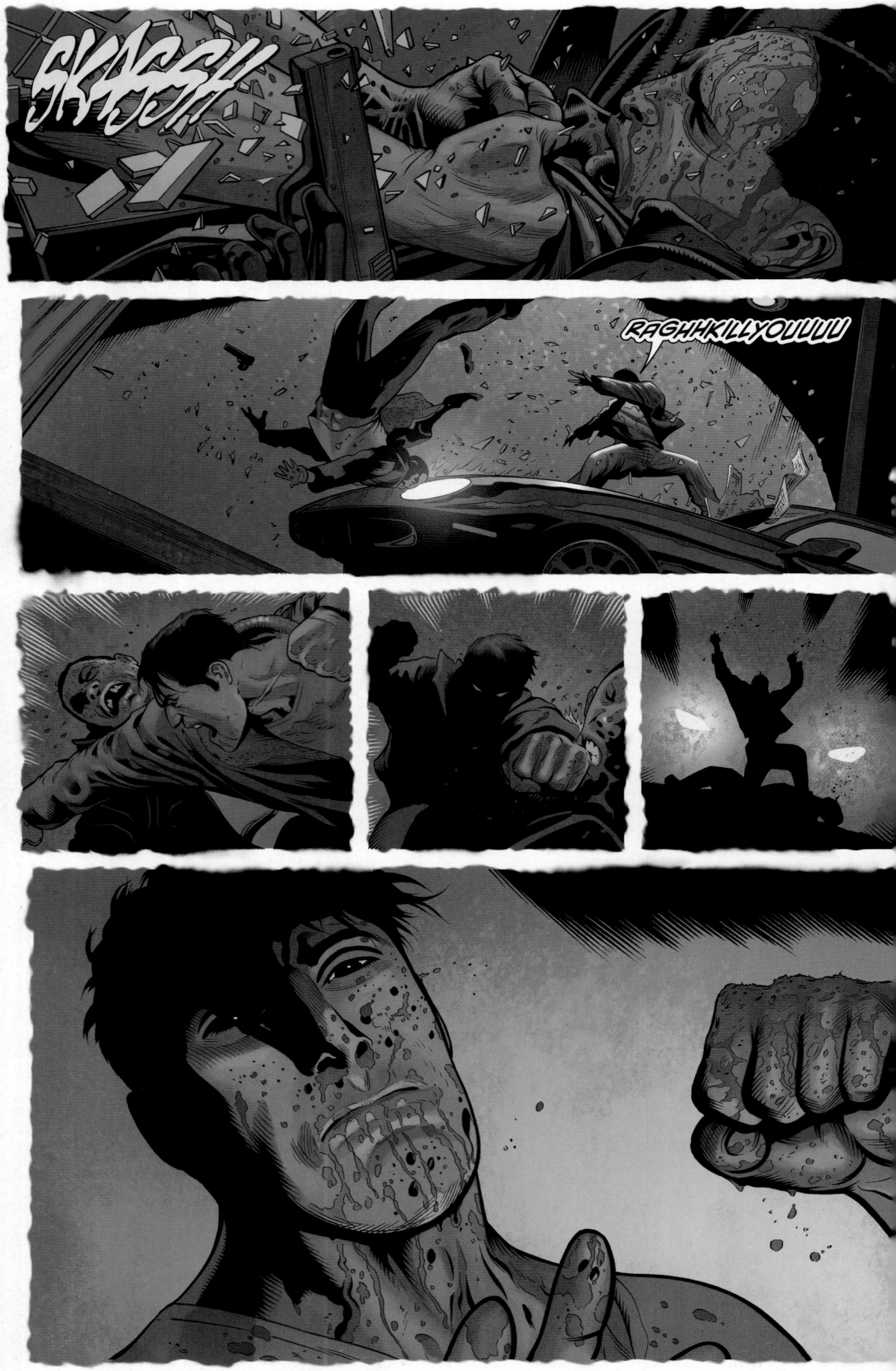
SKASSH
RAGHHKILLYOUUUU

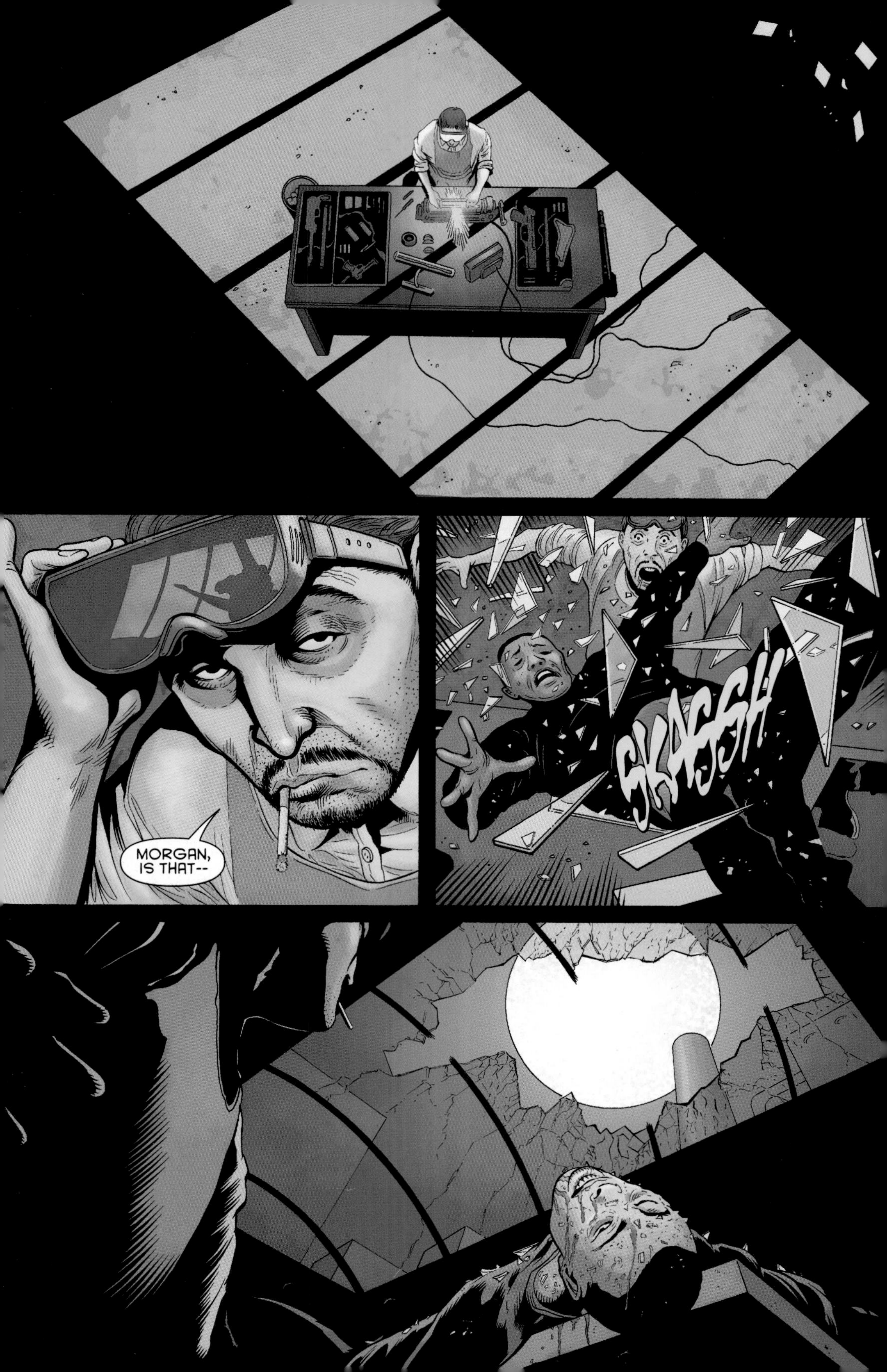
MORGAN, IS THAT--
SKRSSH

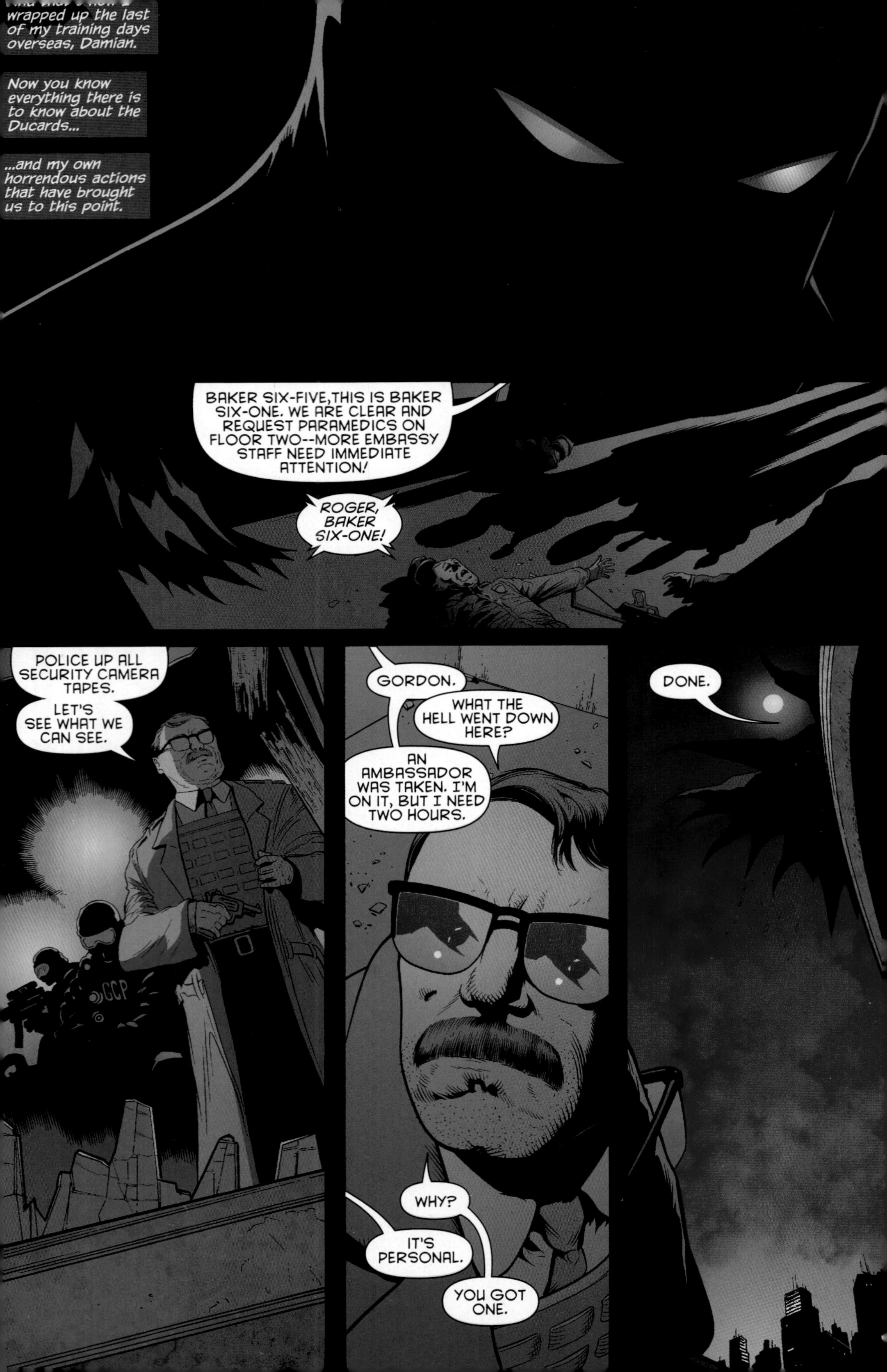
wrapped up the last of my training days overseas, Damian.
Now you know everything there is to know about the Ducards...
...and my own horrendous actions that have brought us to this point.
BAKER SIX-FIVE, THIS IS BAKER SIX-ONE. WE ARE CLEAR AND REQUEST PARAMEDICS ON FLOOR TWO--MORE EMBASSY STAFF NEED IMMEDIATE ATTENTION!
ROGER, BAKER SIX-ONE!
POLICE UP ALL SECURITY CAMERA TAPES.
LET'S SEE WHAT WE CAN SEE.
GORDON.
WHAT THE HELL WENT DOWN HERE?
AN AMBASSADOR WAS TAKEN. I'M ON IT, BUT I NEED TWO HOURS.
WHY?
IT'S PERSONAL.
YOU GOT ONE.
DONE.

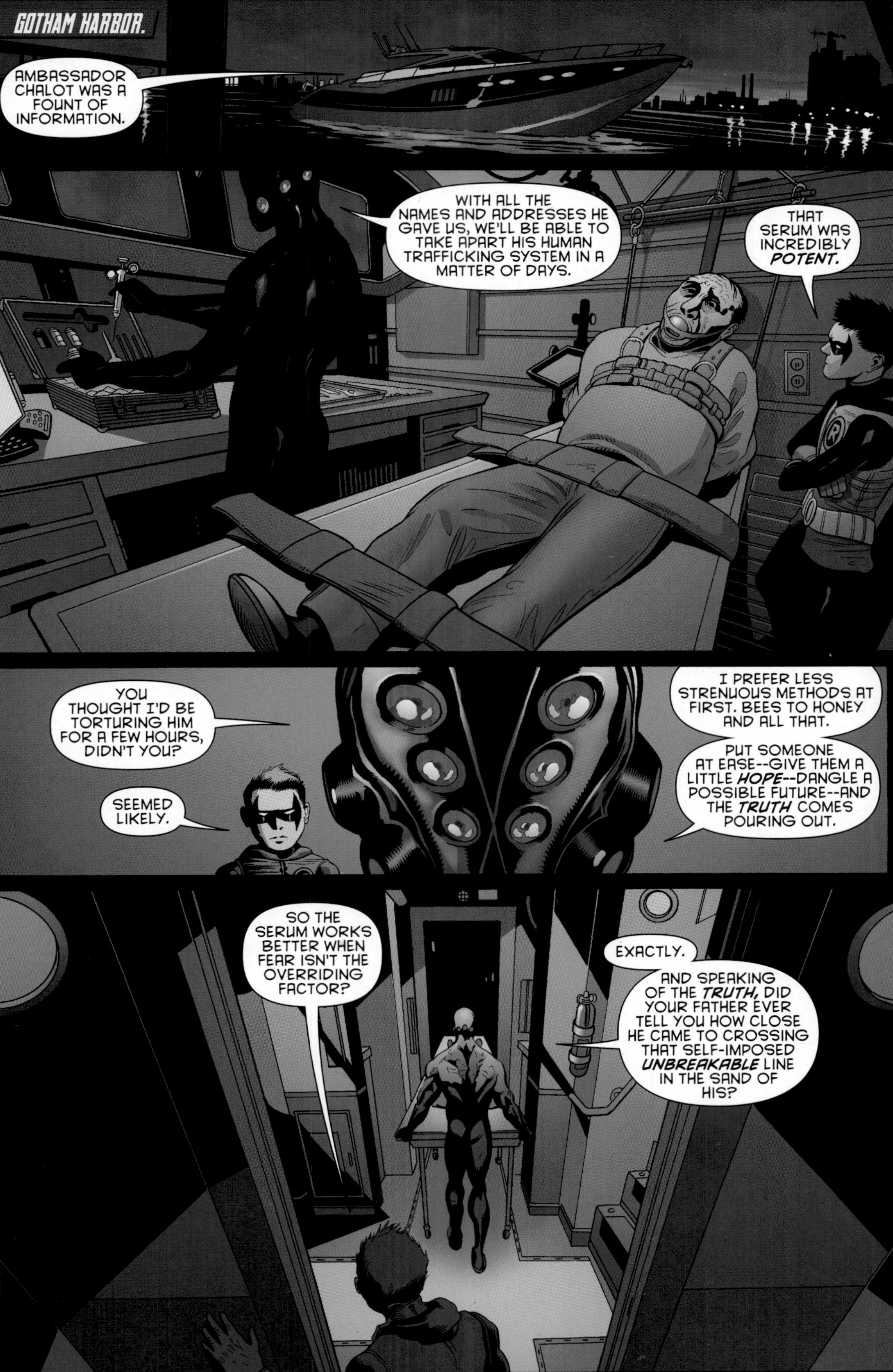
GOTHAM HARBOR.
AMBASSADOR CHALOT WAS A FOUNT OF INFORMATION.
WITH ALL THE NAMES AND ADDRESSES HE GAVE US, WE'LL BE ABLE TO TAKE APART HIS HUMAN TRAFFICKING SYSTEM IN A MATTER OF DAYS.
THAT SERUM WAS INCREDIBLY POTENT.
YOU THOUGHT I'D BE TORTURING HIM FOR A FEW HOURS, DIDN'T YOU?
SEEMED LIKELY.
I PREFER LESS STRENUOUS METHODS AT FIRST. BEES TO HONEY AND ALL THAT.
PUT SOMEONE AT EASE--GIVE THEM A LITTLE HOPE--DANGLE A POSSIBLE FUTURE--AND THE TRUTH COMES POURING OUT.
SO THE SERUM WORKS BETTER WHEN FEAR ISN'T THE OVERRIDING FACTOR?
EXACTLY.
AND SPEAKING OF THE TRUTH, DID YOUR FATHER EVER TELL YOU HOW CLOSE HE CAME TO CROSSING THAT SELF-IMPOSED UNBREAKABLE LINE IN THE SAND OF HIS?

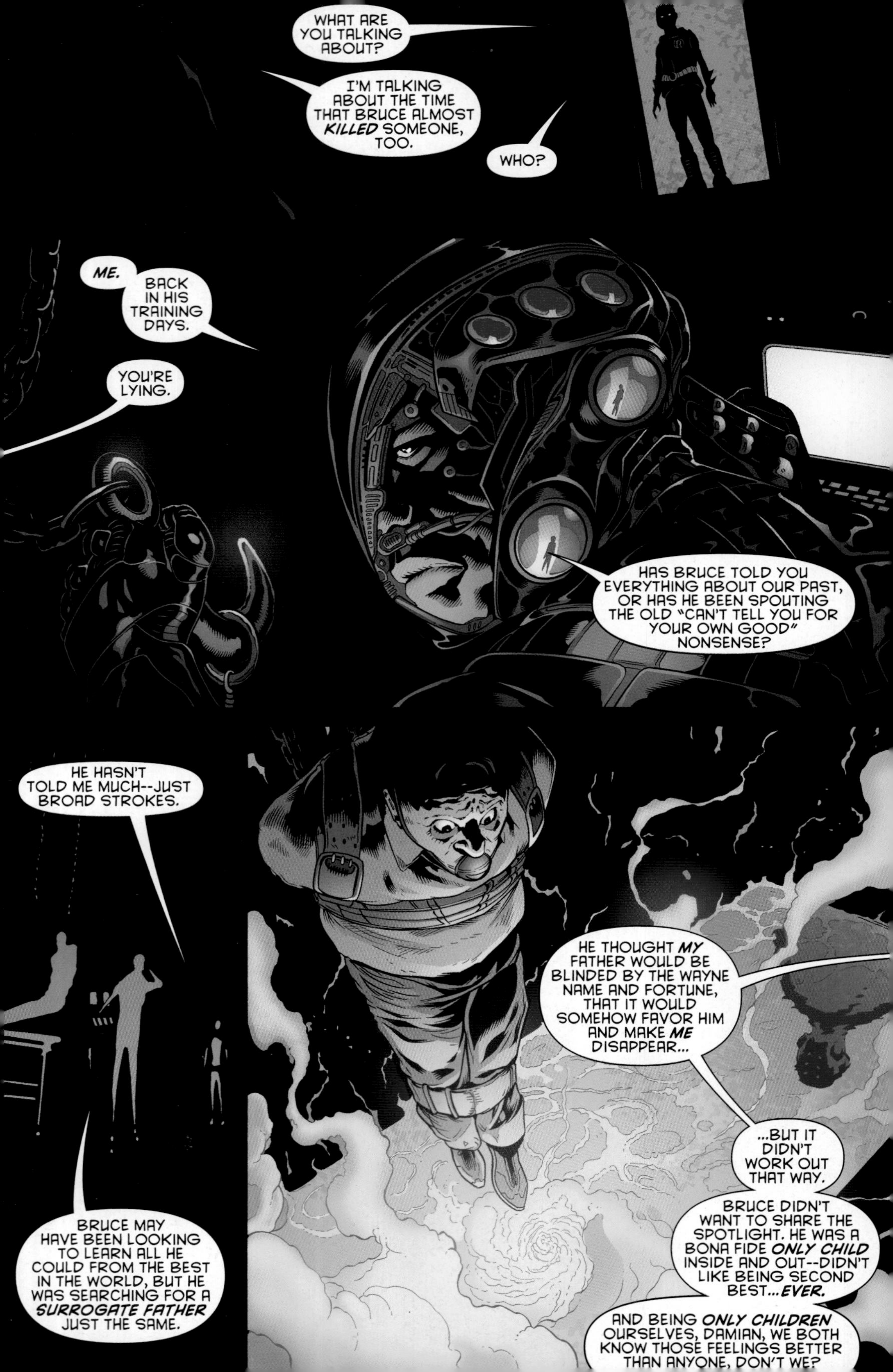
WHAT ARE YOU TALKING ABOUT?
I'M TALKING ABOUT THE TIME THAT BRUCE ALMOST *KILLED* SOMEONE, TOO.
WHO?
ME.
BACK IN HIS TRAINING DAYS.
YOU'RE LYING.
HAS BRUCE TOLD YOU EVERYTHING ABOUT OUR PAST, OR HAS HE BEEN SPOUTING THE OLD "CAN'T TELL YOU FOR YOUR OWN GOOD" NONSENSE?
HE HASN'T TOLD ME MUCH--JUST BROAD STROKES.
BRUCE MAY HAVE BEEN LOOKING TO LEARN ALL HE COULD FROM THE BEST IN THE WORLD, BUT HE WAS SEARCHING FOR A *SURROGATE FATHER* JUST THE SAME.
HE THOUGHT *MY* FATHER WOULD BE BLINDED BY THE WAYNE NAME AND FORTUNE, THAT IT WOULD SOMEHOW FAVOR HIM AND MAKE *ME* DISAPPEAR...
...BUT IT DIDN'T WORK OUT THAT WAY.
BRUCE DIDN'T WANT TO SHARE THE SPOTLIGHT. HE WAS A BONA FIDE *ONLY CHILD* INSIDE AND OUT--DIDN'T LIKE BEING SECOND BEST...*EVER.*
AND BEING *ONLY CHILDREN* OURSELVES, DAMIAN, WE BOTH KNOW THOSE FEELINGS BETTER THAN ANYONE, DON'T WE?

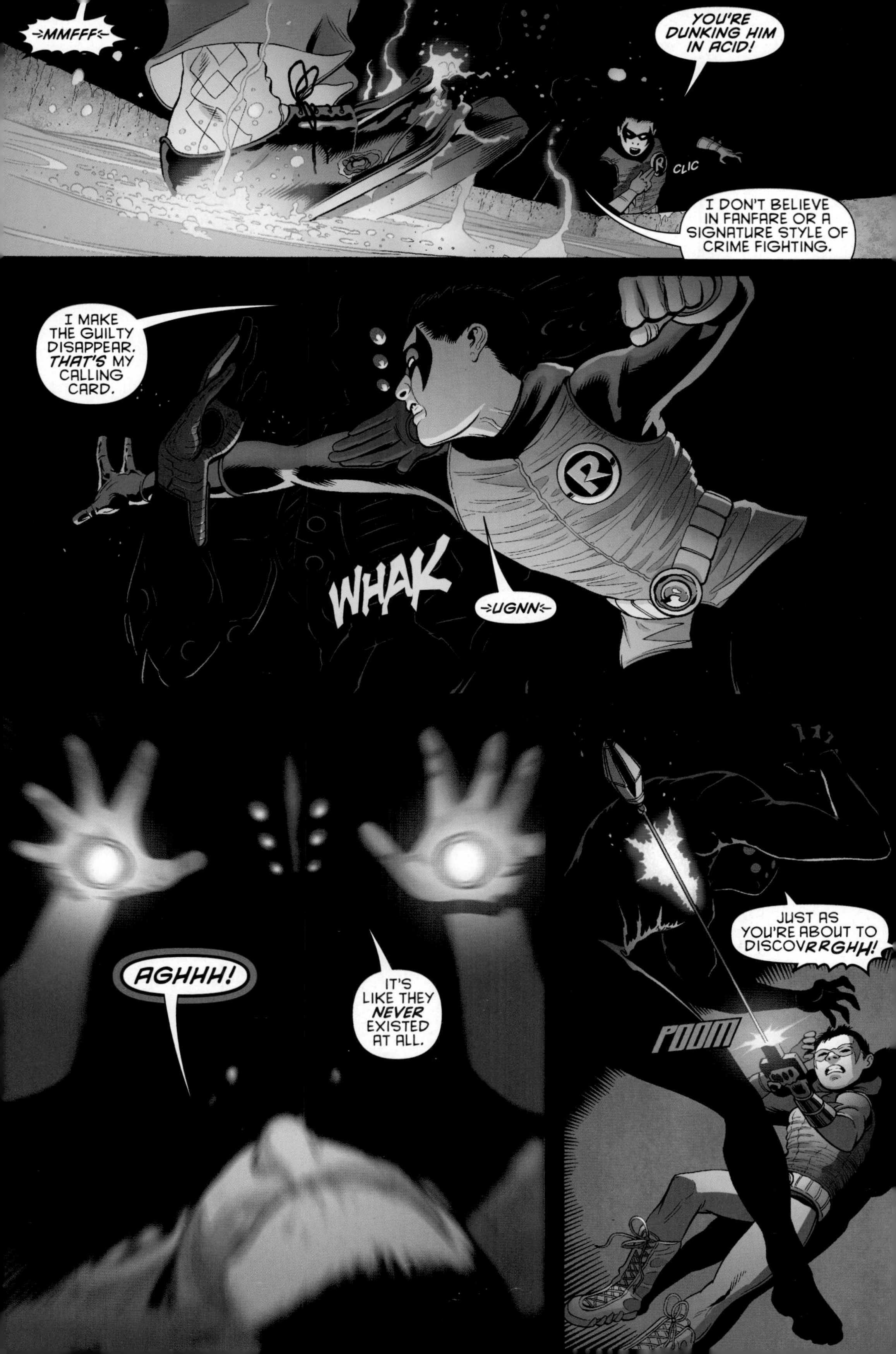

MMFFF
YOU'RE DUNKING HIM IN ACID!
CLIC
I DON'T BELIEVE IN FANFARE OR A SIGNATURE STYLE OF CRIME FIGHTING.
I MAKE THE GUILTY DISAPPEAR. THAT'S MY CALLING CARD.
WHAK
UGNN
AGHHH!
IT'S LIKE THEY NEVER EXISTED AT ALL.
JUST AS YOU'RE ABOUT TO DISCOVRRGHH!
POOM

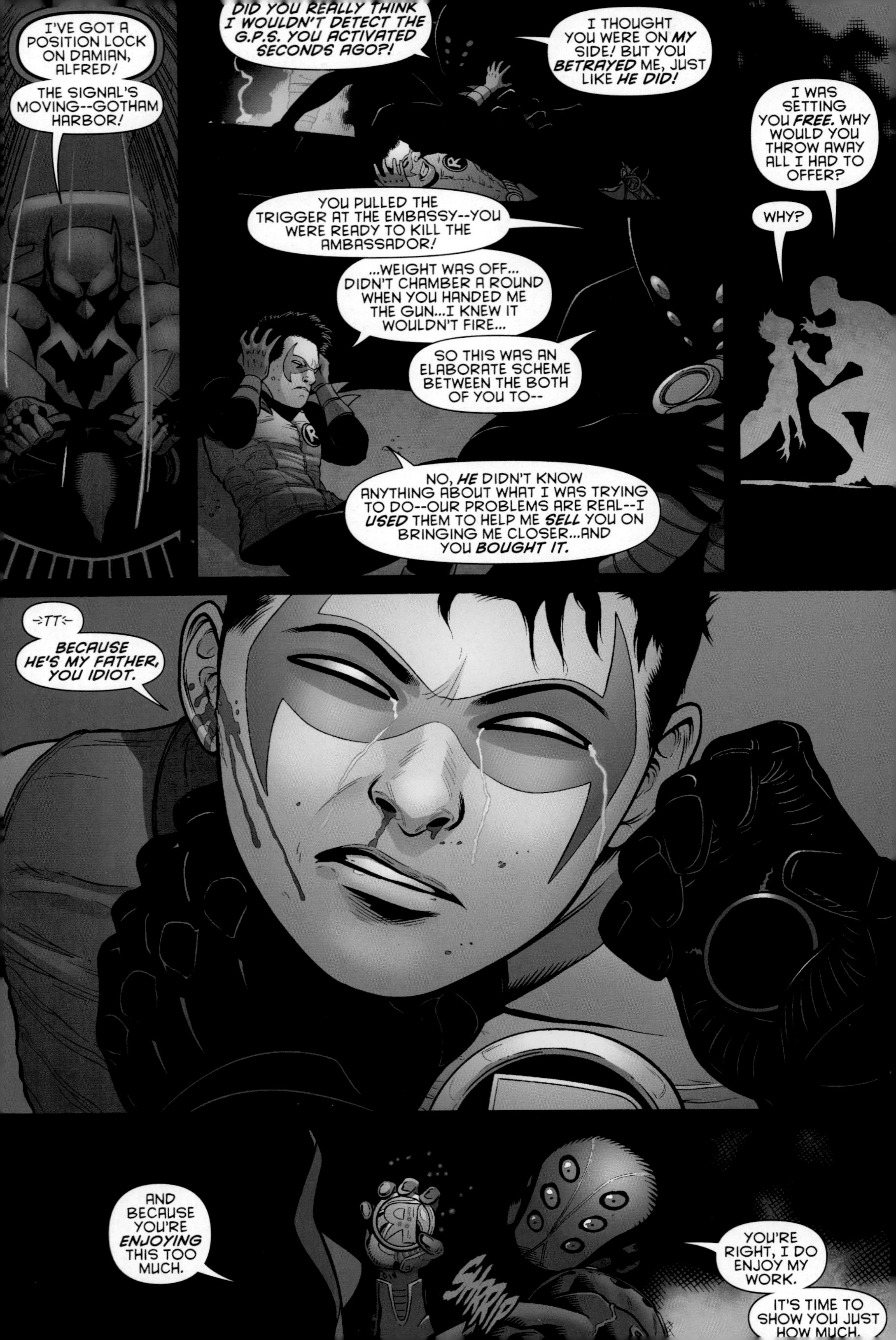
I'VE GOT A POSITION LOCK ON DAMIAN, ALFRED!
THE SIGNAL'S MOVING--GOTHAM HARBOR!
DID YOU REALLY THINK I WOULDN'T DETECT THE G.P.S. YOU ACTIVATED SECONDS AGO?!
I THOUGHT YOU WERE ON MY SIDE! BUT YOU BETRAYED ME, JUST LIKE HE DID!
I WAS SETTING YOU FREE. WHY WOULD YOU THROW AWAY ALL I HAD TO OFFER?
WHY?
YOU PULLED THE TRIGGER AT THE EMBASSY--YOU WERE READY TO KILL THE AMBASSADOR!
...WEIGHT WAS OFF... DIDN'T CHAMBER A ROUND WHEN YOU HANDED ME THE GUN...I KNEW IT WOULDN'T FIRE...
SO THIS WAS AN ELABORATE SCHEME BETWEEN THE BOTH OF YOU TO--
NO, HE DIDN'T KNOW ANYTHING ABOUT WHAT I WAS TRYING TO DO--OUR PROBLEMS ARE REAL--I USED THEM TO HELP ME SELL YOU ON BRINGING ME CLOSER...AND YOU BOUGHT IT.
=TT=
BECAUSE HE'S MY FATHER, YOU IDIOT.
AND BECAUSE YOU'RE ENJOYING THIS TOO MUCH.
SKRIP
YOU'RE RIGHT, I DO ENJOY MY WORK.
IT'S TIME TO SHOW YOU JUST HOW MUCH.

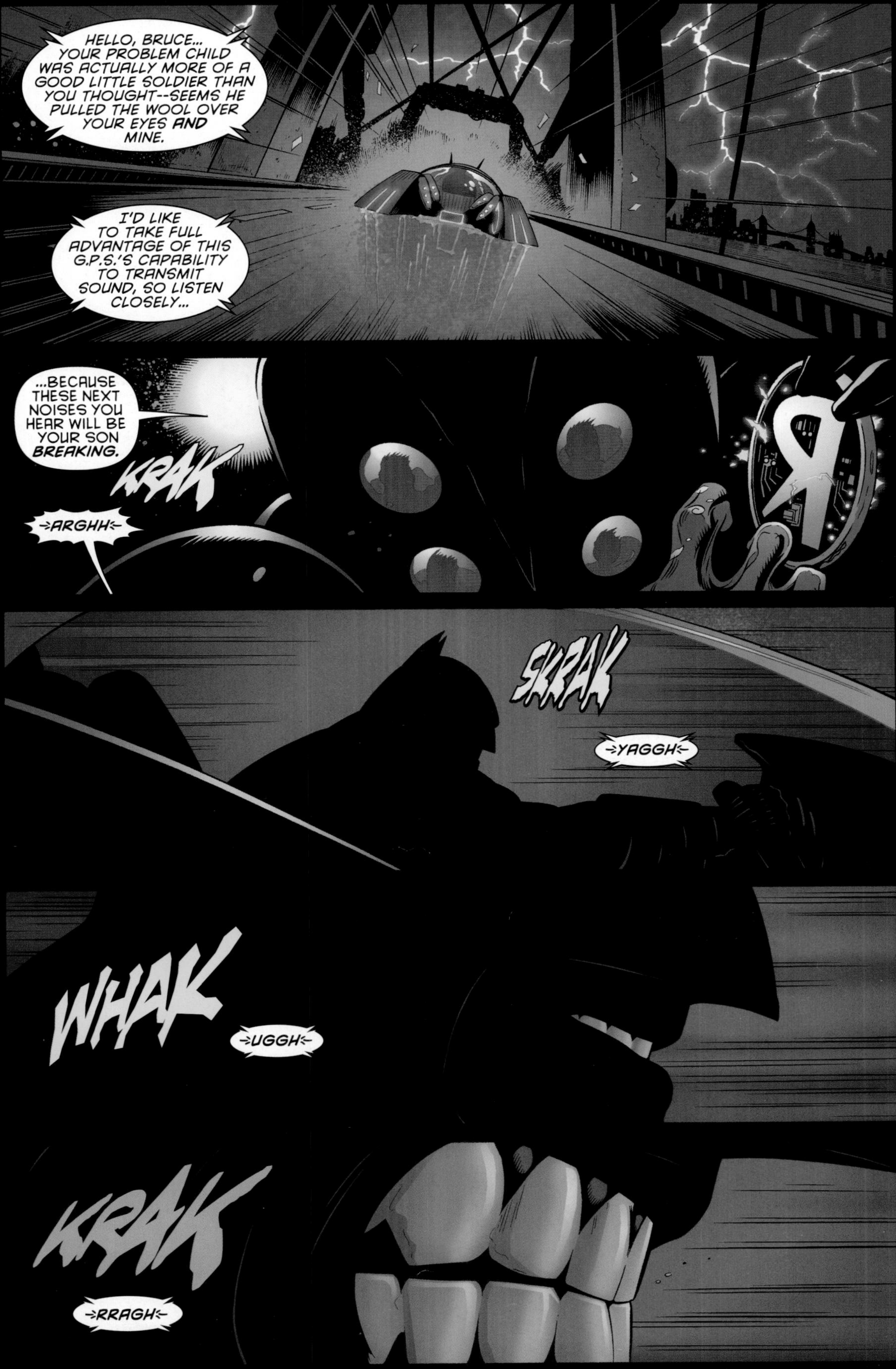
HELLO, BRUCE... YOUR PROBLEM CHILD WAS ACTUALLY MORE OF A GOOD LITTLE SOLDIER THAN YOU THOUGHT--SEEMS HE PULLED THE WOOL OVER YOUR EYES AND MINE.
I'D LIKE TO TAKE FULL ADVANTAGE OF THIS G.P.S.'S CAPABILITY TO TRANSMIT SOUND, SO LISTEN CLOSELY...
...BECAUSE THESE NEXT NOISES YOU HEAR WILL BE YOUR SON BREAKING.
KRAK
ARGHH
SKRAK
YAGGH
WHAK
UGGH
KRAK
RRAGH

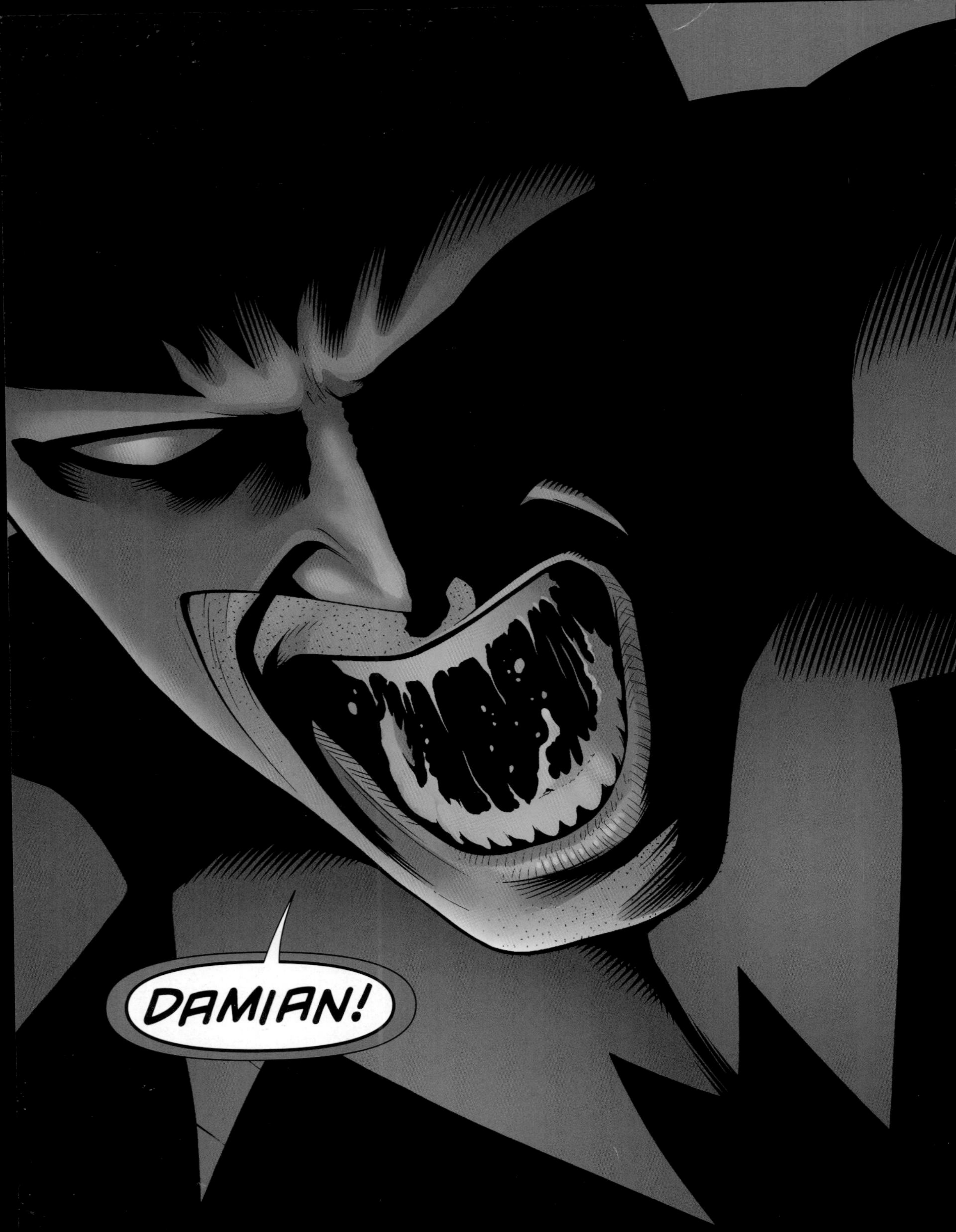
DAMIAN!

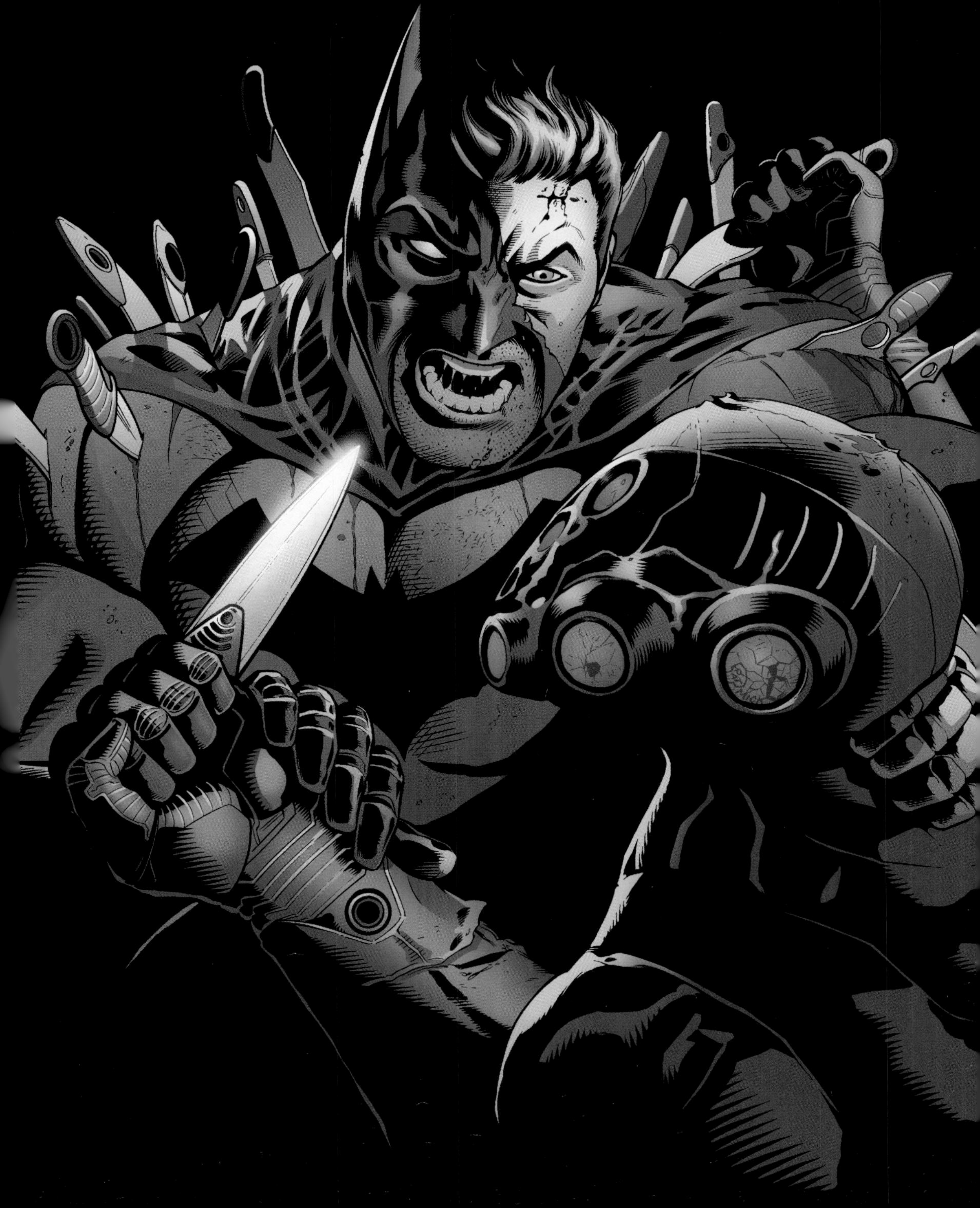

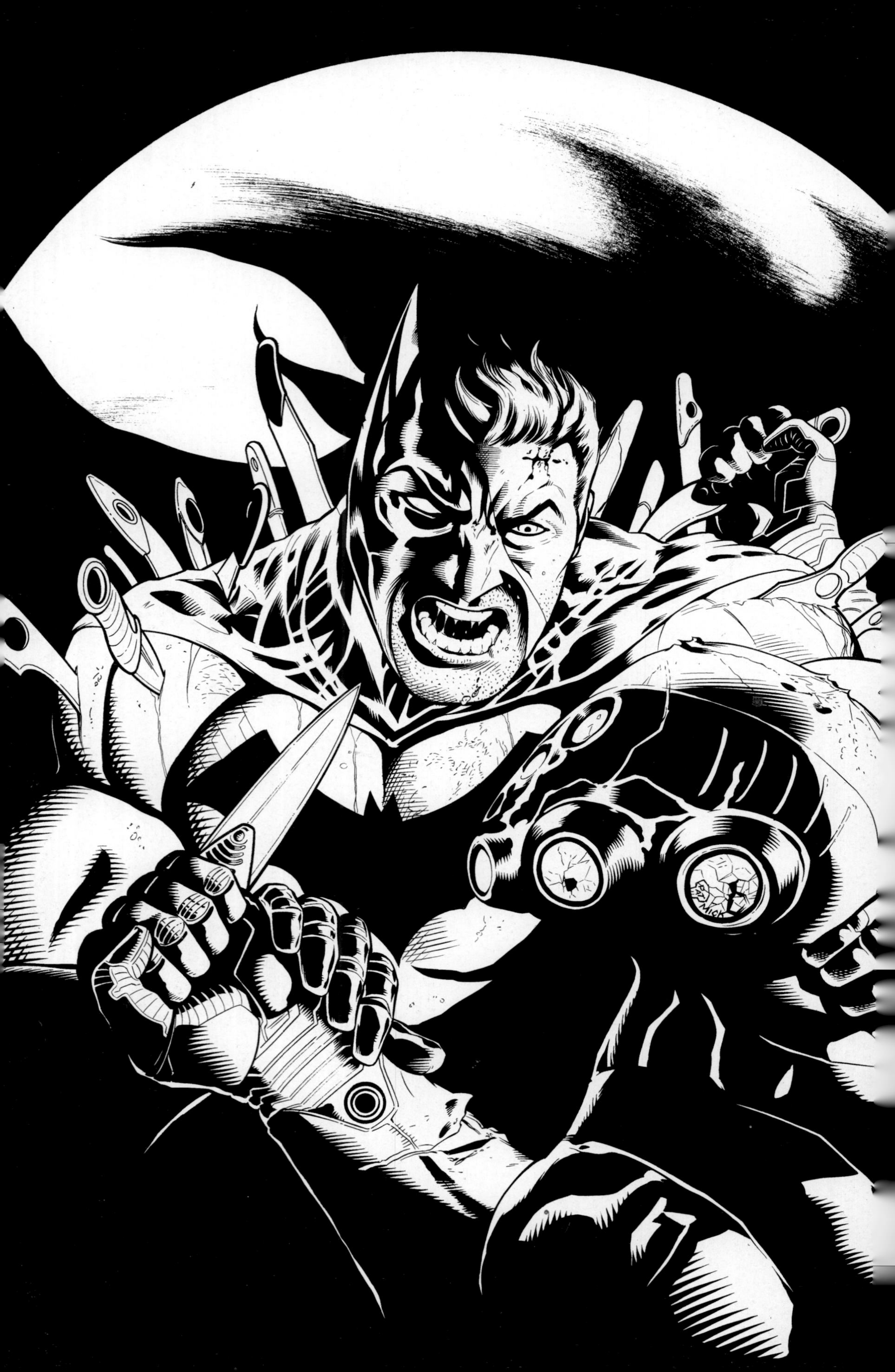

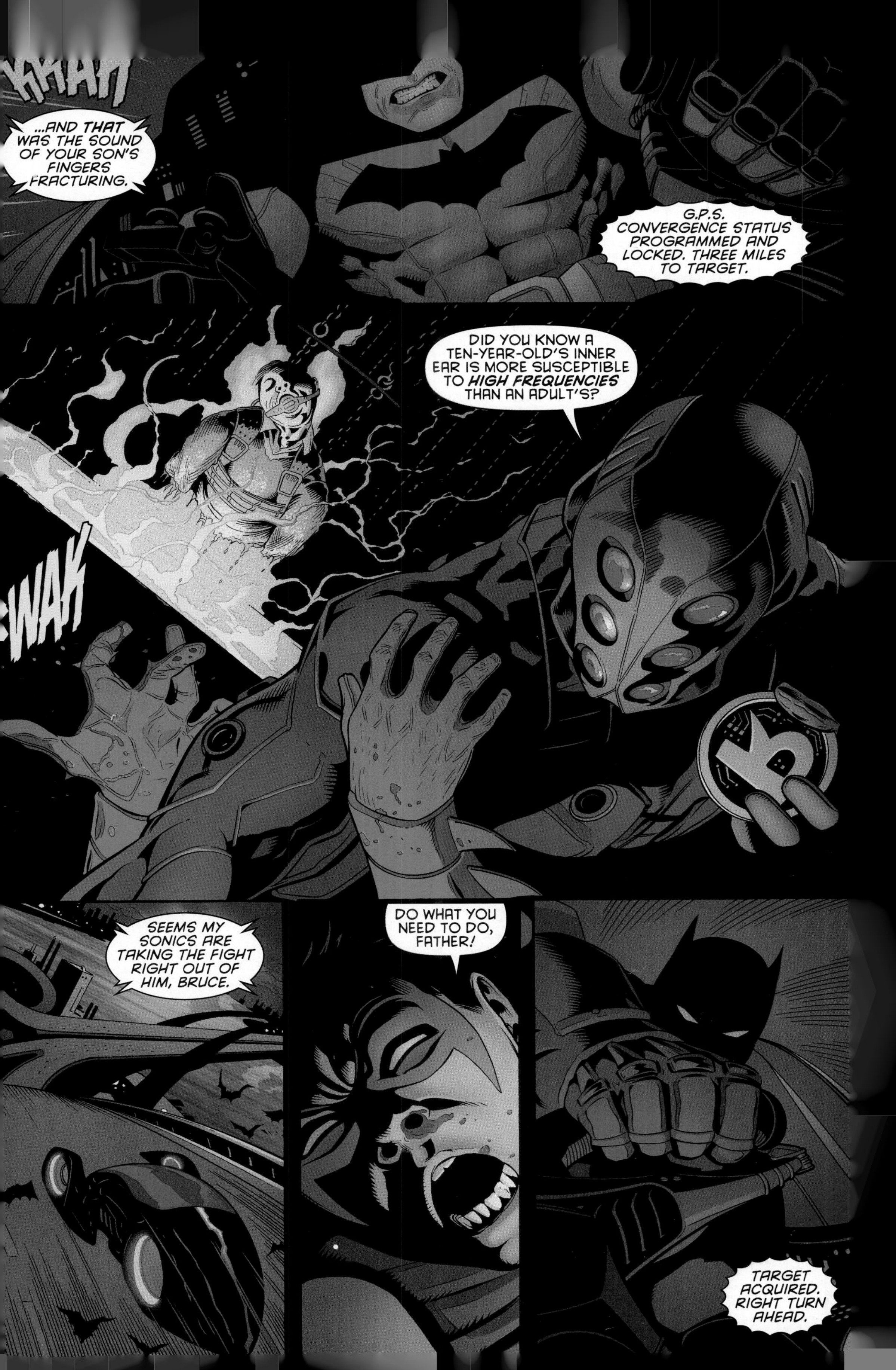
...AND THAT WAS THE SOUND OF YOUR SON'S FINGERS FRACTURING.
G.P.S. CONVERGENCE STATUS PROGRAMMED AND LOCKED. THREE MILES TO TARGET.
DID YOU KNOW A TEN-YEAR-OLD'S INNER EAR IS MORE SUSCEPTIBLE TO HIGH FREQUENCIES THAN AN ADULT'S?
WAK
SEEMS MY SONICS ARE TAKING THE FIGHT RIGHT OUT OF HIM, BRUCE.
DO WHAT YOU NEED TO DO, FATHER!
TARGET ACQUIRED. RIGHT TURN AHEAD.

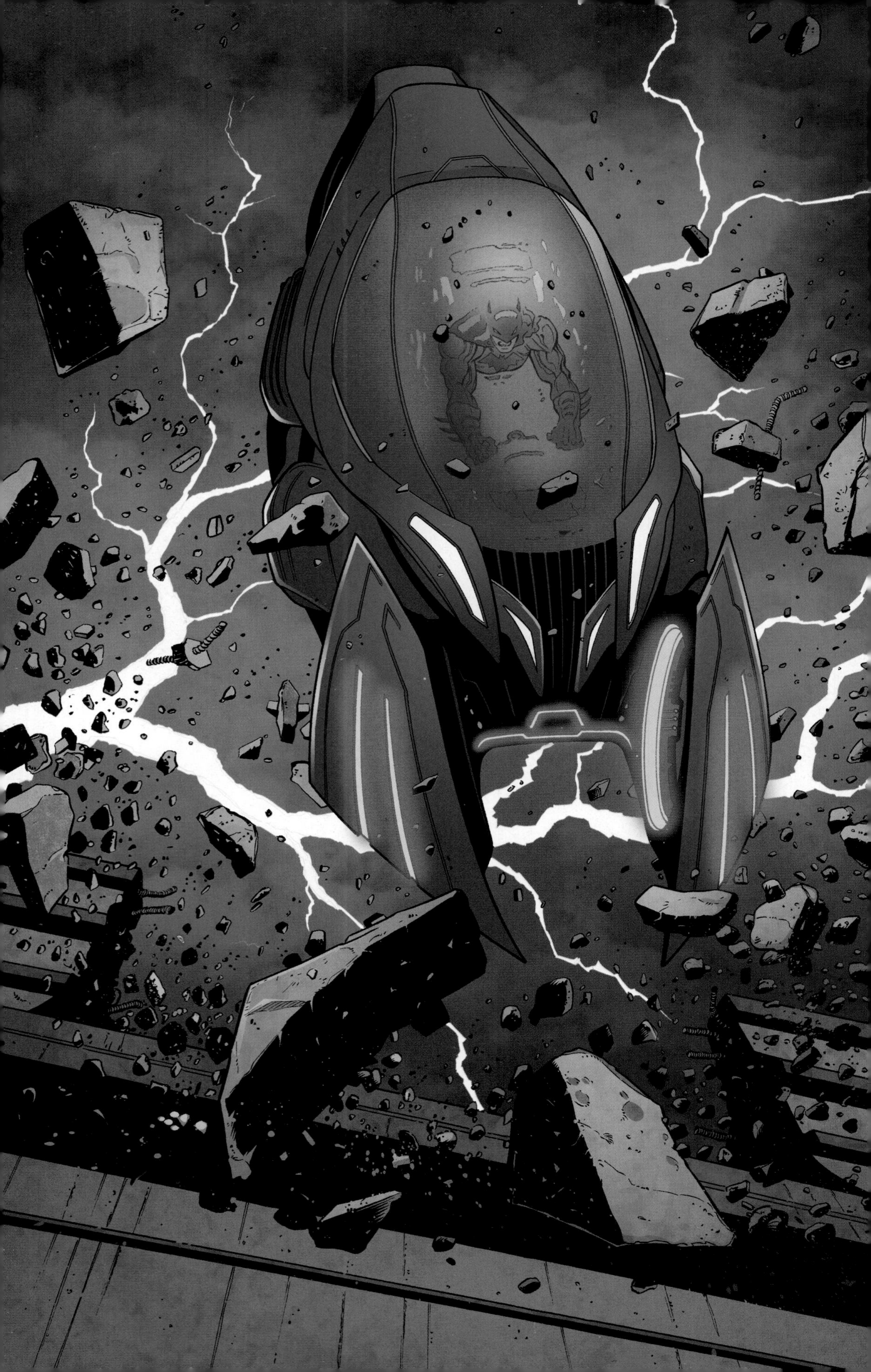

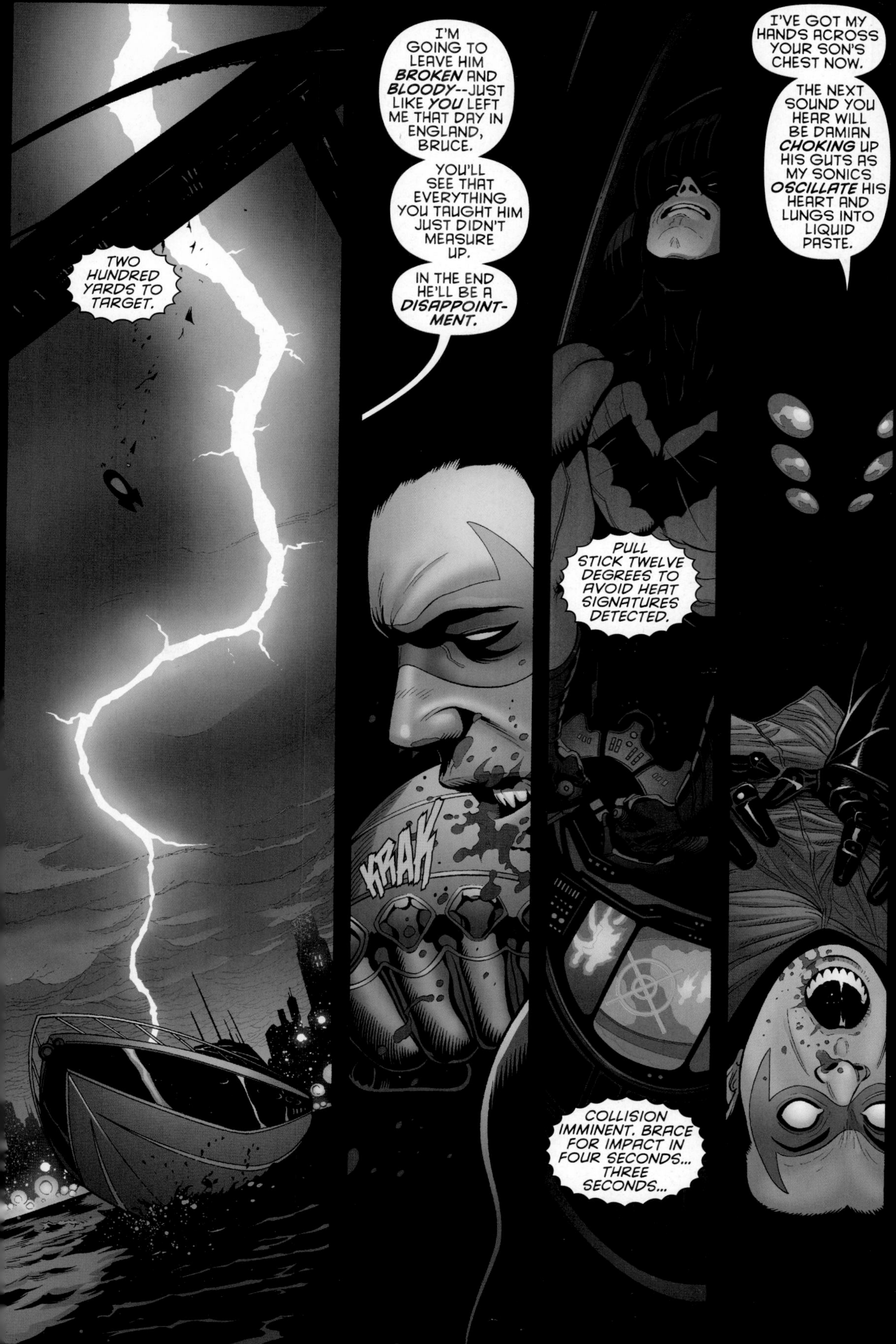
TWO HUNDRED YARDS TO TARGET.
I'M GOING TO LEAVE HIM BROKEN AND BLOODY--JUST LIKE YOU LEFT ME THAT DAY IN ENGLAND, BRUCE.
YOU'LL SEE THAT EVERYTHING YOU TAUGHT HIM JUST DIDN'T MEASURE UP.
IN THE END HE'LL BE A DISAPPOINTMENT.
KRAK
PULL STICK TWELVE DEGREES TO AVOID HEAT SIGNATURES DETECTED.
COLLISION IMMINENT. BRACE FOR IMPACT IN FOUR SECONDS... THREE SECONDS...
I'VE GOT MY HANDS ACROSS YOUR SON'S CHEST NOW.
THE NEXT SOUND YOU HEAR WILL BE DAMIAN CHOKING UP HIS GUTS AS MY SONICS OSCILLATE HIS HEART AND LUNGS INTO LIQUID PASTE.

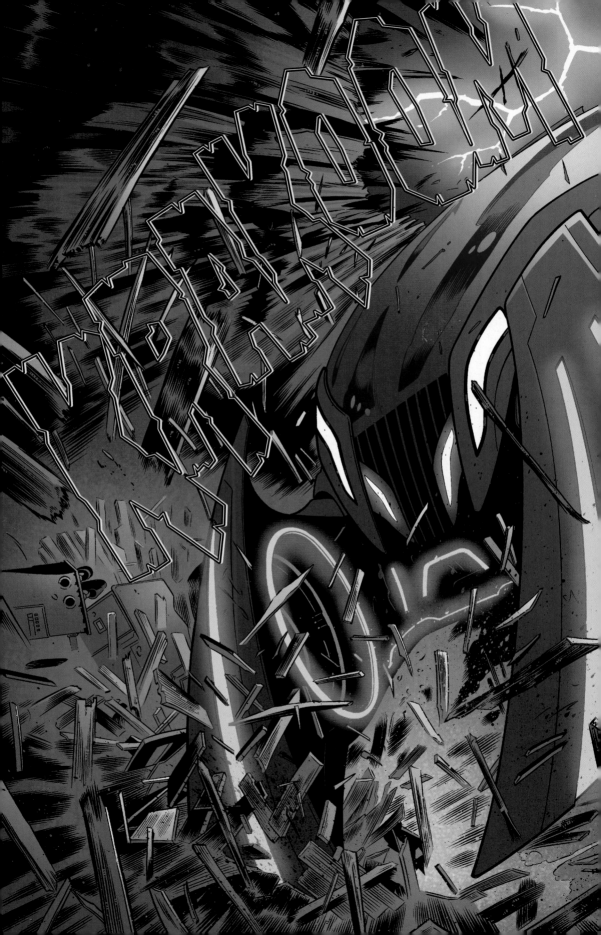

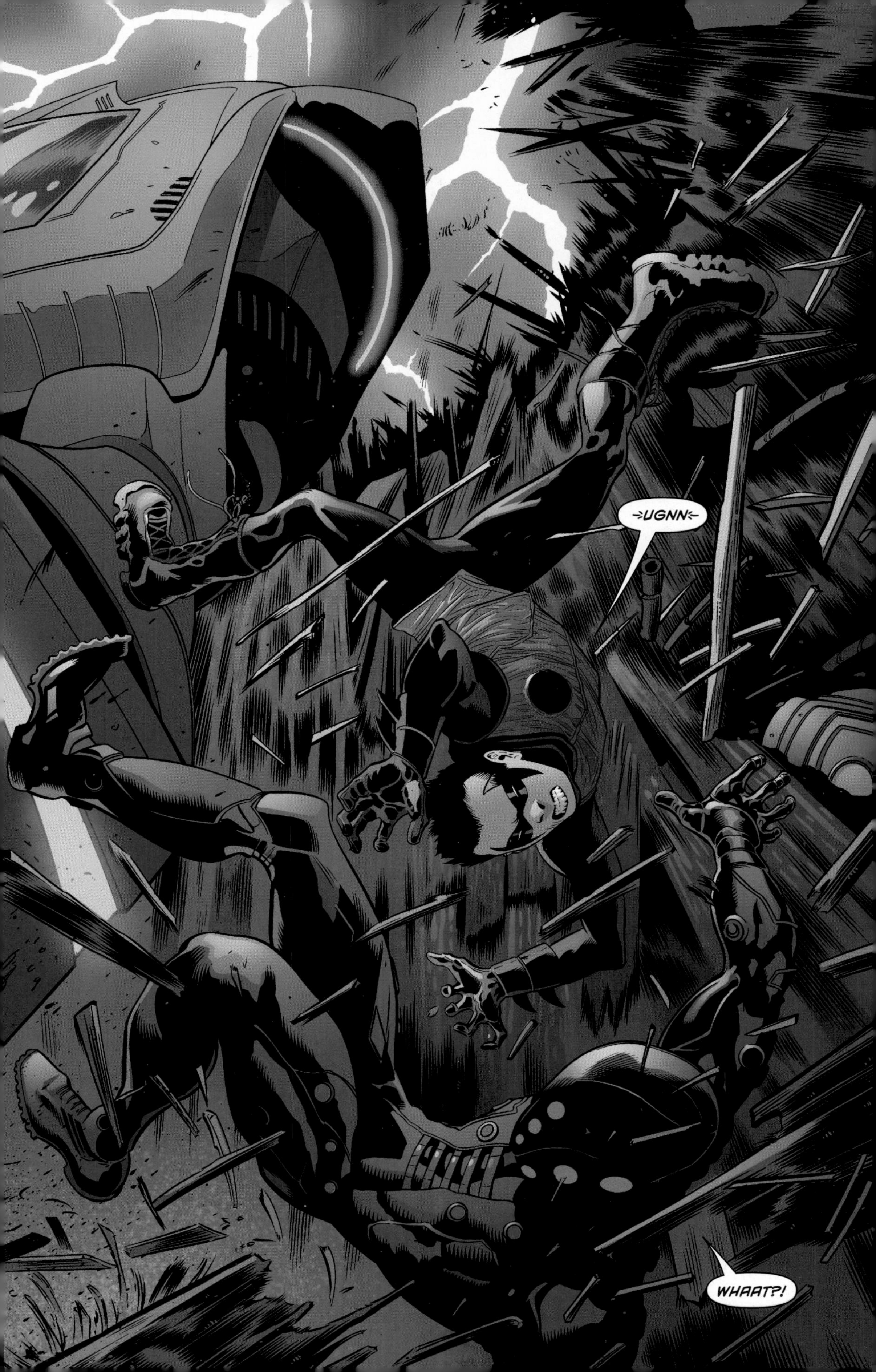
UGNN
WHAAT?!

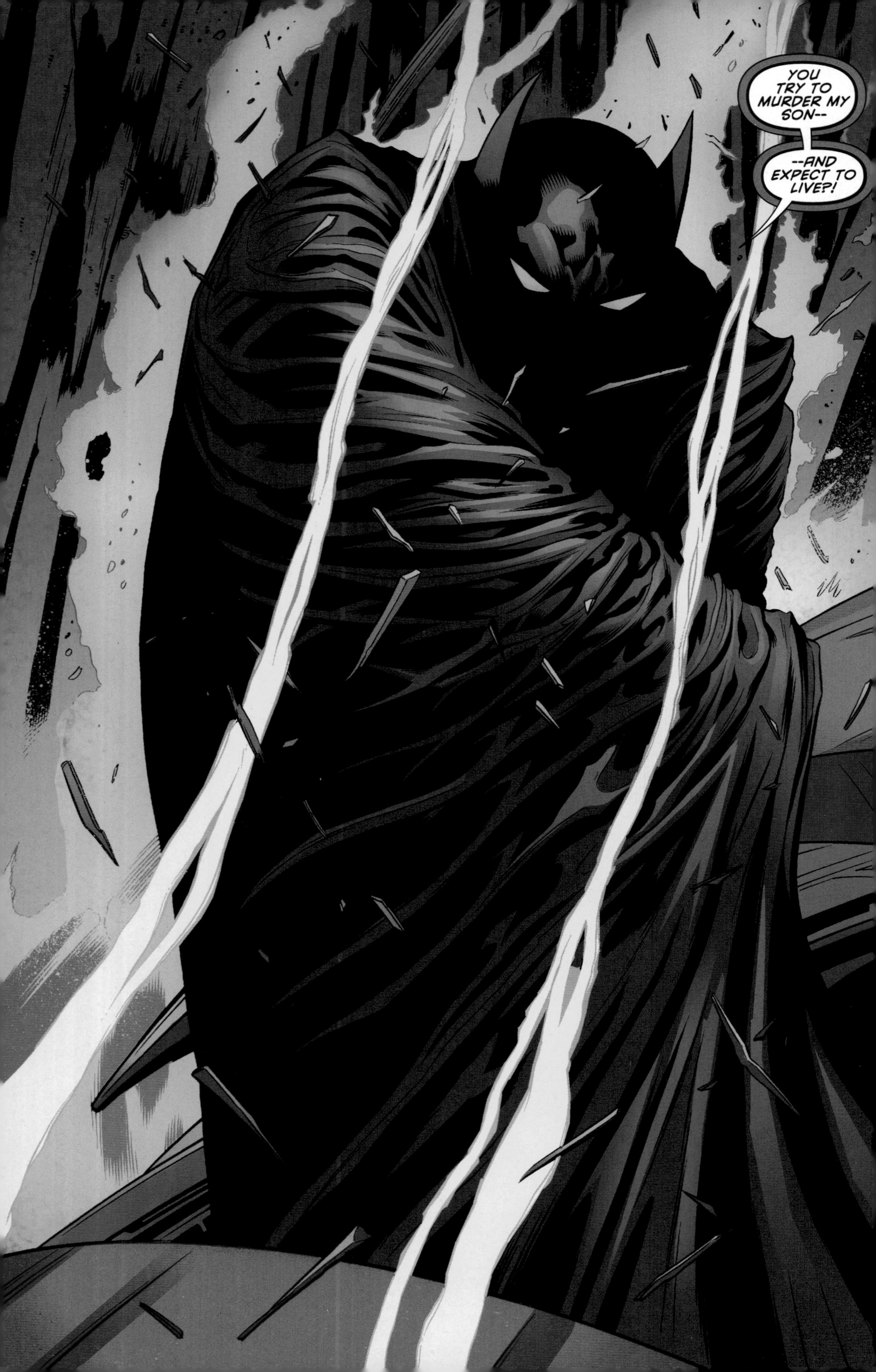
YOU TRY TO MURDER MY SON--
--AND EXPECT TO LIVE?!

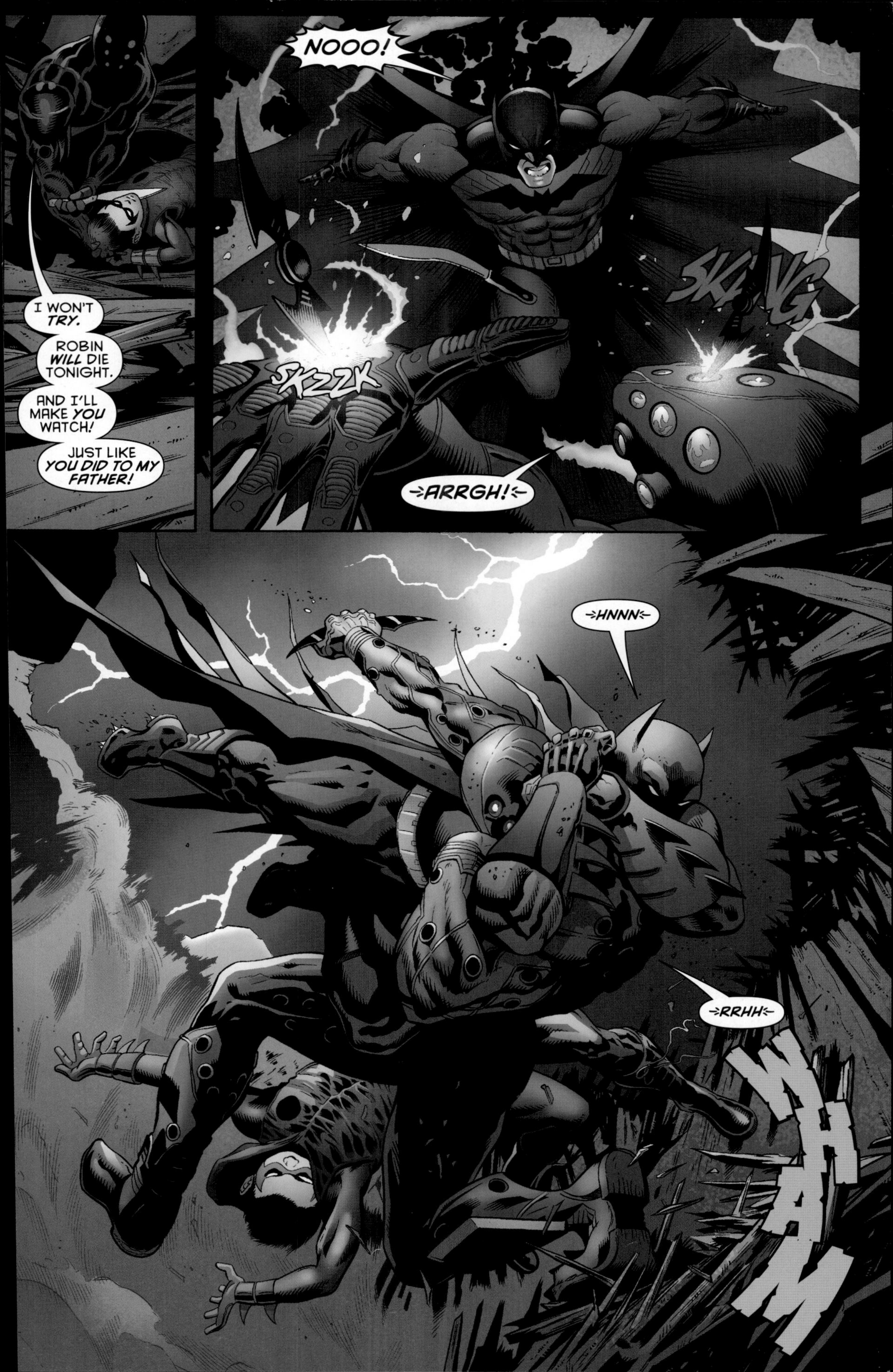
I WON'T TRY.
ROBIN WILL DIE TONIGHT.
AND I'LL MAKE YOU WATCH!
JUST LIKE YOU DID TO MY FATHER!
NOOO!
SKZZK
SKANG
ARRGH!
HNNN
RRHH
WHAM

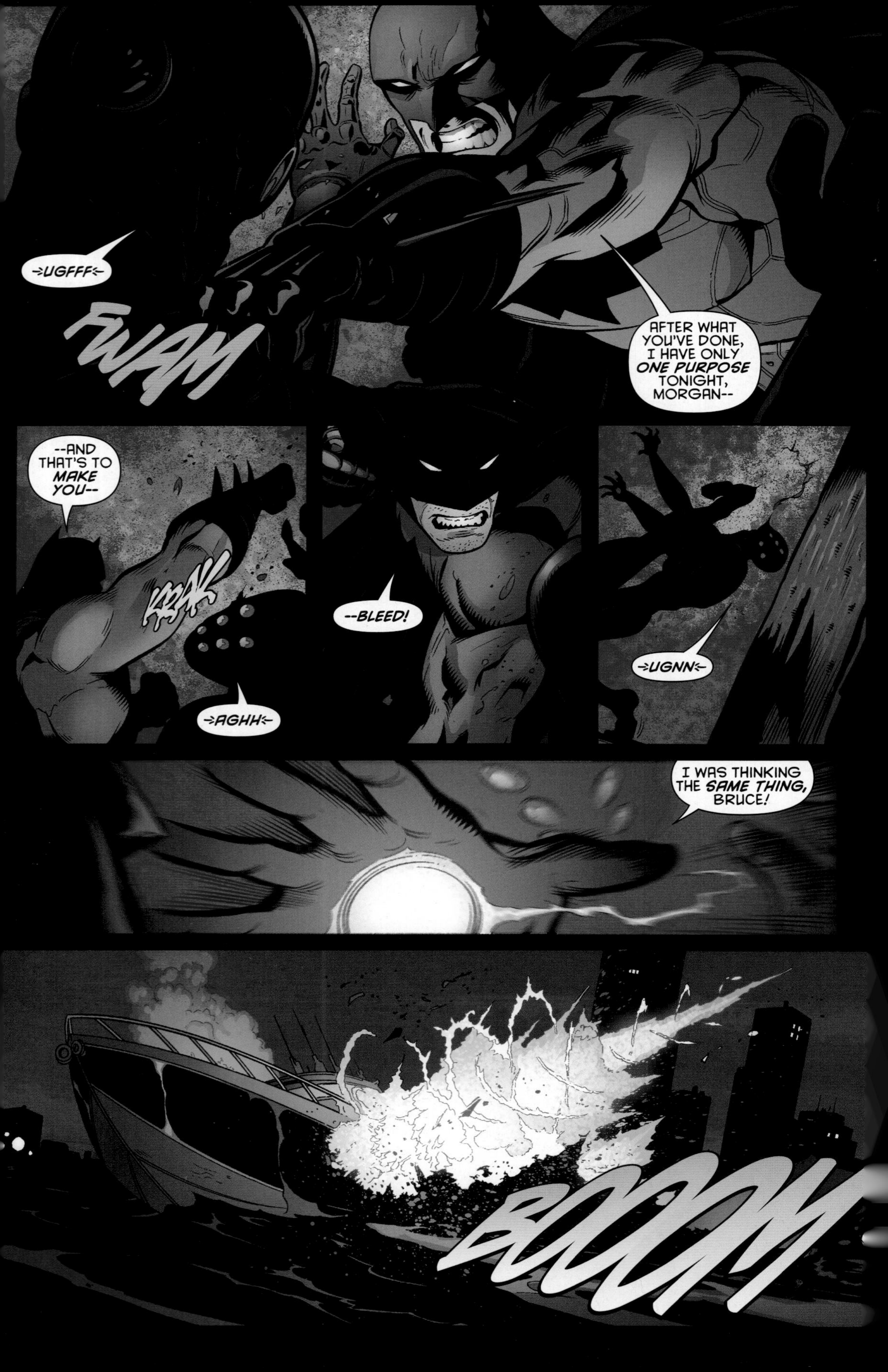

UGFFF
FWAM
AFTER WHAT YOU'VE DONE, I HAVE ONLY ONE PURPOSE TONIGHT, MORGAN--
--AND THAT'S TO MAKE YOU--
KRAK
AGHH
--BLEED!
UGNN
I WAS THINKING THE SAME THING, BRUCE!
BOOM

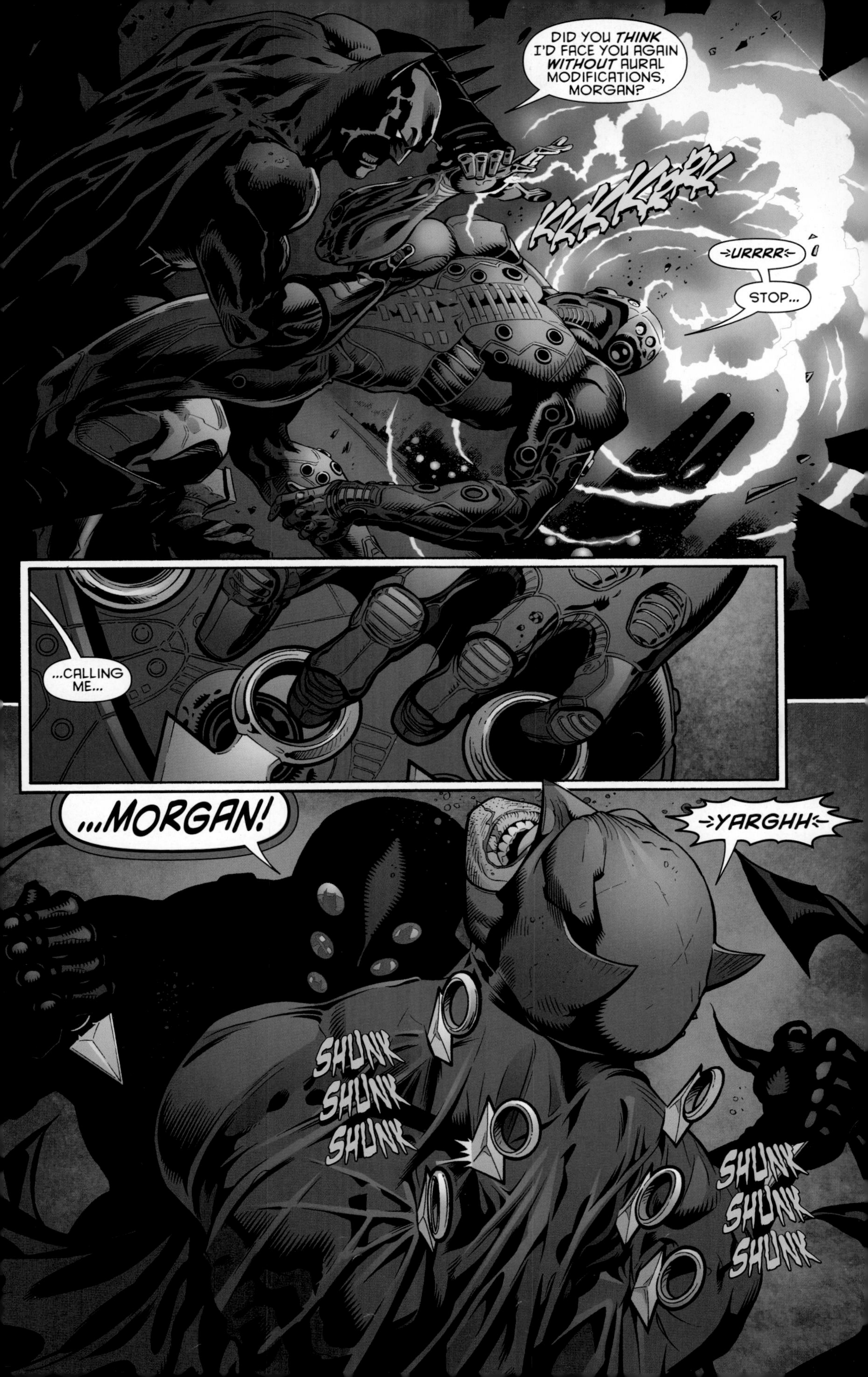
DID YOU THINK I'D FACE YOU AGAIN WITHOUT AURAL MODIFICATIONS, MORGAN?
KKKKKRRK
URRRR
STOP...
...CALLING ME...
...MORGAN!
YARGHH
SHUNK SHUNK SHUNK
SHUNK SHUNK SHUNK

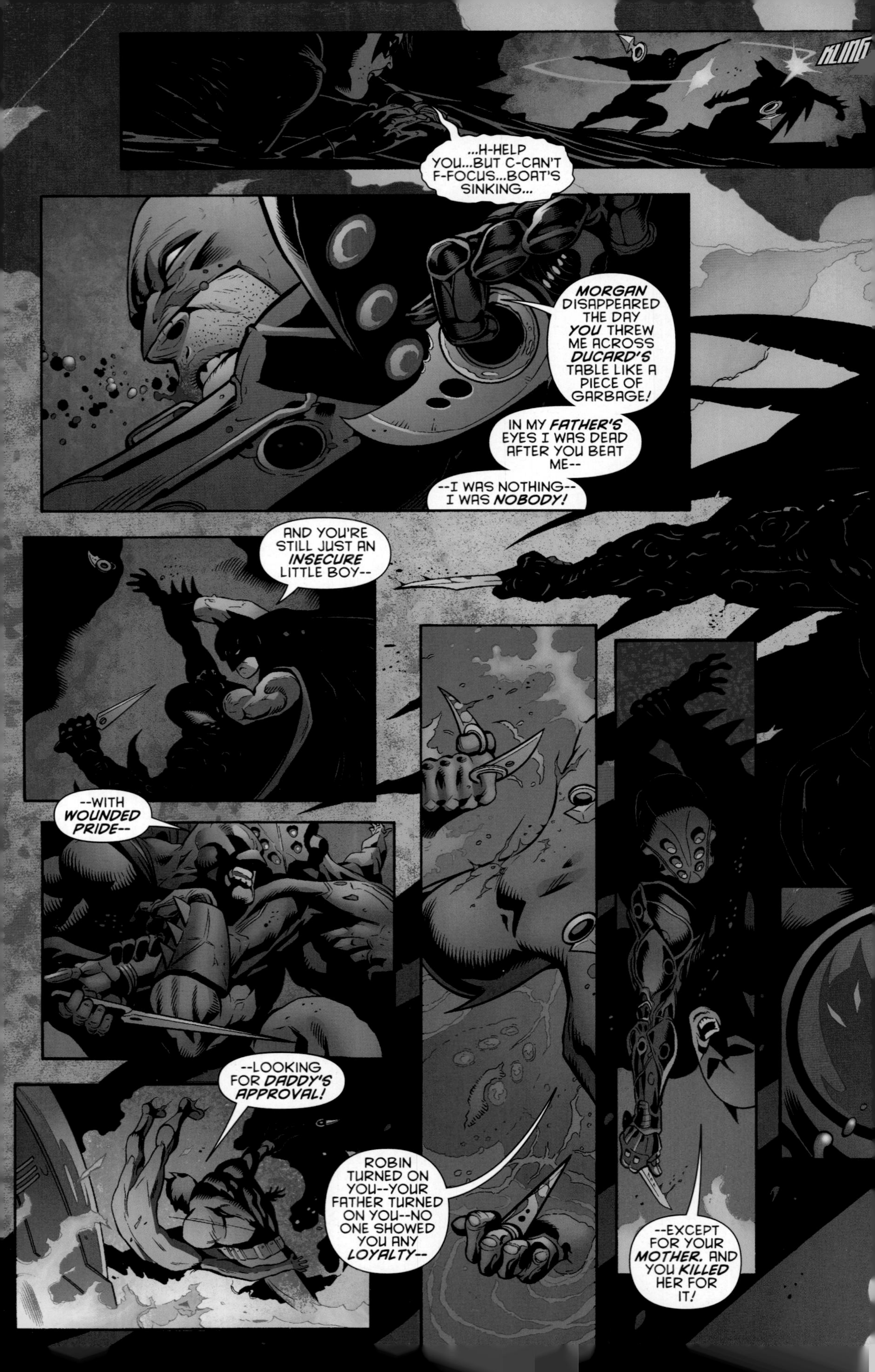
KLING
...H-HELP YOU...BUT C-CAN'T F-FOCUS...BOAT'S SINKING...
MORGAN DISAPPEARED THE DAY YOU THREW ME ACROSS DUCARD'S TABLE LIKE A PIECE OF GARBAGE!
IN MY FATHER'S EYES I WAS DEAD AFTER YOU BEAT ME--
--I WAS NOTHING-- I WAS NOBODY!
AND YOU'RE STILL JUST AN INSECURE LITTLE BOY--
--WITH WOUNDED PRIDE--
--LOOKING FOR DADDY'S APPROVAL!
ROBIN TURNED ON YOU--YOUR FATHER TURNED ON YOU--NO ONE SHOWED YOU ANY LOYALTY--
--EXCEPT FOR YOUR MOTHER. AND YOU KILLED HER FOR IT!

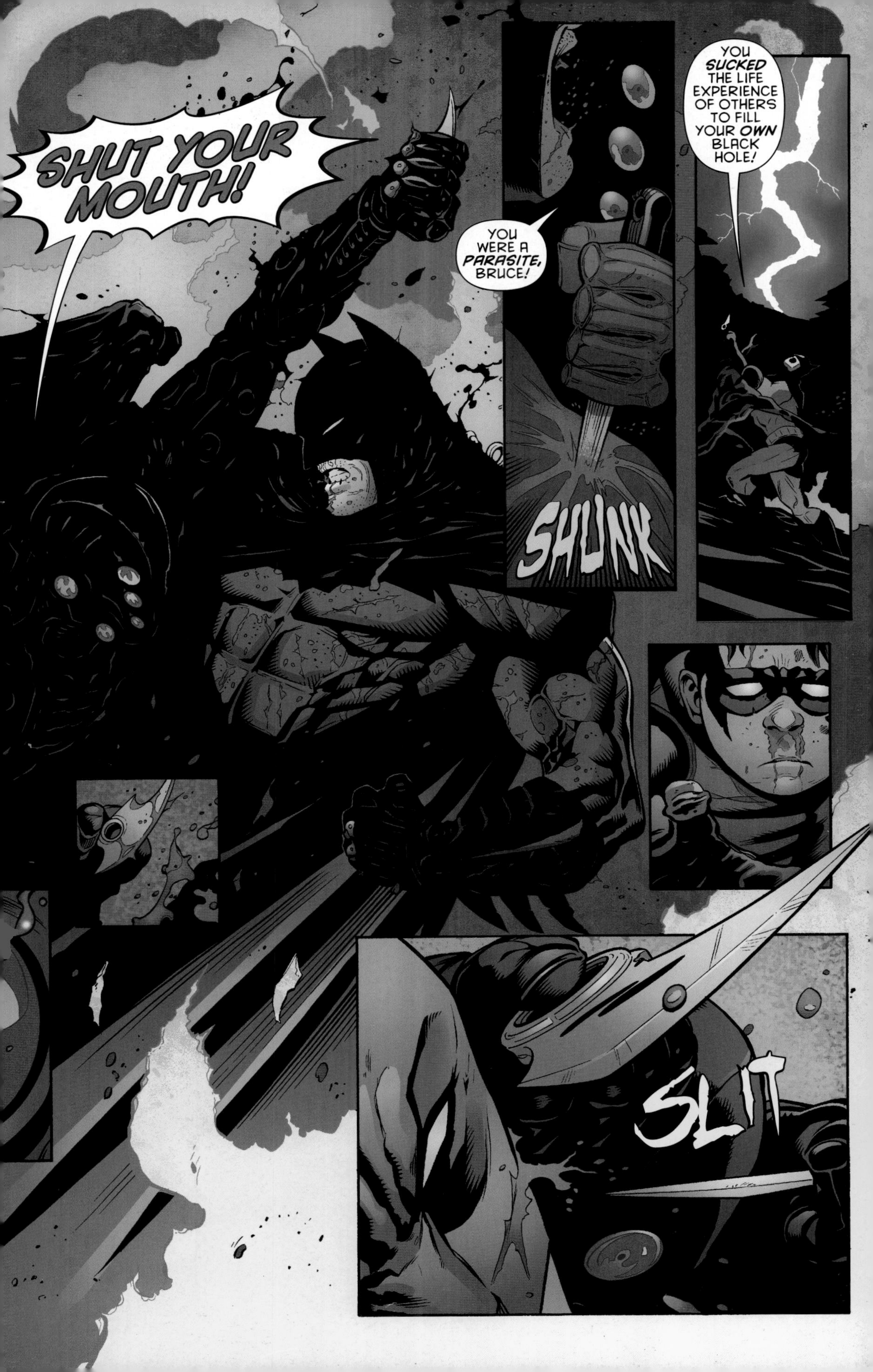
SHUT YOUR MOUTH!
YOU WERE A PARASITE, BRUCE!
SHUNK
YOU SUCKED THE LIFE EXPERIENCE OF OTHERS TO FILL YOUR OWN BLACK HOLE!
SLIT

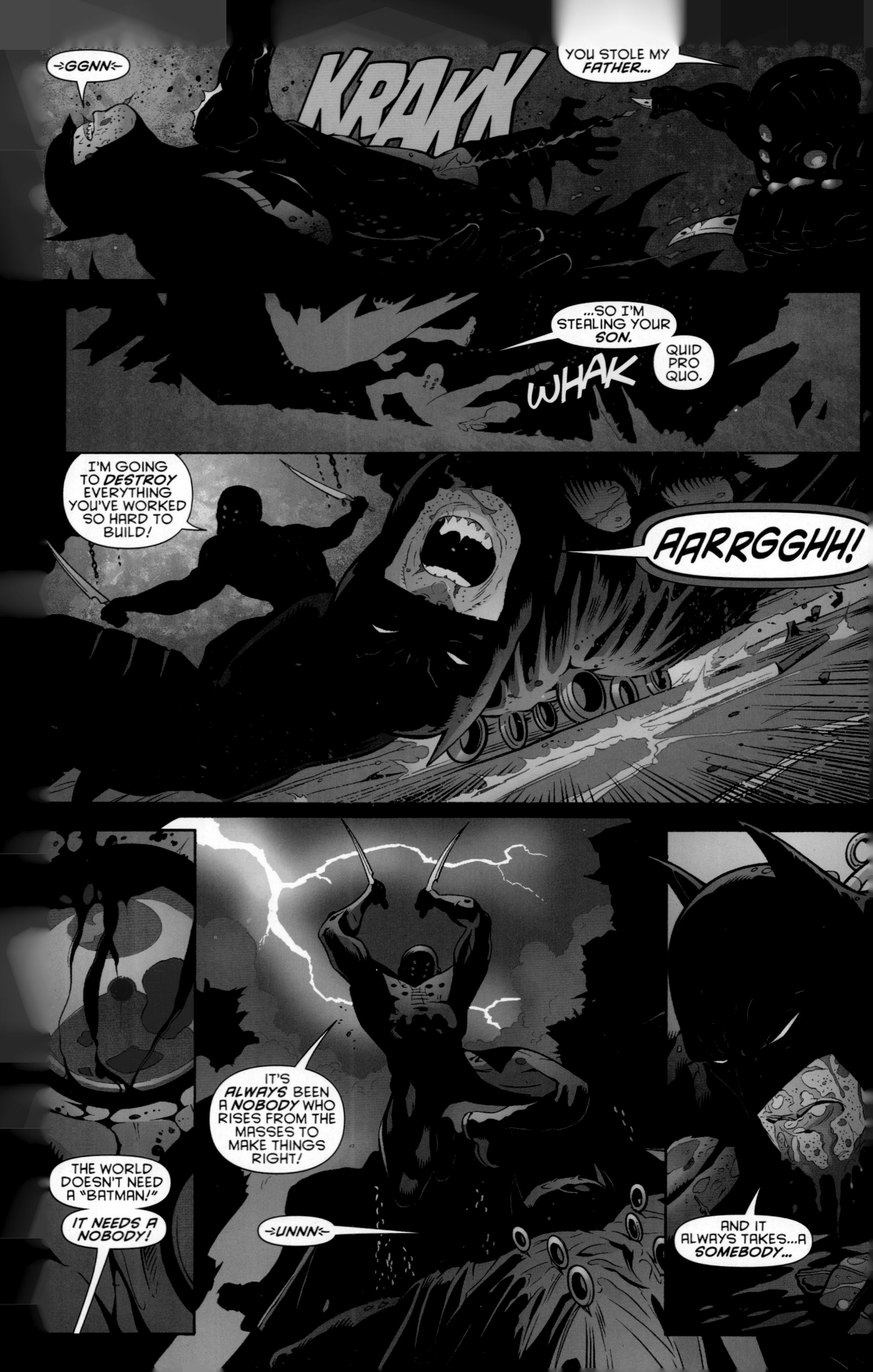

-GGNN-
KRAKK
YOU STOLE MY FATHER...
...SO I'M STEALING YOUR SON.
WHAK
QUID PRO QUO.
I'M GOING TO DESTROY EVERYTHING YOU'VE WORKED SO HARD TO BUILD!
AARRGGHH!
IT'S ALWAYS BEEN A NOBODY WHO RISES FROM THE MASSES TO MAKE THINGS RIGHT!
THE WORLD DOESN'T NEED A "BATMAN!"
IT NEEDS A NOBODY!
-UNNN-
AND IT ALWAYS TAKES...A SOMEBODY...

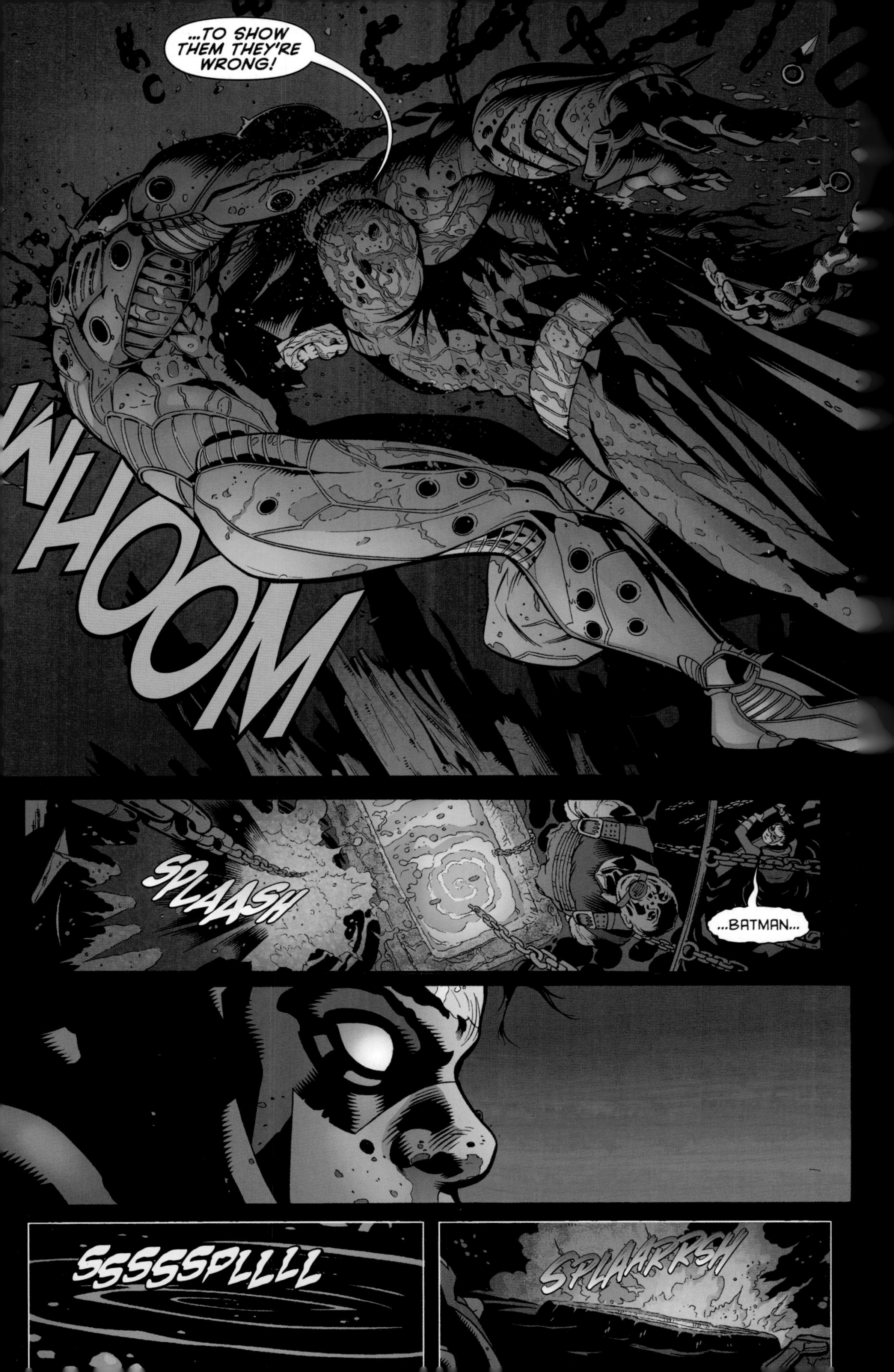
...TO SHOW THEM THEY'RE WRONG!
WHOOM
SPLAASH
...BATMAN...
SSSSSPLLLL
SPLAARRSH

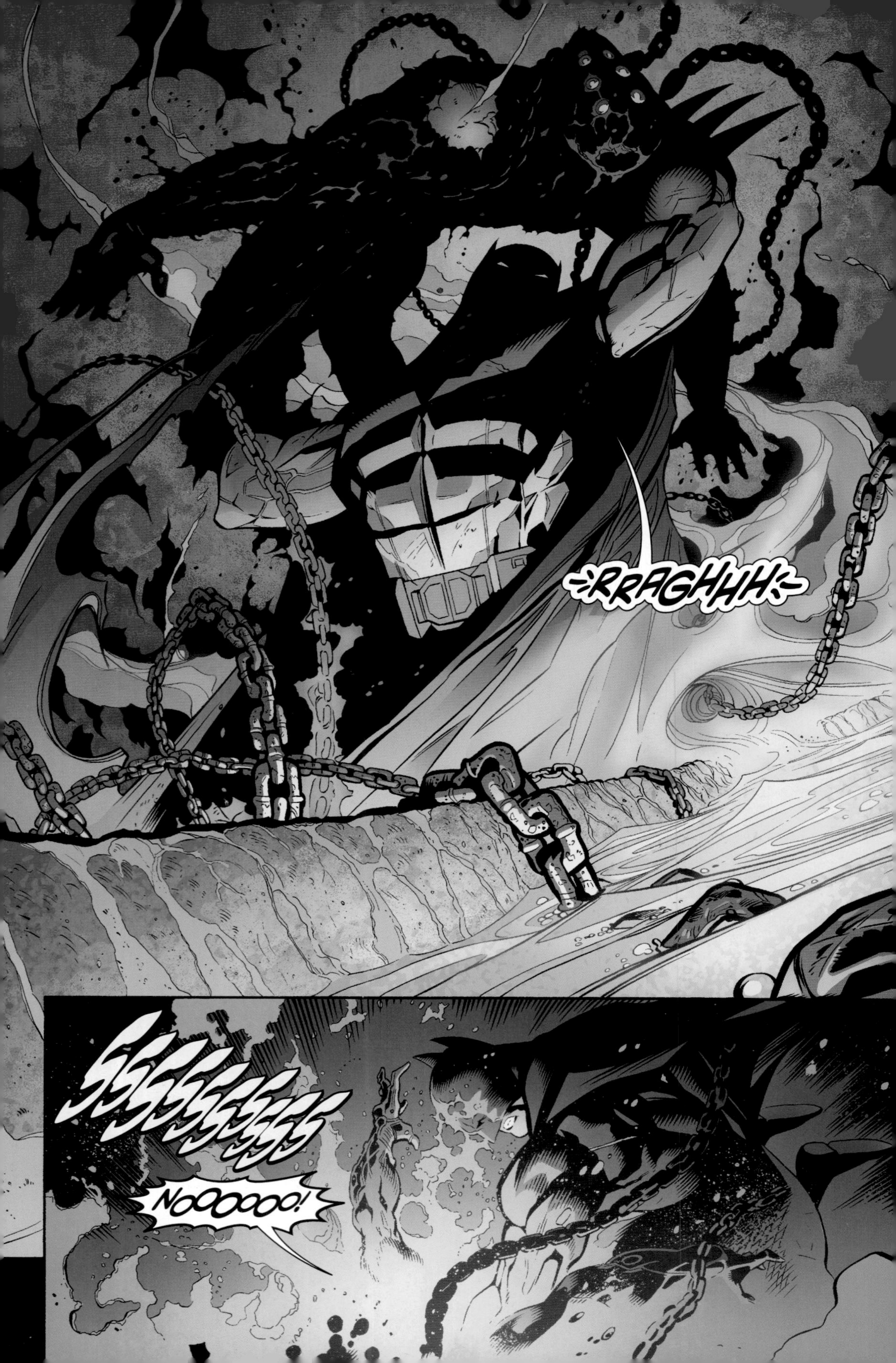
RRAGHHH
SSSSSSSSSSS
NOOOOOO!

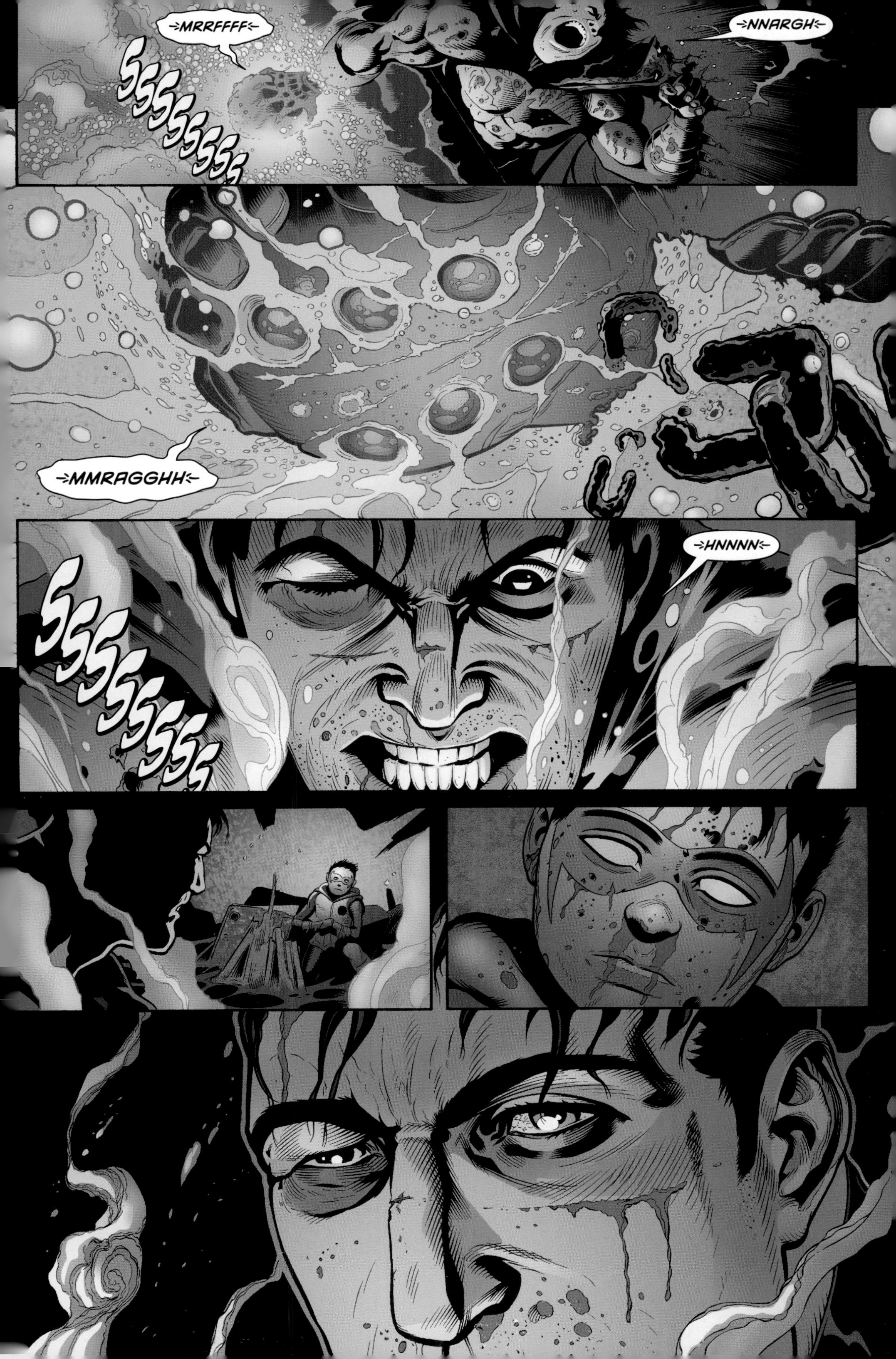
-MRRFFFF-
SSSSSSSSS
-NNARGH-
-MMRAGGHH-
SSSSSSSSS
-HNNNN-

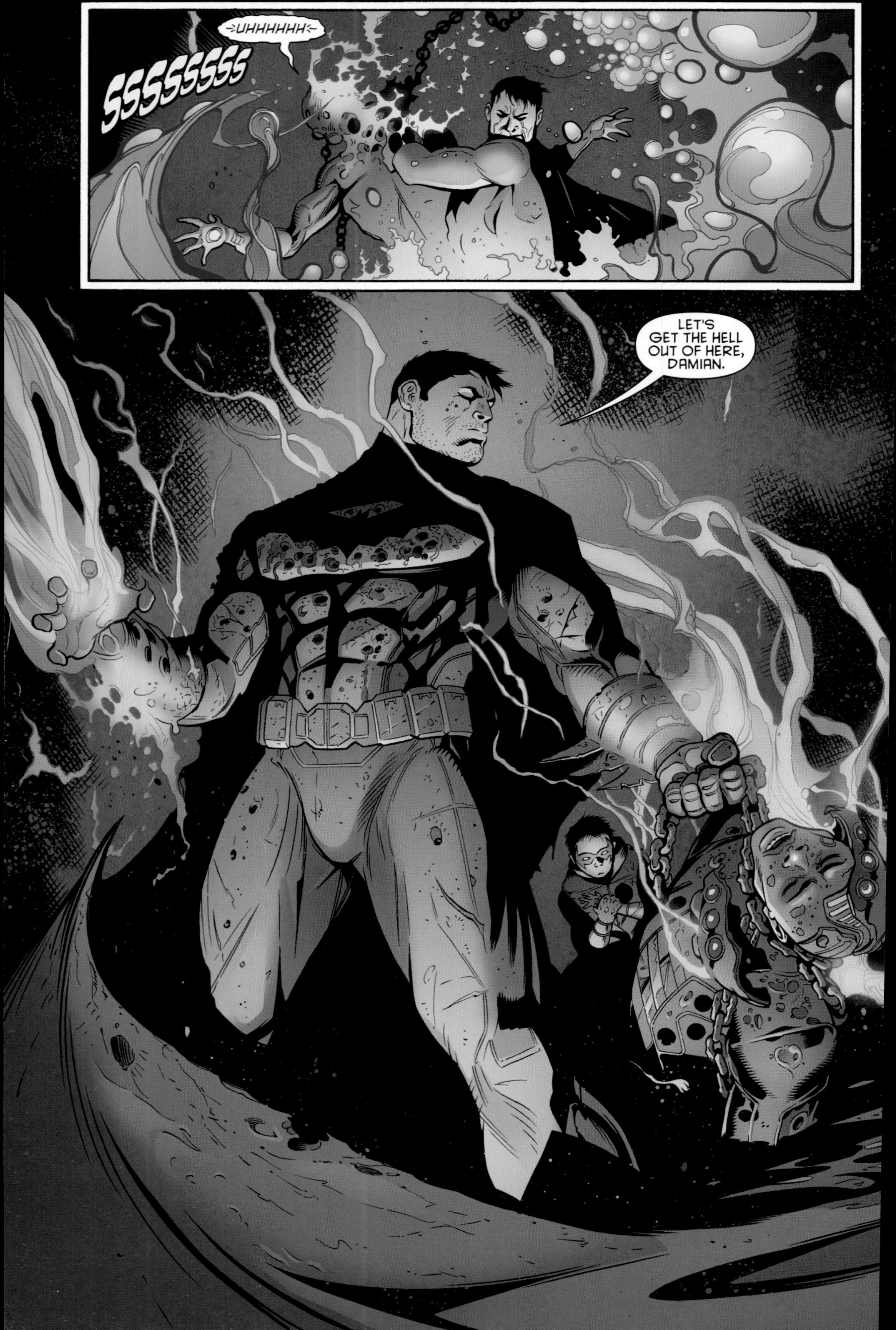

UHHHHHH
SSSSSSSS
LET'S GET THE HELL OUT OF HERE, DAMIAN.

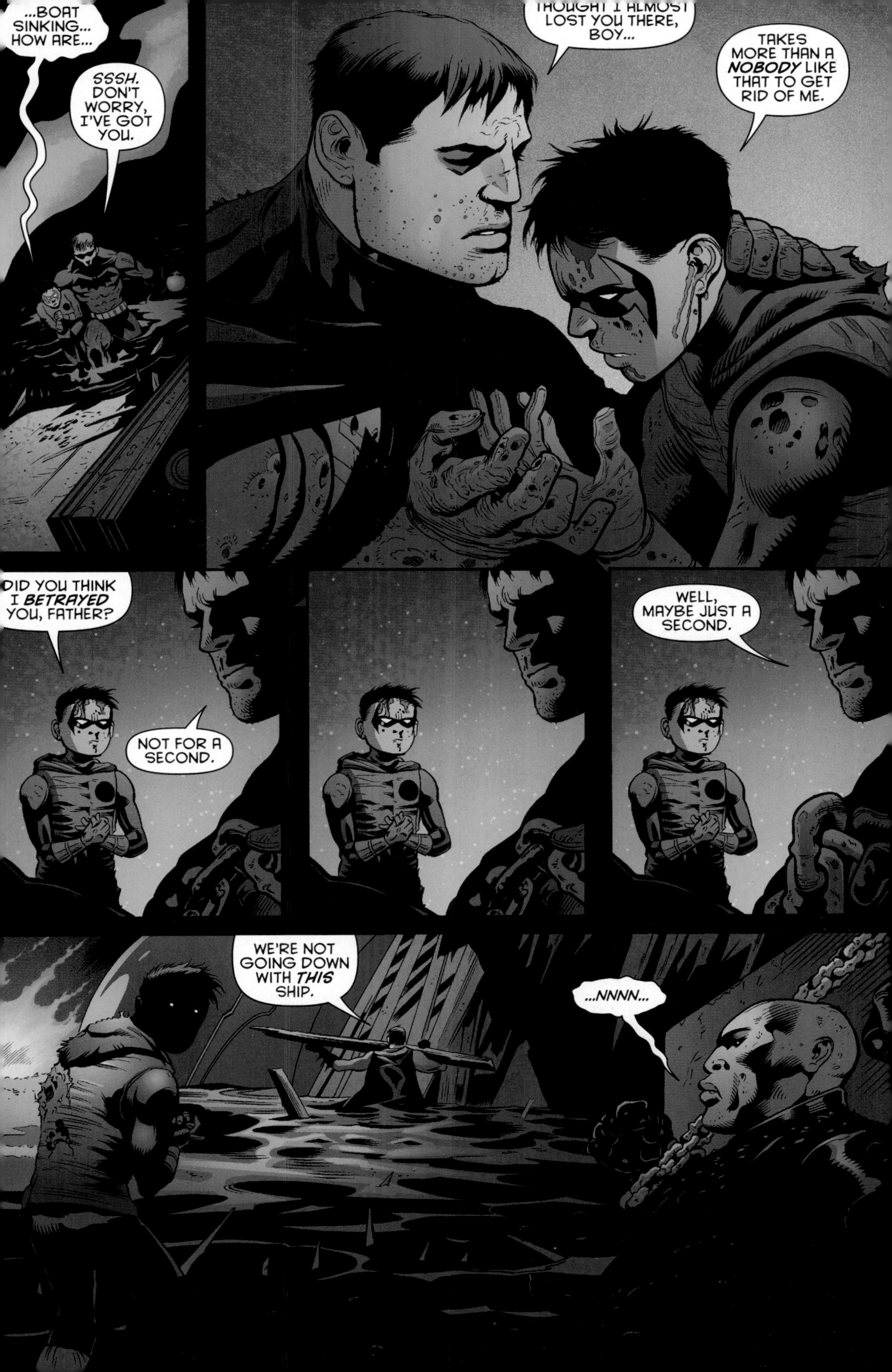
...BOAT SINKING... HOW ARE...
SSSH. DON'T WORRY, I'VE GOT YOU.
THOUGHT I ALMOST LOST YOU THERE, BOY...
TAKES MORE THAN A NOBODY LIKE THAT TO GET RID OF ME.
DID YOU THINK I BETRAYED YOU, FATHER?
NOT FOR A SECOND.
WELL, MAYBE JUST A SECOND.
WE'RE NOT GOING DOWN WITH THIS SHIP.
...NNNN...

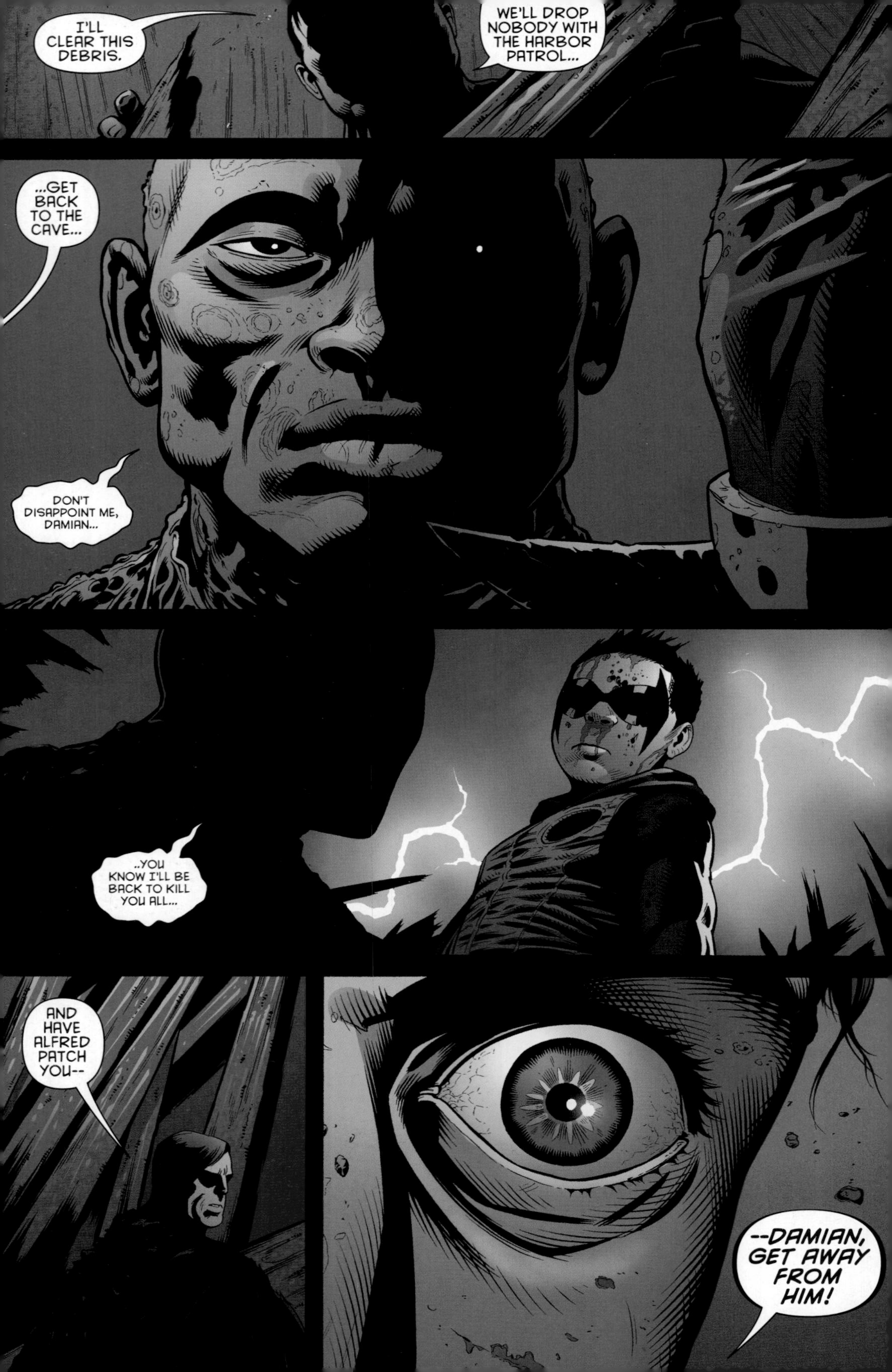
I'LL CLEAR THIS DEBRIS.
WE'LL DROP NOBODY WITH THE HARBOR PATROL...
...GET BACK TO THE CAVE...
DON'T DISAPPOINT ME, DAMIAN...
..YOU KNOW I'LL BE BACK TO KILL YOU ALL...
AND HAVE ALFRED PATCH YOU--
--DAMIAN, GET AWAY FROM HIM!

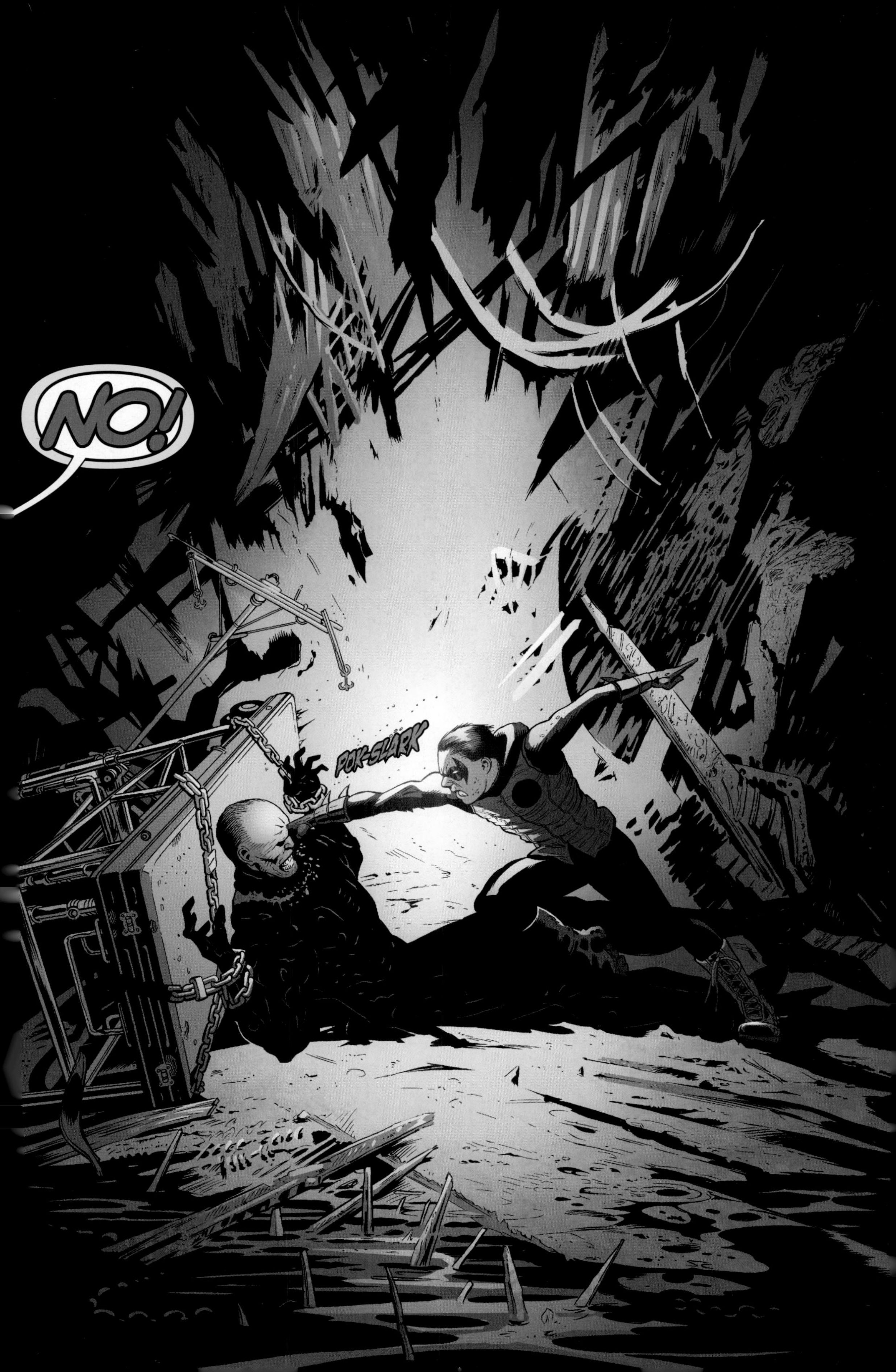
NO!
POK-SLARK

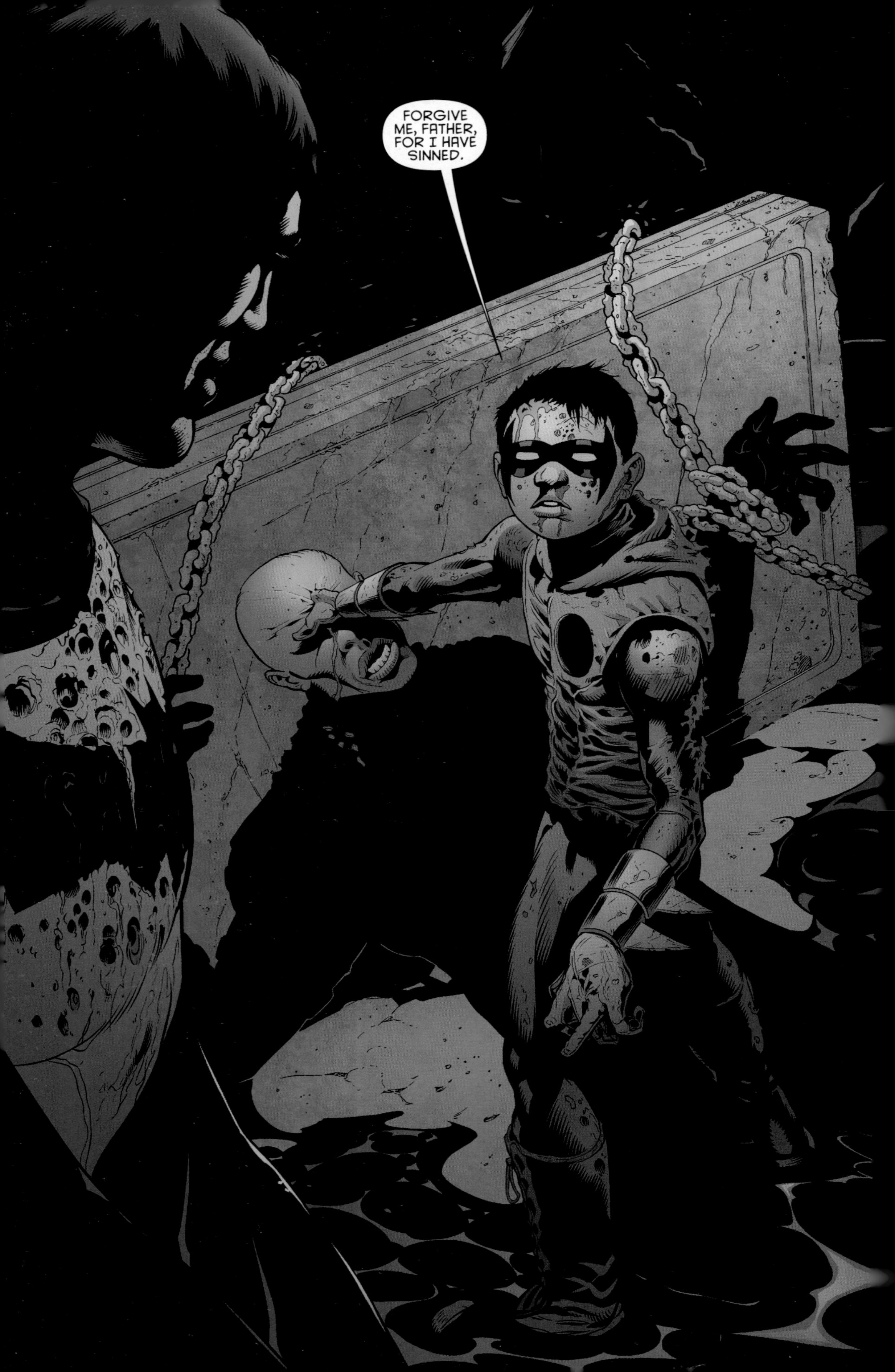
FORGIVE ME, FATHER, FOR I HAVE SINNED.

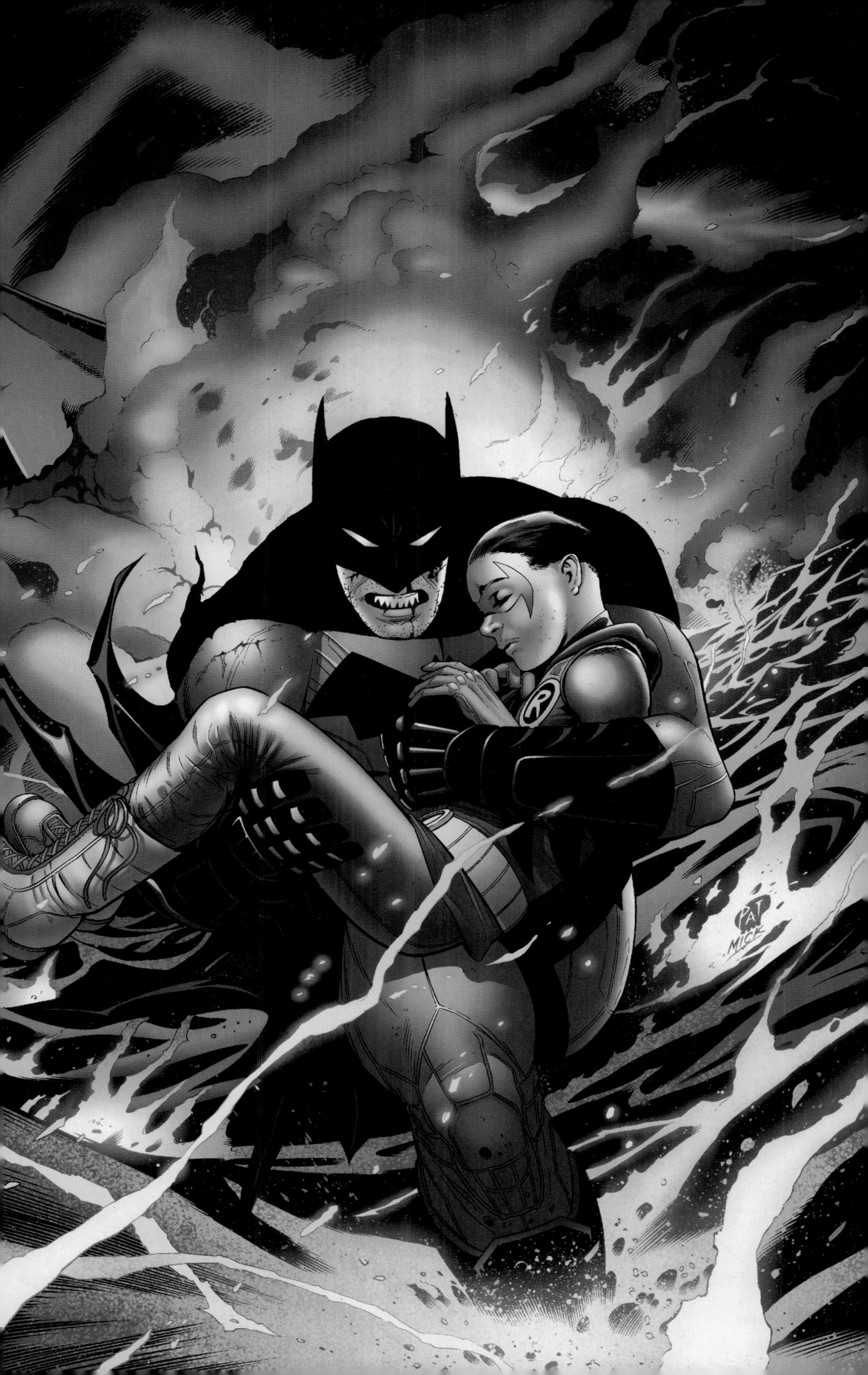

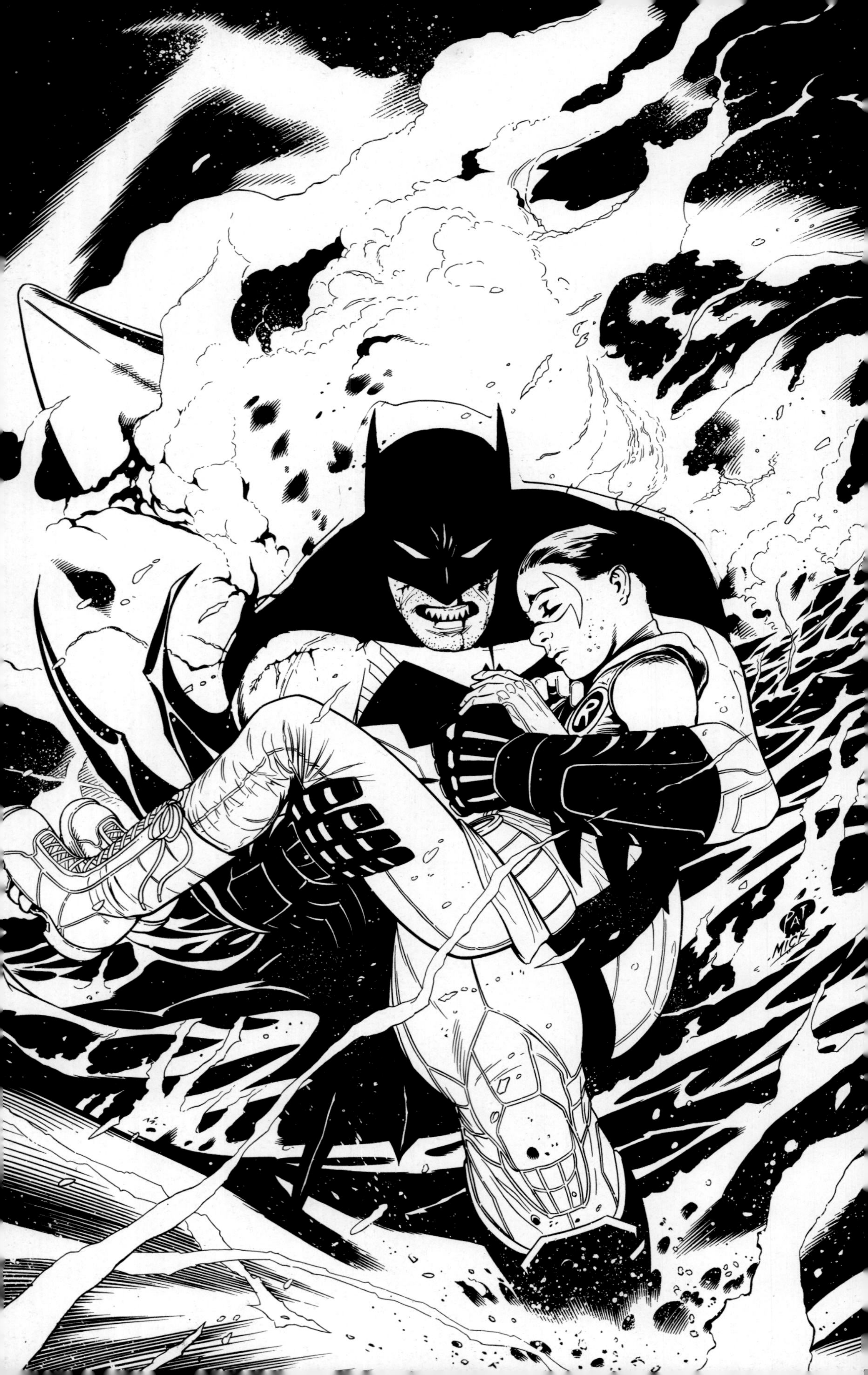
PAT
MICK

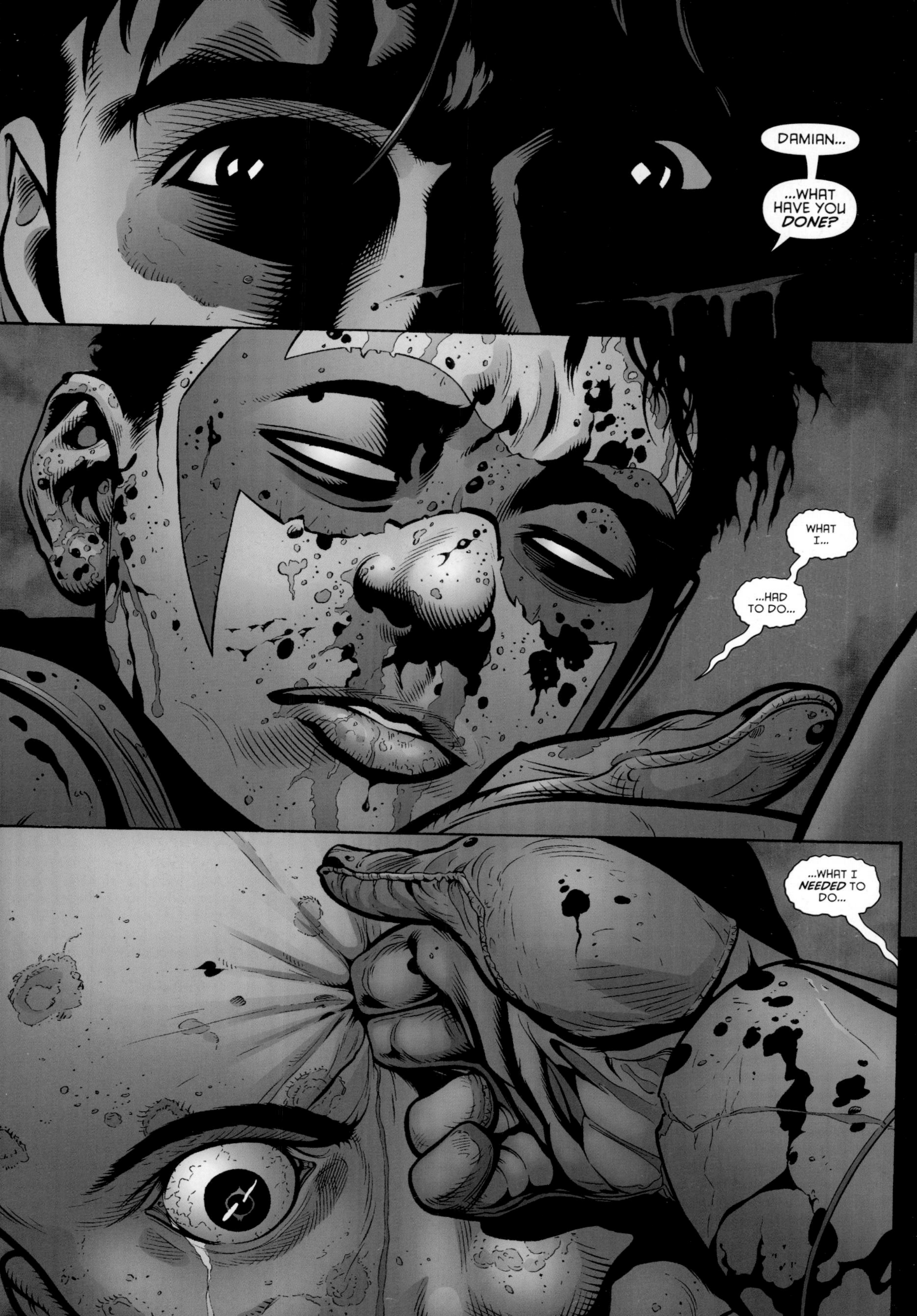
DAMIAN...
...WHAT HAVE YOU DONE?
WHAT I...
...HAD TO DO...
...WHAT I NEEDED TO DO...

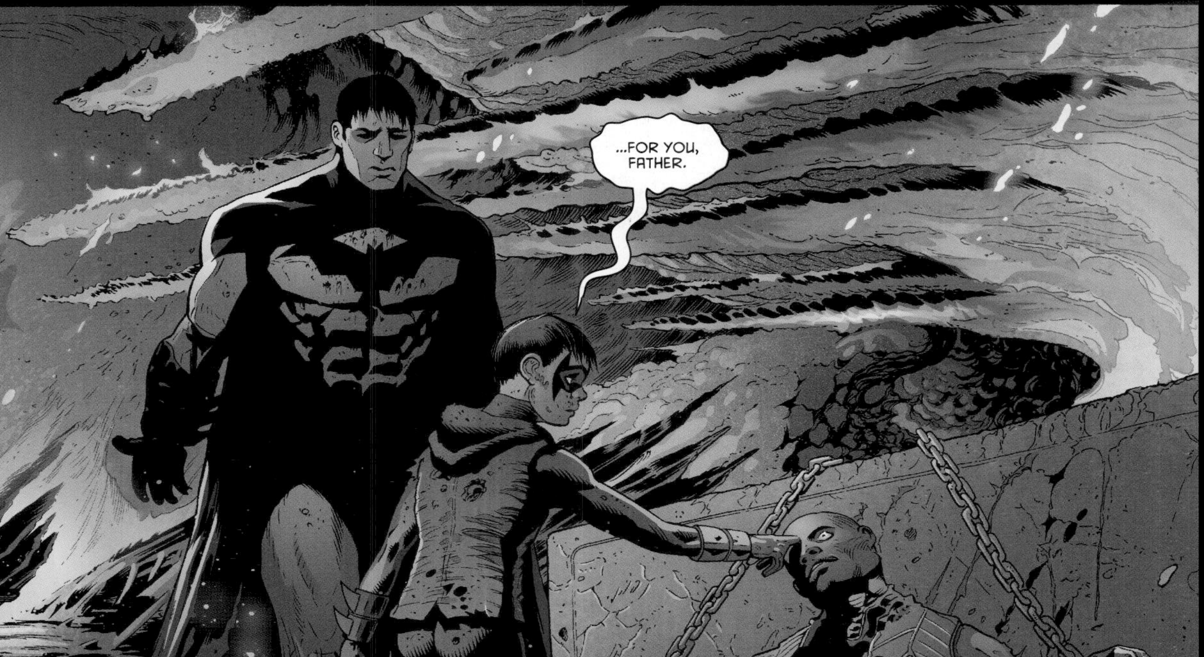
...FOR YOU, FATHER.

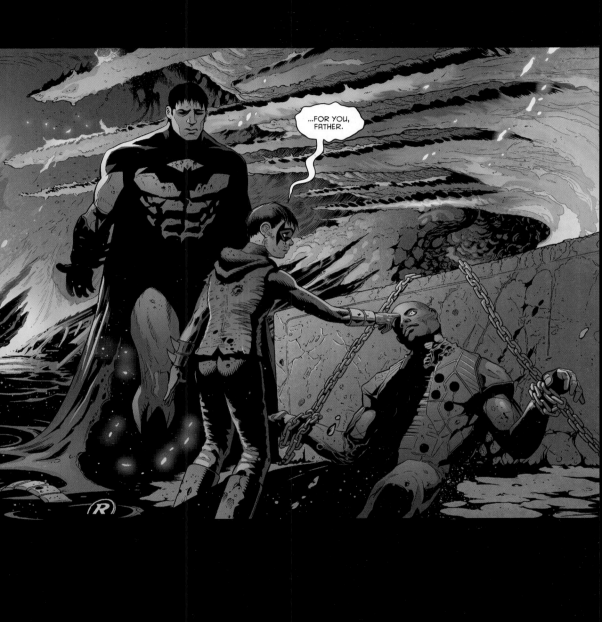

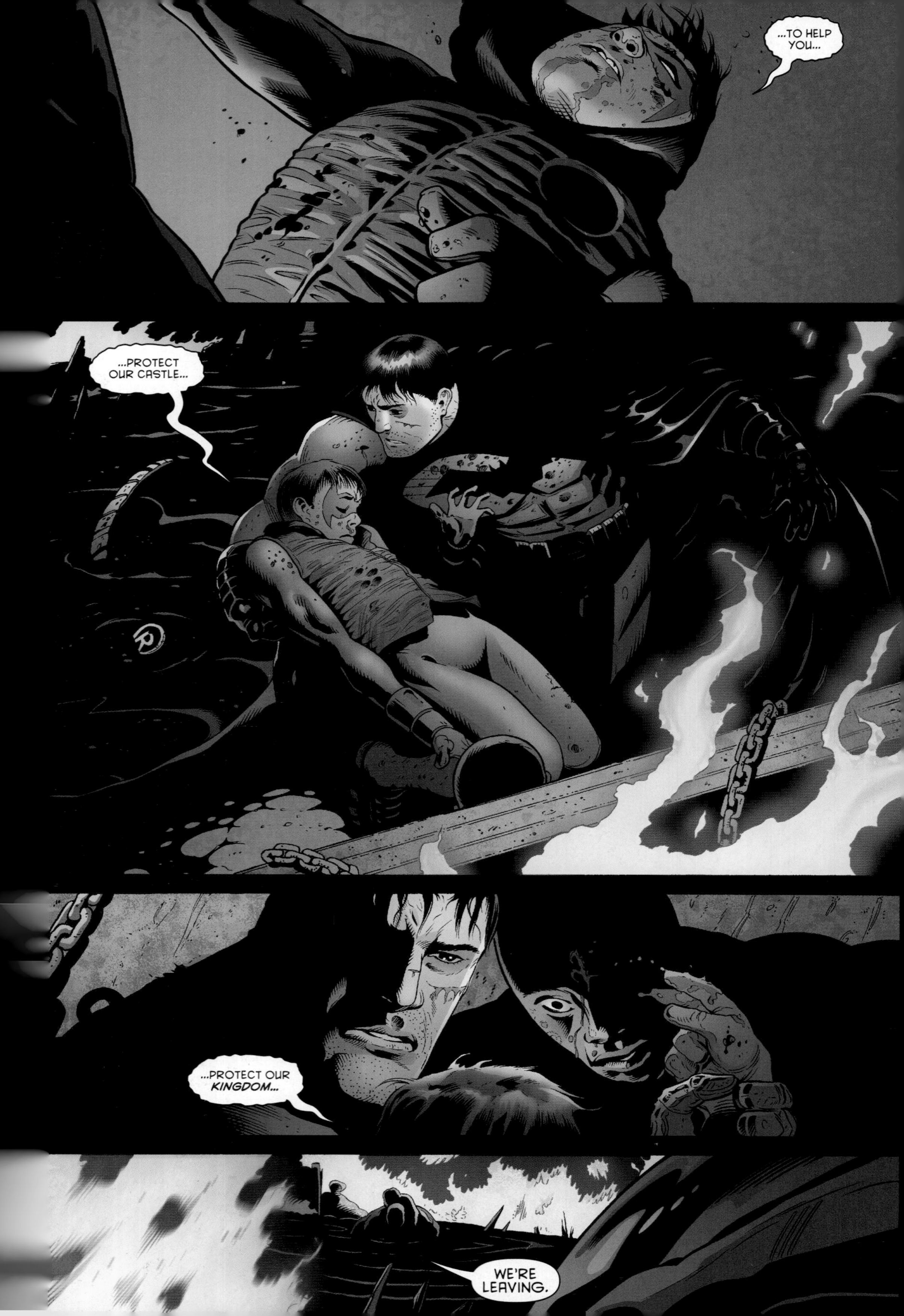
...TO HELP YOU...
...PROTECT OUR CASTLE...
...PROTECT OUR KINGDOM...
WE'RE LEAVING.

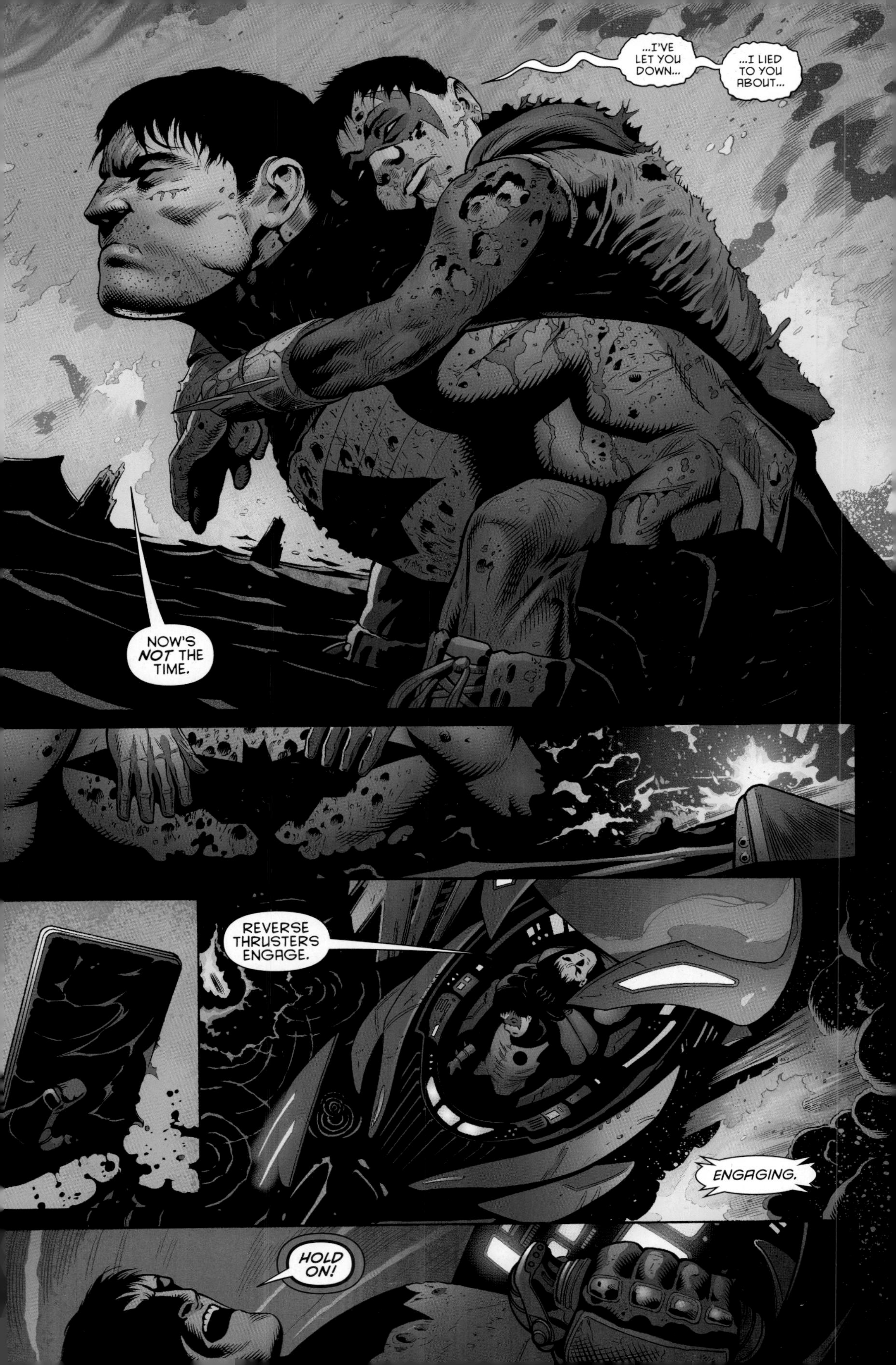
...I'VE LET YOU DOWN...
...I LIED TO YOU ABOUT...
NOW'S *NOT* THE TIME.
REVERSE THRUSTERS ENGAGE.
ENGAGING.
HOLD ON!

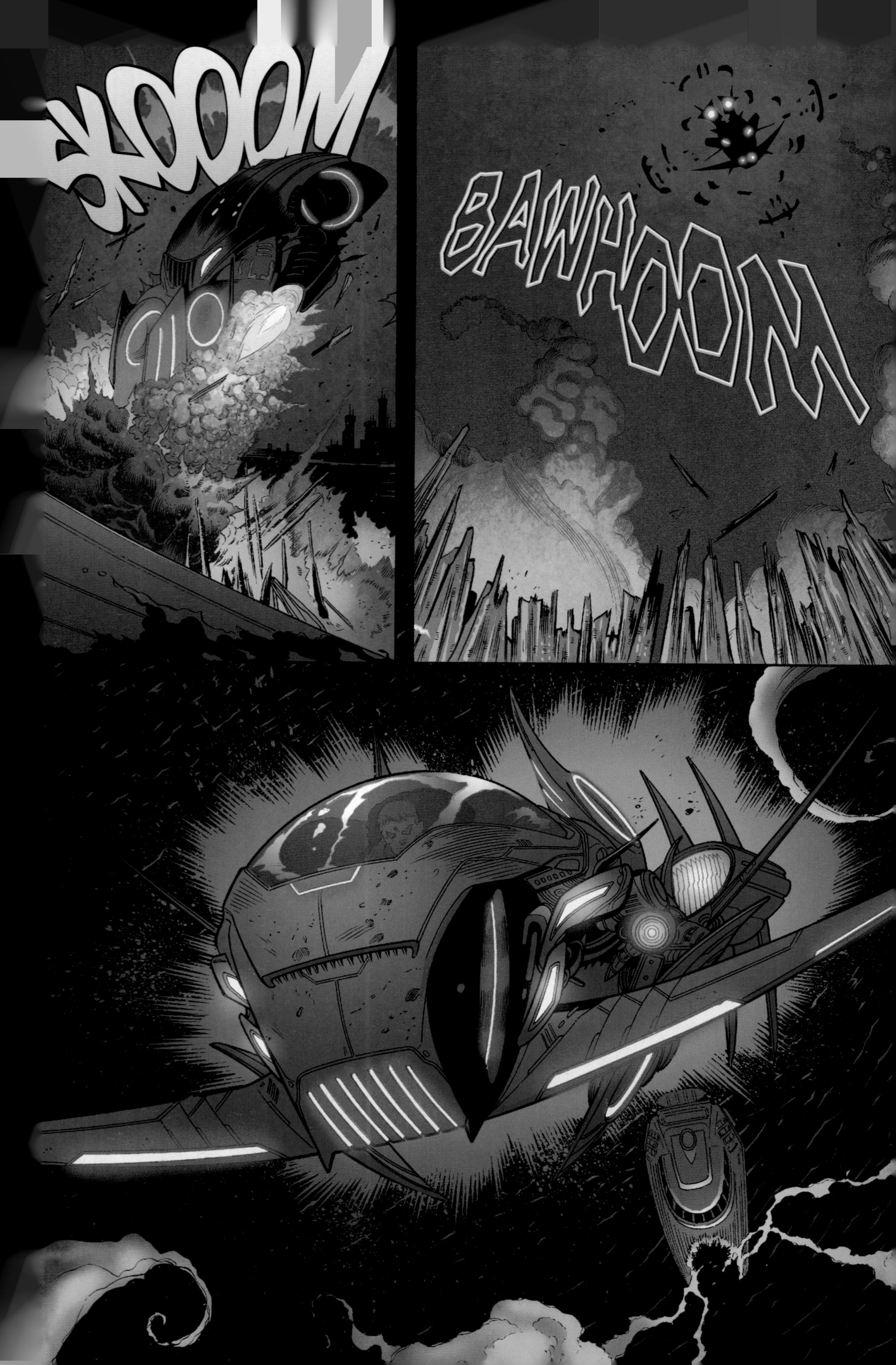
SKOOOM
BAWHOOM

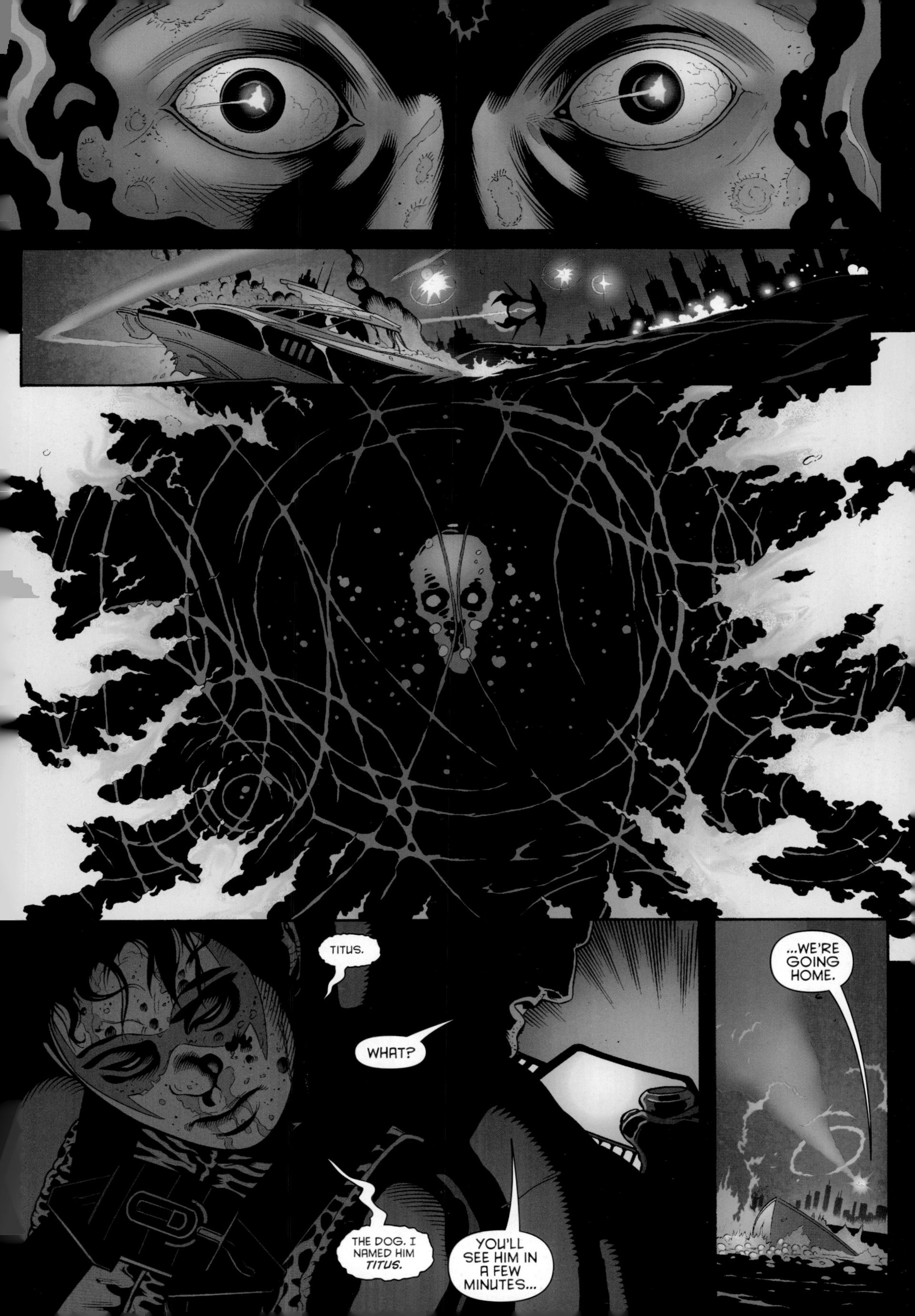
TITUS.
WHAT?
THE DOG. I NAMED HIM *TITUS*.
YOU'LL SEE HIM IN A FEW MINUTES...
...WE'RE GOING HOME.

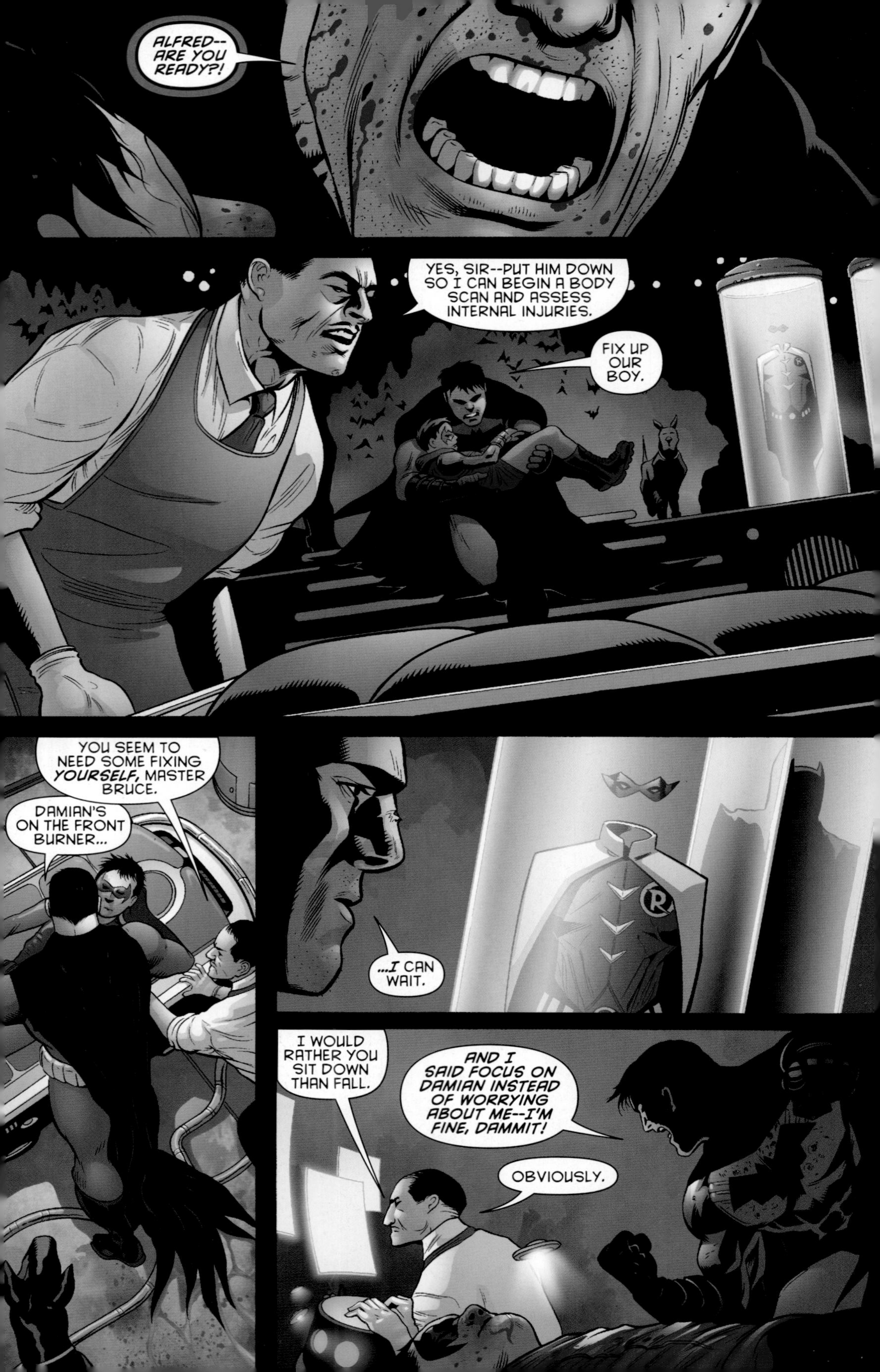
ALFRED-- ARE YOU READY?!
YES, SIR--PUT HIM DOWN SO I CAN BEGIN A BODY SCAN AND ASSESS INTERNAL INJURIES.
FIX UP OUR BOY.
YOU SEEM TO NEED SOME FIXING *YOURSELF*, MASTER BRUCE.
DAMIAN'S ON THE FRONT BURNER...
...*I* CAN WAIT.
I WOULD RATHER YOU SIT DOWN THAN FALL.
AND I SAID FOCUS ON DAMIAN INSTEAD OF WORRYING ABOUT ME--I'M FINE, DAMMIT!
OBVIOUSLY.

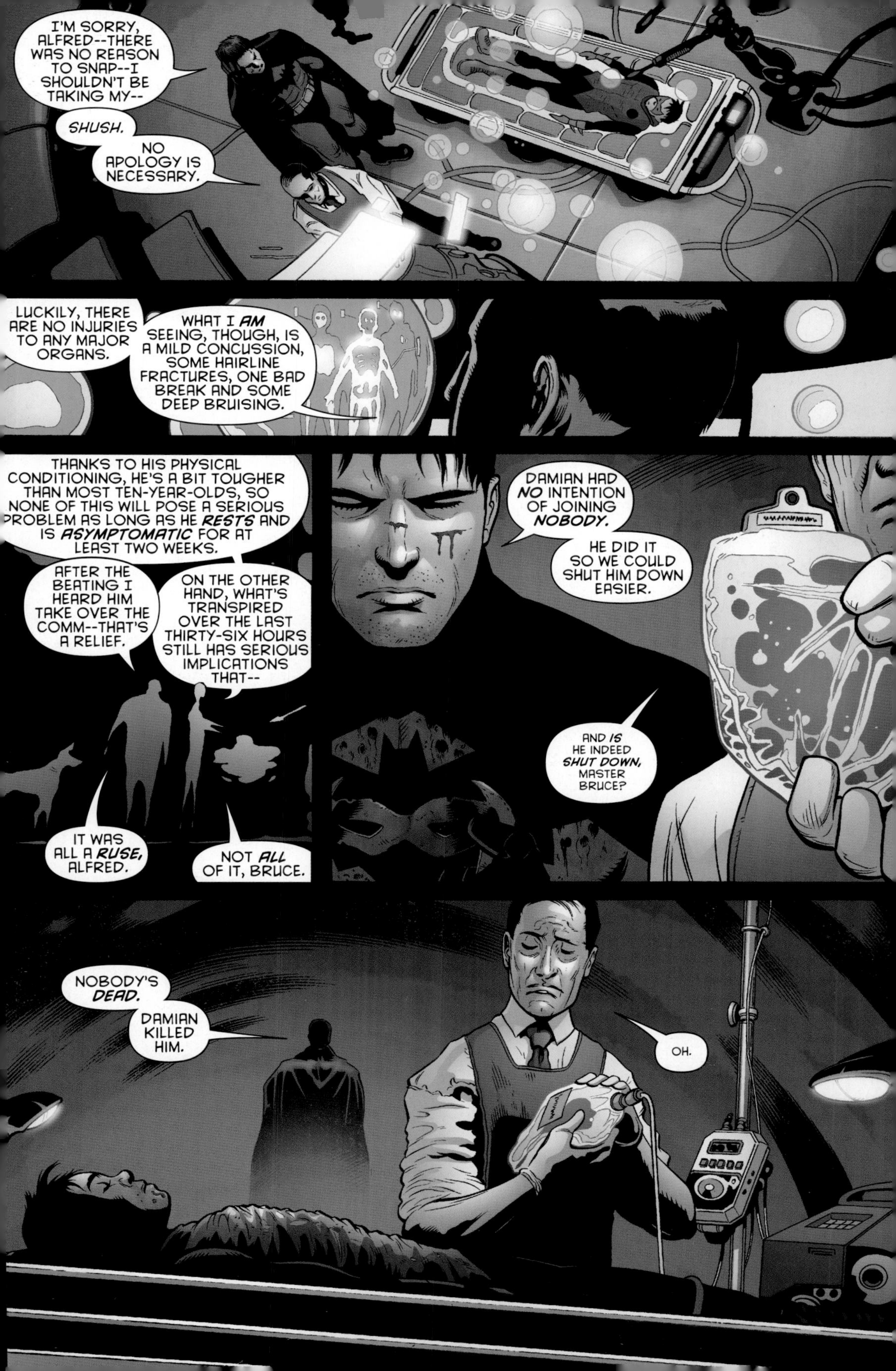
I'M SORRY, ALFRED--THERE WAS NO REASON TO SNAP--I SHOULDN'T BE TAKING MY--
SHUSH.
NO APOLOGY IS NECESSARY.
LUCKILY, THERE ARE NO INJURIES TO ANY MAJOR ORGANS.
WHAT I AM SEEING, THOUGH, IS A MILD CONCUSSION, SOME HAIRLINE FRACTURES, ONE BAD BREAK AND SOME DEEP BRUISING.
THANKS TO HIS PHYSICAL CONDITIONING, HE'S A BIT TOUGHER THAN MOST TEN-YEAR-OLDS, SO NONE OF THIS WILL POSE A SERIOUS PROBLEM AS LONG AS HE RESTS AND IS ASYMPTOMATIC FOR AT LEAST TWO WEEKS.
AFTER THE BEATING I HEARD HIM TAKE OVER THE COMM--THAT'S A RELIEF.
ON THE OTHER HAND, WHAT'S TRANSPIRED OVER THE LAST THIRTY-SIX HOURS STILL HAS SERIOUS IMPLICATIONS THAT--
IT WAS ALL A RUSE, ALFRED.
NOT ALL OF IT, BRUCE.
DAMIAN HAD NO INTENTION OF JOINING NOBODY.
HE DID IT SO WE COULD SHUT HIM DOWN EASIER.
AND IS HE INDEED SHUT DOWN, MASTER BRUCE?
NOBODY'S DEAD.
DAMIAN KILLED HIM.
OH.

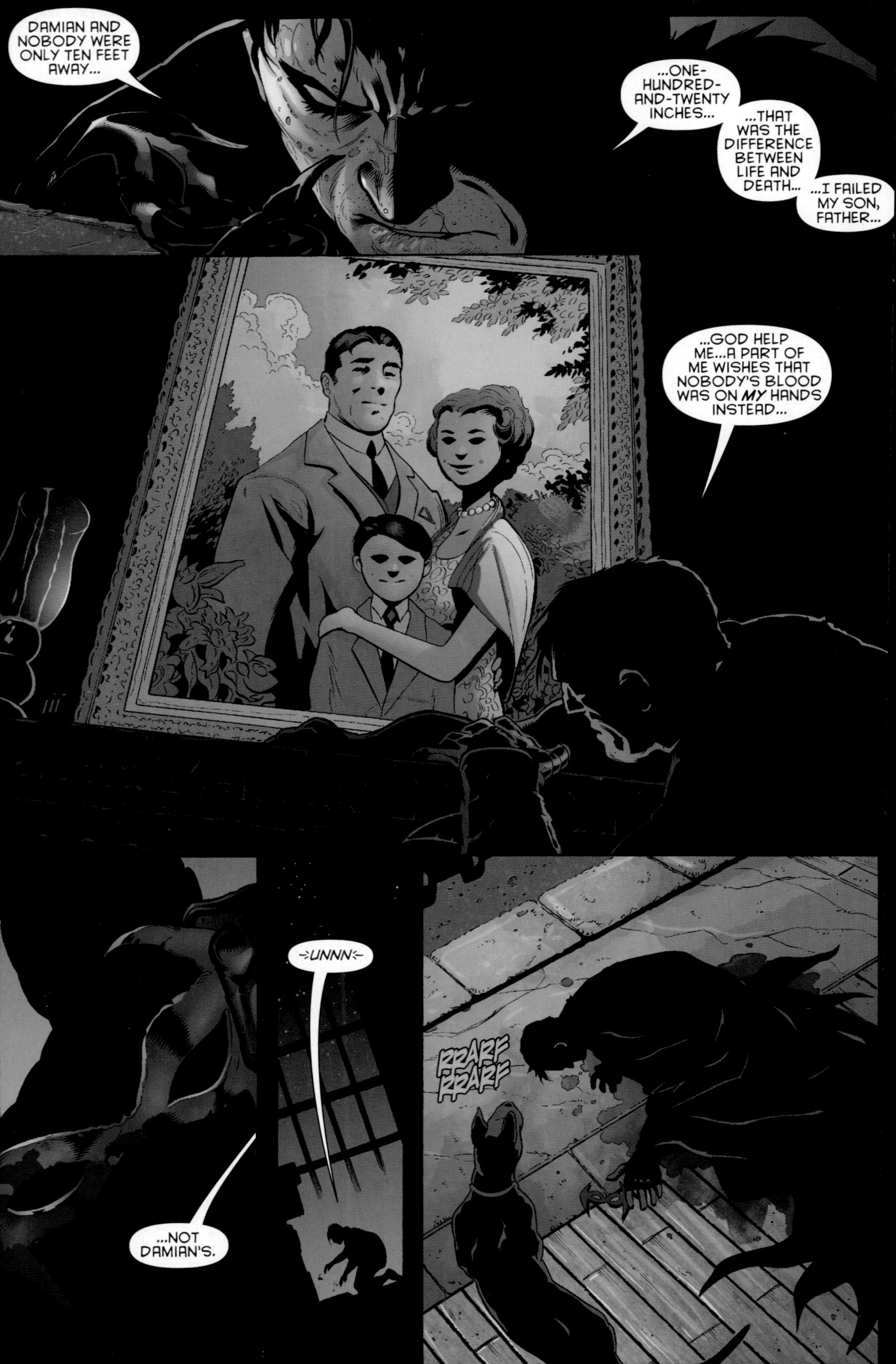
DAMIAN AND NOBODY WERE ONLY TEN FEET AWAY...
...ONE-HUNDRED-AND-TWENTY INCHES...
...THAT WAS THE DIFFERENCE BETWEEN LIFE AND DEATH...
...I FAILED MY SON, FATHER...
...GOD HELP ME...A PART OF ME WISHES THAT NOBODY'S BLOOD WAS ON *MY* HANDS INSTEAD...
...NOT DAMIAN'S.
-UNNN-
RRARF RRARF

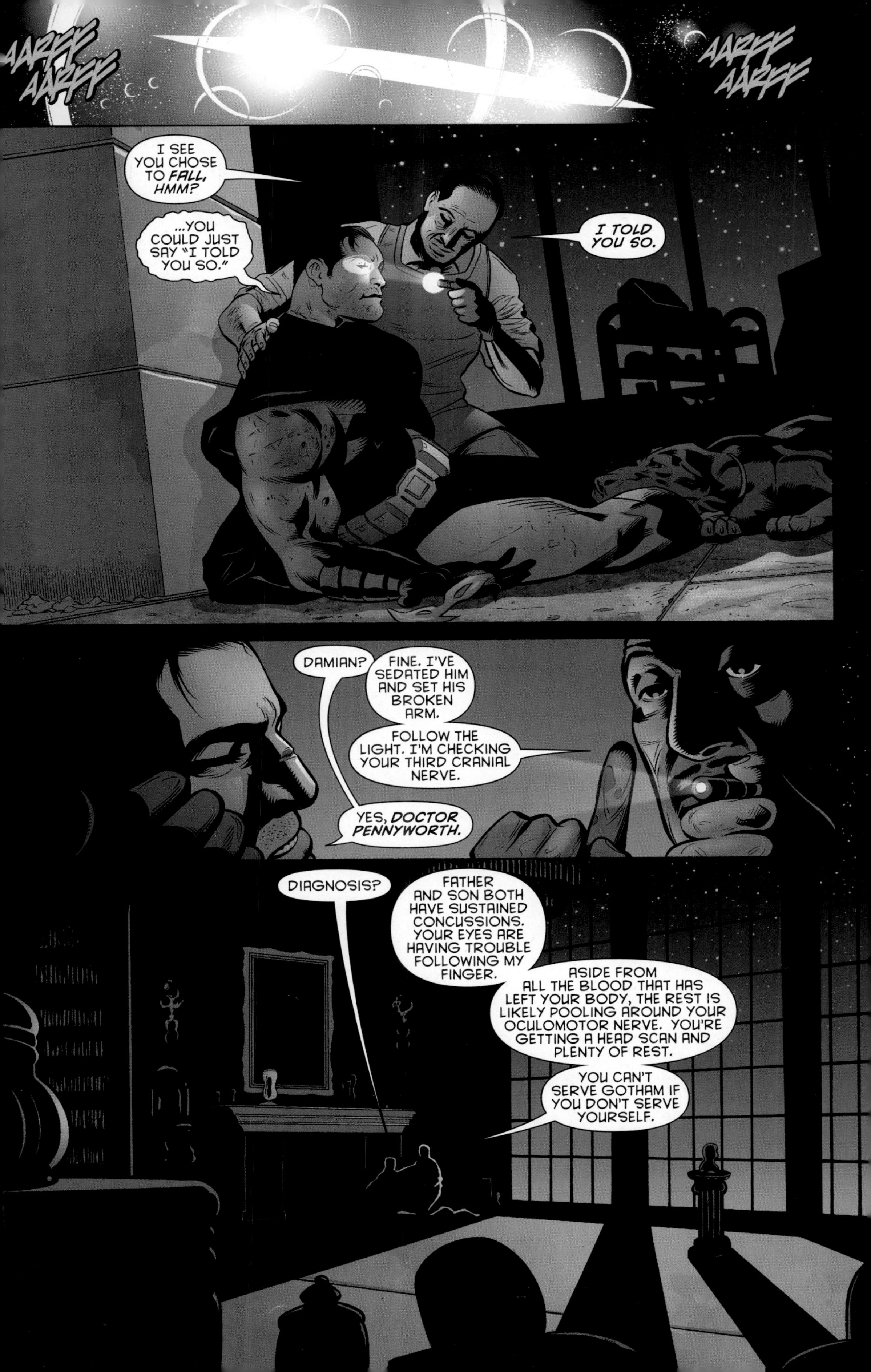
AARFF AARFF
AARFF AARFF
I SEE YOU CHOSE TO FALL, HMM?
...YOU COULD JUST SAY "I TOLD YOU SO."
I TOLD YOU SO.
DAMIAN?
FINE. I'VE SEDATED HIM AND SET HIS BROKEN ARM.
FOLLOW THE LIGHT. I'M CHECKING YOUR THIRD CRANIAL NERVE.
YES, DOCTOR PENNYWORTH.
DIAGNOSIS?
FATHER AND SON BOTH HAVE SUSTAINED CONCUSSIONS. YOUR EYES ARE HAVING TROUBLE FOLLOWING MY FINGER.
ASIDE FROM ALL THE BLOOD THAT HAS LEFT YOUR BODY, THE REST IS LIKELY POOLING AROUND YOUR OCULOMOTOR NERVE. YOU'RE GETTING A HEAD SCAN AND PLENTY OF REST.
YOU CAN'T SERVE GOTHAM IF YOU DON'T SERVE YOURSELF.

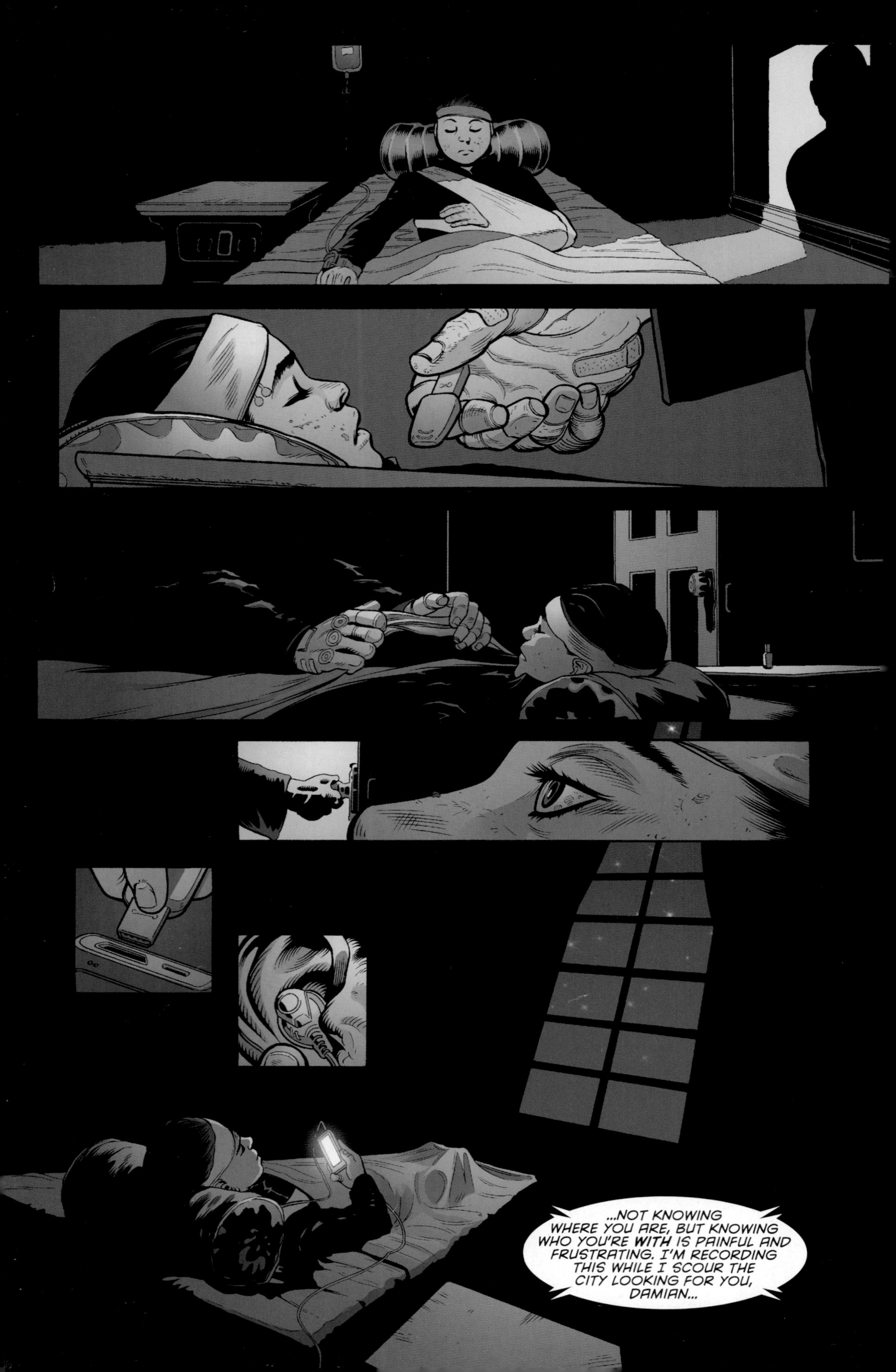
...NOT KNOWING WHERE YOU ARE, BUT KNOWING WHO YOU'RE WITH IS PAINFUL AND FRUSTRATING. I'M RECORDING THIS WHILE I SCOUR THE CITY LOOKING FOR YOU, DAMIAN...

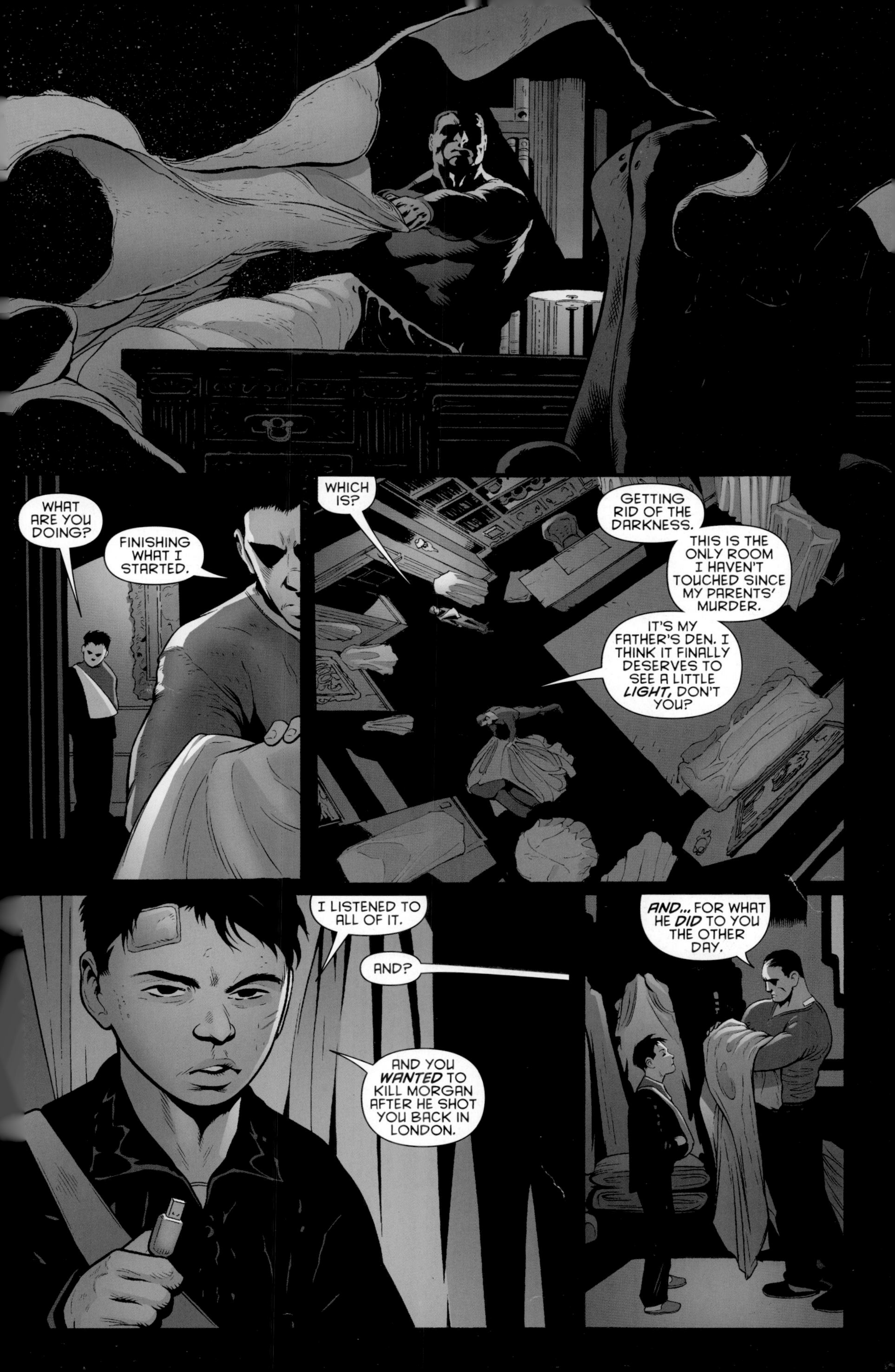
WHAT ARE YOU DOING?
FINISHING WHAT I STARTED.
WHICH IS?
GETTING RID OF THE DARKNESS.
THIS IS THE ONLY ROOM I HAVEN'T TOUCHED SINCE MY PARENTS' MURDER.
IT'S MY FATHER'S DEN. I THINK IT FINALLY DESERVES TO SEE A LITTLE LIGHT, DON'T YOU?
I LISTENED TO ALL OF IT.
AND?
AND YOU WANTED TO KILL MORGAN AFTER HE SHOT YOU BACK IN LONDON.
AND... FOR WHAT HE DID TO YOU THE OTHER DAY.

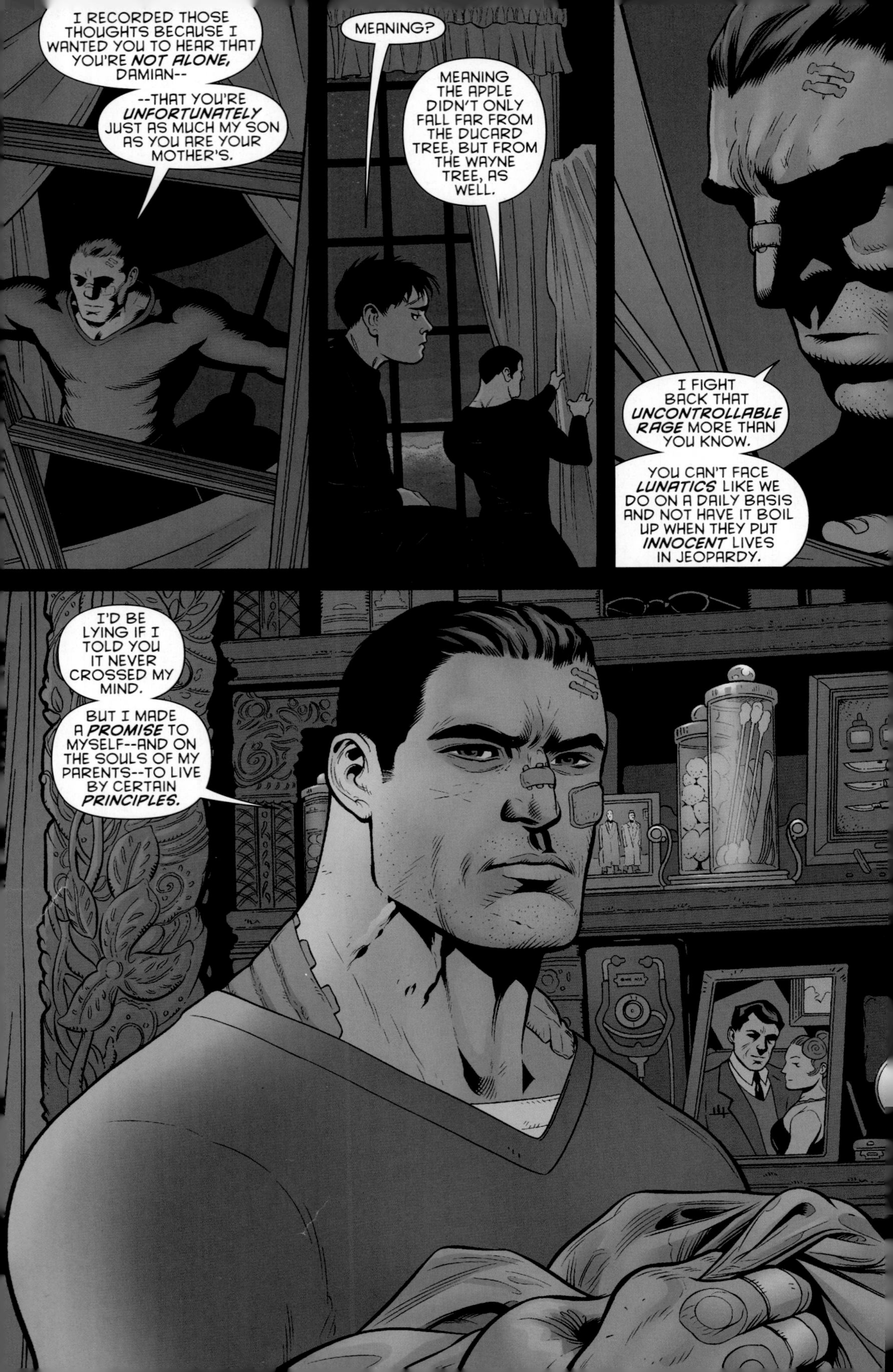

I RECORDED THOSE THOUGHTS BECAUSE I WANTED YOU TO HEAR THAT YOU'RE ***NOT ALONE,*** DAMIAN--
--THAT YOU'RE ***UNFORTUNATELY*** JUST AS MUCH MY SON AS YOU ARE YOUR MOTHER'S.
MEANING?
MEANING THE APPLE DIDN'T ONLY FALL FAR FROM THE DUCARD TREE, BUT FROM THE WAYNE TREE, AS WELL.
I FIGHT BACK THAT ***UNCONTROLLABLE RAGE*** MORE THAN YOU KNOW.
YOU CAN'T FACE ***LUNATICS*** LIKE WE DO ON A DAILY BASIS AND NOT HAVE IT BOIL UP WHEN THEY PUT ***INNOCENT*** LIVES IN JEOPARDY.
I'D BE LYING IF I TOLD YOU IT NEVER CROSSED MY MIND.
BUT I MADE A ***PROMISE*** TO MYSELF--AND ON THE SOULS OF MY PARENTS--TO LIVE BY CERTAIN ***PRINCIPLES.***

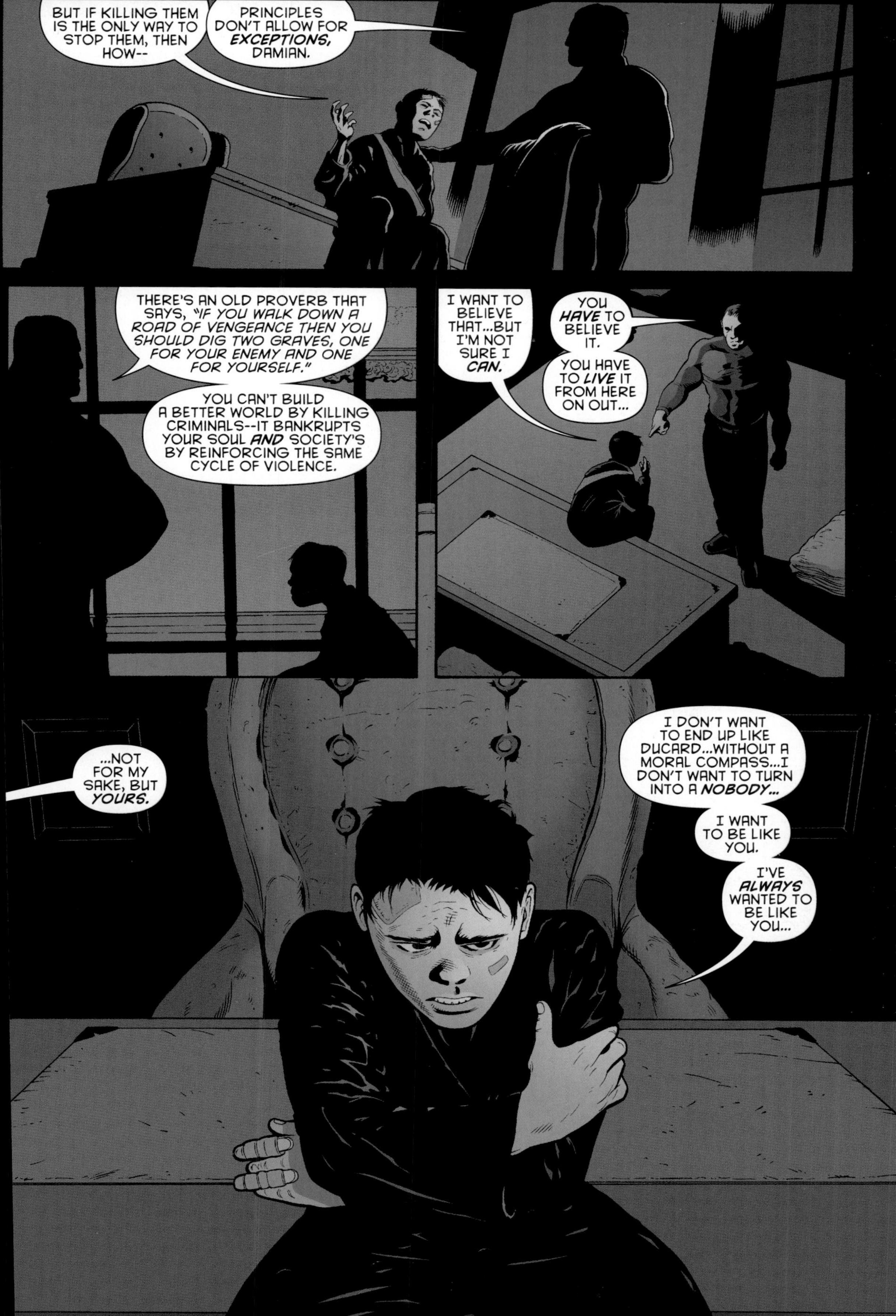
BUT IF KILLING THEM IS THE ONLY WAY TO STOP THEM, THEN HOW--
PRINCIPLES DON'T ALLOW FOR *EXCEPTIONS,* DAMIAN.
THERE'S AN OLD PROVERB THAT SAYS, *"IF YOU WALK DOWN A ROAD OF VENGEANCE THEN YOU SHOULD DIG TWO GRAVES, ONE FOR YOUR ENEMY AND ONE FOR YOURSELF."*
YOU CAN'T BUILD A BETTER WORLD BY KILLING CRIMINALS--IT BANKRUPTS YOUR SOUL ***AND*** SOCIETY'S BY REINFORCING THE SAME CYCLE OF VIOLENCE.
I WANT TO BELIEVE THAT...BUT I'M NOT SURE I *CAN.*
YOU ***HAVE*** TO BELIEVE IT.
YOU HAVE TO *LIVE* IT FROM HERE ON OUT...
...NOT FOR MY SAKE, BUT *YOURS.*
I DON'T WANT TO END UP LIKE DUCARD...WITHOUT A MORAL COMPASS...I DON'T WANT TO TURN INTO A *NOBODY...*
I WANT TO BE LIKE YOU.
I'VE ***ALWAYS*** WANTED TO BE LIKE YOU...

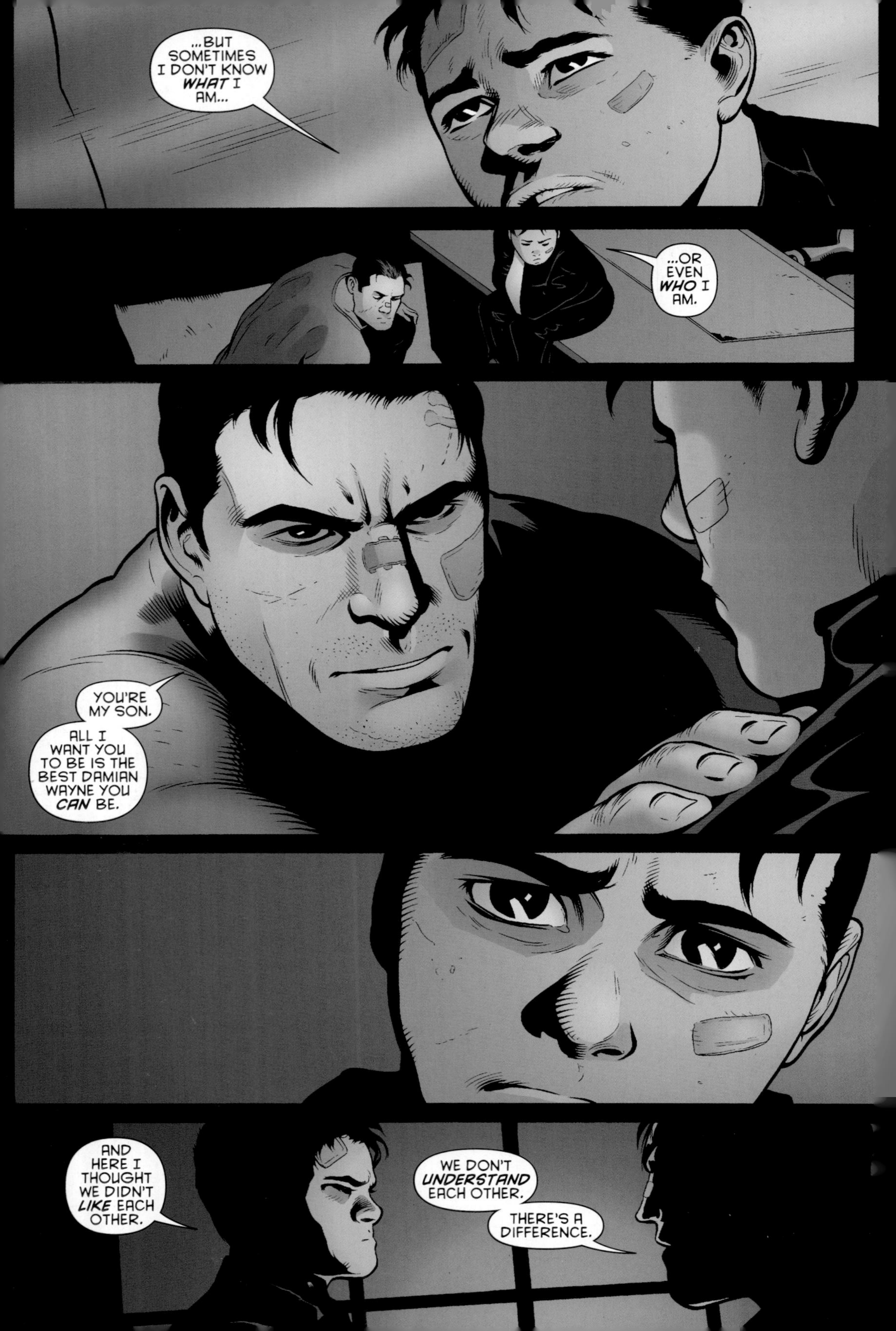
...BUT SOMETIMES I DON'T KNOW *WHAT* I AM...
...OR EVEN *WHO* I AM.
YOU'RE MY SON.
ALL I WANT YOU TO BE IS THE BEST DAMIAN WAYNE YOU *CAN* BE.
AND HERE I THOUGHT WE DIDN'T *LIKE* EACH OTHER.
WE DON'T *UNDERSTAND* EACH OTHER.
THERE'S A DIFFERENCE.

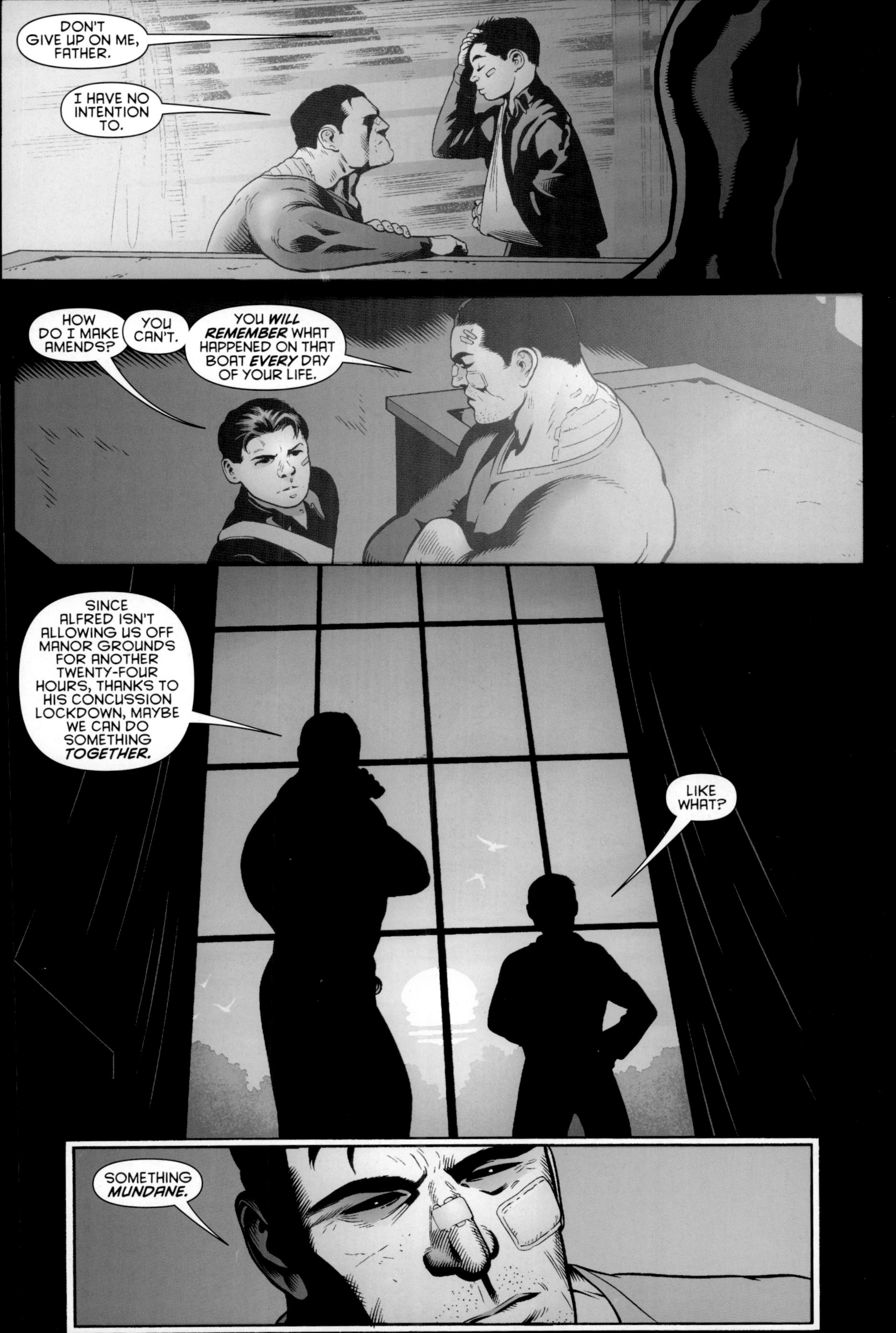
DON'T GIVE UP ON ME, FATHER.
I HAVE NO INTENTION TO.
HOW DO I MAKE AMENDS?
YOU CAN'T.
YOU WILL REMEMBER WHAT HAPPENED ON THAT BOAT EVERY DAY OF YOUR LIFE.
SINCE ALFRED ISN'T ALLOWING US OFF MANOR GROUNDS FOR ANOTHER TWENTY-FOUR HOURS, THANKS TO HIS CONCUSSION LOCKDOWN, MAYBE WE CAN DO SOMETHING TOGETHER.
LIKE WHAT?
SOMETHING MUNDANE.

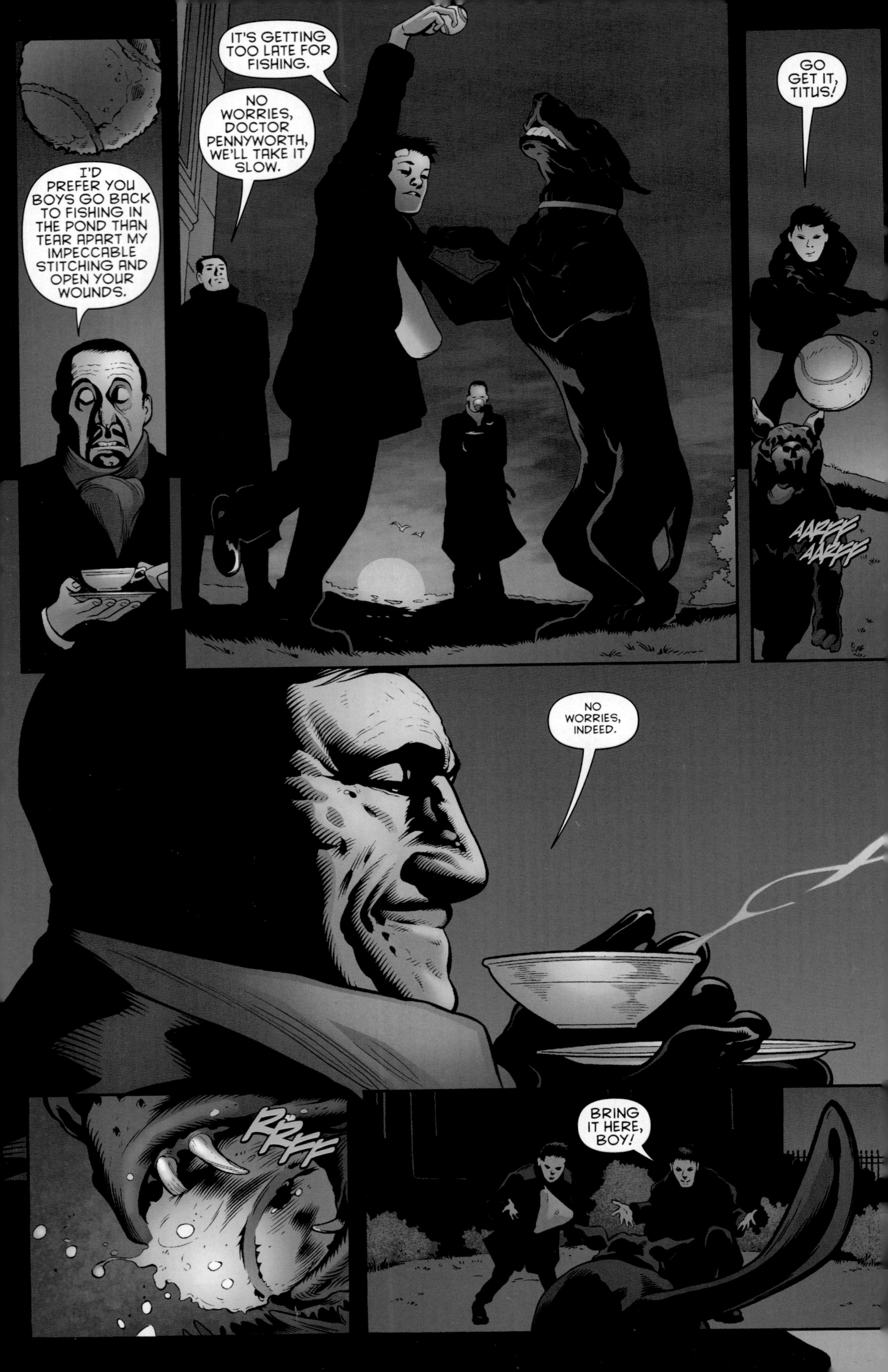
I'D PREFER YOU BOYS GO BACK TO FISHING IN THE POND THAN TEAR APART MY IMPECCABLE STITCHING AND OPEN YOUR WOUNDS.
IT'S GETTING TOO LATE FOR FISHING.
NO WORRIES, DOCTOR PENNYWORTH, WE'LL TAKE IT SLOW.
GO GET IT, TITUS!
AARFF AARFF
NO WORRIES, INDEED.
RRFF
BRING IT HERE, BOY!

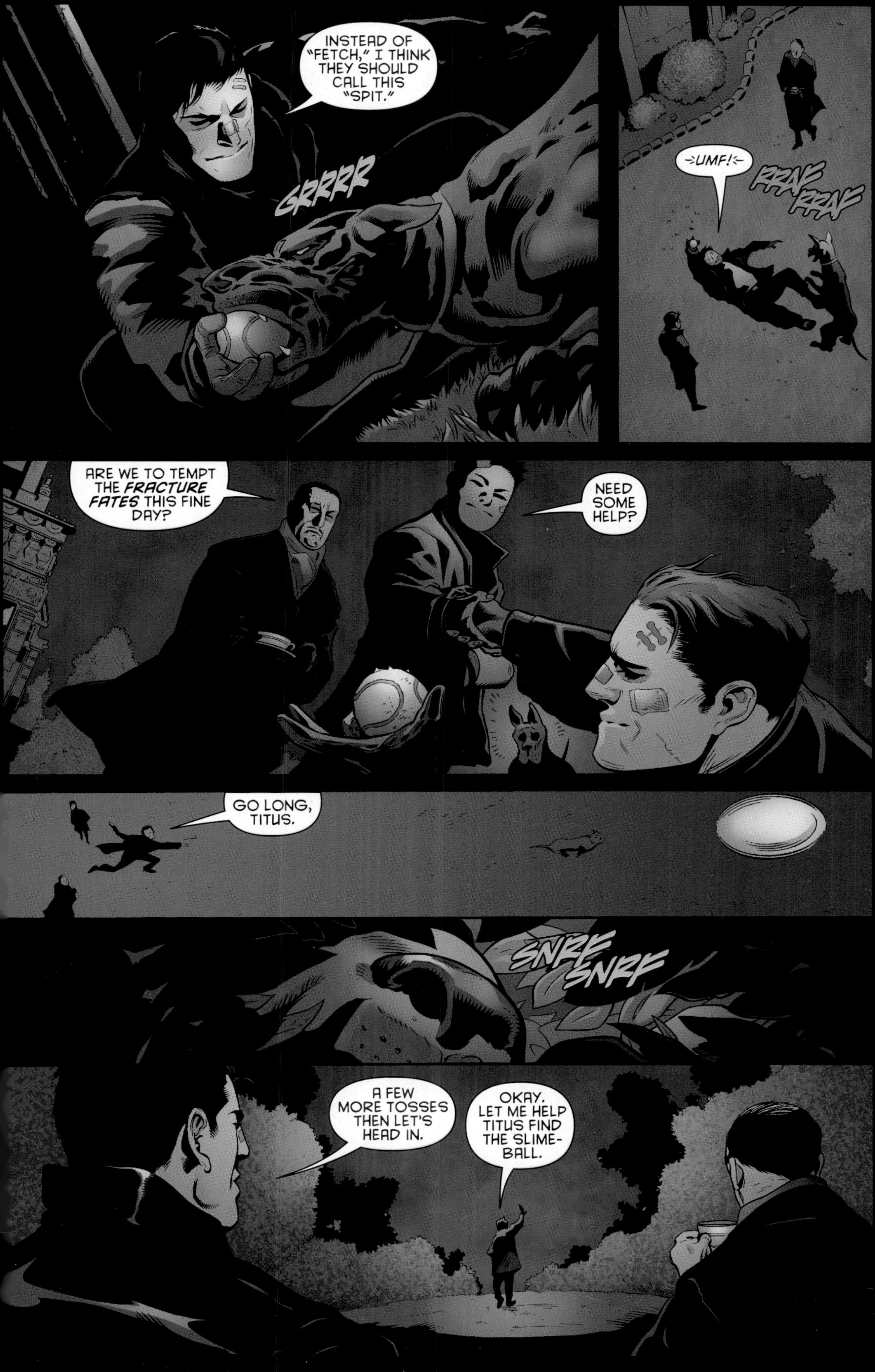
INSTEAD OF "FETCH," I THINK THEY SHOULD CALL THIS "SPIT."
GRRRR
-UMF!-
RRAF RRAF
ARE WE TO TEMPT THE *FRACTURE FATES* THIS FINE DAY?
NEED SOME HELP?
GO LONG, TITUS.
SNRF SNRF
A FEW MORE TOSSES THEN LET'S HEAD IN.
OKAY. LET ME HELP TITUS FIND THE SLIME-BALL.

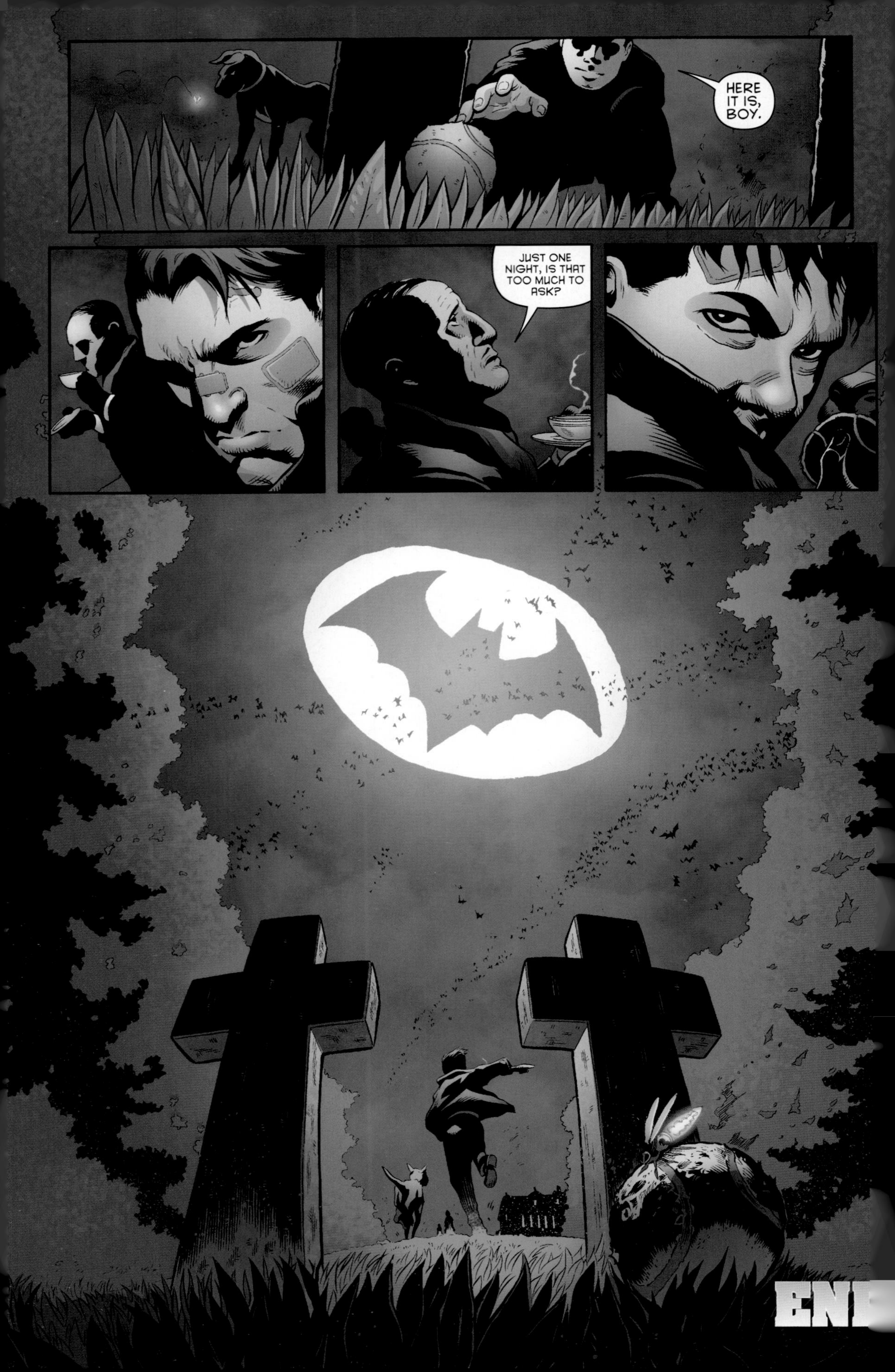
HERE IT IS, BOY.
JUST ONE NIGHT, IS THAT TOO MUCH TO ASK?
END

BATMAN AND ROBIN: BORN TO KILL

WORDS BY PETER J. TOMASI   ART BY PATRICK GLEASON

The following is the story proposal for the first arc of BATMAN AND ROBIN

Bruce may be the 'World's Greatest Detective' but he's still not the 'World's Greatest Dad.'

The premise of this book is simple. It's about a father and son crime fighting team on an adventure ride through Gotham City. But what they come to realize is that the hardest part isn't going up against the villains and freaks every night; the hardest part's trying to live and work together without driving each other insane.

The story begins with Bruce and Damian at odds with each other. Bruce struggles to get a handle on Damian and his past, trying his best to teach his son what it means to be a just and moral person while making plenty of parental mistakes along the way. Due to his upbringing by Talia Al Ghul and the League of Assassins, Bruce sees Damian as being a broken boy and is on a mission to fix him. Damian, on the other hand, only wants to be accepted by his father for who and what he is; he doesn't want to be looked at as some science project that needs to be modified. Deep down though, Damian's conflicted himself; his past and present are locked in a constant battle, a battle between light and darkness that threatens to take a terrible toll on Damian's soul if he lets it.

The emotional spine and theme of the first eight issues of BATMAN AND ROBIN is nature versus nurture, as Bruce and Damian struggle to build a relationship based on love, trust, and respect as internal *and* external forces do their best to keep that from happening.

Our story opens, as a *new character* emerges from the shadows of Bruce's past: his name is NOBODY, and he's reached a tipping point. NoBody's not very happy that an organization like Batman, Inc. is shining a Bat-Symbol into the dark corners where NoBody prefers to operate in his silent but deadly way. Worst of all, that the tactics and mission to combat crime of not only Batman, Inc. but Batman himself, are so distorted and perverted in his opinion they need to be terminated with extreme prejudice. Imagine a cool scene between Batman and NoBody kicking the crap out of each other, justifying their *modus operandi*: NoBody is baffled that they call Bruce by some self-appointed crime-fighting name, that he talks to a Police Commissioner on a rooftop, that they shine a symbol and call him in like some lap-dog to help clean up their mess, that he leaves murderers and thieves dangling like fish in front of police precincts, and worst of all, that he actually lets them live.

Now there's a lot of connective tissue that I don't need to go into at this point, but I will say that as the story evolves/develops, we'll see that NoBody looks to hurt Batman/Bruce in a more personal way due to what happened between them in their youth, and tries to bring Damian over to the 'dark side' so to speak.

NoBody believes crime and the people who perpetrate it should be dealt with quickly, with no fanfare or signature. He sees himself as a living shadow where his method is one of dispatching the guilty and seeing to it that they disappear as quickly as he's killed them. We'll delve into NoBody's origin, where we'll discover that he's the son of HENRI DUCARD, a specialized master of man-hunting that Bruce trained with before he donned the cape and cowl, and juxtapose in certain ways how NoBody's life/upbringing lines up with Bruce and Damian.

And just to be clear, NoBody is our 'B' story.

Our 'A' story, the emotional and psychological backbone of the book will be laser-focused on the relationship between Bruce and Damian.

Deep down, I believe, parents always have a nagging thought in the back of their heads: What if I die or am somehow unable to impart to my child the life lessons I hope will make him a happy and healthy person not only in body and mind, but also in spirit? I feel Bruce Wayne is having these thoughts.

After having been somewhat of an absentee father as of late, Bruce is afraid of what Damian would become if he's suddenly not around anymore. He doesn't want to leave a black hole in a young boy's soul like the death of his own parents did, *especially* a young boy whose soul is as deadly and dangerous as Damian's is.

As Bruce wrestles with what it means to be a father in uniform and out, Damian is wrestling with himself too, using all his willpower to keep his natural instincts and inclinations at bay, trying his best to be the son he knows his father wants him to be, but finding himself failing and not knowing who to turn to, especially when he starts to see Bruce as less of a fantasy father figure and more as a fallible human being. For Damian, it was easy to look up to Bruce when he was gone, but now that his father's back, Damian's finding it was simpler to love and respect the legend more than the man himself.

In my mind, Damian was instructed from birth to be the Eternal Warrior. He's a trained killer, and even though he thought he could control his violent feelings it's starting to bubble to the surface again and manifesting itself at first in small ways like killing a sick bat that's fallen to the cave floor and finally culminating in killing NoBody around issue 7 or 8. Think of Damian as a ten-year-old 'Dexter' — but without the extreme body count, of course.

NoBody's invasion into Bruce and Damian's life juxtaposes the philosophical, psychological, and emotional differences of their crime fighting methods and will, by the end of the story arc, push everyone right to their absolute edge , as NoBody tries to convince Damian that his ways are the true path to battling evil and that Damian is the future.

To boil down the personal dynamic in a nutshell, think of NoBody as the cool Uncle who relates to and understands Damian in ways that Damian feels Bruce can't or won't.

So to wrap it up, this story arc will be a *personal* and *emotional* rollercoaster which I feel will be an important element to help make BATMAN AND ROBIN distinct within the Bat Family of titles in the New 52 launch.

END

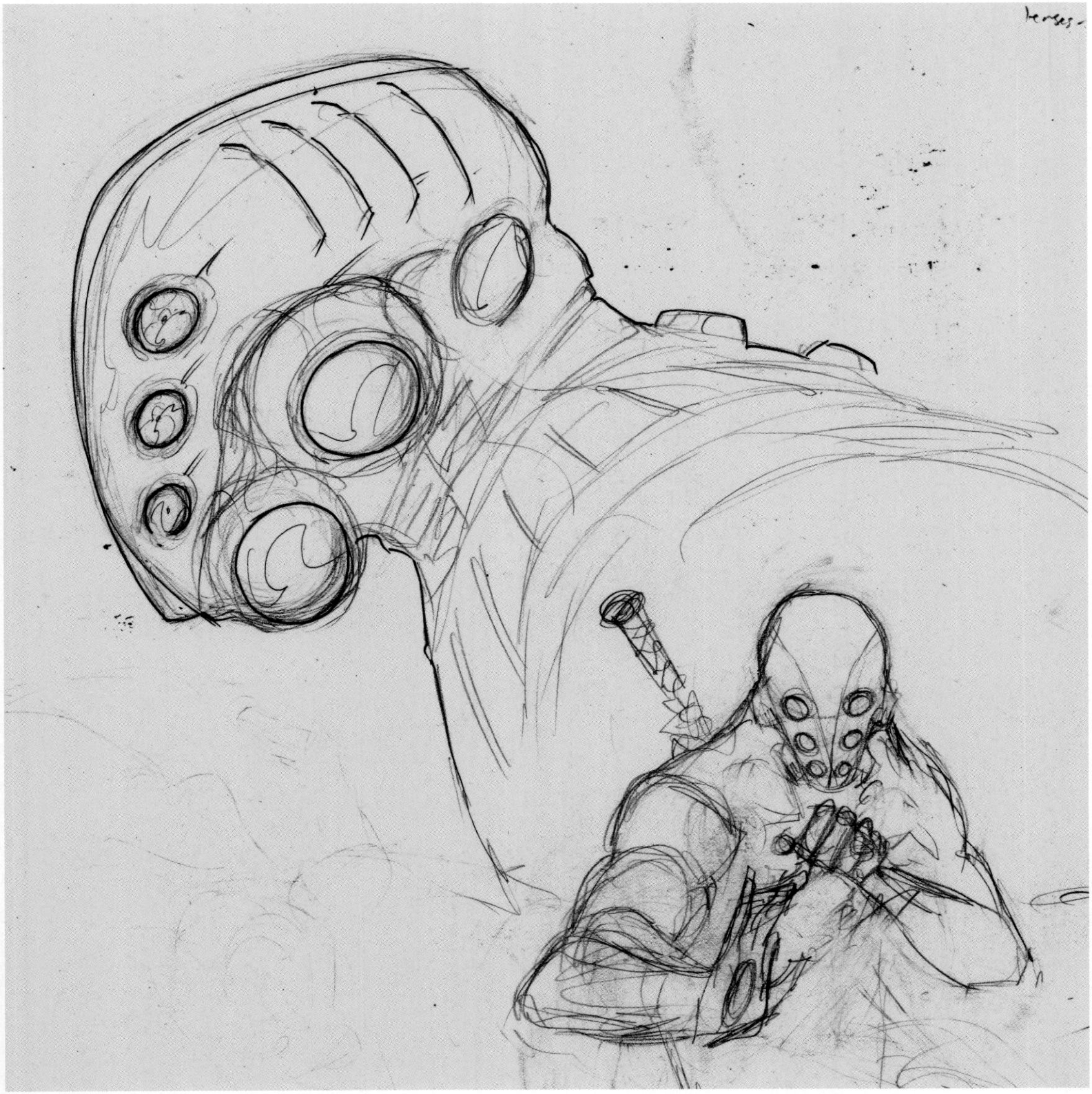

lenses-

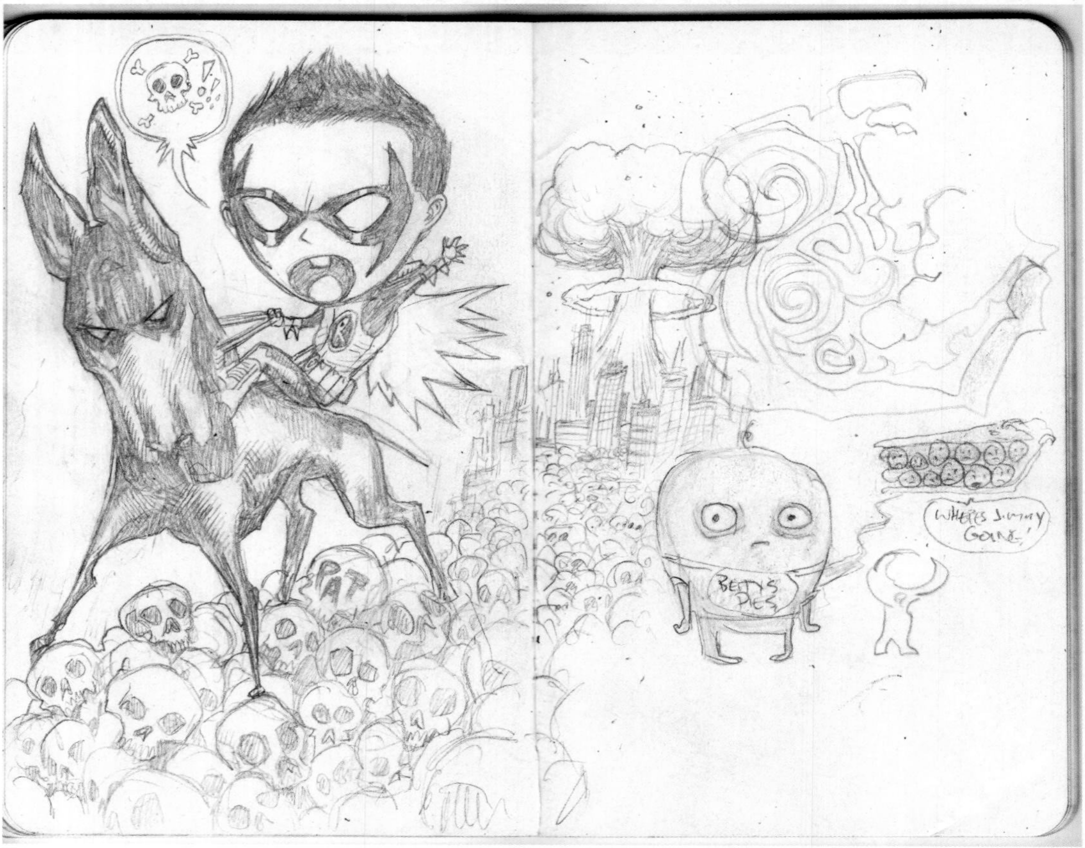
BETTYS PIES
WHERES JIMMY GOING?

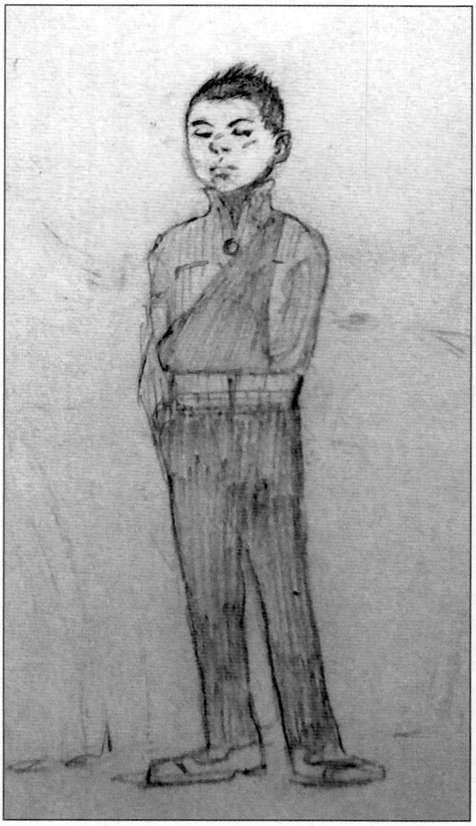

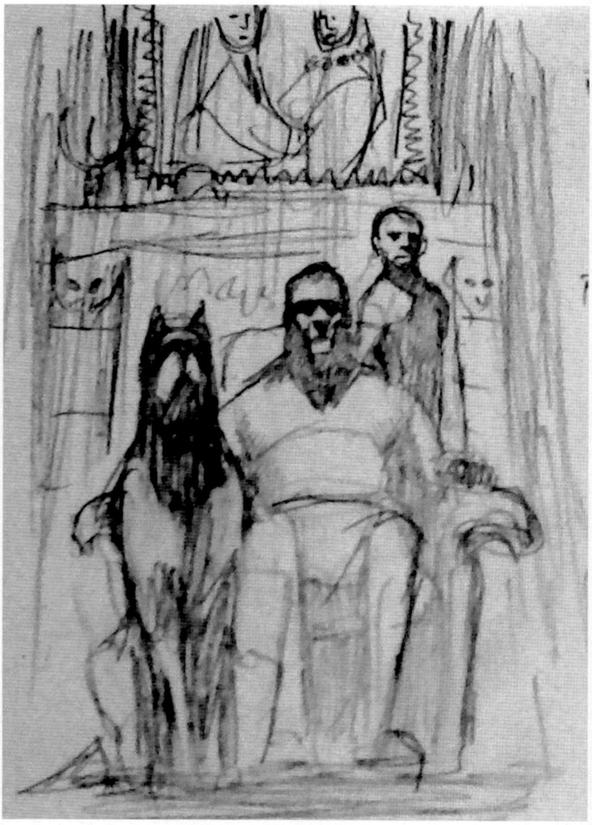

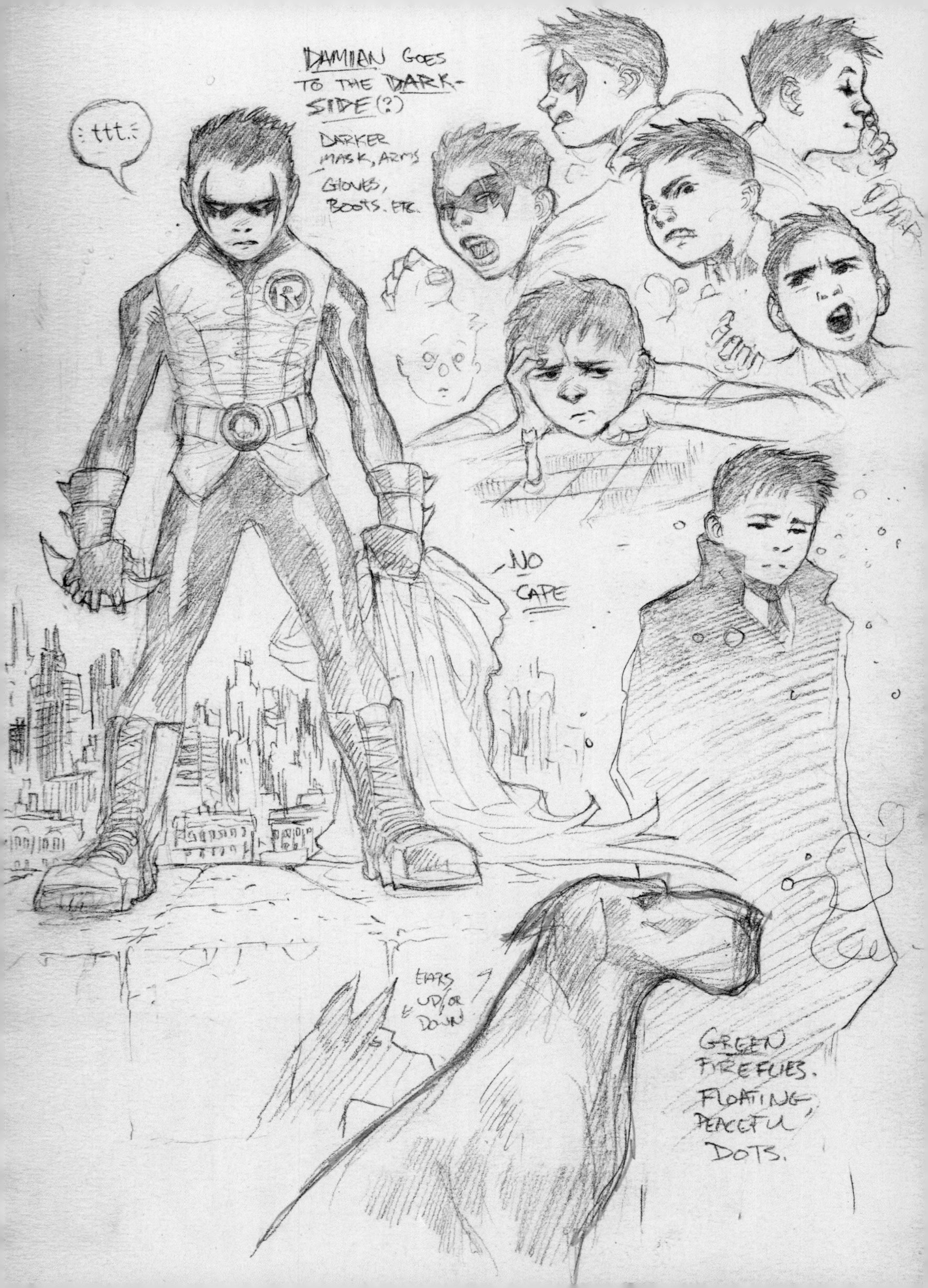
DAMIAN GOES TO THE DARK-SIDE(?)
DARKER MASK, ARMS GLOVES, BOOTS. ETC.
ttt.
NO CAPE
EARS UP/OR DOWN
GREEN FIREFLIES. FLOATING, PEACEFUL DOTS.

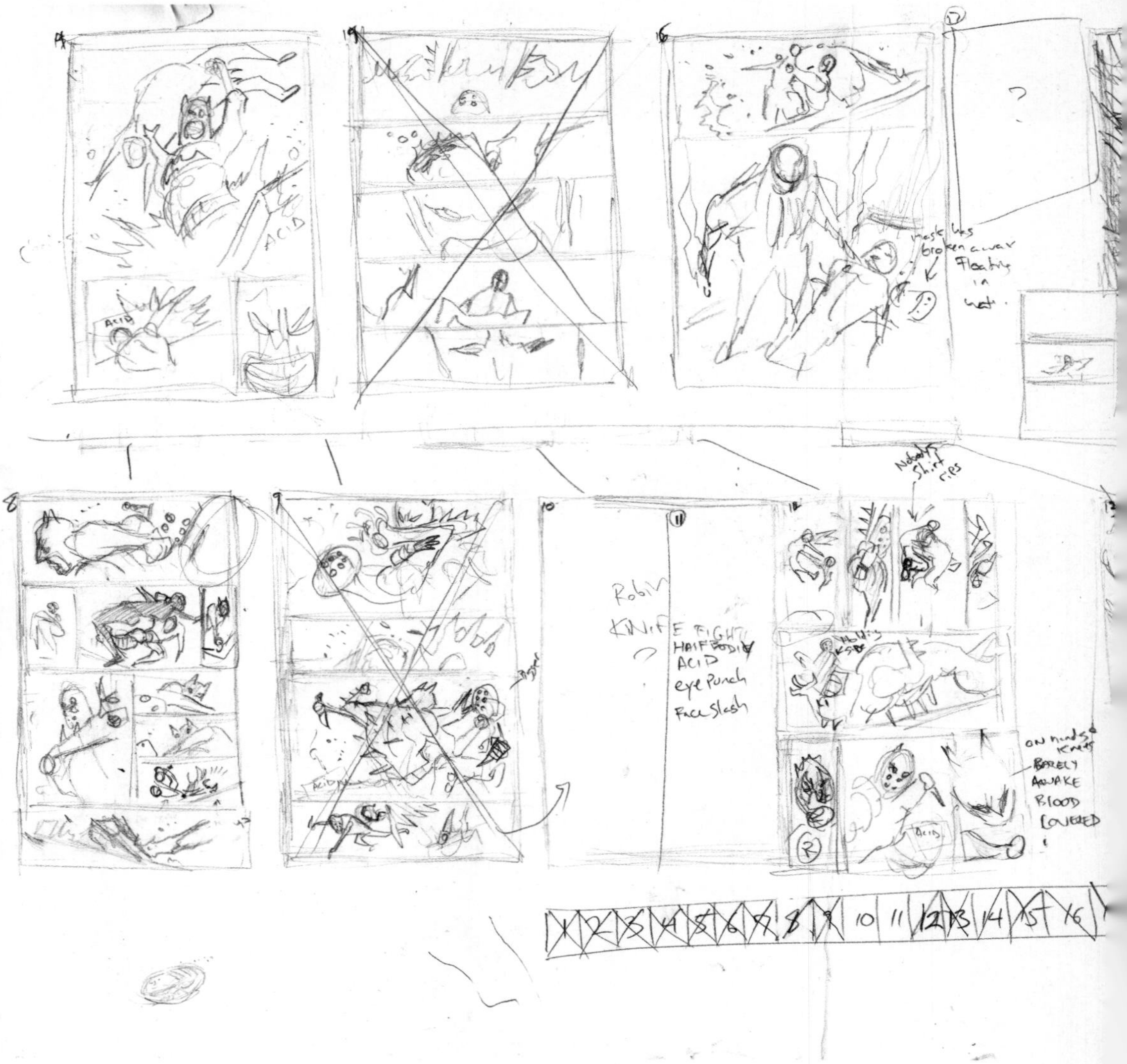
ACID
ACID
Robin
KNIFE FIGHT
HALF BODY
ACID
eye Punch
Face Slash
ACID
ON hands & knees
BARELY
AWAKE
BLOOD
COVERED

A comparison of the initial thumbnail layouts by Patrick Gleason for BATMAN AND ROBIN #7 pages 8-20 and the inked (by Mick Gray) version of the same pages.

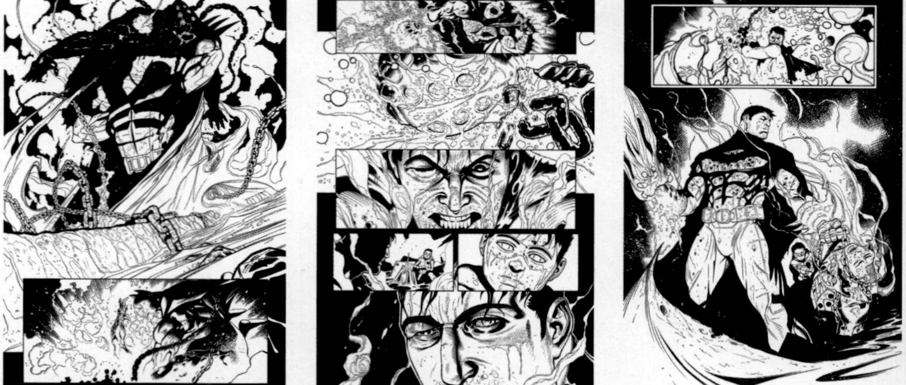

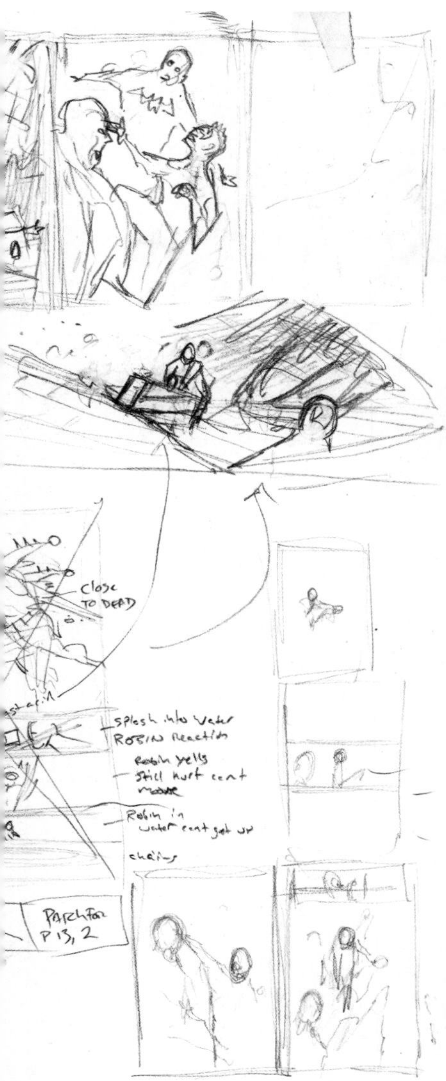
Close TO DEAD
Splash into water
ROBIN Reaction
Robin yells
still hurt cant move
Robin in water cant get up
chains
Patch for P 13, 2

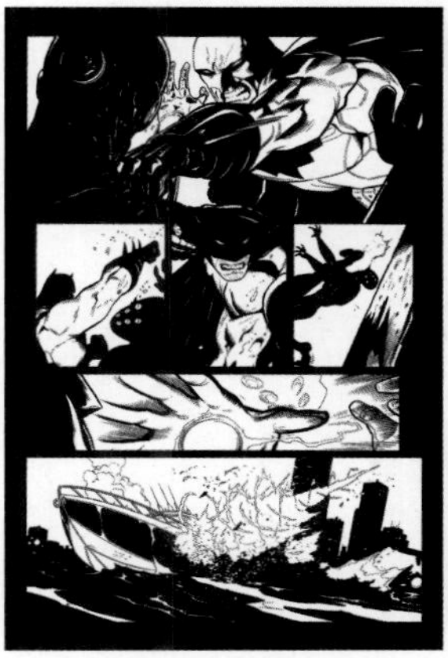

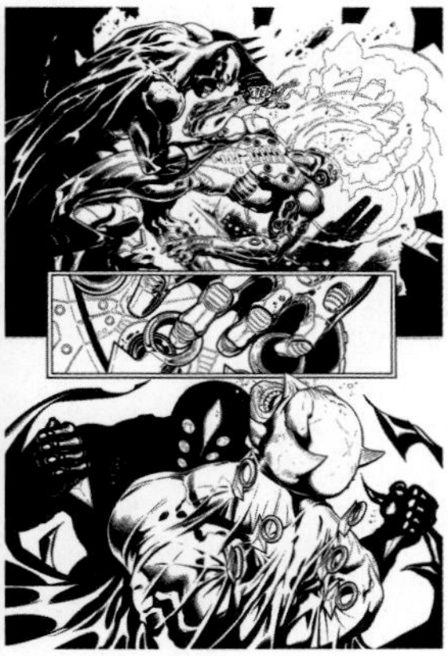

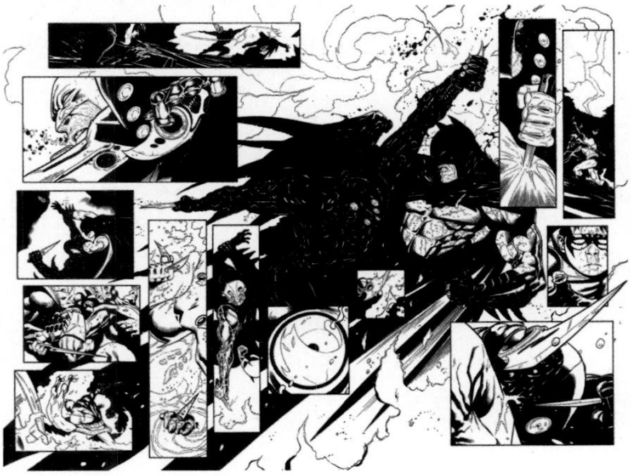

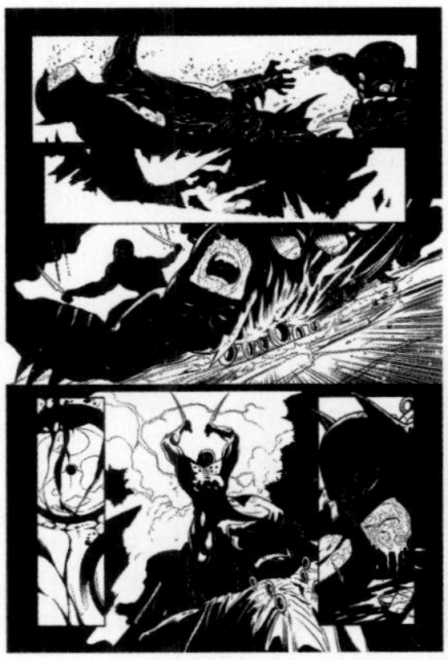

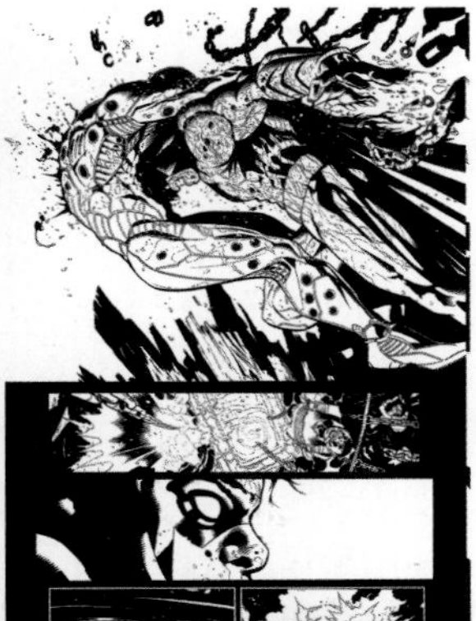

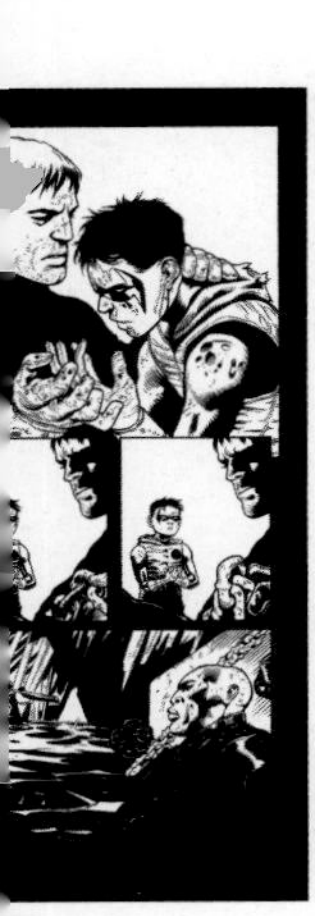

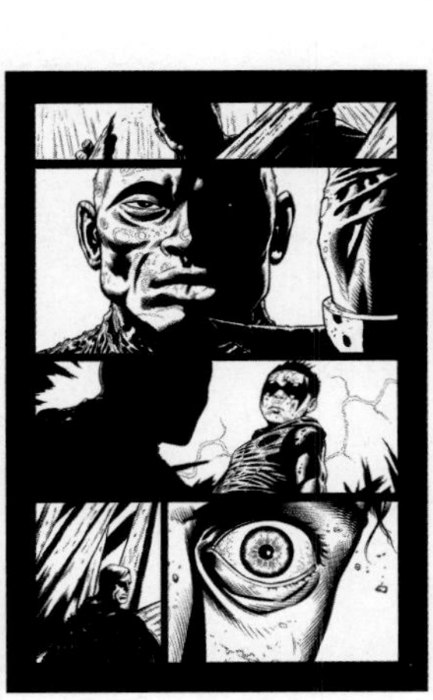

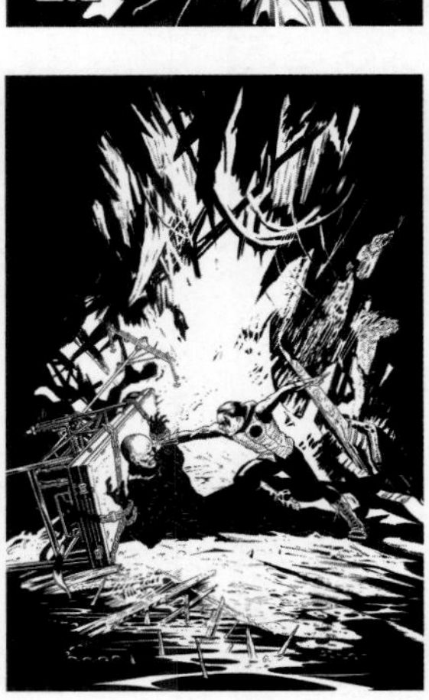

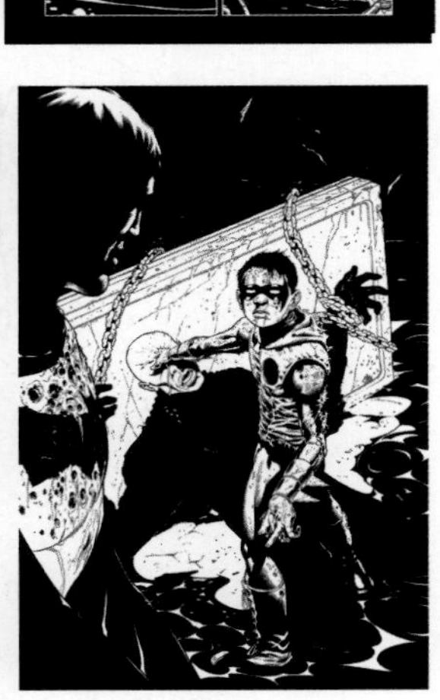

The following is an excerpt of the script for BATMAN AND ROBIN #7.

BATMAN AND ROBIN # 7 - SCRIPT

PAGE 17
panel 1
Angle on Bats as he drags NoBody's unconscious body with one hand and supports Robin with the other. Remember the water level is about up to their knees here. They all look beaten and battered. There's no smiles in this scene, just relief and exhaustion.

ROBIN: ...boat sinking...how are...

BATMAN: Shhh. Don't worry, I've got you.

panel 2
Angle closer on Batman and Robin, as Batman puts his hand on the back of Robin's neck in a gesture of concern and affection as he looks at the wounds Robin's suffered.

BATMAN: Thought I almost lost you there, boy...

ROBIN: ...takes more than a NoBody like that to get rid of me.

panel 3
Angle on Batman as he's leaned NoBody's unconscious body up against the slanted table and is in the process of wrapping the loose straps to NoBody's wrists and arms to keep him upright and out of the water as Robin tries to help through his own pain.

ROBIN: Did you think I betrayed you, father?

BATMAN: Not for a second.

panel 4
Angle on Batman and Robin as they look at each other as Batman cinches the knot. A silent beat. Robin has that "don't gimme that bull" look, but not in a funny way.

SILENT

panel 5
Same exact shot as previous panel, except maybe a little closer.

BATMAN: Well, maybe just a second.

panel 6
Batman wades through the water towards the Batmobile to remove debris. Robin turns to NoBody, who is regaining consciousness.

BATMAN: We're not going down with this ship.

NOBODY: ...nnnn...

PAGE 18

panel 1
Angle on Batman pushing a piece of large debris away from the Batmobile.

BATMAN: I'll clear this debris.

BATMAN: We'll drop NoBody with the Harbor Patrol...

panel 2
Angle only on NoBody, his eyes open as he regains consciousness. They stare right at Robin.

BATMAN(off) ...get back to the cave...

NOBODY(softly): Don't disappoint me, Damian...

panel 3
Angle on NoBody and Robin. Robin looks at him with a scary pensiveness.

NOBODY(softly): ...you know I'll be back to kill you all...

panel 4
Angle only on Batman as he throws off the last of the debris while turning back towards Robin and NoBody who are off-panel.

BATMAN: ...and have Alfred patch you —

panel 5
Angle close only on Bats, his one wide terrified eye that we can see through his torn cowl tells us something horrible is happening off-panel.

BATMAN: — <u>Damian, get away from him!</u>

PAGE 19

Splash.

What comes around goes around.

Robin, looking grim and determined, uses the FINGER MOVE we've seeded/illustrated in the last few issues, but this time Robin is putting all his ninja talent and forceful drive into literally shoving his two fingers INTO NOBODY'S FOREHEAD, right below the brow and just above NoBody's wide pain-filled eyes.

There doesn't need to be blood, by the way.

Now if you want, Pat, and you can make it work in the shot, feel free to throw Batman in the background yelling "No!" But it's your call. I'm fine with just Robin and NoBody in this shot. I could add an off-panel balloon coming from Batman just the same.

BATMAN(off):   <u>No!</u>

PAGE 20

Splash.

Angle looking down at Batman, Robin and NoBody. Not too far though, Pat, keep 'em close. The atmosphere lighting is reddish from the fire.

NoBody is dead.

Robin, battered and bruised, simply stands exhausted beside NoBody in the rising water, his fingers still embedded in his head. Robin is looking at Batman, but not in some evil or demented way. Robin feels what he's done is just and necessary. NoBody was a man who would continue to haunt them until they were dead unless he took this drastic action. Robin should almost be looking at Batman for absolution.

Batman stands there looking at his son. He can't believe what's just happened.

ROBIN   Forgive me, father, for I have sinned.

INITIAL AND FINAL PENCILS FOR BATMAN AND ROBIN #7 PAGES 6 AND 20

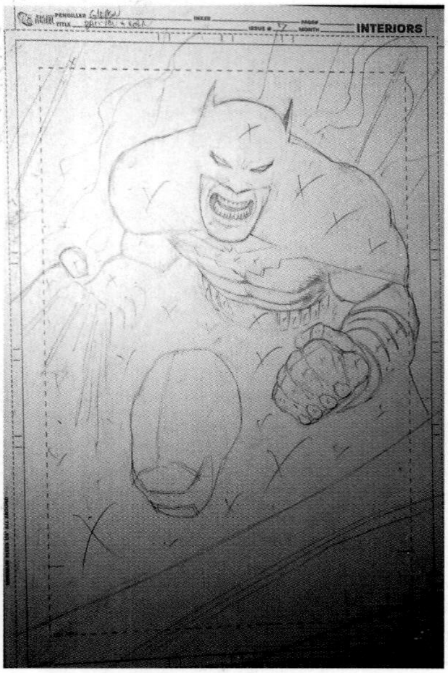
INTERIORS

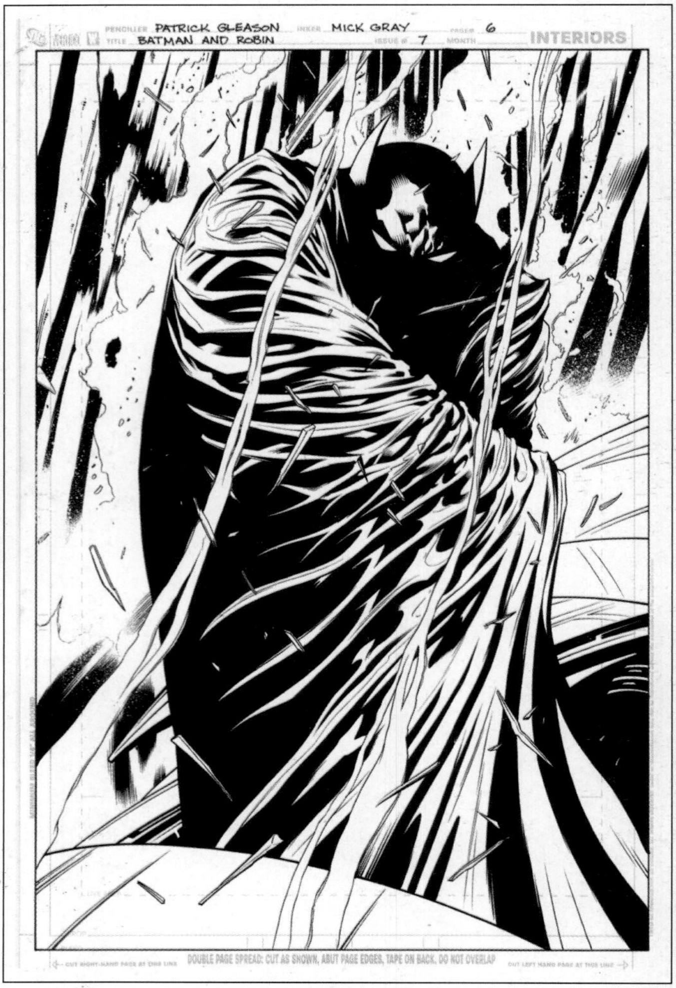
PENCILLER PATRICK GLEASON
INKER MICK GRAY
PAGE# 6
TITLE BATMAN AND ROBIN
ISSUE # 7
MONTH
INTERIORS
DOUBLE PAGE SPREAD: CUT AS SHOWN, ABUT PAGE EDGES, TAPE ON BACK, DO NOT OVERLAP

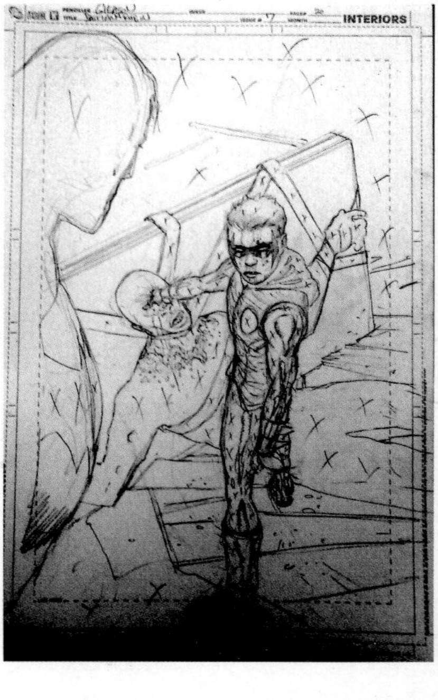
INTERIORS

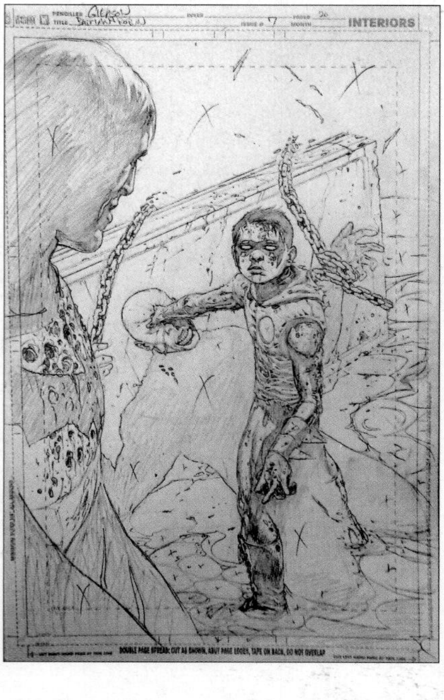
INTERIORS
DOUBLE PAGE SPREAD: CUT AS SHOWN, ABUT PAGE EDGES, TAPE ON BACK, DO NOT OVERLAP

ALTERNATE VERSION TO BATMAN AND ROBIN #8 COVER

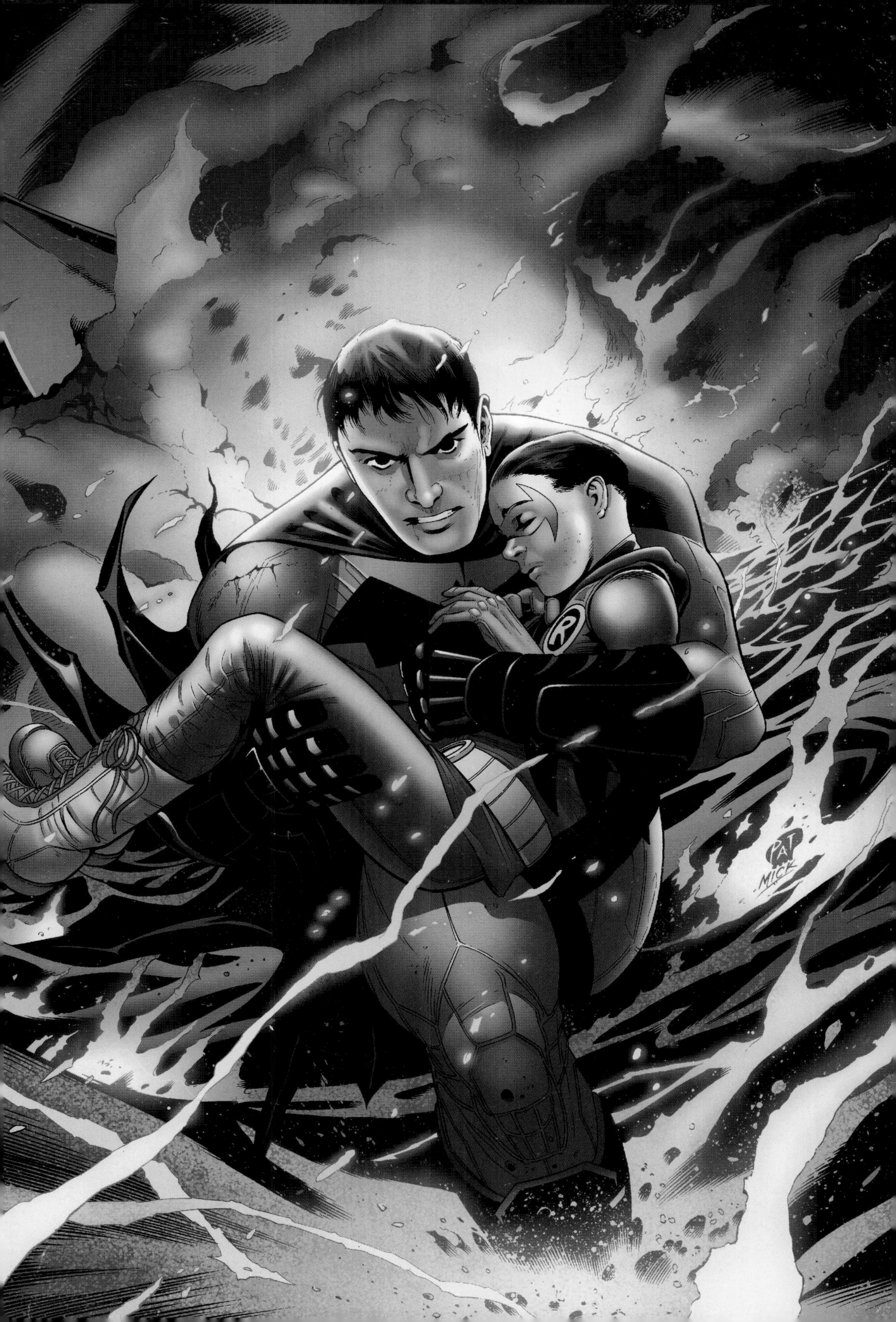
PAT
MICK

BATMAN AND ROBIN
COVER SKETCHES

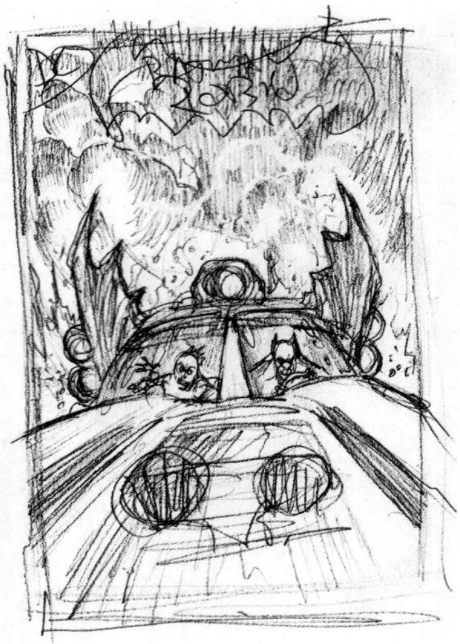

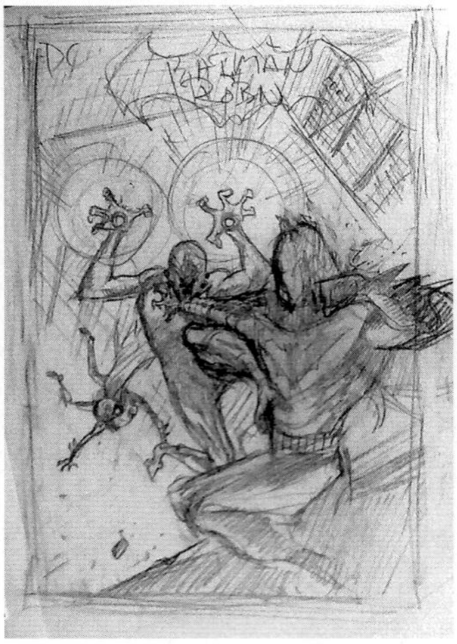

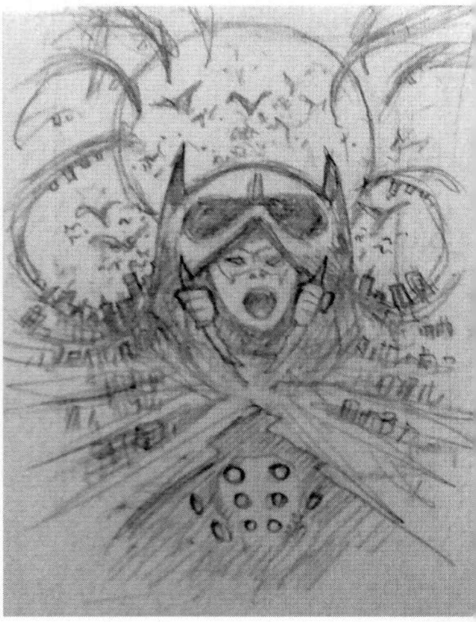

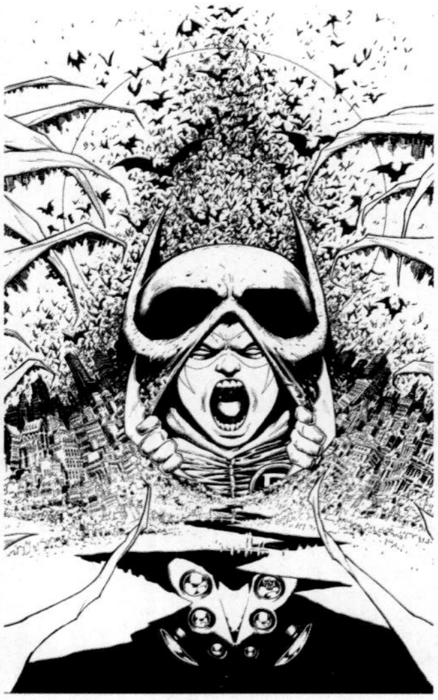

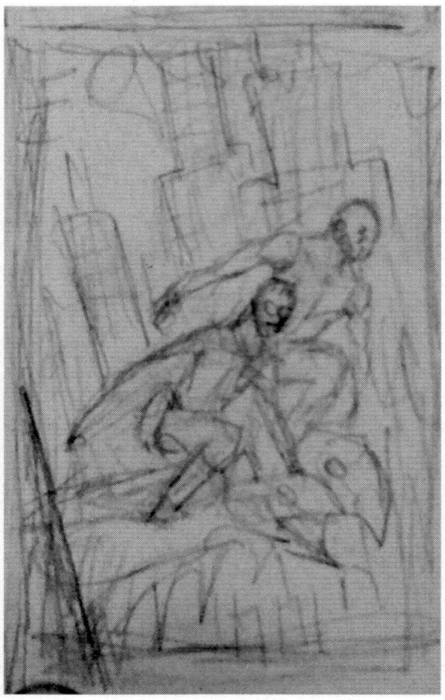

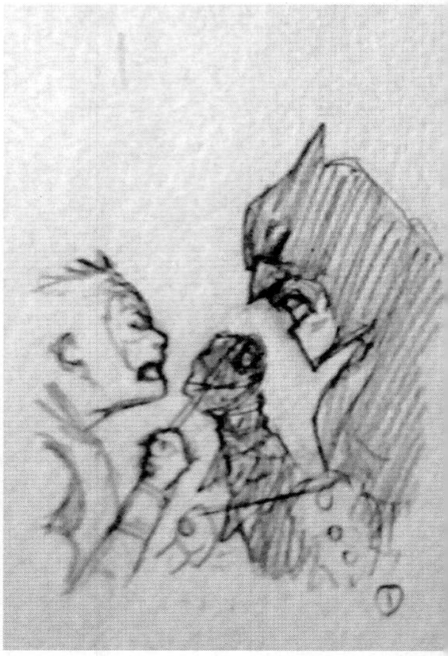

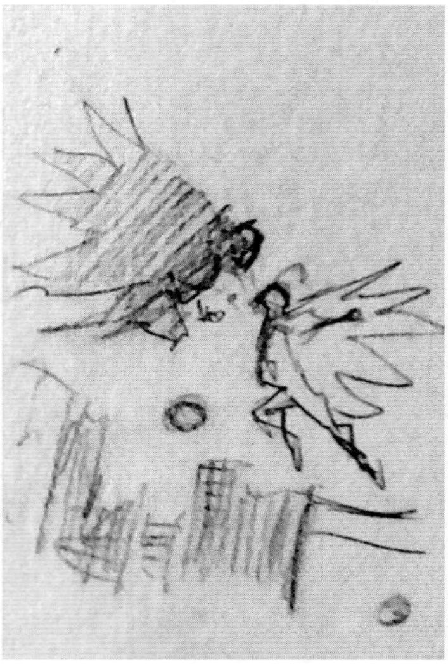

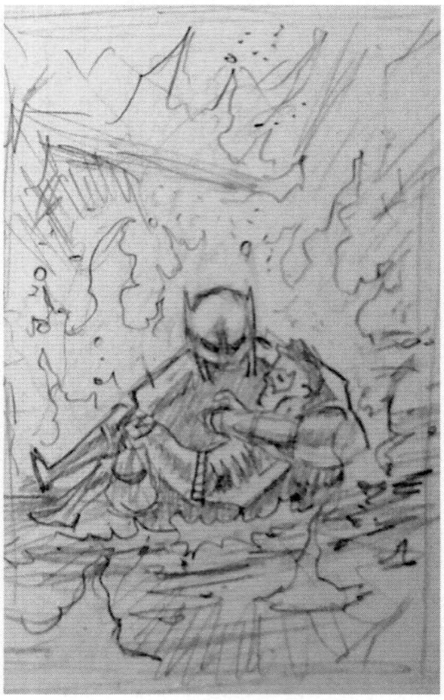

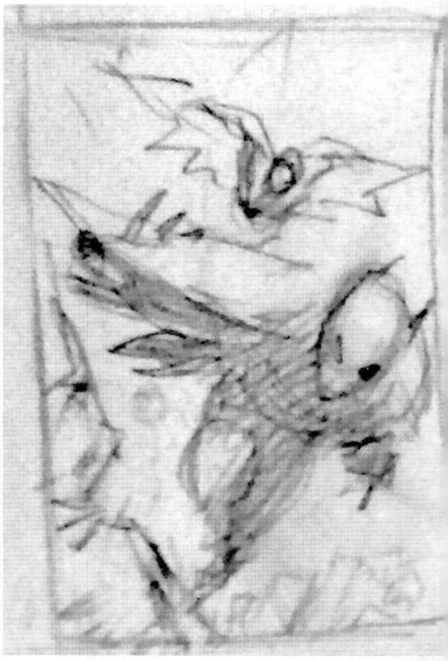